Nationalizing Social Security
in Europe and America

MONOGRAPHS IN ORGANIZATIONAL
BEHAVIOR AND INDUSTRIAL RELATIONS, VOLUME 4

Editor: Samuel B. Bacharach, *Department of Organizational Behavior, New York State School of Industrial and Labor Relations, Cornell University*

MONOGRAPHS IN ORGANIZATIONAL BEHAVIOR AND INDUSTRIAL RELATIONS

Edited by Samuel B. Bacharach,
*Department of Organizational Behavior,
New York State School of Industrial
Relations, Cornell University*

Volume 1. **ORGANIZATIONAL SYMBOLISM**
Edited by Louis R. Pondy, University of Illinois
Peter J. Frost, University of British Columbia
Gareth Morgan, York University
Thomas C. Dandridge, SUNY Albany

Volume 2. **THE ORGANIZATION AND ITS ECOSYSTEM:
A THEORY OF STRUCTURING IN ORGANIZATIONS**
Charles E. Bidwell, University of Chicago
John D. Kasarda, University of North Carolina

Volume 3. **MILITARY LEADERSHIP:
AN ORGANIZATIONAL BEHAVIOR PERSPECTIVE**
David D. Van Fleet, Texas A&M University
Gary A. Yukl, SUNY Albany

Volume 4. **NATIONALIZING SOCIAL SECURITY IN EUROPE AND AMERICA**
Edited by Douglas E. Ashford, University of Pittsburgh
E.W. Kelley, Cornell University

Volume 5. **ABSENTEEISM AND TURNOVER OF HOSPITAL EMPLOYEES**
James L. Price, University of Iowa
Charles W. Mueller, University of Iowa

Volume 6. **INDUSTRIAL ORGANIZATION: A TREATISE**
Joe S. Bain, Professor Emeritus of Economics, University of
California, Berkeley
P. David Qualls, University of Tennessee, Knoxville

Forthcoming
**PUBLISH AND PERISH:
A DYNAMIC ANALYSIS OF ORGANIZATION MORTALITY IN THE
AMERICAN LOCAL NEWSPAPER INDUSTRY FROM 1880 TO 1975**
Glen R. Carroll, University of California, Berkeley

HANDBOOK OF BEHAVIORAL ECONOMICS
Edited by Stanley Kaish, Rutgers University, Newark
Benjamin Gilad, Rutgers University, Newark

Nationalizing Social Security in Europe and America

Edited by DOUGLAS E. ASHFORD
Department of Political Science
University of Pittsburgh

E. W. KELLEY
Department of Government
Cornell University

 JAI PRESS INC.

Greenwich, Connecticut   *London, England*

Library of Congress Cataloging-in-Publication Data
Main entry under title:

Nationalizing social security in Europe and America.

    (Monographs in organizational behavior and
industrial relations ; v. 4)
    Includes bibliographies and index.
    1. Social security—Europe—History—Addresses,
essays, lectures. 2. Social security—United States—
History—Addresses, essays, lectures. I. Ashford,
Douglas Elliott. II. Kelley, E. W. III. Series.
HD7164.N37 1986   368.4′0094   85-23214
ISBN 0-89232-555-0

CONTENTS

LIST OF CONTRIBUTORS

Christa Altenstetter

Department of Political Science
Graduate Center and Queens College
City University of New York

Douglas E. Ashford

Department of Political Science
University of Pittsburgh

Edward J. Harpham

School of Social Sciences
University of Texas at Dallas

Arnold J. Heidenheimer

Department of Political Science
Washington University
St. Louis, Missouri

Ken Judge

Personal Social Services Research Unit
University of Kent at Canterbury
England

E. W. Kelley

Department of Government
Cornell University

François Lagrange

Commissariat Général du Plan
Office of the President
Paris, France

Stephan Leibfried

Faculty of Law
University of Bremen
Bremen, West Germany

Michael Lund

The Urban Institute
Washington, D.C.

B. Guy Peters

Department of Political Science
University of Pittsburgh

Bruno Stein   Department of Economics
                                     Director, Institute of Labor Relations
                                     New York University

Henry Teune   Department of Political Science
                                     University of Pennsylvania
                                     Philadelphia, Pennsylvania

PREFACE

The nationalization of social security programs, a necessary prelude to the emergence of the modern welfare state, was a politically controversial event in all the modern democracies. While there are many books on the contemporary problems of welfare and its associated programs, there are few that deal specifically with the political and historical conditions that affected this transition, and in many ways still shape the social security programs in distinctive ways in western democracies. Although the book is not primarily about economic influences over these changes, the drive to nationalize was a corollary of Western experience in manipulating aggregate demand and achieving full employment. Indeed, the expectations that these goals could be achieved were an essential assumption of the post-war period that helped persuade political leaders that democracies could embark on vastly expanded social security programs.

Our book, then, mainly concerns the politics of policy formation as it relates to the expansion of social security. The essays have been selected to underscore the major differences and similarities among the democracies in the timing of their efforts to increase social services, the political obstacles and coalitions that made change possible, and the key decisions that so often influenced how governments decided to frame and to implement social policies. The mix of policy interests and early commitments to welfare differs from state to state, a measure of diversity in the welfare state that we believe functional studies of social policy often fail to capture.

Viewing the emergence of the modern welfare state in the framework of a major political transformation allows us to enhance the comparative dimensions of the growth of social security programs. Over the past century, very similar results, at least in programmatic terms, have emerged from very different political conditions. Again, one might turn to very general theories concerning the social and economic pressures on modern democracies, but such an abstract approach still does not deal with the particular ways in which democracies sought internal political compromises and dealt with existing bureaucratic interests as the modern welfare state developed. The diversity of the democratic response to similar social and economic pressures is an important measure of changing the political processes of the various democracies, and, in tern, is perhaps a clue as to how they will deal with current difficulties of social security programs.

Most of the papers in this volume were presented at a conference on "Rethinking the Welfare State" held at Cornell University in September, 1981. We are indebted to the Western Societies Program of Cornell's Center for International Studies for assistance toward the conference expenses. In addition, the Council of European Studies contributed toward the costs of bringing a number of European social security experts to our meeting so that we could have the advantage of criticism from those directly involved in recent decisions. The papers have been extensively revised and some key decisions and transitions are highlighted by papers we solicited following the meeting. Our sincere thanks as well to Mrs. Joan Irving, who not only provided for a number of unruly scholars at our meeting, but did most of the retyping needed to prepare the book.

Douglas E. Ashford
E. W. Kelley

OVERALL INTRODUCTION:
POLITICS AND SOCIAL SECURITY

Douglas E. Ashford

A major purpose of our volume is to trace the historical transformation of the Western democracies as they responded to both the intellectual and political justification of vastly expanded social security, and, once programs developed, to the new problems that irrevocably committed the state to national programs of relief and welfare. Most economists, including Keynes, had little interest in the rapid development of social programs between the wars. Much contemporary discussion oversimplifies intense historical controversies between private and public interests as government nationalized a wide array of benefits and costs. First and foremost, nationalization was a consequence of a series of political decisions, not the product of immovable social and economic forces. As will be shown in the historical essays in Part I, politicians were often, at best, confused about the options before them, hesitant to accept new fiscal obligations, and unclear about their priorities.

The nationalization of social security was neither a foregone outcome of occult social and economic forces, nor in most cases was it part of a vision of a new social and economic order for modern states.

A basic argument of our book is that leaders were uncertain about how to respond to increased unemployment and inflation between the wars, and that they acted within a politician's short-term perspective. The diverse political motives and pressures that gradually transformed the early experiments with social security into a political reality of the modern welfare state are considered in Part I. For roughly a century modern democracies have been working out how to respond to the uncertainties, or as some would say, the inadequacies, of the private marketplace. If their efforts have not been entirely satisfactory, it is important to remember that abstract social and economic ideas were not (and probably still are not) easily translated into policy recommendations. The pressure of real political choices complicated the response of each country. The uniformity of the nationalized social security systems is more apparent than real, both in how these systems came into being and how they were organized.

Another purpose of our book is to restore historical awareness of how political leaders responded simultaneously to mass democracy and economic uncertainties as they nationalized social programs. They were seldom certain about why or how to do this. They rarely saw how the full development of nationalized social security over the past two decades would generate a new political setting. Keynes observed that the First World War had "disclosed the possibility of consumption to all and the vanity of abstenance to many" (Skidelsky, 1977, pp. 8–9), but there were even more significant changes taking place as nationalization reached its full proportions in recent years. Mass consumption, of which social security is now a large part, also created its own political forces. Once government entered the marketplace, it too was subject to the same distortions that had made private enterprise suspect. Bureaucracies formed their own client groups, and consumers of public services and benefits organized to preserve their advantages. Public actors, both political and administrative, were as prone to risk aversion as were private producers and consumers. Some of these key decisions are examined in Part II.

Political leaders at the turn of the century, in the interwar period, and even into the 1950s were undecided why they made substantial commitments to maintaining personal incomes. The second political question is how to intervene, a problem that more abstract socioeconomic theories seldom stop to ask. For political reasons, the desirable and possible trade-offs between guaranteed support for the elderly, children, the unemployed and the disabled varied considerably between democracies. None of the early advocates of national insurance foresaw how the state would itself become a political actor in a nationalized social security system.

As social scientists outside the "welfare industry" begin to take more interest in the complications of social security programs, comparative analysis becomes a natural method to explore the similarities and differences of such programs. Several of these possibilities are given in Part III. A comparative context permits us to raise many larger questions about the political and historical development of the welfare state. Heclo's study (1974) is a major step in this direction. But there are numerous additional possibilites. First, single programs can be studied in a longitudinal context with precision in order to extricate the importance of political influence over long periods within one country (see Judge's chapter). Second, the fiscal and tax constraints on growth of social programs vary immensely across countries (see the chapter by Peters). And last, the scale of the welfare state permits us to construct systemic comparisons using the institutional and historical influences that were built into numerous social welfare programs and agencies. In these frameworks social security programs are one of the most neglected dimensions of comparative social policy.

THE POLITICAL PRECONDITIONS TO NATIONALIZING SOCIAL SECURITY

Perhaps the most important reason for assessing the political preconditions of the growth of social security is that so many contemporary critics and advocates of nationalized social security pay so little attention to the historical situation affecting the political leaders of Western Europe and North America when they embarked on their first experiments. In discussions of social security in more functional terms (Lampert, 1980), Germany is often portrayed as the leading innovator of the welfare state, but in political terms it is the enigma. Only the rudiments of political democracy were present when Bismarck enacted health insurance in 1883 and workmen's compensation insurance in 1885. As Altenstetter points out, by the time he felt ready to press for retirement insurance in 1889, a highly decentralized system was constructed. While there is no doubt that the German system stimulated thinking about social security in much of Europe, even in Bismarck's Germany it was controversial. As Altenstetter describes, in the early phase of Bismarck's coalition the Catholics were strongly opposed to state intrusion on welfare and felt their local efforts to be threatened. In the latter period of Bismarck's rule, the programs were used to undercut the Social Democrats and the labor movement. Though certainly propelled by state initiative, there was relatively little actual direct control until white-collar workers were incorporated into the system in 1911. In these maneuvers social security policies were a means of reconstructing the ruling coalition in much the same way as Adenauer's indexation of pensions in 1957 (Hockerts, 1981) was also a device to strengthen his coalition against growing Social Democratic support.

There were important German programs before Bismarck's autocratic government forced through parliament one of the most advanced social security systems of the day, but even Bismarck had to make some political concessions to skeptical Liberals. Feeding on fears of the Social Democrats, his social reforms were more a part of his design for national unification than a genuine response to democratic politics. In Britain, France and the United States, the nationalization of social security was more clearly part of a long political process. Relatively stable and developed national political institutions expressed a variety of uncertainties about nationalizing as effective democratic governance provided increased demand for social protection. The enigma of the early development of national social security in Germany is that the unstable party alignments and relatively untested national institutions permitted leaders to use social policy as a means of achieving political stability. The aim was to preserve conservative rule as the late emergence of unemployment insurance (1927) suggests. German reluctance to use employment as a political tool during the Great Depression is consistent with the delay in providing unemployment benefits (see Wolffsohn, 1981). German social security was state-led long before such radical ideas were acceptable to the more stable European powers, and its development was closely related to the creation of a German state; this condition was obtained in none of the other major democracies.

The early provision of pension and disability benefits in Germany has produced a misleading image of Germany as the first welfare state. From the late nineteenth century Germany had a higher absolute level of social benefits than Britain or France, but this does not probe the political incentives for high social spending nor does it help clarify the political context that became the framework for the contemporary development of social security. Britain is most often used to illustrate German leadership because several leaders in the field of social insurance in the Edwardian period studied the German programs and some visited Germany for this purpose. The implied historical distortion is not negligible because the British had been wrestling with the nature of poverty and the appropriate social response since the 1830s, but even at the turn of the century Britain's main interest was in German labor exchanges which was the major subject of controversy in a highly confused political debate (see Harris, 1972, pp. 278–295). When the British did enact their first pension scheme in 1908, it was the reverse of the German plan, which several British industrial leaders close to the Prime Minister, Asquih, thought too costly (Thane, 1978, pp.107–108). The 1908 scheme was consistent with inquiries that had been going on throughout the 1880s, well before Churchill and a bright young reformer, Beveridge, looked into the German programs. If there are two consistent trends in British social policy early in the century, they are that social assistance must be voluntary and based on self-reliance (Hennock, 1981, pp. 84–106). Indeed, as early as 1889 the *Times* castigated German reforms as "rigid, centralised, and all-pervasive control" (Thane, 1978, p. 88), though, as we shall see in Liebfried's chapter, the German system acquired this reputation more from its early appearance in a generally skeptical political world than because it actually operated this way.

The British social security system developed in an entirely different political context than in Germany. Though it is possible to exaggerate the extent to which Bismarck's reforms were imposed on a "clear field," this was never the case in Victorian Britain (Hay, 1981, p. 112). Politically unified for many centuries, there had been a furious political debate between Whig and Tory forces since the beginning of the century (see Fraser, 1973; Bruce, 1968). The approach to welfare was irrevocably imprinted on policymaking by the 1834 Poor Law Amendment Act. Under Sir Edwin Chadwick, the first of many social engineers who were to try to remodel British government, the Royal Commission on the Poor Laws (1834) outlined a new system of care for the poor whose principles were not eradicated from British practice until 1929. A cardinal principle was that poverty assistance was not to distort the free working of the marketplace, the reverse of the later German *Sozialpolitik* that saw social welfare as an integral part of a benevolent state (Briggs, 1961, pp. 247–251). The historical reasons for such an early clarification, and later stagnation, of the British political debate over welfare are diverse, but basically, as the first industrial power, Britain first experienced the human toll of economic cycles. British concerns with social security in the late Victorian period were the product of growing unemployment but, adhering to classical economic principles, the major dilemma in designing new policies was how to subsidize labor without distorting the labor market (see Harris, 1972).

Under the influence of more classical liberal thought, British policymakers segregated the poor in "deserving" and "undeserving" groups, the latter losing their right to vote, having their homes divided, and their care assigned to special institutions, the workhouses, where they were to learn the virtues of prudence and self-reliance. In this way, Britain nationalized poverty long before she nationalized social security, and produced what Lund calls the "culture of poverty." One must remember that in late Victorian Britain the issues of poverty and unemployment were not joined, nor were there any theories that might have done so. The first response to economic distress was the Royal Commission on Depression of Trade and Industry (1886) where fears were expressed about the risks of overproduction (Harris, 1972, p. 7). The economic sage of the era, Alfred Marshall, was barely concerned with unemployment except for the special case he saw for the aged poor. In Beveridge's first book, *Unemployment: A Study of Industry* (1909), the Keynesian idea of underconsumption was never raised and he rejected Hobson's argument that perhaps *all* factors of production were underemployed in Britain (Harris, 1972, p. 24). Even the Webb's Minority Report to the Royal Commission on the Poor Laws (1909) did not join the issues, but discussed more practical solutions such as limiting immigration, work camps, and so forth to relieve directly the ill-effects of unemployment. As Harris concludes (1972, p. 35), the problem was dimly perceived, "[b]ut for most of the nineteenth century inadequacy of income as such, whether caused by low wages, irregular employment or even by sickness, was not considered a legitimate object of state interference, beyond the conditional assistance of poor relief."

Poor relief was locally organized, though supervised by national inspectors and a constant concern of national politicians, largely because the local taxes used to pay for poverty assistance threatened national tax reform. Local tax increases were politically unpalatable to both Conservative landed-aristocrats and unacceptable to the Liberal Party whose rise in Victorian Britain was associated with reduced spending and decreased income taxes. To avoid the issue of how to pay for increased local costs, the parties could only agree on increasing local government subsidies, as the Royal Commission on Local Taxation (1901) did (see Ashford, 1980a). When Chamberlain, in his brief stint as President of the Local Government Board, suggested increased local public works, he reassured his colleagues that the programs would be "very strict with the loafer and confirmed pauper" (Harris, 1972, p. 76). The next Conservative President of the Board, Ritchie, claimed that "the real remedy was greater thrift, less drunkenness, more industry and fewer marriages" (Harris, 1972, p. 77). In brief, the British solution remained one of self-help and self-reliance, though these ideas were expressed in confused ways by as differing contenders as the Eugenics Society, the Charitable Organizations Society, the Fabians and the Friendly Societies, all of whom, for very different reasons, saw nationalized social insurance as a threat to their interests. The labor movement and the nascent Labour Party were still marginal actors, although a bill to establish the "right to work" (jobs or maintenance) was presented four times between 1907 and 1911.

As Lund points out, the underlying attitudes toward social security changed very little over the 1920s and heavily influenced Beveridge's postwar plans for nationalizing social insurance. The post-World War I Labour Party was much larger, but few persons had new ideas for solving Britain's social problems, except a brilliant and erratic young Clydeside M. P., Oswald Mosley, whose fiery brand of national socialism later made him the leader of the British fascist movement of the 1930s. As Skidelsky writes (1967, p. 41), there was "no suggestion for transferring initiative to the Government itself," and this view was generally consistent, for very different reasons, with both Liberal and Conservative policies. The Liberal Industrial Inquiry of 1925 (of which Keynes was a member) still stressed more public works (Skidelsky, 1967, pp. 50–54) and the Liberal response to the MacDonald government, *How to Tackle Unemployment* (1930), recommended government retrenchment and more agricultural land development (Skidelsy, 1967, pp. 221–222), an echo of the farm colonies and land projects advocated thirty years before. In such a barren policy environment, Beveridge's wartime plans for national insurance inescapably appeared to be revolutionary changes, even though they contained the same values that had governed social assistance since 1834.

The political circumstances propelling France toward nationalizing social security were radically different from those in Britain and Germany. Modern industrialization did not begin to transform French society until the Second Empire. Even so, France remained a heavily agrarian society much later than more urbanized Britain and Germany. As late as 1930, one-third of the French population still gained their livelihood on the land. Nonetheless, France has a tradition—extending back to the Revolution—of caring for the poor through its departmental structure. Social assistance was well described and carefully regulated from its earliest appearance (Godechot, 1968, pp. 440–442, 601—708). A village society still heavily steeped in the Catholic tradition had little need to press for social reforms, and the political crises of the early years of the Third Republic left little time to consider social progress. Nonetheless, once France embarked on the path toward the modern welfare state with its elaborate panoply of social security programs, the rate of growth and the diversity of services were comparable to Germany and Sweden. (I discuss this further in a later chapter.) The political paradox of French social security is how such a conservative society so rapidly progressed toward nationalizing social security.

Practicing a different version of coalition politics than Germany, the combination of Socialists, Communists and Catholics that came to power after World War II found social security one of the policies on which they could all agree. The groundwork had begun with the Popular Front of 1936, but De Gaulle's shaky coalition combined with the nationalism unleashed by the Resistance and the LIberation to make massive social change a natural option (see Lagrange's chapter). But the vested interests in social security programs are no less political than vested interests in any policy area, and in a few years the hope of "generalizing" the system faded and the historically privileged groups, miners, farmers, railroad workers and civil servants, insisted on special treatment. Especially in the area of pensions, the system could only be extended to many industrially-based retirement plans and to white-collar workers by making substantial concessions. Contrary to the stereotype of an all-encompassing French state, the system was organized to operate autonomously from the state, but under the state's "tutelage." As we shall see, nothing could have more successfully politicized the system, providing an endless series of politically defined crises and controversies for the system. Even today, with social security fully nationalized, Mitterrand's hope of reducing the retirement age to 60 years rests on extracting cooperation from the many specialized pension schemes linked to the general pension. As in other areas of French policymaking (Ashford, 1982b), decisions about the future of French social security rested on the ability of the interested parties, who have institutionalized their claims, to reach agreement. Unlike Britain, nationalizing French social security did not insulate it from politics.

For many reasons, the American social security system emerged as late as the French, although the United States was a more industrialized and urbanized country than France by 1930. The frontier mentality, the dispersed and diverse people, and the federal system itself combined to delay reform. More important politically, the Wilsonian reforms, like those in Europe in the previous decades, were mostly concerned with stabilizing business, employment and banking. Many years were needed to assemble a body of advocates and intellectuals who would see federal government as the proper agent of social reform, and the Depression was needed to form a popular Democratic coalition of the poor and neglected under Franklin Roosevelt, as explained by Teune. The minimal security provisions of the 1935 Social Security Act avoided the central-local conflicts of most major policy initiatives in the United States, but the associated "welfare" programs (old age, dependent children, and the blind) were soon immersed in federal-state politics. Indeed, it is largely fortuitous that the main system evaded state and local politics. Roosevelt thought that his program had a better chance of approval by being proposed through the House Ways and Means Committee, where his support was more dependable. This avenue meant that American social security was sheltered from the designs of large, functional departments, and that the appropriations became a fixed charge on the national budget. Even the limited coverage of the early plan drew fire from the economists of the time even though they saw its Keynesian implications (see S. Harris, 1941). The "locals" were pacified by assistance to the states being determined wholly by caseload, an invitation to generous spending that did not seem dangerous when states were still fiscally conservative. Under these conditions, it was possible to index American social security very early (1939) and at the time not regard it as an intolerable burden on government (see the chapters by Stein, and Kelly).

As we saw in Britain, the early politics of social security often hinged on local interests. The American federal system made this doubly so. The creation of the Public Assistance Board in 1936 to oversee welfare administered through the states was greeted skeptically. States were required to administer the three jointly funded programs uniformly, to offer all three forms of assistance, and to organize a single agency for welfare. Nonetheless, the southern states regarded the programs as a potential wedge against states' rights, and as such a threat to the early Democratic coalition which Teune describes. The first federal administrator of social security, Altmeyer, was known for the "reign of terror" he imposed on the states. When the general system of insurance was separated from direct assistance in 1946, his departure was received with relief by the states. By the Truman administration social security had mobilized bipartisan support. When the President tried to veto benefit increases in 1948, he was overridden by 278–75 in the Congress and 65–12 in the Senate. Even a prudent and popular President Eisenhower found it impossible to decrease federal contributions to state welfare programs when it became necessary to increase payments into the general system (ACIR, 1980, pp. 40–42). Whatever the substantive disadvantages of the blend of national and state interests in social security, by 1950 it was fully institutionalized into the structure of American politics.

CRITICAL DECISIONS

The political preconditions for nationalizing social security programs varied greatly. In Britain, social problems had been neglected during the long period of late Victorian Conservative rule, and the Liberals swept into office in 1906 with a huge majority with few firm ideas. An inept Local Government Board resisted enlarging the old Poor Law system and ambitious young Liberal ministers such as Churchill and Lloyd-George seized the issue. In Germany, perhaps the only truly state-led transformation, Bismarck's motives were clearly political, but the continued conservative rule left few opportunities for rapid growth. In France, the issue was debated in the 1890s and postponed in favor of encouraging voluntary, private insurance. In the United States, the critical precondition was to breech the strong states' rights tradition, although the early Democratic coalition recognized that a political compromise had to be made with the states.

The second critically important political feature of nationalizing social security was how to organize the bureaucratic machinery to administer the new insurance schemes and to protect the interests of the beneficiaries. These decisions were heavily influenced by the institutional and political conditions within each state. In Germany, only the limited area of disability insurance was fully under national control, but this was largely because all contributions came from employers who felt secure with the German bureaucracy. Testimony to the power of German bureaucracy, the state stimulus for social security in Germany did not easily overcome the decentralized powers of the Lander civil servants. The 1889 pension scheme was a wholly decentralized system and the early response to unemployment prior to World War I was limited to labor exchanges, largely organized by municipalities with only timid approval from the federal government (Faust, 1981). As in all the democracies, the privileged groups of employees who had extracted special benefits from their employers insisted on special treatment, most often insulating private insurance schemes from governmental control. Perhaps the best illustration of the intricate state-provincial bargaining that went on in Germany was the prolonged dispute over establishing minimum living standards which would, in turn, set the norm for locally administered welfare assistance, as pointed out by Leibfried.

The British legislation of 1946 and 1948 probably represents the most thorough nationalization of social security programs, not only by almost completely excluding local government from social security, but also by generating a wholly national body of civil servants to administer the programs. Political conditions were vital in the systematic organization of special welfare programs by the national government in 1936 when the Public Assistance Board was organized to administer all means-tested benefits (see Gilbert, 1970). Converted into the Supplementary Benefits Commission in 1956, an entire national bureaucracy was established and was a natural, if uncontrollable, object of national policy. As in so many other ways, the British system continued its nineteenth-century precedent of simply excluding diverse political interests at lower levels of the system (Ashford, 1982a). Given a Parliament largely deprived of effective intervention in policymaking, Britain moved more easily toward nationalizaton by a national bureaucracy than did most of Europe. Most of the disputes over social security policy since World War II, like the Beveridge Plan itself, were confined to the national level and conducted by the chief welfare ministers and their officials, often reinforced by academic groups outside government whose political interests escape public examination. Even the reorganization of the small effort assigned locally as personal social services was reorganized according to the designs of a very small number of officials and academics (see Richan, 1981; Higgins, 1978).

Pensions are, of course, the most politically sensitive social security program. Although the real value of British pensions multiplied four times between 1951 and 1978, it is interesting to see how consensual politics might account for this expansion. Judge's chapter underscores a major transformation in the nationalization of social security programs: the construction of broad party agreement that in effect removes important segments of social security from political competition. Not only are the beneficiaries well-organized, but their representatives are in close touch with the national bureaucracy. The effect is that when major structural changes are considered, as in the case of combining public and private pensions in Britain (Ashford, 1980b), the issue is more sectoral than class-based while the problems are often so highly technical that they escape the public. The unification of British pensions spans three governments and was only accomplished by protracted and tedious negotiations with the private insurance firms, largely hidden from either parliamentary or public scrutiny. The inability of any other major Western democracies to reproduce this task is mute testimony to the high degree of central control over policymaking that Britain has imposed.

In the United States, the politics of social security centered on how to pay for inadequate social insurance funds. The paradox of the liberalization of funding in the American social security system is that it came about largely under conservative pressure, as Stein discusses. The crucial compromise was made in 1939 when Secretary of the Treasury, Hans Morgenthau, worked out a plan that in effect permitted the federal government to use some of the contributions on a pay-as-you-go basis in order to keep the level of contributions under control, a reversal in Morgenthau's usual fiscal conservatism that required some delicate explanations before the House Ways and Means Committee. As Stein points out, for fiscal conservatives in the Democratic Party the pay-as-you-go choice carried less risk of deficit spending or the unacceptable possibility of government intervention in capital allocation. What was not anticipated was that the more flexible (more easily expanded) system presented a powerful political temptation to push the system well beyond the limits of its initial aims, once the conservative canons of governmental spending were discredited. In addition, there were few reasons for states and cities to object to increased federal debt, the price paid for increased assistance to local communities in need. Once a President was converted to Keynesian thinking, which is generally associated with Kennedy, the floodgates were easily opened.

The more strongly decentralized United States confronted local resistance to most of its efforts to broaden social security, but given the institutionalized power of states and cities, this resistance was often more effective than in countries where local preferences and procrastination were more difficult to express. As Harpham shows, even unemployment insurance had to make its compromise with state-level interests. Keynesian arguments were introduced as early as 1954 to forestall fiscal reform of employment insurance. In fact, unemployment assistance was conceived more as an instrument of counter-cycle economic policy than as a social policy. As Harpham describes, the Temporary Extended Unemployment Act of 1961 was only part of the broadly Keynesian policies of the Kennedy administration. As was the case with many social programs under Nixon (see ACIR, 1980), the immense cost of basic reform only became clear under conditions of fiscal distress. By the end of 1979, the "reformed" plan of the 1971 Emergency Unemployment Compensation Act was in debt to the Treasury for over $8 billion. From a national perspective, the inability of the federal government to control total expenditure under social security programs became part of the rationale for further nationalization.

In France, Pierre Laroque, the Beveridge of French social security, was determined that the postwar social security system should be organized "outside" the state. But the system could avoid neither the political pressures of its clients nor the state. As coverage was broadened under the Fourth Republic, each occupational group made its own conditions on linking pensions to the general system (see my later chapter and Beattie, 1974). Nor could the presumably self-managed system evade the political interests of its beneficiaries. The privileged pension plans of the white-collar workers were championed by the Confederation Generale de Cadres, their union. The extremely favorable treatment of farmers is guarded by the powerful agricultural pressure group, the FNSEA. Within the system, the elected Administrative Councils, composed of business and labor representatives, fight over the method of election of the councils and the relative weights of each group. Changes in the election system for social security boards by de Gaulle in 1967 were an important electoral issue of the Socialists in 1981, who restored the earlier, more democratic procedures while severely restricting social security deficits. In an intensely political France, virtually no aspect of social security escapes political consideration.

Whether the various forms of political intervention found in these cases makes social security more equitable or more efficient is not our purpose. Our aim is simply to show how politics play an important role within the administration of social security programs. Through the normal political processes of each country, politics helped define the goals and procedures of social welfare. Just as the forms of political competition and governmental stability played a part in justifying why Western democracies should construct new social policies, so also did it work to shape the organization of new programs, the social services bureaucracy and their relation to elected leaders. As the century advanced and social security was expanded, each democracy built a framework which encapsulated the prevailing political characteristics of the system. The democracies may have been alike in pursuing similar social goals, but their ways of achieving them were very different.

COMPARING THE POLITICS OF SOCIAL SECURITY

Given the political variation among and within Western democracies, it is curious that more effort has not been made to extract the political meaning of the rapid growth of social security over the recent decades. One reason, contained in Part II of this book, is that the contemporary dilemmas of social security are often so severe that we fail to analyze the historical and political conditions that persuade leaders to support various programs and to enlarge the system. Social security did not arise from a historical vacuum: progressive German provinces and cities had embarked on a multitude of experiments prior to Bismarck's efforts (Reulecke, 1981); the inadequacies and inequities of Britain's Poor Laws were debated throughout the Victorian age; under the Third Republic an elaborate structure for voluntary, private insurance was encouraged (Levasseur, 1901); and in the United States both states and charities were active in providing the early framework for social assistance.

However inadequate by modern standards, the early programs developed rapidly between the wars and these organizations, and their political and administrative supporters, were active in designing a full-fledged nationalization of social security after World War II. Part III takes up some alternative approaches to isolating how political conflicts and differences influence social security.

Dealing with four countries and a vast array of social programs, it is impossible to consolidate the political significance in a single design. Political influence over social security, like all forms of policymaking, is to some extent germane to a particular set of political conditions and political institutions. One option is to hold such influences constant by studying a single system or benefit longitudinally. The advantages are that the data are usually consistent and plentiful and naturally based on the prevailing social conditions of the society in question. Thus, one avenue is to compare how political variance in major social programs might be isolated, as Ken Judge does in his chapter. Because many of these conditions as well as the data have different meanings across countries, such a design is difficult to use cross-nationally, but there are many possible uses for longitudinal comparisons.

Another comparative approach is to search for the important exogenous factors that may account for differences in total social spending across countries. Peters compares the diverse tax structures in relation to social security and social insurance expenditure. Those immediately concerned with social welfare are less concerned with how national and local politicians see the risks and opportunities of raising and transferring new funds to social programs. These decisions are often more intensely political than are the decisions to build national social security programs. In a later chapter, Ashford outlines the development of bureaucratic and organizational politics in Britain and France. In terms of how benefits are organized, how administrative control is exercised, and how political interests gain access to decisionmaking in the two countries, it would be difficult to image two such different frameworks. This comparison seeks to highlight political influence by using most different systems.

Our book departs from the usual treatment of social security as a functionally distinct and readily separable aspect of modern democratic political systems. In our view, the nationalization of social security was not simply a product of class politics, as those most concerned with internal inequities of social programs might argue (Piven and Cloward, 1974), nor with the fiscal excesses and national expenditure problems of large social transfers, as more conservative critiques of social security would stress. Indeed, in our view an approach which treats social security as though it were immune to political forces and sheltered from political history inescapably underestimates politics. Without in any way diminishing the importance of what we would consider less "political" analyses of social security, our aim is simply to see how the different contexts of party competition and lawmaking influenced the growth of social security. All democratic systems have nationalized social security, but they did so in very different ways and for very different reasons. The nationalizaton of social security is one of the great political initiatives of Western democracies and should be seen as such.

REFERENCES

Advisory Commission on Intergovernmental Relations. (1980), *The Federal Role in the Federal System: The Dynamics of Growth*, Washington, D.C.: U. S. Government Printing Office.

Ashford, Douglas E. (1980a), "A Victorian Drama: The Fiscal Subordination of British Local Government," in D. Ashford, ed., *Financing Urban Government in the Welfare State*, London: Croom Helm, pp. 71–96.

Ashford, Douglas E. (1980b) *Politics and Policy in Britain: The Limits of Consensus*, Philadelphia: Temple University Press.

Ashford, Douglas E. (1982a), *British Dogmatism and French Pragmatism: Center-Local Policymaking in the Welfare State*, London: Allen & Unwin.

Ashford, Douglas, E. (1982b), *Policy and Politics in France: :Living with Uncertainty*, Philadelphia: Temple University Press.

Beattie, R. A. (1974), "France," in T. Wilson, ed., *Pensions, Inflation and Growth*, London: Heinemann, pp. 253–304.

Beveridge, William (1909), *Unemployment: A Study of Industry*, London: Allen and Unwin.

Briggs, Asa (1961), "The Welfare State in Historical Perspective," *Archives Européene de Sociologie*, 2:221–258.

Bruce, Maurice (1968), *The Coming of the Welfare State*, London: Batsford.

Buchanan, James M. and Richard E. Wagner, (1977), *Democracy in Deficit: The Political Legacy of Lord Keynes*, New York: Academic Press.

Faust, Anselm (1981), "State and Unemployment in Germany 1890–1918 (Labour Exchanges, Job Creation and Unemployment Insurance)," in W. Mommsen, ed., *The Emergence of the Welfare State in Britain and Germany*, London: Croom Helm, pp. 150–163.

Flora, Peter and Arnold Heidenheimer, eds. (1981), *The Development of the Welfare States in Europe and America*, New Brunswick, NJ: Transaction Books.

Fraser, Derek (1973), *The Evolution of the British Welfare State*, London: Macmillan.

Gilbert, Bentley B. (1970), *British Social Policy, 1914–1939*, Ithaca, NY: Cornell University Press.

Godechot, Jacques (1968), *Les Institutions de la France sous la Revolution et l'Empire*, Paris: Presses Universitaires de France.

Great Britain (1895), Royal Commission on the Aged Poor, *Report*, London: HMSO, C. 7684.

Great Britain (1901), Royal Commission on Local Taxation, *Report*, London: HMSO, Cd., 638.

Harris, José (1972), *Unemployment and Politics: A Study in English Social Policy 1886–1914*, Oxford: Clarendon Press.

Harris, Seymour E. (1941), *The Economics of Social Security*, New York: McGraw-Hill.

Hay, Roy (1981), "The British Business Community, Social Insurance and the German Example," in W. Mommsen, ed., *The Emergence of the Welfare State in Britain and Germany*, London: Croom Helm, pp. 107–132.

Heclo, Hugh (1974), *Modern Social Politics in Britain and Sweden*, New Haven, CT: Yale University Press.

Hennock, Peter E. (1981), "The Origins of British National Insurance and the German Precedent 1880–1914," in W. Mommsen, ed., *The Emergence of the Welfare State in Britain and Germany*, London: Croom Helm, pp. 84–106.

Higgins, Joan (1978), *The Poverty Business in Britain and America*, London: Martin Robertson.

Hockerts, Hans Bunther (1981), "Background of the Beveridge Plan: Some Observations Preparatory to a Comparative Analysis," in W. Mommsen, ed., *The Emergence of the Welfare State in Britain and Germany*, London: Croom Helm, pp. 315–339.

Howson, Susan and Donald Winch (1977), *The Economic Advisory Council: A Study in Economic Advice during Depression and Recovery*, Cambridge: Cambridge University Press.

Johnson, Elizabeth S. and Harry G. Johnson (1978), *The Shadow of Keynes*, Chicago: University of Chicago Press.

Keynes, John Maynard (1936), *The General Theory of Employment, Interest and Money*, New York: Harcourt Press.

Lampert, H. (1980), *Sozialpolitik*, Berlin: Springer Verlag.

Lekachman, Robert (1966), *The Age of Keynes*, New York: Random House.

Levasseur, E. (1907), *Questions ouvrières et industrielles en France sous la Troisième République*, Paris: Rousseau.

Piven, Francis Fox and Richard A. Cloward (1971), *Regulating the Poor: The Functions of Public Welfare*, New York: Vintage Books.

Reulecke, Jurgen (1981), "English Social Policy Around the Middle of the Nineteenth Century as Seen by German Social Reformers," in W. Mommsen, ed., *The Emergence of the Welfare State in Britain and Germany*, London: Croom Helm, pp. 32–49.

Richan, Willard C. (1981), *Social Service Politics in the United States and Britain*, Philadelphia: Temple University Press.

Skidelsky, Robert (1967), *Politicians and the Slump: The Labour Government of 1929–1931*, London: Macmillan.

Skidelsky, Robert, ed. (1977), *The End of the Keynesian Era*, London: Macmillan.

Stein, Herbert (1969), *The Fiscal Revolution in America*, Chicago: University of Chicago Press.

Tampke, Jurgen (1981), "Bismarck's Social Legislation: A Genuine Breakthrough?" in W. Mommsen, ed., *The Emergence of the Welfare State in Britain and Germany*, London: Croom Helm, pp. 71–83.

Thane, Pat, ed. (1978), *The Origins of British Social Policy*, London: Croom Helm.

Ullman, Hans-Peter (1981), "German Industry and Bismarck's Social Security," in W. Mommsen, ed., *The Emergence of the Welfare State in Britain and Germany*, London: Croom Helm, pp. 133–149.

Wolffsohn, Michael, (1981), "Creation of Employment as a Welfare Policy: The Final Phase of the Weimar Republic," in W. Mommsen, ed., *The Emergence of the Welfare State in Britain and Germany*, London: Croom Helm, pp. 205–244.

PART I

DEVELOPING POLITICAL MOMENTUM

INTRODUCTION TO PART I

Douglas E. Ashford

In all Western democracies, the idea that social security is necessarily connected to national government emerged slowly over the nineteenth century. What is now taken for granted was part of a prolonged and complex political debate in each country and was interwoven with the particular problems of advancing democratic politics in each country. In some respects, launching the welfare state had more political salience than many contemporary disputes about particular services and programs. The early advocates were unsure of the consequences of their decisions and often had only the most elementary notion of how to organize social programs. Political leaders such as Bismarck, Lloyd George and, later, Laroque and Roosevelt knew that their proposals carried immense political risk, but they often did not know how great the risks would become.

There was only a fragmented concept of a nationalized social security system. Each country had its own tradition to care for the destitute and disabled, often rooted in aristocratic charitable traditions or left to each locality. As the early national commitments were made, it became increasingly apparent that the complexity and scope of social welfare could only be coordinated and financed at the national level. Perhaps the single most important stimulus was, of course, the Great Depression that compelled many reluctant welfare supporters to expand and redefine social security. But even this step toward a fully developed welfare state did not predetermine the political nature of the welfare state.

The result was that early development of social security acquired very different emphasis in each democracy, of which we provide four illustrations in Part I. In the United States, as Teune outlines in his chapter, the justification and the political incentives to launch national social programs accumulated over many decades, even though the emergence of the well-developed welfare state occurred dramatically under the New Deal. In countries with a long tradition of political strength on the left, social demands and social responses were better defined, possibly most clearly in Germany where Bismarck more openly used social security as a political weapon than did other democracies. But the struggle within the recently unified country and the pressures of a strong bureaucracy created particular problems that are discussed by Altenstetter.

Although Britain made substantial commitment to national insurance in 1911, the political setting for its welfare state was affected by the prolonged depression and high unemployment of the interwar period. Lund outlines how the Beveridge Plan, the first completely nationalized system of social security, failed to achieve the political legitimacy of less ambitious plans in other European countries. Like the United States, France also made important commitments to increased social security in a very short period of time after the war, as Lagrange describes. Though a highly nationalized system from its inception, it did not involve the conflicts with local government found in Britain nor with the entrenched professionals and local bureaucracies common in federal systems. The historical irony underlined in the first part of the book is that the country most determined to have a comprehensive social security system, Britain, fell behind those who were slower to nationalize social security, such as France, as well as those like Germany, whose social security was riddled with intergovernmental obstacles and complexities, as described by Altenstetter.

In this section, the diverse political forces leading toward the nationalization of social security began to emerge. Each country had to construct a political compromise of the major interested parties as well as those already influential in government. The influence of such early compromises and disputes can be seen in most social security systems long after the initial phases of nationalization. Prolonged unemployment between the wars and the crucial role of trade unions in Labour's postwar government gave a peculiar cast to British social security, as Lund points out in his chapter. In Germany, the grip of the bureaucracy remained a potent force in Bismarck's era, as well as during the desperate efforts to expand assistance under Weimar, as Leibfried describes later in Part II, and Altenstetter shows for the postwar period, at the end of Part I. As Teune outlines in his chapter, the late start of national social security programs was the product of long accumulation of ideas and experience at lower levels of the system, but could not develop without making its peace with American pluralism.

A second observation that emerges from Part I is the vital importance of the bureaucracy in each system. Unlike the early functions of democratic governance, social security required a large administrative staff at many levels of government. In each country there developed a corps of committed bureaucrats, but often located in different parts of the political system and exercising influence over national decisions in very different ways. In Germany, the advocates and the professionals were closely aligned and rooted in the more progressive states and cities who struggled with the Reich over the 1920s, as Leibfried shows in the case of devising welfare guidelines. In contrast, in Britain, the professional and bureaucratic impulse for nationalizing welfare came largely from a group of social policy experts located within Whitehall and with access to top politicians. In France, too, the experts and professionals favoring the nationalization of social services were part of the highly centralized, elitist bureaucracy. In terms of bureaucratic strength, the United States is perhaps the deviant case because the states and cities had a tradition of patronage and administrative independence from federal government that could not be dismantled. Oddly enough, the causal effect was the reverse because federal intervention in social security became one justification for reform of state and local administration and for more stringent standards of local government.

The political element affecting the timing, strategy and formulation is the nature of party competition and political incentives in the various democratic regimes. Compared to the other problems that occupied the democracies in the first half of the century, social security as an issue almost uniformly generated political clout but mobilized little political appeal. This, of course, facilitated the rapid nationalization once leaders realized that social services had to be expanded. Nonetheless, the British Parliament had been debating the nature of poverty since the famous Poor Law Amendment Act of 1834 and clearly saw regulating social spending as one of its major prerogatives. The weak political coalitions of an unstable democracy in Germany were hardly able to intervene effectively once the social security system had taken on a life of its own under Bismarck's rule. In France, social assistance of all kinds were placed in a different context and linked to *solidarité*, readily apparent in the euphoria of Liberation and the new strength of the Left within French government that made the rapid growth inevitable in the postwar period. To the extent that American party politics is the politics of compromise and bargaining among state and federal interests, American social security rests securely in the established history of American pluralism.

THE POLITICAL DEVELOPMENT OF THE WELFARE STATE IN THE UNITED STATES

Henry Teune

The modern welfare state is distinguished in part by governmental activities, both direct and indirect, that transfer resources outside of the private market framework of consumption for more or less explicit political purposes. Polities that engage in high levels of such transfers constitute the class of welfare states. Socially defined transfers are, of course, only part of the total redistribution under the welfare state. Major and significant "transfers" come about, indeed may exceed social transfers, through tax policy, intervention in the market (e.g., price supports), and tolerance of threats of violence, especially by quasi-monopolistic and strategically placed industries and occupations (e.g., transportation and government employees), but at the core of the welfare state are policies of direct government transfers of resources to individuals.[1]

In recent years indirect transfers to individuals have also assumed greater importance. For example, private sector allocations are imposed indirectly by government through hiring and contracting requirements. This phase of the welfare state, it will be argued, began under the Democratic Party when Keynesian policies were used to stimulate demand for

direct social transfers, later to confront resistance both from the global
pattern of slow economic growth and the exhaustion of the will to tax.

The complexity of the development of the industrialized democracies
invites many, even contending, perspectives. Much historical interpretation centered on the search for the dominant dynamic of change is in-
conclusive. For example, for the United States there are Charles Beard's
economic interpretation, J. Allen Smith's clash between democratic and
elite principles structured in the Constitution, and T. Lowi's territorial
expansion (Beard, 1931; Smith, 1907; Lowi, 1976). These are not theories, in that they do not explain why a certain dynamic takes hold, why it
becomes ascendant, and then declines in force. As historical interpretations, they certainly are not abstract. But, the theoretical problem remains: explaining the relative importance of these factors under variable
conditions.

This chapter will employ a mixture of historical factors and theoretical
dynamics to explain the origins of the American welfare state. The historical factors are the setting in which the theoretical dynamics work.
The macro-theory which might explain the broad outlines of social
change in the United States will not be presented, but has been done
elsewhere, in particular, with regard to local and national systems of
government (Teune and Milnar, 1978; Teune, 1981). That theory addresses those dynamics which generate increased production, new products and ideas, and their systemic integration—the general processes of
developmental change. Perspectives from such theories, however, will
be used at various places to point to more general processes of change.
The political development of the welfare state can be interpreted as the
result of the interaction of a political legacy, ideological forces, social and
economic conditions influenced by technology, the international system,
and the thrust for legitimacy of a ruling group, the Democratic coalition.

THE LEGACY: AN INCOMPLETE POLICY

The United States has had several types of political systems. The major
components, the dominant actors, and the fundamental relationships
among them have changed. For example, interest group politics of the
political era of the New Deal were based on labor, business, and agriculture and their relationship to the government shared an interest in
growth, the basis of their legitimacy. Today the major actors are the media, the courts, and the bureaucracy. They assert their legitimacy in
terms of political values of freedom, justice, and equality. A strong na-

tional government is a prerequisite of the modern welfare state. Not until the 1930s was the process of nationalizing local politics and creating national institutions sufficiently advanced to construct a welfare state in the United States.

Prior to 1776, extensive government authority was exercised at the state and local levels. The variable range of powers of the colonial governments within the political economy reflected the prevailing mode of colonial England. Regulation of prices, wages, and other aspects of the economy was accepted, even if the the capacity to do so was limited. Until the late 1780s new state constitutions were put into place. Most states asserted extensive powers over economic matters and democratic control through strong legislators and weak governors (Smith, 1907). Local political control was a matter of local charters and practice, subject to state control. Local, but not state governments, were largely immunized from direct popular pressures.

The central government, established in 1789, assumed only limited powers to intervene in the economy but took authority to limit state controls over their economies, for example, currency and international trade. The exercise of these powers over the states was contested and to some extent that conflict continues today. Even so, until the post-Civil War constitutions, most states had authority to regulate prices, wages, and working conditions. Indeed, there was a close integration of the governors and the societies they governed.

The early growth of the federal government throughout the nineteenth century was almost entirely tied to territorial expansion. In 1802, total federal employment was about 9,237, of which 6,362 were uniformed personnel and most of the rest were revenue collectors, a government of warriors and tax collectors. Of these, about 291 resided in Washington; in the case of members of Congress, only part-time. The eightfold increase in government employees between 1816 and 1860 was almost exclusively in the post office and the military, both critical components for territorial expansion—conquest and communication (Advisory Commission on Intergovernmental Relations, 1980). Post offices often served as listening posts on the peripheries. New land, the primary source of agricultural societies, was owned by the federal government, in part because of the accident of the federal purchase of the Louisiana Territory in 1804. In Europe, in contrast, most land was in private hands—farmers, the nobility, and the church. Substantial public land was the primary resource base of the federal government.

Local politics was democratized during the 1830s with the introduction of locally elected officials. Cities established prior to 1830 had, and continued to have, more encompassing governments, that is, governments with more authority over a larger range of activities (Liebert, 1976). Cities established after 1830 tend to have less encompassing governments—the traditional trade-off in American democracy of greater democracy but less government authority; more authority, less democracy.

The first substantial federal governmental social transfers (there are earlier examples) occurred in the 1860s and set the pattern for later ones. The transfers differed only in terms of land vs. money. In the 1860s there were land transfers to states for education (the Morell Act), directly to individuals (the Homestead Act), and to private organizations (the railroads). Each was targeted to a national purpose. With several exceptions most of the post-Civil War state constitutions limited the powers of government. At the same time the major industrial cities were being formed, generating economic surpluses which were used for local governmental intervention into their economies for public consumption and for building the urban infrastructure that is still being used today (Teune, 1980).

By 1870 the American relation to welfare was mixed: limited government; no national tax on the main sector of growth, industry; and a strong ideological aversion to governmental intervention. The weight of elite opinion was antagonistic to governmental intervention. The growing cities, which were increasingly responsive to democratic processes, however, were pushing for stronger government. The emerging economy was also pressing for central governmental intervention to smooth the way for industrial expansion by providing transportation and communication, and more ominously, by controlling labor after the fears aroused by the industrial strife of the 1870s. One aspect of economic growth in the United States, as well as Europe in the latter part of the nineteenth century, was to increase the industrial work force and to extract increased productivity through the discipline of the factory. Industrial technology, still largely trial and error folk knowledge, was made several times more productive with the use of coal-steam power in industrial cities.

By the end of the nineteenth century, political contradictions made any decisive turn in direction difficult. The question being publicly discussed concerned the "proper" relationship not only between government and society, the old issue, but more urgently between government, and which level of government, and the new economy—a new political economy. The latter issue would take nearly a half century to resolve, and helps explain the delay in developing the American welfare state.

SOCIAL, ECONOMIC, AND TECHNOLOGICAL CHANGE

Preconditions of the modern welfare state are those processes that create an industrial society; retire agriculture as a way of life; shatter the traditional social order of community, church, and family; and integrate people into complex associations in the economy, social organizations, and a national polity. For the United States and Western Europe these changes were accompanied by technological changes that shaped the large city and produced for the first time a society that was almost entirely urban. An urban society and its corollary, a national economy, nationalized the American political system, the entity onto which the New Deal grafted a welfare state.

By 1870 the United States was becoming a fully industrialized urbanized society. The United States, diverse, large, and with a decentralized political tradition, in contrast to Europe, had to experience a massive social transformation to create the social and economic foundation for the development of a modern state. By modern state is meant a government with the organizational capacity to penetrate all sectors of society and economy and, indeed, to control individuals directly. One consequence of industrialization after the Civil War was rapid urbanization, creating a population more accessible to government control.

As growth centers, the cities depopulated the countryside and absorbed population surpluses of Europe. Much of the immigrant population were the young and able-bodied, which further diminished the need for social assistance. The industrial city was made by two types of technological change. First, the coal-steam technology concentrated sources of power and yielded economic surpluses significantly greater than more dispersed forms of industrial production. Industry in large cities was as much as five times more productive in terms of output per worker. Coal-steam power required concentration of labor (Higgs, 1971). Second, electrically powered transportation made the cities "accessible" to hundreds of thousands of people on a daily basis and at a reasonable cost (Owen, 1972; Teune, 1980). By the 1920s the technology of electrical power would undermine the economic rationale for the large city by dispersing sources of power for industry.

THE IDEOLOGY OF THE WELFARE STATE

Policies that shaped the welfare state would not have been possible without clear ideas justifying choice, and confidence that new collective activities might produce the predicted results. A set of such ideas is an ideology. For political intervention in the economy, a requisite to supporting consumption by government spending, a set of normative beliefs must be developed describing just and actual relationships between the constituted political authorities and those groups and individuals that produce goods and services (Teune, 1981). There have been several general theories of political economy in the West, broadly speaking: the mercantilists, the capitalists, and the Marxists. There are also specific ideologies about what particular governments should and can do. The industrial revolution of the 1870s in the United States was a powerful stimulant for the emergence of a new American political economy. To what extent these ideas resulted from social changes or the creativity of individuals is a debatable matter, not directly relevant to this discussion, but does presuppose individual ideas and intellectual movements. Ideological forces and individuals and groups advocating new ideas gave the politicians the confidence to act to transform the political economy of the United States.

The post-Civil War social and economic transformations left millions of people detached from responsive political institutions. The decade of the 1870s was the beginning of a new kind of politics. But the national government was weak and the states committed by and large to an ideology of laissez faire. The political forces created by these changes initially had to focus on the state and local levels.

There were four major streams for political mobilization in support of social welfare (Haynes, 1924). All were rooted in the strong religious basis of American politics. First, the agriculturally oriented utopian movements of the early and middle nineteenth century inspired various philanthropic organizations at the national and local levels in the 1870s. Second, the populistic movement, largely originating in the West, alerted the Midwest to economic inequities. Third, the socialist movement, largely but not entirely inspired from Europe, extended its influence. The first meeting of the Socialist International, after several false starts, convened in New York in 1872. Fourth, the labor movement, tracing its origins to 1800, began to generate a coherent political thrust. Unlike in Europe, American union organization started before the organization of socialist parties rather than the trade union movement and the socialist parties growing together. Religious, labor, and secular groups were uneasy together. America had many religions. As a result, the political forces that might advocate welfare programs were fragmented by states, classes, and religion.

Purposeful political change requires coherent policies to have any chance of succeeding. Even though socialism made little impact in such a divided setting, ideology was especially important because of fragmentation. A small number of people can pronounce and interpret an ideology; a few can design the programs to pursue its stated goals; and most understand only its outstanding symbols, such as jobs and houses. Two streams of American ideology proclaimed both what is good and possible about the imagined welfare state.

In the late nineteenth and early twentieth centuries, a small group of professional political analysts not only founded modern social science but also created the moral base of the contemporary American welfare state. The second generation of these analysts emerged in the 1960s as social scientists. They more or less severed intellectual ties with the founders of social science, but by then the normative basis for national policy had changed. The second wave were Keynesian analysts of the state and were briefly elevated to be philosopher kings of the West. Mostly economists, they were later dethroned by the Keynesian politicians, as will be discussed later.

The initiators of an American welfare ideology were a small group of about one hundred persons who studied in Germany in the 1870s and 1880s, and who were to become perhaps the "most influential men" in American higher education (Fox, 1967). They had seen firsthand the awesome capacity of the Prussian state and its claim to morality. What was important to them was the moral possibilities of the state for mankind. The state should provide economic abundance necessary for human development or, in their term, "betterment." Industrialization assaulted sacred authority but offered the possibility of material wealth for all. They rejected the conclusion of the "dismal science" and assumed for themselves the authority of moral philosophy that challenged the premises of liberal democracy (Haskell, 1977). They were more successful than those holding to the spirit of Adam Smith. Their journals sold better than any others available, and, although "socialist" in tendency, they were not yet tainted with the excesses of socialism in power either at home or abroad. They believed that government could and should act to change society, but within the framework of the American Revolution and the happiness of man.

Among the leaders of this intellectual movement for a new political economy were Richard Ely, Simon Patten, Edmund James, and Henry Adams. They were, as always with something new, associated with fringe individuals, such as Henry George who, although very popular, never influenced the political elites. Most lost influence in the 1920s because of their socialist ideas (two lost positions at the University of Pennsylvania, one through "early retirement"), but they created a generation of students who designed the New Deal, Rex Tugwell among them. What is important about them is that they argued for a new moral foundation for the United States, in particular a strong national government. Defeated by the election of Warren Harding to the presidency, they suc-

14 HENRY TEUNE

ceeded through their students in the New Deal. For political reasons, their legacy was transformed into modern social science justified on a scientific rather than a moral basis. Some of their ideas were even adopted before the decade of their decline, the 1920s.

The Progressive Party not only gave social welfare ideas national visibility but also expressed how to bring them into being. The "social and industrial justice" platform endorsed by Theodore Roosevelt had some impact on the states. Beginning in 1911 and continuing to 1920, 42 states and Hawaii, Alaska, and Puerto Rico adopted workmen's compensation laws. The welfare function of government was made more visible in 1916 when similar coverage was given to federal employees and a system of compensation and insurance was provided for military personnel. In 1920 the federal government appropriated about one million dollars to be given to states having programs for industrial cripples. During this same period 39 states passed "Mother pension" laws and 14 states established minimum wages for women. But little except extensive discussion was achieved for health and old age insurance (Haynes, 1924).

The importance of an industrial social base for government welfare programs can be seen in the pattern of state adoption of social policies. States with little or industry were in the Old South. They neither felt the political pressure nor had the enonomic resources to make changes. The South fully entered the industrial, urban society of the United States in the 1960s, and then under the pressure of increased industrialization and urbanization (Sharkansky, 1975).

In the industrialized areas third parties had many roles, the most important being the nationalization of awareness of social problems and the ideas about what should be done. In contrast, by 1900 the major parties were full-blown patronage parties, helping to dampen demand for governmental services in the cities by themselves providing local welfare. In addition to the problems that social welfare posed for states that were competing for industry, the relative prosperity of the 1920s slowed down the growth of welfare programs. Republicans gained power and were not ideologically disposed to welfare, which was increasingly identified with a confusion of domestic proponents, Germanophiles and destructive Bolsheviks. But with the mass press, expanding communication, and the nationalism of the war, politics in the United States was becoming more national in character. Equally important, by the 1930s the United States had become a national market. Only then could a president assume moral authority of the federal government for prosperity and welfare.

THE IMPACT OF THE INTERNATIONAL SYSTEM

The international system intrudes on a country's domestic politics through the international economy and wars. Both call for strong government, prerequisite to nationalizing social security. Involvement in the international economy requires protection against its volatility; involvement in designing a world order requires central control over a foreign apparatus, including an army, and but also of the economy. World War I strengthened American national government in several ways. It was a period of rapid growth in state level welfare programs, the creation of new federal agencies, and new access to resources through the income tax.

The worldwide economic contraction in 1929 precipitated national politics. The main thrust of the first years of the New Deal was a commitment to find national solutions to problems (Beer, 1978). The New Deal began the process of accelerating intervention in the economy. The primary means was nationalizing the work force by setting terms of entry, wages, exit, and standards to handle industrial conflicts. The demand for national social benefits was virtually assured. Even more important, nationalizing the labor market contributed to the demise of local politics and the ascendance of national politics. The political issues of labor-management were taken away from local and state government and henceforth owners and workers would make their accommodations at the national level. Without this important issue there was a loss of interest in local politics, in controlling the mayor, and having a sympathetic police force.[2] Excepting the courts and the barely visible remnants of the Republican Party, national political solutions to social and economic problems, including individual needs, were accepted in the 1930s as legitimate even though the new "consensus" would be contested several times by the Republicans.[3]

World War II again enhanced the power of the federal government, further nationalized the society by depopulating the rural South, and brought millions more into a new system of federal welfare benefits for veterans. By 1945 the United States was the dominant world power with considerable surpluses both in military and economy capacity and, as after World War I, substantial moral standing. The United States organized the world economic system that would guarantee the dollar as an international currency, open sea lanes for trade, and access to the largest market (the United States itself). With cheap and declining real cost of energy and prevailing stable and declining prices of world commodities, the Western world experienced several decades of high growth. The

Truman-Acheson foreign policy used American resources to contain the expansion of the Soviet Union and to intervene to keep the peace in various world regions that were redefined after the war. But a strong national government for defense helped justify one for welfare. Resources were available for the expansion of the welfare state. The quick start to expand welfare after 1945, slowed down in the 1950s because relative prosperity and full employment reduced demand for welfare, except for Korean veterans.

Expansion of the welfare state resumed in the middle 1960s and continued into the 1970s. But the world order of Truman-Acheson had collapsed, and with it high economic growth. Military involvement in Vietnam drained governmental resources, resumed heavy involvement in government interest payments, and began the inflation of the early 1970s, but even then welfare expenditures continued to expand.

The decline of economic growth of the West today, particularly in the United States, is a worldwide phenomenon as it was in 1929–1930. Several factors converged to transform the world system and to reverse the post-World War II trend of easy accessibility to resources at declining levels or stable costs of commodities, particularly oil. Expansion of government, expenditure on welfare programs, and slow growth resurrect the historic evils of government, inflation and taxes. Contemporary democratic politics requires growth to smooth conflicts. What has to be analyzed is why, apart from the considerable international constraints, did the Democratic Party put aside its commitment to growth in favor of consumption.

THE EARLY DEMOCRATIC COALITION: THE RISE OF WELFARE POLITICS

The welfare state was created by the Democratic Party and its coalition; the configurations of the American welfare state must be understood in terms of that coalition. For nearly 50 years the Democratic Party was the dominant ideological force in American politics at the local, state, and national levels. It was the party of "innovation," as was so often stated in American government textbooks. The logic of Democratic politics passed through two phases. The first, say between 1935–1965, was characterized by national investment (electrification, TVA) and social insurance (social security and income maintenance). The Party did not attempt to nationalize industries, but it did nationalize the industrial labor force, regulating points of entry, retirement, and some aspects of wages. This was a slow process but by 1980 about 90 percent of the work force was also nationalized into the social security system and most of it was regulated in other ways to construct a national incomes policy. The nationalization of labor policies is obviously important for developing the capacity for direct transfer payments to individuals. With the nationalization of labor, along with strengthening unions, the Democratic Party created a new political economy.

The second phase began in the mid-1960s with President Kennedy's support for national economic planning, expressed in terms of growth targets. His espousal of higher living standards, based on Keynesian economics, was soon replaced by President Johnson's Great Society, or full-blown Keynesian politics. Kennedy subscribed to economic growth; Johnson turned to stimulation of political demands or increased consumption. Initially, Keynesian politics proceeded to bringing aggrieved groups into the political process, which helped produce indifference to economic growth and imposed additional obligations for increased consumption on the private sector.

The New Deal was based on the votes of industrial workers in the large cities, and the traditional South, including the agricultural sector; and the ideology and ideas of the universities. The main "interests" of the country were business, labor, and agriculture, all organized by the 1930s but then in a more or less fragmented fashion. Until the 1930s interest group politics focused on the states and localities, not on the federal government. Although "big business" was the symbolic political enemy, Roosevelt worked with them. He had to, because if the labor force were nationalized, the core political conflict would center on labor and business.

The Democratic Party organization was basically southern and metropolitan, constructed from various forms of local patronage. The party organization survived the onslaught of more radical social reform movements, such as the Townsendites, as well as the 1938 purge by Roosevelt. His programs were justified by revived economic growth. As in Britain at the turn of the century, the most visible form of intervention was public works, such as rural electification, public parks, TVA, roads, etc. All interests shared the interest of economic growth, but it would not be possible to increase personal consumption until the Second World War.

The Democratic political coalition can be characterized as market "democracy" where organized interests were arbitrated or bargained. In return such organized interests gave political support. The arena for these bargains shifted from state and local government to the federal government, and welfare has become part of this process. The local government system is now used to administer "programs," the label for the laws, transfers, reviews and bureaucracies that are national governmental transfers. Political federalism was replaced by administrative federalism.

SOCIAL SCIENCE AND THE LEGITIMIZATION OF FEDERAL INTERVENTION

The 1920s fragmented both the conservative and the liberal thrusts of social science. It became quiescent. Economics was uninteresting and the founders were in retreat. There was discussion of the role of the state, in particular its control of the economy and economic planning. The professionalization of social and political analysis, the trappings of a new legitimacy, shifted to the University of Chicago, which replaced Columbia, Johns Hopkins, and the University of Pennsylvania as the main center of social science. The debate over the role of the state was a response to communism and fascism, the ascendant nationalizing forces in Europe. The retreat from moral philosophy, at least a first step, was toward science, a science of man. Merriam's *New Aspects of Politics* was printed in 1925. Seven years later the first scale analysis was published in political science, reporting correlations (Beyle, 1932).

The 1940s, especially the war years, involved a variety of social scientists in the actual conduct of government. Whereas previously the influence of the social analysts in the construction of the modern welfare state was indirect—through students—from the Second World War to the height of the Vietnam War, social scientists were part of the Democratic Party's mobilization, mostly during the war but also after 1960 with the introduction of Keynesian economics and politics.

By the late 1960s, following the relatively quiet decade of slow federal government growth and private prosperity, a "revolution" occurred in the social sciences, called various things including "behavioralism." From small nineteenth-century beginnings, by the end of the 1920s there was a blossoming of literature expounding the principles of science which by then claimed the power to provide economic prosperity. The principles of science (philosophy of science) were to be applied to the social sciences and to various agents of change, including, of course, the government. The moral basis of the social sciences was rejected in favor of scientific legitimacy. Social science entered the marketplace.

Previously the connection between political analysts and the welfare state was through moral philosophy. Political agents and political parties were the avowed agents of principles. Now advocacy would take place through a neutral, objective science and the public bureaucracy. More than that, there were new reasons to proclaim the virtue of the national over local government. The nation stood for freedom and prosperity; the locality for elite tyranny and inefficiency. Politics and administration could be separated and the best solutions found in ways compatible with democratic principles. When the government increased its efforts to build a welfare state in the 1960s, social scientists were enlisted as "scientists," professional and technical personnel to design and direct welfare programs. Not only did the federal government confer full legitimacy on social science, it also began funding large-scale social research. In exchange, social scientists cooperated by defining the categories of the deprived and aggrieved, locating them in the population, and setting up programmatic and institutional mechanisms to reach them. The most dramatic of these efforts was a federal definition of poverty and the subsequent war on it.

THE LATE DEMOCRATIC COALITION: THE DECLINE OF WELFARE POLITICS

The federal government asserted full control over the economy in 1960. This was in the Kennedy platform, and a similar commitment was made by Nixon in exchange for political support from Rockefeller. But the Democratic Party, as part of its endorsement of national economic planning and Keynesian economics, maintained its allegiance to the principle of economic growth. This was clear in the Kennedy campaign and his subsequent efforts to stimulate the economy. Although it could be argued that the United States was not a completely nationalized economy until the final erosion of local markets during the 1950s, the assertion of national capacity contained explicit promises that the government could solve individual problems and satisfy economic needs. The international corollary in the Kennedy program was that a strong military could intervene anywhere in the world and "pay any price" for freedom.

A problem of political parties that mobilize the poor, or relatively less well-off, is that success in reducing poverty will erode their political base. As the sentiment of past recipients deteriorate, they are not completely reliable supporters. Put in other terms, the Democrats needed the poor. Whatever the number of the poor, in 1960 most were blacks and most did not regularly participate in elections. Just as it did with the poor immigrants in the nineteenth century, the Democratic Party sought to mobilize new groups of voters. But rather than using the local party organization, the federal government would do this directly. The party organization had declined, the South was poor, and the cities were decaying and losing population. Further mobilization of blacks would strain the Party's alliance with the South. The memory of the 1948 split over civil rights instilled caution.

In fact, the 1960s was a decade of substantial growth. Real family income increased about two-thirds and that of black families nearly doubled. Union members were getting wealthy and sensitive to taxes. The Civil Rights movement mobilized the blacks nearly all of whom, if they

voted, voted Democratic. But more mobilization required federal control of state voting laws if the Democratic Party was to retain its position
of political dominance in the South. This was achieved in the Civil Rights
Act of 1964.

In 1965, the Great Society initiated yet another transformation of the
American political system. Rather than a "market democracy,"
Keynesian politics stimulated demands not only of the poor but also of
certain sectors of the middle classes. On an unprecedented scale, the
federal government created demands for its services, and Congress,
rather than being a focal point of a politics of accommodation, allowed
that responsibility to be assumed by the courts and the bureaucracy. A
major step in this was the War on Poverty, conceived as an easy war. A
study published in 1962 and co-authored by Wilbur Cohen, who later
became Lyndon Johnson's Secretary of Health, Education and Welfare,
saw this as a small matter: "The United States has arrived at a point
where poverty could be abolished easily and simply by a stroke of the
pen. To raise every individual and family in the nation now below a subsistence income to the subsistence level would cost about $10 billion a
year. This is less than 2 percent of the gross national product" (Morgan,
et al., 1962, pp. 3–4).

The War on Poverty was based on a new political organization,
bypassing both the Democratic Party and city halls through federally
created poverty committees. The bureaucracy would get its own political
precincts. That was a major miscalculation because the poor are difficult
to mobilize and the old urban political order was not yet dead, although
increasingly subservient to the federal government. Between 1968 and
1972 the Democratic Party intensified its politicization of new groups. It
created political demands and the growth of government increased
exponentially. The effect is unmistakable: there was a fivefold increase
in federal expenditures between 1958–1978. Although much of this was
state and local, most of that was in response to federal programs. This
growth is a well-known story (Advisory Commission, 1980).

By 1968 the Democratic Party ceased appealing to existing organizations and groups and searched for aggrieved aggregates, in some cases
mandating local government agencies to stimulate political organization.
The logical extension was the Democratic Party reforms of the late
1960s that diminished the influence of old organized interests of the
New Deal. Delegates were now defined by sharing certain characteristics
rather than representing interests. Why the Democratic Party abandoned its concern with investment and economic growth is difficult to
explain. That it did so is clear. Its new policies were delivering welfare
and appealing to new categories of the population to seek governmental
aid. Part of the explanation perhaps derives from the "accidents" of

United States involvement in Vietnam where for the first time Soviet resistance to regional military intervention by the United States gained strength.

The Democratic Party also succeeded in stimulating political demands to remove a large range of injustices. Its most important client group became the government itself, those involved in actually administering the welfare state. Put simply, those working for government became the Democratic Party.

The worldwide recession shrank the tax base, but tax rates continued to increase in real terms. Rather than seen as provider, government was mistrusted. Although by 1972–1973 the working "middle classes" began to resist increased taxes, a weakened Republican administration was not able to resist the Democratic strategy for increased welfare. From 1969–1972, 57 new federal programs were established; in 1973 alone 23 new ones (Advisory Commission, 1980). In 1974 still another new government clientele group was created through the Comprehensive Employment Training Act (CETA) which would add hundreds of thousands of new government employees at the state and local levels.

Until 1974 the costs of maintaining and preserving the political base of the Democratic Party were met through tax transfers. But the will to tax in the face of recession, slow growth, and inflation was reaching the point of exhaustion. What was done in the middle of the 1970s was to transfer the costs of the newly formed Democratic Party coalition to the private sector by various regulations on employment, which gave additional employment to the reliable beneficiaries of the new strategy. Pollution regulation could satisfy middle-class activists; new life-styles could appeal to feminist and young voters. Regulation served both the old mobilizing strategy and the new clientelist strategy. What these policies did for growth is difficult to determine, but economic growth was among the lowest in the industrialized world.

WHY THE UNITED STATES WAS A LATE WELFARE STATE

The welfare state and its origins in the United States is certainly a more complex question than has been suggested. So far a few political factors have been selected and highlighted. But perhaps the best explanation is the formation of the industrial state discounted by demography.

Though unadjusted to national political differences, macro-comparative statistical analysis shows a simple pattern of similarity. To quote Harold Wilensky: "On the basis of a cross-sectional analysis of sixty-two countries, I conclude that economic growth and its demographic and bureaucratic outcomes are the root cause of the general emergence of the welfare state—the establishment of similar programs of social security" (Wilensky, 1975, p. xiii). In other words, wealth and people who seek it cause social security. But there were decades of difference between the United States and other countries putting together a welfare state. Why? One obvious answer is American federalism.

Two other factors could account for the "lateness" of adoption in the United States. First, the United States had among the lowest demographic dependency ratios—the number of people requiring support, the young and the old. This was largely because the immigrants who came after 1870 were ready to work and did not require rearing and education. The immigrants diluted the proportion of the old and young. This demographic damper, of course, diminishes as the number of immigrants declines and the years pass.

A second factor that might have contributed to less political pressure for welfare in the United States is private welfare. For many reasons—a free agriculture, the frontier culture, the self-governing churches—the United States has and continues to have a philanthropic tradition. Around 1960, for example, survey data revealed the following: "Public transfer amounted to some $25 billion in 1959, and private pensions another $2 billion. But private charity and aid to friends and family amounted to at least $21 billion including the free food and housing provided by relatives" (Morgan, et al., 1962, p. 7). If projected to 1980 dollars, that is a considerable amount, and private help must also be taken into account. Then, of course, to paraphrase one Democratic Party boss, the Democratic Party was the best welfare program in the world.

Having pointed to these factors, compared to parts of Europe, the United States was not really that late in developing social policies at the state level. But not only was great political effort required to establish welfare in a decentralized system, it also was doomed to fail. Local and state politics could not cope easily with industrial problems. More than this, local welfare put localities in difficult competitive positions with one another. By nationalizing labor and welfare policies, the problems of states competing with cheap labor and low taxes were moderated. It could be argued that it took from 1920–1936 to learn this lesson, the years of American "lateness."

CONCLUSION

The future direction of the welfare state depends again on economic growth. But clearly all industrialized democracies, except possibly Japan, a relatively strong economy, are making efforts to control welfare.

In the United States, the legacy of the generation that created the modern welfare state after 1965 is one of several trillion dolllars of debt for past welfare consumption. For example, the legally incurred debt to pay civil service retirees is $450 billion, for veterans about $375 billion, and billions in unfunded retirement programs at the local level. The welfare state shifted the structure of current and future political conflict from ethnic groups and socioeconomic classes to those privileged with indexing by the government against inflation and to those neither young nor old. Shifting welfare programs to the private sector is one response (medical, dental, retirement). But even this is based on assumptions of growth from the 1950s and especially the 1960s.

If the next two decades are ones of modest growth, conflict will intensify but perhaps be manageable. If they are ones of poor growth, then the magnitude of reallocations of resources may revive the intense levels of political conflict that has characterized American politics for much of its history. Then, of course, there are the unexpected international events.

NOTES

1. Although a more general definition of the welfare state is required for theoretical analysis, the one given is suitable for the "contextual" discussion. Its empirical referents are transparent.
2. I thank Oliver P. Williams for this insight.
3. The 1980 election of Ronald Reagan, representing the most recalcitrant part of the Republican objectors, was at last a concession to the legitimacy of the welfare state.

REFERENCES

Advisory Commission on Intergovernmental Relations (1980), *The Federal Role in the Federal System,* Washington, D.C.: U.S. Government Printing Office.

Beard, Charles (1913), *An Economic Interpretation of the Constitution of the United States,* New York: Macmillan.

Beer, Samuel (1978), "In Search of a New Public Philosophy," in A. King, ed., *The New American Political System,* Washington, D.C.: The American Enterprise Institute, pp. 5–44.

Beyle, Herman (1932), "A Scale of the Measurement of Attitude For Elective Government Office," *American Political Science Review,* 26:527–544.

Fox, Daniel (1967), *The Discovery of Abundance: Simon Patten and the Transformation of Social Theory,* Ithaca, N.Y.: Cornell University Press.

Haskell, Thomas (1977), *The Emergence of Professional Social Science: The American Social Science Association and the Nineteenth Century Crisis of Authority,* Urbana, IL: University of Illinois Press.

Haynes, Fred (1924), *Social Politics in the United States,* Boston: Houghton Mifflin.

Higgs, Robert (1971), *The Transformation of the American Economy: 1865–1914,* New York: Wiley.

Liebert, Roland (1976), *Disintegration and Political Action: The Changing Functions of City Government in America,* New York: Academic Press.

Lowi, Theodore (1976), *American Politics: The Imcomplete Conquest,* Hinsdale, IL: Dryden Press.

Morgan, James, et al. (1962), *Income and Welfare in the United States,* New York: McGraw-Hill.

Merriam, Charles (1925), *New Aspects of Politics,* Chicago: University of Chicago Press.

North, Douglas (1966), *The Economic Growth of the United States, 1790–1860,* New York: Norton.

Owen, Wilfred (1972), *The Accessible City,* Washington, D.C.: The Brookings Institution.

Sharkansky, Ira (1975), *The United States: A Study of a Developing Country,* New York: Longmans.

Smith, J. Allen (1907), *The Spirit of American Government,* New York: Macmillan.

Teune, Henry (1980), "Nationalization of Politics and the Governance of Cities in the United States," *International Political Science Review,* 1:280–295.

Teune, Henry (1981), "Political Developments and the American Local System of Government," *Acta Politica,* 812:217–240.

Teune, Henry and Zdravko Mlinar (1978), *The Development Logic of Social Systems,* Beverly Hills, CA: Sage Publications.

Wilensky, Harold (1975), *The Welfare State and Equality: Structural and Ideological Roots of Public Expenditures,* Berkeley, CA: University of California Press.

THE POLITICS OF A NATIONAL MINIMUM INCOME:

THE POOR LAW COALITION

IN POSTWAR BRITAIN

Michael S. Lund

Although probably not on its way out, the Western "welfare state" once again is controversial. Beginning in the late 1960s or early 1970s, well-established health and social service programs in the industrialized democracies encountered rising criticism and debate, in marked contrast to the broad support these programs enjoyed in the preceding two or three decades. Certain concerns are being expressed almost everywhere in one form or other: alarm over the rapid rise in social spending; backlash against welfare freeloaders; complaints about higher taxes, over-regulation, and bureaucratic inefficiency; criticism of welfare's disincentives for work, savings, and productivity; anxiety about threatened or actual deficits in social insurance funds; renewed philosophical doubts about whether the state has much of a role in social welfare (OECD, 1981; Heclo, 1981, pp. 399f.). These issues have been put on national agendas alongside more familiar indictments, such as that the welfare state's meager benefits are inadequate for alleviating the problems they are directed at, and that its benefits have served the well-off as much as or more than the needy.

The latest attacks have been made before, of course, but they did not have much importance in public attitudes, electoral politics, and government policy until recently. The relatively tranquil postwar climate, in which inter-party agreement behind gradual expansion of welfare's scope and levels had been the norm, has been disturbed. In some nations, parties identified with social reform appear to have lost ground over these issues to more centrist or conservative parties; in others, anti-tax movements have emerged.

All the democracies are having questions raised about prevailing assumptions and policy trends, but the amount of controversy, the main issues raised, and the responses to these issues differ from nation to nation. Indeed, it has been argued that certain Western systems are more vulnerable than others to the popular manifestations of current welfare state attacks. Among the handful of democracies that several cross-national rankings of anti-welfare state behavior have listed as especially susceptible to phenomena such as welfare backlash, tax resistance, and the weakening of parties on the left, stands Britain (Wilensky, 1976, 1981; Coughlin, 1980, p. 131). Scholars noted this even before 1979, when the election of Margaret Thatcher's stridently anti-welfare government signalled to some observers that the British electorate had repudiated postwar "Butskellism." In office, that government has aggressively tried to reduce spending on long-standing social services.

Students of modern social policy must find it ironic that the particular welfare state regarded after World War II as something of a paragon for other allied democracies to emulate is now one of the most besieged in the West. The phrase "welfare state" itself was coined in wartime Britain (Flora and Heidenheimer, 1981, p. 19). When soon afterwards Britain established a centralized, administratively unified panoply of benefits for the "cradle to the grave" that were guaranteed to all Britons as a right of national citizenship, it was viewed as a bold and unique experiment. The 1942 Beveridge Report and the social legislation based upon it that was enacted from 1945 to 1948 received wide recognition among the allies, and although not followed in all specifics, the Beveridge plan was regarded as a model for the sort of social reforms that modern industrialized democracies could and should attain (Brady, 1950, pp. 307f.; Milhaud, 1943, p. 2).

The influence of the British model was especially great in the English-speaking democracies, which already shared a social policy tradition. In the United States, for example, the postwar generation of trained social welfare professionals have often looked to British policies as a major source of inspiration and implicit standard of comparison. Social work thought and literature have been greatly influenced by the field of "social administration" in Britain; influential texts define "welfare state" in terms that correspond closely to the goals, scope, and structure of the British system (Wilensky and Lebeaux, 1965, p. xii).[1] In national politics, "liberal" welfare reformers have sought to extend America's social insurance network and enact a federally-guaranteed income floor much along British lines.

How is it that Britain's welfare state over the past 35 years has exchanged an illustrious international reputation for a sort of notoriety? How did its initial popularity fade, and what led to the current attack on its fundamental principles? This chapter does not offer a full explanation of this multi-faceted transformation, but it does propose certain important contributing factors that have been generally overlooked.

A great deal of speculation and systematic research is attempting to explain the apparent decline in the legitimacy of the Western welfare state as a whole. The theories offered are very diverse, naming factors as different as continuing class conflict (Wolfe, 1978), the declining influence of political parties and parliamentary discipline (Janowitz, 1976), interest group structures (Wilensky, 1976, 1981), deterioration in the quality of the social services relative to public expectations (Hirschman, 1980), the inability of governments to cope with an "overload" of demands (Crozier, et al., 1975), the visibility of a nation's tax structure (Wilensky, 1976, 1981; Coughlin, 1980, p. 153) and the progressive achievements of the welfare state itself (Logue, 1979). Undoubtedly, all these factors have played some role; a complete explanation would have to examine the complex interactions among social structures, economies, political systems, and national policy legacies.

The argument that follows does not directly dispute or support any of these general theories. What it tries to do in regard to Britain in particular is uncover certain neglected linkages between the specific characteristics of major welfare policies and their wider political milieu, linkages that may help to explain the special vulnerability of Britain's welfare institutions. Understanding these relationships might yield useful hypotheses about the "crisis" of the welfare state in general. Britain is a "critical case" not in the sense of being representative, but in the sense of representing a major alternative type (cf. Furniss and Tilton, 1979). Practically, this study suggests some cautions for those American welfare reformers who mark progress in social policy, consciously or unconsciously, by the standards Britain has set.

One common explanation of Britain's predicament can be quickly dismissed. American conservatives often express the view that Britain has been a lavish social spender, living beyond its means, and that Thatcher's rise to power shows that the effect of this profligacy on its economic

instability is finally being understood and corrected. But if Britain is indeed among the more threatened welfare states, the reason cannot be
found in any tendency to spend extraordinary amounts on social welfare. Britain spends a smaller portion of its total production on social
programs than most other industrialized democracies.[2] The relationship
between spending levels and popular acceptance of the welfare state
does not appear to be inverse, since higher spenders than Britain, such
as West Germany, France, and the Netherlands, are considered among
the least affected by anti-welfare state sentiment (Coughlin, 1980, p. 52;
Wilensky, 1976, 1981; Hibbs and Madsen, 1979).

POSTWAR POLICIES AND BRITISH POLITICS

An analysis of the postwar evolution of three major social security programs suggests that a major reason Britain still seems to allow for basic
doubt about many of its social programs is not that its welfare state has
attempted to do too much, but that its policies in certain ways were not
allowed to do enough. The comparative vulnerability of the once-
renowned British welfare model is rooted in certain striking and peculiar characteristics of its social welfare policies themselves and in the effects of these features in changing widely-accepted perceptions of the
function and social impact of the welfare state. Conceived in the midst of
a national crisis, Britain's universal, comprehensive income maintenance
network was meant as a simplified, efficient, effort at collective self-help.
It was supposed to benefit the nation as a whole by alleviating basic social
distress while at the same time stimulating economic productivity. Only a
few years after it was enacted from 1945 to 1948, however, this system
was being viewed in political discourse as a governmentally-sponsored
relief operation that redistributed income from the average worker and
middle class to poor and dependent groups, from a growing majority of
"haves" to an increasingly distinct minority of "have-nots." It was not
long before the conclusion was tacitly drawn that the welfare state had
little to do with the needs and interests of the mainstream of the economically active population. A corollary was that social programs were
parasitic on the growth of the economy and social policy was unproductive and inherently in conflict with the goals of economic policy (cf.
Klein, 1980, pp. 24–31).

Such perceptions were based on the emerging benefit allocations and
administrative structure of the major income programs and the controversies these features generated. Certain policy characteristics stand out.
Although virtually universal in coverage, many of Britain's major social
security benefits have been quite low, and do not compare favorably in
level of payment with those of other European nations. This is clearest

with regard to national contributory insurance benefits and other programs geared to active wage-earners, such as family allowances. Britain's basic retirement pension, for example, provided 35.1% of the net earnings of the average ex-wage-earner and his wife in 1971. The comparable percentages for other major nations were: Netherlands, 64.3; Germany, 60.0; Belgium, 56.8; Sweden, 52.5; France, 51.5; and Italy, 33.3 (Wilson,1974, p. 354). Social insurance for unemployment and sickness in Britain also generally falls below those of other EEC countries, and family allowances levels in 1972 are similarly ranked (Lawson, 1975, pp. 22f.). Two studies conclude that Britain's postwar social security payments have tended to treat the great majority of manual and white-collar workers and their families less generously than do the European continental nations (Lawson, 1975, p. 1; Lawson and George, 1980, p. 240).

The slow development of contributory insurance can put state programs in a weak economic and political position vis-à-vis fringe benefits provided to workers commercially, such as occupational pensions. With respect to British pensions, for example,

> the better off and some not too well off expect their occupational scheme, not the state scheme, to provide them with the bulk of their pension. As a result, the more prosperous section of the population does not identify with National Insurance and demand better state pensions. (Abel-Smith, 1973, p. 210)

Efforts of postwar British governments to improve state pensions through adding an earnings-related component to the flat-rate scheme were either half-hearted or were frustrated by trade union concerns about their own negotiated plans and a growing insurance lobby that resisted state encroachment on benefits above the basic level.

If Britain's contributory insurance and family allowances are comparatively underdeveloped, its means-tested public assistance has undergone considerable improvement and expansion in clientele since the 1940s. Because of low insurance benefits, large numbers of old people and insured persons have relied on means-tested payments from the National Assistance Board (NAB), which was dignified in 1966 with the new name Supplementary Benefits Commission (SBC). NAB/SBC payments have been set at high levels and, because they include rent and other discretionary items, often exceed benefits received from contributory insurance. New categories of needy persons have been added to the scope of the SBC rather than incorporated into the national insurance network or left to local welfare. The result has been the progressive institutionalization—against all expectations in the 1940s—of a sizeable, centralized, and politically salient relief agency devoted exclusively to caring for the poor and disadvantaged. Thus, despite official rhetoric that it would eventually be abolished, the Poor Law has been institutionalized further and made more acceptable through administrative reforms.

The goal of contributory insurance, family allowances, and means-tested assistance in Britain is to provide minimum support in circumstances of social distress or earnings loss. This stands in contrast with the idea more characteristic of the continent that income transfers ought to maintain the income levels of active earners beyond a minimum, because they are an inherent portion of one's total earnings. What stands out as unique to Britain's postwar social security policy agenda is its continued and exclusive preoccupation through the postwar period with the problem of poverty and its identification of social security with that problem (Coughlin, 1980, p. 110; Abel-Smith, 1973, pp. 203–207). At least until the 1970s, moreover, Britain's treatment of the low-income population in terms of benefits and administrative procedures may have been relatively more benevolent than continental Europe's (Lawson, 1975, pp. 24–28). As one British civil servant closely involved in much postwar policymaking has observed:

> What has made our own position unique is the emergence of the "poverty" and the "insurance" approaches to social security as fully developed universal systems, running in double harness since 1948 and now, since 1966, actually joined in a single administration. (Walley, 1972, pp. 102ff.)

A related factor contributing to the British system's susceptibility to political conflict and differentiating it from continental European systems is its centralized and unified structure and its management wholly by civil servants. Continental European systems are more organizationally fragmented along occupational or other lines and have workers and employers playing some role in administration. As the original distinctions in Britain between contributory insurance and unilateral relief were blurring in terms of payment levels, program purpose, and clientele, welfare and social services administration was being further consolidated, and its problems were being defined increasingly by an emerging social welfare profession. The consequence was that the system's inadequacies, inequities, and dysfunctions were left increasingly exposed in the public domain.

Thus, despite the much-celebrated advances made by the postwar establishment of a universal, comprehensive, uniform, and centralized social security system, and certain social and administrative advantages such a highly "public" structure may have over more incomplete, differentiated, quasi-private systems, high political costs have been paid for this structure in the degree of legitimacy accorded to the welfare state. Scholars have claimed that individualistic values are latent in the mass belief systems of all Western nations (Wilensky, 1976; Coughlin, 1980, pp. 25–31). If so, the priorities and structures built into national social benefit systems may either exacerbate the tensions between this individualism and governmental welfare or minimize these tensions. British policy changes have exacerbated them. It is not that publics totally resist providing for the poor, especially the "deserving" poor (Coughlin, 1980, p. 120). But political support for conspicuously altruistic charity run largely through the state and financed to a large extent by general revenues does have its limits, especially under conditions of slow economic growth (cf. Alt, 1979, pp. 261f.). These limits are severely tested when not only is tax money very "visibly" going into higher and higher benefits for an unproductive group, but furthermore, this government largesse is not perceived as achieving its goal of eliminating poverty—an impression that the vocal poverty lobby in Britain may have succeeded in conveying over the last fifteen years (cf. Lund, 1977; Banting, 1979). A seemingly expensive but ineffective national system of public relief becomes an easy target for anti-welfare state ideologies.

To what can we attribute these trends? The historical narrative that follows describes the evolution of pensions, national assistance and family allowances from 1942 to 1979, pinpointing the proximate forces responsible at critical decision points for steering these policies in one direction or another. What we find is a constellation of political forces that has consistently inhibited the growth of national insurance and family benefits, on the one hand, and has encouraged the growth and reform of national assistance, or supplementary benefits, on the other hand. We call this constellation the Poor Law Coalition not because it acted in conscious collaboration. In actuality, these forces were separately motivated and mobilized, often taking positions in direct conflict on issues of public debate. This was a coalition in the sense that their separate actions led to a consistent result over time, an abiding national approach to the uses of social security.

Prominent at the initial stages of formulating new proposals were individual reformers or small groups of them. Heclo is correct to observe that in general major proposals for change in social security were initiated by middle-class experts, such as William Beveridge, Eleanor Rathbone, and the researchers associated with Richard Titmuss at the London School of Economics (LSE) (Heclo, 1974).

The identification of postwar British social security with the poverty problem is due in part to the continuation of the tradition of poverty research by these reformers. Although their immediate concern was the alleviation of poverty and through their influence the British policy agenda defined that as the primary target problem and policy goal, the proposals of these reformers also justified state intervention in social security on grounds that went beyond the goal of reducing poverty.

It is in relation to nontraditional components of the reformers' proposals that the role of the other members of the Coalition comes into
play. It is not generally noted that the success of reformers in getting
their specific ideas adopted by politicians differed greatly between the
wartime 1940s and the subsequent period of peace. Beveridge and
Rathbone were helped by the societal dislocations, social solidarity, and
nonpartisan politics of the wartime period and the memory of the
politically-divisive unemployment issue of the 1930s. But Titmuss and
other postwar researchers and activists saw their reforms blocked or
significantly compromised by the combined forces of other parts of the
Poor Law Coalition.

Acting as veto groups in reaction to major reforms of social security
were the Labour and Conservative parties as electoral competitors and
as the bearers of conflicting ideologies; large interest groups that ex-
erted influence within each party—especially the trade unions and insurance industry, respectively; the Treasury; and the established social
security bureaucracies. During the war and until 1948, this combination
was largely overwhelmed by the popular pressures behind major social
reform. With the waning of mass demands, however, this coalition succeeded in blocking or greatly modifying major policy changes. They are
the key political forces over the years that have been responsible for
keeping flat-rate national insurance benefits low, notwithstanding their
gradual improvement, and for consistently frustrating the extension of
state control over pensions and other social insurance business, such as
through a liberal earnings-related scheme. Generous non-means-tested
benefits for the families of low- and middle-income workers have also
been blocked by these interests. In the meantime, and sometimes as incremental surrogates for failing to enact major reforms after the partisan disputes over them, governments continuously raised minimum-
level flat-rate insurance and national assistance benefits and made
efforts to remove the stigma and increase the take-up of the latter.

The multilateral influence on policy reflected the postwar rekindling
of partisan and ideological conflict over social security that had been
suppressed during the wartime party truce, and a consistent outcome of
the interactions among these forces was a policy trend representing the
most common denominator among them: the steady improvement and
administrative reform of national assistance, or the Poor Law. Thus
much of the current design of the British system is the accumulated resi-
due left by the breakdown of efforts to achieve an agreed-on theory between the parties concerning the proper role of state intervention in social security—a role, that is, beyond that of providing a subsistence
minimum—and policy has rarely been the result of goal-directed, deliberate decision. Changing social security in response to social and eco-

nomic trends has been a low priority of postwar governments, preoccupied as they were mostly by economic and foreign policy. As a result social security policy has been highly susceptible to the short-term pressures of electoral, interest group, and budget politics.

Our method for reaching this conclusion through historical analysis of policymaking starts with an analytic distinction between two major goals national social security policies have pursued. One is the provision of a basic subsistence floor through either social insurance or assistance, or a combination of the two. The other is the replacement of workers' incomes at substantial levels above subsistence, either through contributory social insurance benefits or tax-supported "demogrants." Paralleling this distinction are two types of concrete decisions that policymakers can be observed making. Some decisions involve minor, gradual incremental changes in the role of the public sector while others significantly expand the role that a social security program, and thus the state, plays vis-à-vis the wage system and the other forces shaping policy in the private sector (cf. Derthick, 1979).[3]

The distinction is applied to history by selecting for close examination those critical episodes in a program's development when its basic goals and structure are at stake, and determining the political forces that acted to move decisionmaking toward one type of policy or another. Though the time period is long, it includes only a few of these important decision points. The gain of this method over the usual one-shot case study lies in discerning whether there are certain political factors and institutional processes which consistently play a determining role in steering policy over time, and avoiding the pitfalls of interpreting "the politics of" an issue area through naming those forces that influence only one or two instances of change. If certain factors appear again and again over many decision episodes, they can be identified as making up a continuing political "structure" that shapes a nation's policies in a given field.

THE SHALLOW CONSENSUS, 1942–1948

If Beveridge had amalgamated his objective of a minimum floor of income with Bismarck's objective of compulsory fringe benefits, the fate of social insurance in Britain might have been very different over the past thirty years. Indeed, social insurance in Britain might have been playing as large a role as it plays in Germany.

Brian Abel-Smith (1973)

A major turning point in Western welfare policy occurred when social insurance for the general worker was first introduced by Bismarck in the 1880s, and schemes for job injuries, sickness, retirement, and unemployment began to spread throughout Europe and abroad. From the late nineteenth century until the 1960s, Western democracies were engaged in extending these programs to more and more social risks, incorporating more segments of the population, and liberalizing benefits and the terms of their provision. Some countries, such as Sweden, extended coverage to the whole population from the outset of their plans. Their plans tended to organize the financing and administration of the various benefits around a few national funds. More frequently, as new risks and groups were made eligible, governments would establish distinct funds with separate financing and administration and semi-autonomous powers, especially where the state was coming in to mandate and extend the standards created under previously-organized voluntary arrangements.

In the 1930s, Britain's network of state health, pensions, and unemployment insurance schemes was incomplete, fragmented, and inconsistent in terms of benefit standards, contribution levels, and organization. Further development of benefits, financing, and administration could move in one of two basic directions: toward more equity or more equality. It could improve the benefits and upgrade the standards within each of these schemes for their respective beneficiaries, but not endeavor to equalize them, expand entitlement, extend coverage to new risks, or consolidate financing and administration. Or national policy could try to extend the population coverage of the system and eliminate differences in operating rules and administration. The fact that Britain moved mostly in the latter direction is due to William Beveridge's unique impact as a policy thinker and entrepreneur and the popular support he received for egalitarian policy changes arising from the war.

Under pressure in 1941 from a Trade Unions Congress (TUC) delegation to equalize standards among various workmen's compensation and health benefit schemes, the Coalition Government appointed a committee to review the social services with an eye to postwar changes. The Government appointed Beveridge chairman, expecting this would keep him on the sidelines of wartime manpower planning (Weale, 1979, p. 289), but Beveridge seized the opportunity to develop a comprehensive program of social reforms which he linked with a new approach to economic planning.

Beveridge proposed an array of income transfers and a health service in order to abolish the main domestic problems anticipated at war's end: unemployment, poverty, and ill health. The centerpiece of his plan was a nationally-administered and simplified set of contributory social insurance programs that would provide basic benefits for unemployment, old age, and industrial injury in an efficient and non-stigmatizing way. All citizens would be enrolled and classified in the scheme, not by occupation, industry, income, or region, but by their status in relation to full-time employment—as employee, employer, self-employed, dependent of an employee, and so on.

The contributory programs were to be accompanied by allowances for families raising children and a National Health Service, both to be financed entirely by general revenues. A National Assistance Board was to be established as a centralized relief agency providing a basic income floor for those residual segments of the population who could not initially qualify for the national insurance plans. Benefit levels under the NAB were to be set lower than national insurance benefits, but the numbers receiving means-tested relief were expected to dwindle as more of the population was covered by the contributory, more adequate national insurance system. Both the contributory and the means-tested benefits, as well as family allowances, were to be administered by a single, central government Ministry of Social Security. The whole scheme was to be underpinned by a government commitment to maintain maximum employment.

Although elements of the Plan, such as its all-in insurance and free health service, were original with Beveridge, the distinction of the plan was not in its new content. Family allowances had been proposed by reformers in the 1930s and by Keynes in 1942, when the Treasury had considered them as a way to compensate workers for wage controls and to control inflation (MacNicol, 1978). Beveridge's unique contribution was to pull these various pieces together in a single plan that in pushing social security one step further, appealed to a restless public in the midst of a war, but at the same time maintained consistency with the liberal traditions in British social policy.

The features of Beveridge's program that got the most recognition were its egalitarian measures and spirit. The main doctrinal breakthrough was its principle that a comprehensive panoply of social benefits was inherent in any citizen's rights in an industrialized democracy and ought to be enforced by the state. This view was embodied in the plan's sweeping scope, categorical eligibility criteria, and its unified administration under the central government. The replacement of a patchwork of private and state-sponsored insurance funds differing in privileges and burdens and incomplete in coverage of risks and affected populations by a comprehensive, universal, uniform system was perceived as a blow against status distinctions among the classes. Social protections that were the exclusive privilege of the wealthy and certain occupational groups, and left the majority to fall back on the begrudging, paternalistic poor relief of the local authorities, would persist no longer.

Beveridge's egalitarianism had its roots in his commitment since the

1920s to the idea of "all-in" insurance; it was given an outlet with the spirit of social solidarity that arose with Dunkirk and the Blitz. But Beveridge's egalitarianism was tempered by his roots in liberalism.

First, Beveridge's was a plan for compulsory self-help organized by government on a national scale. By definition, social insurance requires contributions by the covered members themselves, to be used to protect them from designated risks. Beveridge's endorsement of a largely contributory scheme was based on the belief that contributions by employee and employer would protect the beneficiary's right to benefits and guard against governmental or political tampering for the purposes of social control. "Payment of a substantial part of the cost of benefit as a contribution irrespective of the means of the contributor is the firm basis of a claim to benefit irrespective of means" (Beveridge, 1942, p. 12).

Second, social security would treat all citizens equally only up to that point at which destitution would be overcome, for benefit payments would be set at subsistence levels. The obligation of the state was only to require a minimum benefit sufficient to prevent poverty, as measured scientifically through a poverty index geared to the cost of nutritional and other basic needs. Above that level, individuals were to provide for themselves through savings or private insurance; it was not the business of the state to influence the distribution of income above the poverty line.

Beveridge's equality also dictated that each participant receive equal treatment *within* the state scheme; no one should benefit at the expense of others. He thus set contributions and benefit levels at a single flat-rate for all participants, so that no matter what wages or salary a person earned, their contribution to and benefit from the state would be the same amount.

The combination of Beveridge's minimal anti-poverty objective of social security and his flat-rate principle departed from the option of using state compulsory social insurance as a vehicle for allowing workers and employers to set aside proportionally more contributions as their wages went up, and thus providing a level in times of adversity that came close to maintaining their normal standard of living. This task was delegated to the voluntary sector. The flat-rate principle also proscribed any way of directing proportionately higher benefits to lower income recipients. Wage differences among individuals, occupations, or regions would not be recognized, either for the sake of income redistribution or individual equity.

A less recognized element of Beveridge's plan that was important in giving it an aura of legitimacy was its economic rationale. Much of its genius lies in the way the plan linked the achievement of social justice with economic efficiency in a "positive-sum" relationship. Comprehensive and universal benefits were not simply justified on the grounds of citizenship rights, but also were essential to the functioning of a modern industrial economy. The two principles entailed the belief that certain vulnerabilities to an individual's livelihood and health were the general condition of all of society's members, or at least the mass of workers, and not the outcome of individual failings. Therefore, these risks ought to be pooled. Such preventive action to allay insecurity caused by these risks was not simply social justice, but conducive of a productive, growing economy through stimulating consumption and strengthening social capital. Universal benefits at a basic level would boost worker morale and thus productivity and instill a spirit of national solidarity. Contributions were also essential in the economic rationale for social security, for they inculcated a greater proprietary sense of investment in the scheme on the part of its contributing members than would be possible through tax-supported outright grants. At the same time, contributions would help to discourage lavish benefits and would thus help to discipline social spending: "The insured persons should not feel that income for idleness, however caused, can come from a bottomless purse" (Beveridge, 1942, p. 12). The same incentives justified the principle of less eligibility, whereby payments from the National Assistance Board would be held below those provided by national insurance.

Besides the provision of benefits in itself, another feature that implemented Beveridge's economic reasoning was his recommendation that unemployment insurance payments be conditional after a certain period upon attendance at retraining centers. A necessary corollary for his linkage of social benefits with economic development was his "Assumption C": that government must be committed to maintaining for the mass of workers "a reasonable chance of productive employment" (Beveridge, 1942, p. 163). Adopting a national contributory scheme for which the payments of benefits was obligatory, and abandoning discretionary assistance, was in fact a means to prod government to attack the underlying causes of social needs. "The Government should not feel that by paying doles it can avoid the major responsibility of seeing that unemployment and disease are reduced to a minimum" (Beveridge, 1942, p.12).

Heretofore, social programs had been conceived largely as antithetical to economic growth and economic policy. To Beveridge, however, social benefits and interventionist economic policies were differing but interdependent methods to achieve the same goals of national welfare, and the two policy sectors needed to be coordinated.

Beveridge had developed his plan in close consultation with the trade unions and civil servants, but it was his own intellectual vision and initiative that made his report so astutely sensitive to a wide range of interests and gave it the potential for receiving wide political support. Beveridge disarmed the two major contending models of welfare legislation that had been represented by the Conservatives and Labour during the divisive 1930s. Conservative policy was epitomized in the stigmatizing means-test of the Unemployment Assistance Board and its potential use in "regulating the poor." Labor and trade union policy up until the eve of the war had been heavily influenced by overtly redistributive, left-wing schemes for tax-financed demogrants.

The distrust and ambivalence felt by both sides toward the use of state power in income distribution could be allayed by the extension of the principle of contributory insurance up to the point of a national minimum. The compromise offered by Beveridge was to neutralize the role of the state in social security. On the one hand, the detested means test would be abolished and replaced by the right to benefits by virtue of contributions. Greater interclass status equality, though not income equality, would be increased by granting universal membership in the new national insurance plan and by guaranteeing uniform flat-rate and stipulated benefit levels in the event of a wide range of commonly-feared contingencies. On the other hand, raids on the Treasury on behalf of massive income redistribution would be forestalled by the plan's safeguards against fiscal irresponsibility and slackening individual work effort. Increasing benefits would require increasing contributions. State responsibility would be limited to provision of subsistence needs. Above that level, individual circumstances and initiative would be left unaffected. The doctrine of "less eligibility" would be retained as benefits for the insured would be maintained above the level of means-tested assistance. The pace of improvement in benefits would be governed by the prior achievement of full employment and economic planning to maximize industrial efficiency. Much of the appeal of the Beveridge plan lay in this seemingly automatic, self-regulating operation, which offered to place the use of public resources beyond the reach of partisan controversy and political manipulation by the right or the left.

The Beveridge Report's appealing content was no guarantee in itself that the plan would be adopted, however, after it was issued in late 1942. News about Beveridge's costly plan alarmed the Treasury and Churchill even before it was published, and both Labour and Conservative ministers in the Coalition were anxious not to destroy the moratorium on partisan debate by opening up controversial issues about postwar reconstruction while the war was still being waged. This reluctance was overcome by a set of fortuitous events arising from the war itself.

With the beginning of a serious war effort in May, 1940, there had been increasing public discussion of the obligation of the government to achieve greater social justice after the war. This talk increased in the dark days after Dunkirk. After France fell, Britain felt totally isolated, and the feeling increased that if burdens were now to be borne for the sake of national survival, the government should demonstrate that the struggle was worth the effort, by laying plans for reforming society after the war (Titmuss, 1950). This mood of reform was mobilized after a critical turning point on the military front. In 1940 and 1941, the war did not go well for the Allies, and Britain received heavy bombing until 1942. When Germany shifted its attacks to the Eastern Front, however, the bombing let up. The threat of invasion lessened, and the Allies secured victories in North Africa. Public attitudes were mightily affected.

> Before that time, the strain of war was so intense that the overriding question was not what kind of society there would be after the war, but, rather, whether Britain would exist at all. By December, 1942, however, there was growing confidence about the future. (Dorfman, 1973, p.43)

Published at that moment, the Beveridge Report focused public feelings on a concrete plan for the future, and it became a best-seller within a week. A poll indicated 95% of the country had heard of the report, and the public's enthusiasm was mirrored by organizations representing major interests in British society and backbenchers of all the political parties.

Despite this public acclaim, the government made no official mention of Beveridge until February, 1943 when a Commons debate was forced by a back-bencher resolution that called for support of the now famous Report. Faced with the possibility of an adverse vote from both Labour and Conservative backbenchers, the Government was saved from defeat only by a tactically effective speech by an influential Labour Cabinet member and by strenuous persuasion directed at rebellious Tories by the Chancellor. Reluctantly, the government endorsed Beveridge's broad principles and announced that work would be started on postwar legislation, with no decisions made until the war's end.

In this way, then, it was Beveridge who set the agenda and outlined the basic structure of postwar social security reform. To be sure, the acceptance of Keynesian theory within the Treasury by this time made the Government more receptive to increased social spending as integral to fiscal policy. But notwithstanding the potential appeal of his proposals for Treasury and many interest groups, it was clearly the war's evoking of popular enthusiasm for the Beveridge Report that compelled the Government to start its planning with the Beveridge proposals in particular.

Immediately, however, little-recognized but ultimately important differences appeared between the plans and policy rationale Beveridge had envisioned and the specific legislation that the Treasury and the party politicians were willing to adopt. The first evidence of these differences appears in the White Papers of 1944. After completing his report, Beveridge had set about developing his full employment proposals in a separate, privately-funded study. The Government was anxious to preempt Beveridge on this subject, and it rushed to issue three White Papers on the Beveridge Plan. Modifying Beveridge's assumptions considerably, the three papers left doubt whether the Government treated social security as a complement to a positive national economic plan to secure steadily expanding production, or as an independently operated, upgraded relief system that would function largely to compensate for the failure to attain that goal.

In principle, the government accepted a national, unified, universal insurance system with higher benefits, family allowances, the health service, and full employment (Bruce, 1966, pp. 272–278). But its social insurance paper rejected Beveridge's goal of a guaranteed subsistence minimum, lowered his recommended family allowance levels, and proposed maintaining a semi-autonomous assistance board within a new Ministry of Social Insurance, rather than a totally integrated Social Security Ministry. The government would not wait twenty years, moreover, to start the new pension benefits, but would begin them immediately, albeit at a level lower than Beveridge advised.

The White Paper on employment also revealed the gap between Beveridge and the newly-converted Keynesians at the Treasury. Beveridge had proposed using taxation, borrowing, and deficit spending to determine public expenditure, business investment, and consumer demand. A new planning-oriented Ministry of Finance would use fiscal policy to influence the location of industry, encourage mobility of labor, and supervise both public and private investment (Harris, 1977, p.438). The White Paper restricted itself to varying social insurance contributions and local authorities' spending as the means to regulate consumer demand, however. Beveridge as well as Keynes had wanted sufficient control by government over industry to prevent all fluctuations in the business cycle, but government planners were skeptical of their ability to control private investment and the balance of payments sufficiently, and they believed that only anti-cyclical action was possible. Beveridge reacted to the government's timidity by calling the White Paper "a public works policy, not a policy of full employment," and complaining that the document treated British industry "as if it were a sovereign independent State, to be persuaded, influenced, appealed to and bargained with by the British State" (Beveridge, 1945, pp. 261–262).

The legislation adopted from 1945 to 1948 then put into effect the compromises outlined in the White Papers. Churchill's brief National

Government passed family allowances in 1945, announcing increases in school meals as a justification for the allowances' sub-Beveridge levels. The large majority of Attlee's Labour Government ensured that the rest of the Beveridge Plan would be completed, at least in overall outline. Labor ministers had encouraged and followed Beveridge's work all along, and the obvious electoral advantage of Labour's identification with the Report also kept it on Labour's agenda. To a great extent, external influences were responsible for the fact that Labour moved quickly to implement Beveridge. But Labour's victory did not guarantee that important details in Beveridge would remain unaltered.

Labour acted fast to enact Beveridge's social insurance plans, viewing that merely as an administrative task that required setting up the appropriate social security machinery at the new headquarters in Newcastle. The creation of the Health Service was seen as the greater social policy challenge, and Attlee was mainly interested in concentrating on Labour's program for nationalizing British industry. The result for social security was that seemingly unimportant changes were made in Beveridge that were subsequently critical in holding back the development of contributory insurance and accentuating the growth of national relief. Insurance benefits were set below levels Beveridge recommended. Existing national assistance levels were maintained, placing these benefits above insurance benefits, and the NAB was kept as a separate agency. Beveridge's automatic cost of living mechanism was dropped, and his proposal to nationalize industrial assurance, or death benefit, plans was ignored. The contributory principle was weakened further when a group of eligible insured were allowed to receive benefits before they would have accumulated sufficient contributions. Beveridge's retraining centers were not enacted, and his planning unit to coordinate social and economic policy through the budget was disregarded.

Although these were ad hoc changes brought about to accommodate interest groups, administrators, and the Treasury, the deeper explanation for this legislation was the lack of a substantial commitment to the doctrines of contributory social insurance within Labour's leadership and ranks. Labour had its social security program in the Beveridge Report, but it adopted Beveridge uncritically, neither understanding the Plan thoroughly nor adding anything substantial to social security of its own.

Labour's left wing under Silverman and Bevan was the only potential source of a distinctly different approach to reform, but it failed to gain enough support to make major changes. More representative of the attitudes of the Party was Ernest Bevin, chief spokesman for the trade unions and a key figure on the Cabinet committee that had issued the 1944

White Papers. The social insurance paper had reflected the residual suspicion of this trade-unionist toward contributory benefits. Bevin had regarded the Beveridge Report as merely a "coordination of the whole of
the nation's ambulance services on a more scientific and proper footing"
(Bullock, 1960, p.242). Believing that providing unemployment insurance benefits could be an excuse for government in failing to take necessary structural measures to deal with unemployment itself, he had opposed social insurance providing the full guarantee of subsistence and
preferred that it provide only a portion, leaving the rest to be made up
by the National Assistance Board.

There were other major differences between the chief spokesman for
the trade unions in the government and the Beveridge philosophy. For
Bevin, social insurance could have a distinctive effect on work, even if it
only covered subsistence. To avoid this complacency, he was willing to
use the means test of the Assistance Board as a prod to work—an attitude that was curiously compatible with the paternalistic philosophy attributed to the Poor Law and to Conservative Party policy in the past. To
be sure, Bevin supported strong measures to ensure full employment
through government control of industry if necessary; social insurance or
the assistance benefits would be needed then only for a very few. But if
the required controls were not implemented, nor full employment
achieved, the Bevin policy and that of the Poor Law in practice would
amount to the same thing. For both, social security was the last resort, a
method for compensating those who could not support themselves.

A common explanation of the foundation of the postwar welfare state
under the 1945–1950 Labour Government is that the Beveridge Report
formed the basis for a wartime bipartisan consensus that then lasted beyond the 1940s. Beveridge's key principles (universal coverage, comprehensive protection, a national minimum, flat-rate contributions and benefits) and his panoply of national insurance, family allowances, national
assistance and the health service were indeed endorsed in broad outline
and were implemented by Labour without any changes seen as
significant at the time. But as we have seen, the depth of the understanding and commitment to policy that existed within that consensus is ques-
tionable. Thus, it may be more illuminating to consider the Beveridge
package as a fragile accommodation brought about during an extraordinary time because the leaders of both major parties did not otherwise
agree fundamentally on how the compulsory power of the state ought to
be used in the area of social security. This shallow consensus made social
security policy subject to a set of interests that stood in the way when
subsequent reformers sought to introduce proposals for earnings-
related national insurance and increased family benefits in the following
decades.

THE FAILURE OF PENSIONS REFORM,
1951 TO 1960

Only three years after the widely-celebrated edifice Beveridge designed was put in place, the welfare state debate was re-opened once again. Neither Beveridge nor everyone else had expected that unemployment would be so low after the war, and inflation so high, as these were in the late 1940s and early 1950s. Events not anticipated in Beveridge's reasoning quickly revealed how superficial and tentative the party agreement on social security had been. The absence of a deep commitment to contributory insurance or any other new approach soon became clear for no institution or body of experts stepped forward to play the role of advocate and planner that Beveridge had played for a certain time. Conceivably a steering function that could show the way that Beveridgean assumptions and legislation needed to be adjusted to fit new circumstances could have been performed by the central planning unit Beveridge had proposed. But neither Labour nor the Treasury had created such a planning and coordinating body. Adaptation of the newly-created structure was left therefore to several separate forces, each with a different interest in social security. The development of a new structure and different goals in response to a changing economic and political environment occurred slowly over the next thirty years with many starts, stops, and divisive political controversies.

The first pattern emerging in social security policy in response to the new conditions was to make national insurance and national assistance into politically-governed benefits distributed to a distinct clientele within the welfare state: the pensioner. The fact that unemployment was low meant that able-bodied, active workers did not come to need unemployment benefits in large numbers, and, in fact, were experiencing rising wages. This weakened one of the main social and economic arguments in the Beveridge Report. Britain's historically unprecedented economic growth rate, on which the rising wages were based, also vitiated a key economic argument: that state benefits were essential to promoting growth through boosting consumption. But while unemployment was low, prices were higher than expected, and the largest group to become dependent on and invested in welfare state benefits became those on fixed incomes.

Labour had rejected Beveridge's recommendation that flat-rate insurance benefits be adjusted routinely through an automatic benefit review. This made pension levels an inevitable issue for electoral politics and stimulated party competition for the votes of a growing segment of the electorate and their sympathizers. A recurring theme in all General

Elections from 1950 to 1979 has been the plight of the pensioner, and each party has endeavored to present itself as more compassionate than the others toward these widely-acknowledged beneficiaries of governmental support. Herein lies a great deal of the much-vaunted postwar consensus on the welfare state. At the same time, as pensions benefit increases emerged as a "sacred cow" in national politics over the years, a central legitimating rationale of the postwar program—that its clientele was the mass of active workers—was being undermined. Pensions incrementalism was making the welfare state into a redistributive measure for a minority interest and less of a national self-help program for the entire population.

Gradual improvement of elderly payments was hardly an adequate long-term policy response to inflation and other changes in the economy and social structure. Proposals to restructure social security through departures from Beveridge began to be outlined by small groups of Young Turks within each of the parties as early as 1951. Each reform effort attacked key Beveridge principles, especially the notion of universalism, but on the basis of widely-differing assumptions, and very different solutions to Beveridge's structure were proposed. Because these proposals opened up partisan and ideological issues that had been circumvented earlier, it was going to require a great deal of conflict, bargaining, and delay before anything like the new proposals were adopted within the two parties or their governments, and even longer for the new approaches to be institutionalized as continuing national policy.

The Conservative group that first attacked the social security consensus explicitly drew on the public mood of retrenchment which had helped their party to power in 1951. Korea and the Cold War were interpreted widely as requiring more defense spending and less social spending. Combined with the perception that a new era of economic growth was imminent, the international climate with its Stalinism, Red Scare, and anti-communism began to be used as a warrant for restraining the growth of the social services. The fragility of Beveridge's idea that national defense and welfare were compatible became evident as the argument was heard that Britain no longer needed the welfare state and could no longer afford the escalating costs of its universalistic benefits. As inflation raised pensions and health service costs, the welfare state was described more frequently as a national burden that increased inflation and harmed productivity by coddling its beneficiaries (Townsend, 1958, pp.95f.)

In two unofficial party pamphlets, a group of Tory backbenchers led by Enoch Powell spelled out the implications of recent social changes for Conservative social policy (Conservative Political Centre, 1950; MacLeod and Powell, 1954). The actual redistribution in universal services ought to be openly acknowledged, and more efficient means of delivering benefits to those who really needed them ought to be devised, in view of the competing demands on public expenditure. Among other recommendations, this meant increasing reliance on NAB benefits and reducing their stigma, rather than continuing to increase flat-rate pensions.

The response of the Conservative government to this early "crisis of the welfare state" was to appoint three special commissions to investigate the rising costs of pensions and the health service and the problem of the "work-shy" (Great Britain, 1953, 1954, 1956). The Phillips Report on pensions recommended that workers be encouraged to work longer and retire later, in order to ease the burden on retirement pensions, and it suggested that tax incentives might stimulate the growth of private, occupational schemes so that they could ease the future costs for national insurance of the rising population of the elderly. It was the first government statement proposing major changes in post-Beveridge policy. But in the election of 1955, the Government ignored the Phillips reforms and took the conventional path of improving flat-rate pensions to attract pensioner votes (Beer, 1965).

The new "selectivism" had little direct impact on Conservative policy toward pensions, but the critics of the welfare state on the Left were to have some success with the Labour Opposition. The main concern of a small group of social researchers under the tutelage of Professor Richard Titmuss at LSE was that national insurance benefits were too low to alleviate old age poverty, one of the main objectives of postwar policy. Rising prices were forcing increasing numbers of pensioners to turn to National Assistance to supplement their pensions, while many others were unwilling to apply for the assistance they needed because of the degradation of the means test that they anticipated at their local welfare offices.

The critique of the Left started out in 1951 as an attack on the subsistence criterion on which national insurance and assistance benefit levels were nominally based. A few weeks before the 1951 General Election, Seebohm Rowntree had published the results of his third survey of living standards among the working class of York. The study indicated a significant proportion of old people and workers with large families still living below Rowntree's standard of subsistence—the same criterion used by Beveridge—but the fact that he reported a sizeable decrease in these numbers since the previous survey in 1938 was widely interpreted as evidence that the legislation of the 1940s had virtually eliminated serious want. The finding was used in the election by Labour as a vindication of their social program and by the Conservatives as a justification for arguing the welfare state was obsolete.

On the tenth anniversary of the Beveridge Report, Peter Townsend published a critique of Rowntree (Political and Economic Planning, 1952), arguing that the subsistence concept of need did not reflect the actual circumstances of the poorer groups in the working class. The poverty standard ought to be relative, he asserted, based on the amounts and types of goods regarded within the working class community as an adequate minimum.

Disturbed by the glib assumption by both Conservative and Labour officialdom that the work of the welfare state was virtually complete, and by the threat to contributory pensions and other non-means-tested social services that was posed by the climate of retrenchment, Townsend teamed up with Brian Abel-Smith to reform Beveridge national insurance pensions. Any proposal to improve pensions by right in order to avoid increased means testing would have to solve two problems. The first was the problem of avoiding hardship for low-income workers caused by any increase in flat-rate contributions for the sake of financing improved benefits; hardest hit by flat-rate levies would be those workers with the smallest income to begin with. The other obstacle was the resistance of the government and Treasury to increasing the government's contribution, derived from tax revenues, to the insurance funds. Despite Beveridge's intention that the Treasury provide one-third of the funds, its contributions were declining. The Treasury was in fact borrowing for general purposes from the surplus in the unemployment fund that had been created by unexpectedly low levels of unemployment.

The solution Townsend and Abel-Smith devised to avoid both higher flat-rate contributions and more tax revenues introduced the principle of earnings-based contributions and benefits, a method they knew was used in the United States and several continental countries but had been explicitly rejected by Beveridge. A scheme in which contributions rose with a worker's wages provided the means to redistribute improved benefits to the low-income worker by raising additional revenue without requiring added burdens on the low-income worker or a change in tax levels. While generating revenue to raise universal pensions for the current poor was their main motive, their proposal also represented a major departure from the postwar doctrine of uniform treatment from the state in that benefits as well as contributions would rise with wages. A new notion of the role of the state was reflected in the argument that workers should get a level of retirement benefit that was sufficient not only to avoid poverty but also to avoid a drastic decline in their individual incomes, whatever their levels.

In one way, earnings-relation was responsive to the political mood of the times for it allowed social policy to reflect income differences and thus would implement meritocratic criteria of distribution, as well as egalitarian values. Also compatible with the mood of the era was the re-formers' proposal that accumulated contributions would be "invested aggressively" to increase national productivity. But the plan departed from the Government's outlook and from that of the Phillips Report in its basic assumption that the state plan, not occupational plans, ought to be the vehicle for providing pension benefits higher than a subsistence minimum.

The Townsend-Abel-Smith plan was bound to face great political op-position. Not only did it challenge Conservative preferences for limiting state intervention and employing means-testing, but it also offended so-cialist sentiments through perpetuating the inequalities of the workplace into the retirement years. Scrapping the flat-rate principle would offend both Beveridge proponents still active within the Labour Party—such as James Griffiths, the Labour Minister of National Insurance who set up the 1948 system—and it would also offend the Left Wing under Aneuran Bevan.

Civil servants in the Conservative insurance ministry had discussed earnings-relation, but the idea went no further within the Government because of lack of interest by the Minister (Walley, 1974). Townsend and Abel-Smith believed their most receptive audience was Labour in oppo-sition, in any case. Titmuss arranged for them to present the idea to Pe-ter Shore, Labour's Research Director, at the 1954 annual conference, but earnings-relation did not take hold in the party until after Labour's second defeat in the 1955 General Election. Its successful introduction into the party so closely identified with the Beveridge system was due to the partly accidental, partly calculated way in which a young Bevanite, Richard Crossman, was able to thrust the idea as a compromise plan into the midst of the ideological fights in the party between the Bevanites and the "revisionists."

Fearing a party battle over the Bevanites' annual resolution calling for politically unrealistic tax increases to save pensions, Labour's spokesman on the social services assigned Crossman to answer the debate for the Executive Committee, fully aware of his Bevanite tendencies. Crossman turned to Shore for a way out of his predicament, and Shore had Titmuss brief Crossman on the new idea of "national superannuation." The predicted resolution was made, but Crossman was able to get a standing ovation from the conference when he proposed the Party study a new plan for earnings-relation. Crossman was made chairman of a study committee comprised of Titmuss and his two protégés, party officials, and trade unionists.

The main specific obstacle to getting Labour support for earnings-relation was the opposition of certain trade unionists who feared the ef-fect of a new state scheme on the occupational plans they had established with various employers. Crossman bargained aggressively, but was forced to accept a compromise through which occupational schemes could "contract-out" of the state plan if they met government standards. This mixed structure combining state and occupational schemes in response to union and employer pressure, was to characterize every subsequent pensions proposal from either party, including the plan finally established by Labour in 1975 and now in effect. The planning and bargaining went on under Crossman from 1955 until an unofficial Report was issued in 1957.

The plan Labour was cooking up for "half-pay on retirement" picked up attention all during its formative stage, and by the time the Party agreed in 1958 to bring the plan into the next General Election, it was clearly destined as a controversial election issue. Initially, the Government resisted any movement away from flat-rate pensions and attacked Labour for its radical plan to take over British industry through increasing government control over pensions funds investment. But before the 1960 General Election, the government felt compelled to come forward with a promise to present its own pensions alternative. The Boyd-Carpenter pensions scheme enacted in 1961 by the Conservatives was the first legislation to change the Beveridge structure. But the plan extended contributory insurance as national policy very little, for it provided lower benefits for middle-income workers than Labour's, required no increases in state contributions, made no provision for cost of living adjustments in response to inflation like Labour had, and, of course, allowed for contracting-out. Correctly, Labour saw it as aimed principally at easing the immediate financing pressure on the Treasury and on contributions from rising flat-rate benefits, not a new departure that raised pensions substantially and changed government's role.

THE LEGITIMATION OF THE POOR LAW

Following the 1960 Election, Crossman's committee continued to develop a pensions plan they believed would compete well with the Boyd-Carpenter stop-gap program. But with the question now being asked after its third defeat—"Can Labour Win?"—the business of raising issues and developing policy proposals to bring to the electorate intensified within the party, and a host of party study groups were set to work on social security issues other than pensions, as well as problems in education, housing, and so on. To earnings-related pensions was added earnings-relation in unemployment and industrial injuries, a plan to finally abolish the National Assistance Board, proposals to increase family allowances, and a plan for reorganizing the local social services.

No episode in postwar social policymaking illustrates better the new political forces that had come to govern social security since the late 1940s than the failed attempt from 1960 to 1966 of the Labour party to stem the growth of the National Assistance Board. The absence of any new program of improved contributory pensions meant that the numbers of pensioners relying on the NAB continued to rise through the 1950s, a trend contrary to Beveridge's intentions, although arguably foretold in Labour's enactments of 1948. The trend was accompanied by a gradual transformation in the attitudes of both the Government and Opposition toward Britain's central relief agency. Much along the lines proposed by the Powell backbencher group earlier, the NAB began to be treated less and less as the undesirable alternative to national insurance and more and more as an agency with a distinct and proper mission. Talk of reducing its role gave way to praise for the difficult and noble job the NAB was doing in assisting the nation's worst-off. In 1959, the actual practice of the NAB to occasionally raise benefits in response to the cost of living rather than using a strict subsistence standard, was explicitly affirmed when the Government set levels even higher than what the cost of living required and justified the action with the principle that assistance recipients were due a growing share of national prosperity. This emerging policy of means-tested selectivity was, of course, consistent with some strands in Conservative thought, as expressed for example by the Powell group in the early 1950s, and the Government's act was also a way to buy off criticism of the low pensions offered by the Boyd-Carpenter plan. But it demonstrated a way that social security could cater to the increasingly narrowed constituency of the welfare state with apparent compassion while at the same time avoiding costly increases in contributory benefits.

Inevitably, Labour was to be affected by this growing toleration of the Poor Law. Labour-oriented policy researchers such as Townsend did not like the extent to which the National Assistance Board was becoming an established and legitimate function of central government, but the needs of the growing clientele it served and of those eligible for it but not benefiting became a growing concern of theirs, nevertheless. Several surveys were undertaken by poverty investigators during the 1950s, following Townsend's initial effort to develop a standard of relative deprivation. One outstanding explanation of the large numbers of pensioners and other persons whose incomes were below NAB rates but who were not applying to the Board was the discouraging effect on take-up of the NAB means test. How to reform the procedures of the NAB to reach more eligible clients and thus reduce poverty became a subject that stimulated several studies and reform proposals (Lynes, 1962; Glennerster, 1962). By the 1964 election campaign, each party had its own plan.

The Conservatives argued that the NAB should be retained but should be transformed into a professionalized welfare service better equipped to ferret out the cases of worst need and deal with them in a sensitive and appropriate manner. Fabian researchers at LSE attacked the means test as the basic problem and the Labour Party devoted one of its study groups to an alternative that would abolish the NAB altogether, Beveridge's old goal. The task of developing such a reform was given to a new member of the Crossman Committee, Douglas Houghton, who had led the trade union representing Inland Revenue employees. The result was the promise in Labour's 1964 Manifesto of a new Income Guarantee. The Guarantee would replace the NAB entirely with a negative income tax. Means testing would be eliminated by using Inland Revenue offices and tax forms for determining eligibility and distributing benefits to everyone below a designated poverty line (Labour Party, 1963).

Despite the prominence given to its pensions, national assistance and other social services proposals during the election and the electoral gain Labour derived from being perceived as the party best equipped to carry forward popular improvements in social policy (Butler and Stokes, 1969, p.343), Wilson's new Government did not assign top priority to these issues. The Prime Minister assigned Crossman to Housing and Local Government, rather than the Ministry of National Insurance, thus postponing further development of National Superannuation. The social security position was placed outside the Cabinet and given to a less aggressive personality in Margaret Herbison. Responsibility for the social services was further fragmented between current programs and future plans, moreover, when Wilson gave the post of Chancellor of the Duchy of Lancaster to Houghton and asked him and a tiny staff to tackle the new plans through a "Review of the Social Services." None of the promised reforms was actually undertaken; the only immediate action taken was to increase flat-rate pensions in order to build political support for the next election, which Wilson knew would be soon because of Labour's slim 1964 majority.

The contrast between the results of the Houghton Committee and those of the Beveridge Committee are instructive. Houghton worked first and primarily at his pet project, the Income Guarantee. In working with Inland Revenue staff, Houghton immediately encountered technical problems which the opposition study group had not anticipated. Many old age pensioners had incomes below the taxable level and thus were unreachable by Inland Revenue for the purpose of determining eligibility. Inland Revenue staff resisted the reform, moreover, on the grounds that their department was not a social welfare agency. Furthermore, the staff of the NAB, which had instituted new administrative procedures to increase efficiency and reduce stigma on its own, was not eager to be abolished. Negotiations were time-consuming, and with Houghton soon diverted to other issues such as family allowances by a new outside poverty lobby, progress was slow.

Pressure to do *something* to woo NAB recipients before the next election was building. Unable to resolve the snags in the Income Guarantee idea, Houghton reluctantly scrapped the plan and took up a method of revamping the NAB instead. The result was a bill the Powell group and Conservative Government might well have sponsored. To reinforce the idea that national assistance was a right and to remove its stigma, the National Assistance Board was renamed the Supplementary Benefits Commission (SBC) and merged with national insurance into a single Ministry of Social Security. The respected Richard Titmuss, who had actually not endorsed Houghton's Income Guarantee, was made the SBC's new chairman. Such a unified Ministry had been Beveridge's intention, of course, but the similarity is misleading. Beveridge had not intended that the creation of such a ministry would be the occasion for strengthening the standing of the national agency responsible for means-tested relief through linking it with national insurance administration. It was ironic that Labour in office should now be making selectivity under the NAB more tolerable, through administrative reorganization and benefit take-up publicity campaigns, rather than opposing the means test altogether. The Poor Law had been reformed, not transcended.

Labour went into the 1966 election promising the SBC reform and earnings-relation for unemployment and sickness insurance. Both were enacted without difficulty after the election, and the focus of Houghton's "Review" turned to family allowances and pensions.

FAMILY ALLOWANCES SHIFT TO THE "NEW POOR"

The lack of development in national insurance pensions and the acceptance of a permanent, means-tested relief service in the SBC are not the only illustrations of the extent to which the universal network of social security programs was being aimed increasingly at the problems of certain poor and dependent minorities and was being disengaged from its wartime constituency of the mainstream of the working class. Another example of this trend is the revival of family allowances under the aegis of the new poverty lobby of the 1960s.

The poverty research of the late 1950s and early 1960s uncovered other low-income groups besides old age pensioners which were below the poverty line but not eligible for, or not applying to, the NAB. The

largest such category was large families headed by full-time workers.
Family allowances had virtually languished since the war. A combination
of low unemployment, rising wages, and broad suspicion that allowances
were spent on frills rather than family needs had meant that government increased payments only twice between 1946 and 1967, and family
allowances had been allowed to suffer a decline in their real value. The
unemployment of 1962–63, high by postwar standards, helped to rekin-
dle an interest in family allowances by the TUC, which had ignored
them up until then. But the TUC took even more interest at the time in
extending earnings-relation to unemployment insurance, and the Conservative government left family allowances unchanged. The missing
constituency for family allowances was supplied by the poverty researchers who proposed increases in the benefit as a means to improve the income of low-income workers.

In 1965, Peter Townsend and Brian Abel-Smith completed one of the
most authoritative surveys of poverty to date (Abel-Smith and
Townsend, 1965). Disturbed by the evidence it suggested of poverty
among large families, the two researchers decided to organize a small
group of activists to publicize the study's findings and to press for increased family allowances as the way to alleviate family poverty. Just before Christmas, 1965, the group effectively focused press attention on
family poverty by presenting a demand at Ten Downing Street that the
problem be addressed by the Labour Government.

There were two alternative ways to deal with poverty in large families,
each of which had major difficulties. One way would simply increase the
level of family allowances. But the problem here was high cost. The alternative method of increasing NAB benefits or developing a new selective family benefit for the poor was equally objectionable because it would
entail a means test. From 1965 until 1967, family poverty was the dominant issue in the social services area, and a multitude of proposals were
aired in the pages of *The Times* and *New Society*.

The proposal the Cabinet studied most seriously and eventually approved in 1967 was an outgrowth of the work of Richard Titmuss and
his former research assistant, Tony Lynes, who in 1964 had joined the
staff of Margaret Herbison in the national insurance ministry. Titmuss
and Lynes developed a controversial plan for recouping the costs of a
family allowance increase through reducing the child tax allowances that
benefited largely middle-class families. This "clawback" approach went
through many changes in the Government from 1965 to 1967 because
of its overtly redistributive character in pitting the poor against the middle class, pressure on the government to reduce spending, and technical
problems. But family allowances were finally increased through a
modified "clawback" strategy in 1967 and 1968.

CONFLICTS OVER SOCIAL SECURITY POLICY IN THE 1970s

By 1970, poverty and related causes on behalf of dependent groups had come to dominate and unify national debate concerning social security policy. Up until then, the most innovative reforms that were proposed against the Beveridge network of income transfers had come from the Labour Party. These proposals had been directed toward alleviating poverty among the "rediscovered poor" largely because of the motivations of the Fabian social researchers who influenced the party and because of the lobbying of the action groups these researchers subsequently organized. But in 1967, the Conservative Opposition under Edward Heath tried to seize Labour's initiative in social policy by developing a Conservative approach to poverty that went beyond the party's traditional promotion of means-tested assistance. The poverty issue was becoming less of an asset for Labour and more of a liability the more prominent it became on the policy agenda and the more successful the poverty lobby became in publicizing the problem as a national issue.

Abel-Smith's action group was organized into an ongoing lobby organization called the Child Poverty Action Group (CPAG) by Tony Lynes, after Lynes left the Ministry of Social Security in 1966. The two issues the group tackled were the procedures and results of the new Supplementary Benefits Commission and family allowances. The group successfully publicized poverty surveys; criticized the SBC on its wage-stop policy, the means test, and its seemingly arbitrary rulings. It continually pressed Houghton and Herbison on a family allowances increase. After Lynes left as director in 1968, CPAG entered a new phase as it turned its attention to organizing local action groups to pressure the SBC. From 1966 until 1970, CPAG and similar middle-class, reformist groups on other issues such as Shelter, became thorns in the side of the Labour government, as it tried to live up to its reputation as the party most responsive to social needs, but also faced pressures to restrain social spending to maintain the balance of payments.

The political costs of the poverty issue that Labour had helped to create culminated in the 1970 General Election campaign. CPAG attacked Labour with the damning charge that the poor were worse off under Labour than they had been in 1964. If some of Labour's middle-class constituency was moved by this argument, other constituents, mainly in the trade union movement, still felt resentful toward what they considered to be excessive attention under Labour to the poor. Clawback had been especially unpopular (Banting, 1979, p.107). Although it is difficult to verify the effects of this controversy on voting in the election, Labour's political strength was undoubtedly damaged by these new cross-pressures over poverty.

Pensions policy in the 1970s continued to reflect the difficulty of achieving agreement between the parties on a way to establish a state earnings-related insurance scheme. In 1968, Richard Crossman had been put in charge of a new, consolidated Department of Health and Social Services and was thus finally able to perfect his national superannuation plan. Negotiations were begun again with the trade unions, and this time the insurance industry was brought in. A Green Paper on the Crossman Plan was issued and a bill introduced in 1969. But before the Commons could debate the bill and vote, the Prime Minister called a General Election. The calculations of electoral politics had once again displaced long-term pensions planning.

The see-saw alternation between Labour and Conservative earnings-related pensions schemes continued under the two subsequent governments. The Conservatives' 1973 plan was rejected by Labour in 1974 on its benefit levels and its terms for allowing occupational plans to "contract-out." But occupational plans had been growing in numbers during the time pensions reform was blocked and Labour's 1975 pensions act necessarily had to concern itself even more than Labour had before with gaining the cooperation of the insurance industry.

Family benefits policy reflected the continued difficulties both parties had in trying to improve benefits for the poorest families, while at the same time retaining Britain's universal family allowances demogrant. During the 1970 campaign, the Conservative Party suggested it would introduce a non-means-tested family benefit based on a negative income tax mechanism. When it was unable to do so soon after assuming office, and instead introduced a means-tested Family Income Supplement for the working poor in 1971, it was attacked bitterly by the poverty lobby for its broken promise, and the program came under criticism for its accentuation of the "poverty trap" problem. A second effort at a negative income tax was made in the Tax Credit Scheme of 1972. The Conservative Government appointed a bipartisan committee to develop the proposal, but Labour members were unwilling to agree to a plan.

But Labour in 1974 encountered the same political problems posed by any universal family benefit with its Child Endowment proposal in 1975. This proposed a single child benefit to replace family allowances and child tax allowances. The inflation of this period meant that any increases that would maintain or improve the real value of the benefits would be very costly. Labour passed a trimmed-down benefit as an interim measure in 1974. It then proposed the more complete original version in 1976 but backed away from it because of Treasury opposition to its price tag and trade union opposition to the abolition of tax allowances (*New Society*, 1976). The measure was finally passed in 1979 through CPAG pressure. But in the absence of a family lobby combining CPAG's interest in poverty and the TUC's concern over workers' income, the prospects for retaining the real value of universal family benefits under the Thatcher government were doubtful (*New Society*, 1979).

Meanwhile, as policy differences between the two parties persisted in pensions development, and conflicts within each party's governments between costs and adequacy continued to frustrate family allowance reform, the Supplementary Benefits Commission continued to expand its responsibilities and draw controversy. The numbers of pensioners on its rolls increased to 3 million by 1977. This clientele provided an increasingly thin "political 'cover'" (Donnison, 1976) for the less politically popular groups that the SBC was now protecting under its welfare umbrella, such as one-parent families. The SBC continued to be at the center of the recurring criticism from the popular press that it catered to welfare "scroungers" and subsidized workers on strike, and at the same time, it was attacked for its low take-up rate, the wage-stop, and other issues for which the poverty lobby is known. The continued increase in discretionary payments created frequent public relations problems for the Commission when it treated apparently equal beneficiaries differently. The political visibility of Britain's central relief agency was increased further when, under Labour in 1978, the SBC was officially given the mandate to be a government monitor of the extent of poverty and to act as an advocate within government for the poor.

CONCLUSION

A dominant motif in the story of postwar British income security policy was the failure to build a generous system of contributory social insurance and family allowances on top of the universal framework of basic supports that Beveridge had designed. What emerged instead as in many ways the core of the British welfare state was an increasingly explicit policy of national public relief devoted mainly to pensioners and other categories of "new poor" perceived to be economically unproductive. This evolving meaning of social welfare is what may explain why the British version of the welfare state experience has become one of the most vulnerable to recent attacks on the general welfare state idea.[4] Inflation, low unemployment, demographic change, increasing affluence in a comparatively slow-growing economy, international pressures, and public resistance to increased government spending and tax increases were all broad constraints that successive British governments had to contend with as they sought to adjust the Beveridge legislation to new postwar realities. But these factors do not account for why other European nations faced similar conditions during this period as well but came out with policy responses quite different from the British solution. This chapter has argued that the sources of the British formula lay in British politics, and in particular, the concept of the Poor Law Coalition. A certain constellation of political actors with conflicting reactions to policy debates interacted to produce a consistent trend in collective policy over time. A trade union movement jealous of its bargaining gains and ambivalent toward state social welfare schemes; a Labour Party unsure of its own social security philosophy and distracted by electoral imperatives, internal disputes, and (when in power) recurrent economic crises; a Conservative party preoccupied with the same things but more sure of its preferences for selective benefits and means-testing; a budget-conscious and domineering Treasury; and a small, adroit corps of social policy researchers *cum* activists who were caught between their desire to restructure national policies for the long run and their immediate concern to improve benefits under the existing system for those in present need: these were the main parts of the inadvertent alliance whose net result was to refurbish the Poor Law, rather than abolish it.

NOTES

1. One recent study of the Western welfare state takes Britain as representative of all the others (Janowitz, 1976, p.32).

2. In an OECD study comparing spending on education, income maintenance, and health in 18 democracies (OECD, 1978), Britain ranked 18th, with 16.7 percent of its Gross Domestic Product going to welfare in the mid-1970s. The average in the OECD area was 18.8 percent. For an argument against the view that Britain's welfare spending has retarded its economic growth, see Lenkowsky (1977).

3. The explanatory argument here may help to resolve differences that have arisen between various postwar interpretations of British politics and policymaking. Initially, most interpretations of British government and politics stressed the power and initiative wielded by the political parties in power and the institutional powers of the central government. This "strong government" view was later eroded by American-style studies of interest group politics and by the observation of "pluralistic stagnation" in British politics in the late 1960s. To some extent, these scholarly trends may reflect the changes actually occurring through the postwar years. But another variable that may determine the strength or weakness of Britain's central political institutions could be the nature of the policy issues at stake. The present study suggests that British government may meet little resistance when it makes "minimalist" social policy decisions, such as increasing flat rate pensions or reforming the NAB. But the "weak government" model may be more appropriate when policies are likely to increase the authority of the state over the private sector or affect the status and economic interests of organized groups, such as the trade unions.

4. A comparative study of welfare backlash that develops a policy-oriented explanation similar to that in this chapter, but which appeared after it was written, is found in Rosenberry (1982).

REFERENCES

Abel-Smith, Brian (1973), "Perspectives on Income Inequality and Income Maintenance: Some Dilemmas from the British Experience," in Philip Booth, ed., *Social Security: Policy for the Seventies*, Ann Arbor: University of Michigan Press.

Abel-Smith, Brian and Peter Townsend (1965), *The Poor and the Poorest*, London: G. Bell and Sons.

Alt, James E. (1979), *The Politics of Economic Decline: Economic Management and Political Behavior*, Cambridge: Cambridge University Press.

Banting, Keith (1979), *Poverty, Politics, and Policy: Britain in the 1960's*, London: Macmillan Press.

Beer, Samuel (1965), *British Politics in the Collectivist Age*, New York: Alfred Knopf.

Beveridge, Sir William (1942), *Social Insurance and Allied Services*, New York: Macmillan.

Beveridge, William (1945), *Full Employment in a Free Society*, New York: Norton.

Brady, Robert (1950), *Crisis in Britain*, Berkeley, CA: University of California Press.

Bruce, Maurice (1966), *The Coming of the Welfare State*, New York: Schocken Books.

Bullock, Alan (1960), *The Life and Times of Ernest Bevan*, Vol. 1, London: Heinemann.

Butler, David and Donald Stokes (1969), *Political Change in Britain*, New York: Macmillan.

Conservative Political Centre (1950), *One Nation: A Tory Approach to Social Problems*, London: Conservative Political Centre.

Coughlin, Richard M. (1980), *Ideology, Public Opinion and Welfare Policy*, Berkeley, CA: University of California Press.

Crozier, Michel et al. (1975), *The Crisis of Democracy*, New York: New York University Press.

Derthick, Martha (1979), *Policymaking for Social Security*, Washington, D.C.: Brookings Institution.

Donnison, David (1976), "Supplementary Benefits: Dilemmas and Priorities," *Journal of Social Policy* 5:337–58.

Dorfman, Gerald (1973), *Wage Politics in Britain, 1945–67*, Ames, IA: University of Iowa Press.

Flora, Peter and Arnold Heidenheimer (1981), "The Historical Core and Changing Boundaries of the Welfare State," in Peter Flora and Arnold Heidenheimer, eds., *The Development of Welfare States in Europe and America*, New Brunswick, NJ: Transaction Books, pp. 17–34.

Furniss, Norman and Timothy Tilton (1979), *The Case for the Welfare State*, Bloomington: University of Indiana Press.

George, Victor (1968), *Social Security: Beveridge and After*, London: Routledge and Kegan Paul.

Glennerster, Howard (1962), *National Assistance: Service or Charity?*, London: Fabian Society.

Great Britain (1953), National Advisory Committee on the Employment of Older Men and Women, *First Report*, October.

Great Britain (1954), Committee on the Economic and Financial Problems of the Provision for Old Age, *Report*, December.

Great Britain (1956), Committee of Enquiry into the Cost of the National Health Service, *Report*.

Harris, José (1977), *William Beveridge: A Biography*, Oxford: Clarendon Press.

Heclo, Hugh (1974), *Modern Social Politics in Britain and Sweden*, New Haven, CT: Yale University Press.

Heclo, Hugh (1981), "Toward a New Welfare State?" in Peter Flora and Arnold Heidenheimer, eds., *The Development of Welfare States in Europe and America*, New Brunswick, NJ: Transaction Books, pp. 383–406.

58   MICHAEL S. LUND

Hibbs, Douglas and Henrik Jess Madsen (1979), "Public Reactions to the Growth of Taxa-
    tion and Government Expenditure," Paper prepared for delivery at the 1975 Annual
    Meeting of the American Political Science Association, Washington, D.C.
Hirschman, Albert O. (1980), "The Welfare State in Trouble: Systemic Crisis or Growing
    Pains?" *The American Economic Review* (May):113–16.
Janowitz, Morris (1976), *The Social Control of the Welfare State*, Chicago: University of
    Chicago Press.
Klein, Rudolf (1980), "The Welfare State: A Self-Inflicted Crisis?" *The Political Quarterly*
    (January-March):24–34.
Labour Party (1963), *New Frontiers for Social Security*, London: Transport House.
Lawson, Roger (1975), *Social Security in the European Community*, London: Chatham House.
Lawson, Roger and Victor George (1980), *Poverty and Inequality in Common Market Countries*,
    London: Routledge and Kegan Paul.
Lenkowsky, Leslie (1977), "Welfare in the Welfare State," in Emmett Tyrell, Jr., ed., *The
    Future That Doesn't Work*, Garden City, NY: Doubleday and Company, pp. 144–166.
Logue, John (1979), "The Welfare State: Victim of its Success," *Daedalus* (Fall):67–87.
Lund, Michael S. (1977), "Maintaining the Poor: Politics and the Function of the Welfare
    State in Britain, 1939–70," Unpublished Ph.D. Dissertation, University of Chicago.
Lynes, Tony (1962), *National Assistance and National Prosperity*, Welwyn, England: Codicote
    Press.
MacLeod, Iain and Enoch Powell (1954), *The Social Services: Needs and Means*, London:
    Conservative Political Centre.
MacNicol, S. (1978), "Family Allowances and Less Eligibility," in Pat Thane, ed., *The Ori-
    gins of British Social Policy*, London: Croom Helm.
Milhaud, Edgard (1943), *Le Plan Beveridge*, Geneve: Les Annales de L'Economie.
New Society (1976), "Killing a Commitment: The Cabinet vs. The Children," *New Society*
    (June 17):630–32.
New Society (1979), "Not the Family Way," *New Society* (October 4):3.
OECD (1978), *Public Expenditure Trends*, Paris: OECD.
OECD (1981), *The Welfare State in Crisis*, Paris: OECD.
Political and Economic Planning (1952), *Poverty: Ten Years After Beveridge*, London: Political
    and Economic Planning.
Rosenberry, Sara A. (1982), "Social Insurance, Distributive Criteria and the Welfare Back-
    lash: A Comparative Analysis," *British Journal of Political Science* (October): 421–448.
Titmuss, Richard (1950), *Problems of Social Policy*, London: His Majesty's Stationery Office.
Townsend, Peter (1958), "A Society for People," in Norman MacKenzie, ed., *Conviction*,
    London: MacGibbon and Kee.
Walley, John (1972), *Social Security—Another British Failure?* London: Charles Knight and
    Co.
Walley, Sir John (1974), Interview, London.
Weale, Albert (1979), "William Beveridge: The Patriarch as Planner," *Political Studies*
    (June):287–93.
Wilensky, Harold and Charles Lebeaux (1965), *Industrial Society and Social Welfare*, New
    York: The Free Press.
Wilensky, Harold (1976), *The "New Corporatism," Centralization, and the Welfare State*, Los
    Angeles: Sage Publications.
Wilensky, Harold (1981), "Democratic Corporatism, Consensus and Social Policy:
    Reflections on Changing Values and the 'Crisis' of the Welfare State," in OECD, *The
    Welfare State in Crisis*, Geneva: OECD, pp. 185–92.
Wilson, T., ed. (1974), *Pensions, Inflation and Growth*, London: Heinemann Books.
Wolfe, Alan (1978), "Has Social Democracy a Future?" *Comparative Politics* (Octo-
    ber):100–125.

SOCIAL SECURITY IN FRANCE FROM 1946 TO 1982

François Lagrange

In France, as elsewhere, the system of social protection is at the heart of the political, economic, and social life of the country. Its structure and its characteristics reflect the entire history of the country. Before becoming an economic and financial reality, the system was the object of a long struggle over many years involving conflict, force and negotiation. Certainly, the extraordinary economic growth of the period 1950–1974 dampened these conflicts, and the progress of social security has on the whole been encouraged by this growth. But even during this period, social conflicts and political vicissitudes played a decisive role in the evolution of social security. This explains why the system of social protection in France presents itself today as such a disparate collection of programs, produced by successive efforts over time and without the power to make radical change and to create a rational system.

Without doubt the system today is as universalized as possible. It extends to the entire French population. It covers all risks: sickness, disability, old age, pensions, unemployment, and family allowances. But it remains extremely complex. After a brief description of the French system, this chapter includes two parts. First there will be a description of the positive and voluntary efforts by the government. Here it is a matter of demonstrating the evolution of social security over the period 1950–1982 and how it resulted from deliberate choices by successive governments. In fact, certain governments put into effect a conscious policy of social transfers. Second, there is a discussion of the problems that have been inadequately handled. This part reviews the problems and constraints that escape public control and which play an important part in the evolution of social protection.

If it is impossible to measure precisely the respective importance of social factors and the deliberations of government, it is nonetheless certain that official influence has been considerable. One is reminded of this today, when, with the economic crises created by two oil shocks, the major problem is precisely to find a means to control the growth of social expenditures, that is to say to convert this constraint to a coherent and conscious public policy.

THE STRUCTURE OF FRENCH SOCIAL SECURITY

The most important part of social benefits are distributed by regimes financed by obligatory contributions charged on salaries and paid for by the employed and employers. Contributions are based on the salary within a limit (*plafond*). The actual system of regimes originated with the Liberation. Major social reforms were accomplished by the governments of General De Gaulle associated with three large parties—the Communists, the Socialists, and the Popular Republican movement—known as the period of tripartism. Before 1945 the institutions meant to protect employees against social risks were only a heterogeneous effort and were very incomplete. In 1945–1946, the idea arose that social protection should be extended to everyone and to all risks. However, universality was lacking because certain salary groups, already covered by particular regimes, whose benefits were generally more advantageous, and because of the more flexible form, allowed autonomous or occupational regimes.

A "general regime" was created to cover all industrial and commercial employees. But there are also special regimes, principally for the public and parapublic sector which were covered before 1945, and in addition the autonomous regime for the nonsalaried. The different regimes covered three major social needs: family allowances, which were made uniform and largely unified; the risks of old age and sickness to which was added maternity; and disability and death benefits in case of occupational accidents. The general regime became the most important, protecting 75% of the population for sickness, 90% for family allowances and 60% for old age.

Each regime has its own institutions. The special regimes are managed by each profession, and the autonomous regimes are managed by elected councils. The general regime since 1967 includes three distinct branches (sickness, old age and family) managed by administrative councils (*conseils d'administration paritaires*) made up of members chosen by employer and union organizations. The decision in 1967 to compose the administrative councils from designated members, nominated by social groups, was severely resented by the left and is now being returned to an elected system under the Mitterrand government. From 1982, two-thirds of the councils will be directly elected by employee organizations and one-third by employer organizations.

To these basic regimes should be added the complementary regimes for old age added to pensions under the general regime. These complementary regimes were created on the initiative of the social partners (CNPF, CFDT, FO, CGT and CFTC) who were strongly attached to their contractual rights. Nevertheless, the regulation of the system was made obligatory by the state in 1972 when Chaban-Delmas was prime minister and Jacques Delors was his social advisor. Mutual insurance companies provide complete coverage for sickness insurance, but largely as a complement to the other regimes, and are not obligatory.

Social benefits also include unemployment protection. In France it is not part of social security, although based on a system of obligatory contributions charged to employees and employers. This system was put in place by the social partners and managed equally by employer organizations and unions with the assistance of the state. In 1979 unemployment protection was the object of a major reform which was to merge the contributions and benefits provided by the public sector with the system of obligatory insurance. It was one of the last social reforms under President Giscard d'Estaing.

Finally, social benefits in the sense meant here also include a certain number of funds provided by the state, such as the fund for National Solidarity. Providing an additional benefit for the elderly, poor, and in particular those who have not contributed for a sufficient number of years to other pension plans, this fund was created in 1956 under the Socialist government by Guy Mollet. The idea of a social expense expenditure is not entirely clear. The definition varies according to the point of view adopted. It has evolved over the course of time and makes historical comparisons difficult. For present purposes, I do not use the notion of social protection in the large sense, which includes local social assistance financed by the state and local government, as well as sums given by the state and employers for professional training and lodging. Rather, I refer to the direct expenses of social security in the accounting sense, that is to say, the expenses of the administration whose principle

Table 1. Major Social Programs in France,
from 1959 to 1983, in Percentages

	1959	1965	1970	1978	1983
Total social benefits (in billions of francs)	25	59	101	377	928
Social benefits as percentage of GNP	9.6%	12.3%	13.0%	17.7%	44.1%
Sickness insurance	26.7%	32.0%	33.6%	34.1%	28.1%
Occupational disability	6.2%	6.3%	5.8%	4.9%	3.3%
Old age pensions	36.2%	37.6%	40.4%	43.4%	44.4%
Family allocations	30.6%	23.4%	19.3%	13.3%	11.9%
Unemployment benefits	0.4%	0.6%	0.9%	4.2%	11.8%

object is to provide social benefits. The totals of these social benefits have grown rapidly since 1959 and their part in the GNP has grown from 9.6% in 1959 to 44.1% in 1983 (see Table 1). In 1984, the expected expenditure by the basic regimes is 962 billion francs plus 109 billion francs by the complementary regimes.

POSITIVE AND VOLUNTARY EFFORTS BY THE STATE

After putting in place the overall system of social security between 1945 and 1947, subsequent governmental policies centered around three principles: (1) extending the protection to all occupational groups; (2) improving protection; and (3) searching for ways of redistributing the income among the various social security programs.

The most important problem since the war has been to generalize the system to the entire population. In 1945 only employees benefited from social security. But from 1946, the right to family allocations was recognized for both salaried and nonsalaried workers. Ever since 1948, merchants, artisans, and professions were included under separate regimes for old age pensions, and agricultural proprietors were added in 1952.

From 1960, under the government of General de Gaulle, these piecemeal extensions were pursued more actively. In 1960 sickness insurance was extended to include the services of all doctors and medical services. A new regime for sickness insurance was created specifically for agricultural proprietors in 1961. In 1966, merchants, artisans and the professions created their own regime for sickness insurance. Finally, the 1967 orders (*ordonnance*) offered voluntary sickness insurance to all persons residing in France.

Although only 53% of the population was covered in 1945, 96% were covered in 1974, thanks to the creation of autonomous regimes and the attachment of new groups to existing regimes. In 1974, at the beginning of Giscard's presidency, the law established the principle of financial redistribution between the regimes, opening the way for the balancing of resources among regimes (*harmonisation*) and the generalization of social security to all French people. Generalization became effective for family allocations from January 1978. For old age pensions, the generalization reached a minimum for all persons and the minimum for 1960 was extended to all retired persons. In addition, the law of 1978 added certain professions that were not covered under the categories of nonsalaried persons. Another law of 1978 created a particular regime for priests and nuns that came into effect in 1979 insuring the only category of French persons who had not yet benefited from old age insurance.

Many laws promoted the expansion of sickness insurance since 1974: improvements in the benefits in kind for sickness; support for certain categories of persons such as the young in search of their first job, the families of young persons undergoing military service; and encouraging the use of private insurance. Under certain conditions contributions could also be charged to welfare assistance for the poor or to the funds of the family allocation program for low income families.

A second major improvement was to work toward a universal pension plan with the complementary pension regimes. As in Britain initially, in 1945 pension contributions were limited to a certain platform, but were extended over 1947 by the development of a complementary regime for white-collar workers (*cadres*) by a special organization, AGIRC, which collected contributions above the social security platform based on the calculations of the basic pension fund. Managed equally by employers and unions without state control, the success of this operation quickly stimulated other complementary pension regimes for other nonsalaried groups.

These modifications were integrated in 1961 to include all salaried employees affiliated with the CNPF (National Council of French Employers). The creation of another new organization, ARRCO, federated 42 complementary pension systems from different professions. In 1972, a law achieved a full generalization in establishing the obligatory affiliation of all employed persons in one complementary or additional regime for old age.

The third major evolution of the French social security system toward universal coverage has been to standardize benefits among the various regimes for similar risks, usually called the problem of *harmonisation*. Prior to 1974, the nonsalaried (self-employed) persons in particular hoped to acquire equal benefits to salaried persons who had in 1945 and

1946 decided not to be part of the general regime. This meant that the nonsalaried were not able to profit from the financial assistance provided to that regime by the state or the improvement of benefits for salaried persons which increased regularly. Sickness insurance, for example, created in 1966 for nonsalaried persons, was much more limited than that under the general regime for salaried. In particular, their system did not anticipate covering "small risks" (ambulance services, etc.). But from 1970, the small risks were covered for the nonsalaried but with a limited charge (*ticket moderateur*) paid by the insured. Another step toward standardization was the law of 1972 which provided for the direct alignment of old age insurance for artisans, workers, and merchants based on the benefits of the general regime so that since 1973 the contribution and the benefits are the same for those in regimes for the salaried and nonsalaried.

The law of 1974, mentioned above, anticipates creating a legally obligatory system of standard benefits. But this standardization was jeopardized by the attachment of privileged groups to the advantages of their particular regimes, as well as by the financial difficulties created as standardizaton led to increasing benefits and costs. As a result, the law of 1974 was not widely applied, reaching only the more important risks for both salaried and nonsalaried and improving the old age pension for the professions.

A second major area for improvement was to increase benefits. Unemployment insurance was increasing in importance with the economic dislocation of 1970. A voluntary professional agreement of December, 1958 added public support to the unemployment insurance which had been wholly financed by contributions, 80% from the businesses, 20% from the workers. The platform for unemployment contributions was based on the social security platform, but at four times that level. The system is managed by the social partners with equal representation. The Association for Employment and Industry and Commerce (ASSEDIC) supervises the work of the National Interprofessional Union for Employment in Industry and Commerce (UNEDIC). An order from the Minister of Labor in 1959 extended the system of unemployment insurance to all nonunionized businesses associated with the CNPF. However, all of the employees were not yet covered. Not until the reforms of 1967 were most of the employees included. Agricultural workers were only covered as of 1974. Further improvements involved adjusting the maximum benefit to the age of the person as well as gradual increases in the level of benefit. Since 1974, the unemployed receive 40% of their previous salary for three months.

The problems of unemployment insurance became more severe following the economic crisis of 1974 and the growth of unemployment.

The social partners decided to create a new benefit to aid persons who were dismissed for economic causes by providing their full unemployment benefits for an entire year. The supplementary allocation (ASA) by the government paid 90% of the previous gross salary for one year. Some relief was also provided under the 1972 reform of Fontanet, Minister of Labor, who negotiated an interprofessional agreement with the social partners intended to relieve the problems of unemployed workers over 60 years old. A special regime was created to provide them with resources equal to 70% of their previous salaries. This precedent was revised in June 1977 in a new interprofessional agreement extending this benefit to all employed over 60 years who lost their jobs. The agreement was originally made for two years but has been renewed by the social partners. Under these conditions it becomes a form of early retirement which complements similar incentives under the old age pension system. In 1985 this system will be replaced by a new plan for voluntary retirement from the age of 60.

The sophistication and progressive improvement of the various benefits of ASSEDIC which were financed by the state have increased the complexity of the unemployment insurance system. The law of January 1979 simplified the system after negotiations with the social partners by Prime Minister Barre. The reform was based on four principles: unification (direct public contributions ended but the benefits were partially subsidized by the state), the extension to all employees overseas, unification of management under ASSEDIC, and creative incentives for beneficiaries to seek jobs (ASA gradually diminishes over time).

A second substantial source of increased benefits has been the growth of sickness insurance costs, largely because the system can control neither costs nor demand. When the system was first conceived in 1945, the anticipation was that 80 to 100% of medical cost would be covered. This goal was not achieved until 1960, when a system of agreements were negotiated between the social security agencies and the doctors. Under these conventions, the doctors agreed to accept fixed fees in exchange for a number of physical and social advantages given them by the state. Under the Debré government in 1960 the enlarged structure was put in place. In 1961 a new step was taken automatically to include all doctors in the national system unless they decided to exclude themselves.

A major controversy among beneficiaries in the system is the creation of fees (*ticket moderateur*). Approximately 20% of medical charges are still paid by the patient, although these are frequently reimbursed through private health insurance. In 1969 it was decided that the expenses of prolonged illness or intensive treatment would be fully reimbursed, on the advice of doctors. With a number of other serious medical problems, totaling 26 different illnesses, the personal charge is no longer applied.

A third major increase in costs is from pension increases. As in most European countries, the growth of old age pensions has been remarkable. The most important expansion in recent years was in 1972 when Boulin, Minister of Health and Social Security, restructured the conditions for qualifying. The period of contribution for full benefit was extended to 37.5 years in place of the previous 30 years, which made it possible to standardize retirement at the age of 65 years at between 40 and 50% of the person's salary. At the same time, the base salary for calculating pensions was defined more advantageously, in particular for workers whose salaries had diminished toward the end of their working lives. The base salary is now defined as the average of the ten best years of a person's earnings and no longer as the ten last years.

Other improvements included a system of reevaluating pensions each year in order to maintain their purchasing power. Since 1974 pensions and contributions have been recalculated twice a year so that the growth of pensions follows average wages. This indexation favors lower salaries and from 1974 to 1979 permitted an average increase in purchasing power of 14% each year.

Additional measures were taken to assist women who are the majority of the elderly population. The age at which they qualify for pensions as widows has been lowered from 65 to 55 years. The calculation of resources in arriving at the pension benefit has been increased to the minimum wage level (SMIC). There are also special provisions which allow spouses to combine pension rights. A special effort has been made to enhance the rights of women in order to compensate for the short period many have contributed. Two years of additional pension rights are automatically added for each child. In addition, a special insurance program for single parent families was created in order to provide special support for the education of children. Finally, diverse measures have been taken to lower the age of retirement for certain categories of workers that are forced to retire for work-related health disabilities. In 1972, this program provided pensions at full levels at the age of 60 years for all persons that were 50% handicapped for work reasons. In 1975 all manual workers were included, and, in 1977, all women having a full period of pension contributions. The full effect of these measures was not negotiable. Between 1974 and 1977 the proportion of special pension support taken from the basic regime for retirement at 60 years of age increased from 11 to 25%. The new Socialist government has agreed that from 1983 all those who have contributed the full term (37.5 years) may retire at 60 years of age with a pension equal to half the average of the best ten years of a person's employment. Negotiations are continuing on how the complementary pension plans will adjust to an earlier retirement later.

In summary, successive governments have recognized social solidarity and the importance of income redistribution. At its origin, the system envisaged little more than horizontal redistribution from active toward less-active citizens, from well to the sick, and from the single toward families. Certain solidarity was present insofar as benefits could be provided without contributions in certain cases, but it remained nevertheless a concept of insurance as indicated by the ceiling or platform above which the salary could not be taxed. In a more recent period, on the contrary, redistributive aspects or vertical redistribution from the rich to the poor have been accentuated, in part by having adjustable ceilings or platforms, and in part by the creation of benefits without considering other contributions.

In the adjustment of resources to the increased costs of social security, the most important decision was to remove the platform or ceiling on contributions to medical insurance, the only program within the system where contributions are not limited by a platform. For old age insurance, the variety of complementary regimes in effect means that persons with higher incomes are paying larger contributions, but until now any effort to remove the platform on general pensions has been resisted.

The third major tendency within the French social security system has been to redistribute income in order to reduce social inequalities. As outlined above, the social security system was based on contributory principles. Some exceptions were made for the unemployed, the sick without resources, or youth, but basically the French system has retained characteristics of an insurance-based system. The only major form of benefit that was not viewed as based on contributions was poverty assistance (*aide sociale*), normally provided when the needy were unable to care for their families or for a family with no other form of support. But over many years there has been a movement toward including welfare assistance under the rubric of social security without finding new contributions. The trend has several explanations.

The general reason put forward is the desire to eliminate the degrading character of assistance and the social controls which were attached to it. But the true reason should be looked for in terms of financing. Welfare assistance is financed by a tax. A tax conforms to the French tradition of social service solidarity because it is progressive, unlike most contributions to social security. But the contributions through taxation have the attraction that they are largely unnoticed, particularly by salaried persons (see Table 2). In practice, they do not know the contributions made for them by the employer. The effect has been that institutions supporting welfare assistance remain largely invisible.

The gradual transfer of welfare assistance to social security began with the creation of special funds in 1952 and of a National Solidarity Fund (FNS) in 1956 to provide the minimum old age contributions for persons with resources. Since 1970, the same practice has been undertaken for disability insurance. In addition, over the 1970s a number of benefits

Table 2.   Rate of Contributions in 1982 to the General
Regime, in Percentages

	Employers	Employees	Total
Family allocation			
(CNAF)	9	–	9
Pensions (CNAV)	8.20	4.70	12.90
Sickness (CNAM)			
on platform salary	5.45	–	5.45
on total salary	8	5.50	13.50
Unemployment (UNEDIC)			
(Based on 4 times the			
basic platform)	2.76	0.84	3.60

were attached to the system of family allocations such as education for
handicapped children and adults which were a supplement to earlier
forms of assistance. In 1975 all these allocations were integrated and the
family allocation system was put in charge of them. The change was very
controversial and gave rise to continuing dispute over unjustified
charges (*charges indues*) imposed by the state on the social security system. This tendency was reinforced in 1976 when an allocation for single
parents was added.

The result was to strengthen the social solidarity characteristics of the
system and to accentuate vertical redistribution. But a reverse effect was
also felt as benefits were increasingly linked to personal resources. The
most important benefit of this kind is special assistance to housing. But
the idea of selectivity of benefits in relation to resources continued to
grow in the family allocation system as a way of increasing the efficiency
of social welfare. The principle was clearly established by 1972 when
special assistance for low income families directly recognized income differentials in providing welfare assistance. For the total of welfare assistance to families in 1980, 116 billion francs, direct family assistance represents 20 billion francs. The new government of President Mitterand
has tried to accentuate this redistributive effect by reducing family assistance to those with high income. A family can no longer receive more
than 7,000 francs per year per child.

PROBLEMS YET TO BE RESOLVED IN FRENCH
SOCIAL SECURITY: THE BURDEN OF SOCIAL AND
ECONOMIC CONSTRAINTS

The rapid growth of social spending in France results from a number of
factors that are difficult to control by public means. There are also factors contributing to this growth that are explained by the development

of very different and diverse assistance for new kinds of risks, changes which are often not clearly perceived by government.

Perhaps the most important factor in France has been the demographic evolution of the country which plays a determining role in the structure and growth of social spending. The importance of family assistance depends, of course, on the number of births, family size, and family structure. Family allocations in France always favored larger families with considerable increases for the third and fourth child. Like most Western countries, the French population has stabilized since 1964. Birth rates increased rapidly following World War II, but in 1972 there were 870,000 births and in 1976 only 720,000, a rate of birth that will not sustain the present population. But within these overall figures there are also important changes in the size and structure of families. Between 1964 and 1974 the number of first children increased from 284,000 to 343,000, while the birth of second children remained at the same level. Third and fourth children are becoming increasingly rare, so that the typical French family now has two children. The effect on social spending has been very dramatic. Expenditure for family and maternity assistance in 1959 was 30.6% of social benefits, but by 1978 represented only 13.3% of benefits. In addition, family benefits have not always been adjusted to inflation and prices, principally because the managers of the system hope to remove resources from family allocations in order to finance other social services, principally, health. The growth of social expenditure for pensions results in part from improvements which have already been described and were deliberate choices by the managers of the system. Nevertheless, it should be noted that in the case of old age these choices were not always taken with the full appreciation of the subsequent cost. The political tendency is to announce favorable changes but to acknowledge the financial pressures some years later. Improvements do not affect existing pensions, so that the cost of improvements can provide short-term political rewards with minimum immediate cost.

The period from 1960 to 1980 was also marked by the retirement of many persons born after the First World War. At the same time the government was confronted with pressing public demands to lower the age of retirement and increase unemployment benefits for the aged. These adjustments were exacerbated by the demographic problem so that, between 1960 and 1980, the number of elderly (over 65 years of age) increased by more than two million persons, from 5.3 to 7.5 million in 1980. Of course, the total population also increased over this period, from 45.5 to 53.6 million persons. However, the population growth was not sufficient to sustain the financial equilibrium of pensions. The highly differentiated pension system of France means that active citizens must provide the resources for the inactive without adjustment to demographic changes. The number of persons between 20 and 64 years in relation to those over 65 years has constantly diminished, decreasing from 4.8 in 1960 to 3.9 in 1980, an enormous change. The problem was compounded by low economic growth since 1974, which increased the dismissals of elderly persons and rapidly increased the need for early retirement. The total effect of these factors explains why pensions have not ceased to take a larger and larger part of total social expenditure, increasing from 36% in 1959 to 43% in 1978.

The most dramatic change has clearly been in the areas of sickness and health benefits. From 1960 to 1978 the consumption of medical services by families increased from four to seven percent of GNP. Over the same period, the cost of medical services provided by social security increased much more rapidly, from 47.6% in 1960 to 71.1% in 1976. In doing so there was a natural tendency on the part of the public authorities to extend coverage to the entire population and to improve the quality of care. Parallel to this transformation there was an enormous increase in hospital costs. To 1968 hospital costs remained constant at roughly a third of the total of medical costs, but by 1977 were nearly half of all medical costs. The total effect of these changes was to rapidly expand the importance of sickness and health care in the total system, increasing it from little more than one-quarter of the costs in 1959 to over one-third in 1982.

A number of studies have been done to try to explain how the pattern of medical and health consumption has changed in France. Basically, the pattern of medical consumption outside hospitals is very high among young children, diminishes with adolescence and increases with age. During old age the increments are very large, increasing by roughly one-third between persons aged in their sixties and those aged in their seventies. After 80 years of age, oddly enough, consumption outside the hospital tends to diminish while hospital-based care increases very rapidly. Thus, the aging of the population between 1960 and 1980 is one of the critical factors explaining the increased cost of health. Not only did the elderly population rapidly increase, but this population grew older at the same time that persons over 75 increased from 1.9 to 3 million and those 85 increased from 290,000 to 580,000. To deal with these problems it would be necessary that the government have some effective control over the provisions of services, which has been severely resisted in France. Over the early 1970s there were some efforts to establish a legal control over the use of hospital equipment and the selection of medical specialists. Efforts have also been made to try to control the number of hospital beds in different regions, so that between 1963 and 1978 the increase in the number of hospital beds was only 1.5% per year. More recently, a law in 1979 enabled government to close hospitals when local needs are filled.

The law of 1971 on growth of the medical profession has never really been applied and there was no reduction in the number of candidates for medical school before 1977. But this control, too, has proven ineffective in that there were 68,000 doctors in 1970, 100,000 in 1980 and 140,000 in 1985. The reform of medical studies now being put in place is intended to decrease the number of medical graduates from 9,000 to 5,000 per year, but this reform will not take effect for many years and the shortage of doctors has already been filled. In summary, it is extremely difficult to find any way to voluntarily or forcefully control the growth of social spending. A study done by the General Inspector of Social Affairs for the period 1972–1974 showed that roughly three-fourths of the growth can be explained by demographic factors and improvement in social services. One might infer that in effect no more than one-third of public expenditure for social services could have been controlled by government under the most favorable conditions. The need for medical care is more and more a fundamental need, while technical progress and medical science encourage and make more expensive health care. At the same time, modern societies tend more and more to seek medical solutions to social problems, that is to say, increased highway accidents, occupational hazards and sicknesses, psychological maladjustments, etc. Nor are public authorities unwilling to make some response to the rapid increase in unemployment. From 1970 to 1978 the increase in unemployment expenditures rose on the average of over 40% per year. Simultaneously, the estimate is that a billion francs in contributions are lost with each 100,000 additional unemployed. Thus, the unsolved problems of French social security, not unlike those in other Western countries, represent a confluence of a number of factors, few of which can be directly or rapidly manipulated.

In conclusion, since 1960 social benefits have increased rapidly in France for a number of voluntary reasons and in order to improve social conditions, but also under the impact of a number of demographic and economic conditions which public authority could not control. The result has been that contributions to social insurance have increased from 9.6% of GNP in 1960 to 12.9% in 1970. In more recent years the increase in contributions has been even greater, reaching 16.5% of GNP in 1978 and expected to be 19.6% for 1983.

Economic growth enabled public authorities to accept these charges over the past 20 years, and in particular to choose to improve social benefits without simultaneously considering how new revenues would be raised. The economic crisis since 1974 has changed the situation. More than ever before it is now a problem of finding ways of limiting increases in social benefits to the growth of national wealth. In effect, over the 1970s the total increase of GNP was diverted to improve the social security system. The result was that the variety of social assistance and benefits provided by France compares favorably among all of the industrial countries, although France still occupies an intermediate position. Like other Western countries, France must find a way to slow the rate of increase of social expenditure and to limit the multiplication of obligatory benefits to acceptable social and political conditions.

In this respect, the dilemmas of the Socialist government in France since 1981 are similar to those of the previous governments. Mitterand's victory was an irresistible impulse to increase social benefits, and in July 1981 roughly 35 billion francs were added to social expenditure. These increases were to enhance the redistributive potential of the social security system, but it proved impossible to continue the high rate of growth of social spending. After a change of ministers, it was decided to implement far-reaching reforms to limit future growth of social spending and to increase the direct charges on the stick towards the cost of health. For both the right and the left, the costs of social security have conflicted with the primary economic and social objectives.

At the same time, it is virtually impossible within democratic systems to find reliable measures to control social expenditures. No one can say what the system will be or what optimum level of protection is workable in given economic and financial conditions. Only well-conducted negotiations between those responsible for services can help provide reasonable evolution of social security. Such negotiations should include all the responsible actors: the state, but also unions and professional organizations. All should help build a better system of information, including a better knowledge of the costs and the redistributive effects of social security. In other words, it is necessary that very self-conscious arbitration be carried on to understand the evolution of the modern welfare state. It would be vain to denounce the welfare state under the pretext that there are difficult years to come. It is more a matter of how to reconstruct and to direct the evolution of welfare states differently in the future.

GERMAN SOCIAL SECURITY PROGRAMS:

AN INTERPRETATION OF THEIR DEVELOPMENT, 1883–1985

Christa Altenstetter

The social security programs of most industrial countries have grown dramatically over the last century. The German programs, among the first to be initiated, are no exception. More restrictive interpretations of program stipulations have given way to more comprehensive ones. More importantly, the boundaries of the risks to be covered have expanded qualitatively and quantitatively (Van Langendonck, 1975; Kaim-Caudle, 1973), resulting in considerable cost pressures (Maxwell, 1975). Individual programs have become more interdependent on and complementary to other programs, even though they sometimes remain organizationally and financially separate.

The older a welfare state and the older its individual programs, the more complex, even confusing, becomes the interdependence of policy and structural arrangements of programs. The more programs are integrated into overall national policy, the more they constitute a more or less comprehensive and complementary "net" of entitlements to services and financial benefits. If they retain their organizational identity, the interprogrammatic dynamics become ambiguous and confusing. For example, when public pensions in Germany were indexed in 1957, other transfers were also indexed as appropriate changes were made through legislation. In this case it is fairly easy to identify these interprogrammatic dynamics. But other programs involve hidden transfers of responsibilities and costs, whose dynamic effects are more difficult to demonstrate. Two inferences can be made: (1) to treat a program as if it were isolated from other programs is inappropriate; (2) interprogrammatic dynamics readily become important determinants of new legislation. Many studies of German programs demonstrate how new policy decisions were adjusted to both the existing decision-making structures and the previously existing networks of implementation (Heclo, 1974, 1981; Mayntz, ed., 1980; Hanf and Scharpf, 1978; Hull and Hjern, 1983).

Ashford (1978) and others have urged a return to structural analyses that would identify both the institutionalized biases (Schattschneider, 1960) and what Ashford (1981) recently called the structural regularities of social service policy areas themselves. Preliminary findings of a comparison of four health programs in Germany from 1955 to 1985—one old (1883) and three relatively recent programs (1972, 1974, and 1976)—suggest that because of the complexity of joint action, structural analyses are as important at the community and regional level as they are at the macropolitical system and societal levels (Altenstetter, 1982a, 1982b, 1985).

In the case of German social security administration, the responsibilities for raising the funds and for spending them are frequently separate, which translates into a unique situation: one set of people decide how many funds should be raised, from whom, and by what methods; a second set of people decides for whom, on what and how much is needed. In Germany, implementing agencies are frequently caught in the middle and have to honor the mandates of both sets of decision-makers.

Over time, all programs separately and jointly exert incremental pressures on the center. Such pressures become stronger and more politicized in times of economic austerity than in times of prosperity. Spillovers from one program to another and pressures from one program onto another are additional "push" factors. Multiple funding in implementation frequently results in complicated and confusing financial arrangements and creates administrative situations that hardly resemble the features foreseen in Max Weber's rational-legal model of bureaucracy.

The first part of this chapter contains a brief sketch of the political and economic circumstances that conditioned social policymaking from the early nineteenth century to the present time, and provides background to the developmental path of the four core programs of the German social security system: the health insurance program of 1883; the work-injury program of 1885, which later became the accident insurance program; the public pension or social insurance program of 1889; and the unemployment insurance program of 1927.[1] Next, the chapter presents a diachronic comparison of benefits, populations, eligibility, administration, and financing. The analysis will show the organizational complexity and the administrative complexity of financing each social security program. Because of the large amount of prior research on health, more details are offered for the health insurance program than for the others. The third section of the chapter examines how the legal unification of individual provisions by central legislation has had an impact on local implementation and how efforts to nationalize German entitlements and benefits affect the heterogeneous and decentralized implementing agencies.

HISTORICAL PHASES IN HEALTH AND SOCIAL POLICYMAKING, 1839–1982

Except for the years 1839–71 and 1871–90, the developmental path of German social security programs spans several periods that correlate with four radically different political regimes (Lampert, 1980, pp. 122–165). Lampert, for example, argues that in each period, distinct political, economic, and institutional configurations influenced decision-making on health and social policy, and structured and restructured the political debate over policy proposals and final solutions. But antecedents of social and health policies and the earlier implementation strategies imposed considerable constraints on successor regimes. Moreover, the failure to address certain political and economic issues bequeathed problems to successor regimes that could not be ignored. After 1918 and 1945 respectively, postwar political leaders could not ignore the social effects of war. Because of their severity and magnitude, those problems often set the governmental agenda and influenced governmental action regardless of regime preferences. Even under these severe conditions, one discovers a remarkable degree of continuity in organization, financing, and incremental change. New programs conform to the pattern that existed previously, even though amendments and cutbacks can be attributed to particular governments or to coalition parties in power over shorter periods.

The political reformers of the pre-Bismarckian period (1839–78) were concerned with improving the inhuman and unsafe working conditions of the industrial labor force, especially to protect children and women. They were successful in obtaining some changes in poor laws and introduced insurance schemes in several parts of what was to become the German Empire. Some schemes were voluntary, others compulsory (Peters, 1974, pp. 19–43; Mommsen, 1981, pp. 71–83, 133–204, 315–339).

Bismarck's Government (1871–1890) marked the beginning of the German social security system on a nationwide scale. It had two separate objectives: (1) the provision of some economic security in exchange for the political integration of dissatisfied laborers, and (2) political stability. The government offered economic protection for only the top segments of the blue-collar working class against the temporary or permanent loss of one's ability to earn a living because of disease, old age, accident, death, and unexpected expenditures for some family crises. In response to increasing political threats to his regime, Bismarck co-opted dissenting and/or dissatisfied groups. Bismarck was not interested in income equality for all working people.

The second phase spanned the period from 1890, the year of Bismarck's resignation, to 1918. That year marked not only the end of World War I, but the end of a monarchical aristocracy and its repressive political regime. Under the Kaiser, several improvements were made in the initial programs. The Imperial Insurance Order of 1911 (*Reichsversicherungsordnung*) integrated separate provisions into a unified social security system. Compulsory coverage and benefits were extended to a new group—white-collar workers. In 1916 survivors' benefits were increased, and the retirement age was reduced from 70 to 65. Because the cooperation of labor, leftist parties and the working class was needed to maintain the war effort, they acquired some political influence. Efforts were also made to develop mechanisms for settling labor disputes and organizing voluntary employee committees.

The fall of the monarchy, especially the period between November 9, 1918, the date on which the Emperor resigned, and the final enactment of the Weimar constitution of August 11, 1919, inaugurated the third phase of development. The interim People's Council (*Rat der Volksbeauftragten*) exercised governmental authority, restored collective bargaining, and recognized the binding force of master contracts negotiated between management and labor in individual enterprises. These measures recognized the right of labor and management to control the governance and the administration of three main social security programs. Moreover, the council centralized decision-making and the implementation of the unemployment program. The Weimar constitution incorporated these advances, but the new republic had still to face the realities of the immediate postwar period.

Inflation rates surpassed the imagination of the most pessimistic forecasters. The acceleration of the inflation rate was no longer measured in increases of 1, 10 or 100 percent. Instead, between 1919 and 1923 the increase amounted to more than 1.8 million percent (Lampert, 1980, p. 137). After the stabilization of the currency in 1923, Germany, like other industrial nations, experienced a short period of economic growth during the "roaring twenties" (*Goldene 20er Jahre*) from 1924 to 1928. The economy began to pick up, unemployment was slowly reduced, and wages and salaries increased. However, the bank crash of 1929 destroyed any hopes for economic and political stability.[2]

Despite generally unfavorable internal and external conditions, the government of the Weimar Republic introduced several important innovations in order to ameliorate the considerable financial difficulties of insurance funds and to rescue the economy and stabilize labor markets. The *Reichsknappschaftsgesetz* of 1923 centralized the administration of the social insurance programs of miners. Instead of 110 separate associations, one central agency assumed responsibility for the administration of programs against the risks of disability, old age, and disease. In 1925, the accident insurance program was reformed substantially, and occupational diseases became insurable risks. In 1927, the previously federalized, need-related unemployment program became an unemployment insurance program. The *Reichsanstalt für Arbeit*, today the *Bundesanstalt für Arbeit*, was designated as the responsible agency (Lampert, 1980, p. 144; Leibfried, 1977, pp. 289–301).

From 1930 to 1932 substantial reductions were imposed not only in the social insurance programs but also on wages and salaries. State contributions to the unemployment insurance programs were increased substantially to pay for the increasing number of unemployed. Because of high unemployment, contributions to the social insurance and the health insurance programs decreased. In brief, all social security and assistance programs were on the brink of bankruptcy (Lampert, 1980, pp. 146–147).

The ascendance of Hitler in 1933 marked the beginning of the fourth phase of the development of German social policy. The Nazi regime introduced major changes in individual programs and made drastic departures in the administration of programs. In 1934 the self-governance structure of all social insurance programs was abolished. The regime appointed a director for each insurance program, who reported directly to the central authorities, instead of to management and labor. Many improvements in benefits and coverage in social insurance and need-based programs served the political and ideological goals of the Nazi regime rather than the goals of management and labor. Moreover, social insurance funds were used for armament, and later, for the war effort (Lampert, 1980, pp. 153–156).

Following the collapse of Germany in 1945, a constitutional government was not established until 1949. Yet the interim period between 1945 and 1949 was significant for the development of social security under the Bonn democracy. The political realities of the immediate postwar period constrained governmental action. Both political and social priorities focused on the nearly 10 million refugees from the East and the social cost of the war. Forty percent of the population consisted of widows, orphans, war veterans, refugees, and displaced persons (Lampert, 1980, p. 157). Even before the new constitutional order was established in 1949, health, accident, social insurance, and unemployment programs were enacted, incorporating some features of Weimar legislation and some provisions of the Nazi regime.

Legislation affecting the four core programs extended benefits and provided different mixes of better and more costly service to larger population groups. Legislation and court decisions amended the objectives of the health insurance[3] and turned it de facto into a completely different program. In addition, legislation and court rulings altered the organization of the implementing agencies, and the administration of health insurance funds (Altenstetter, 1982a).

Local sickness funds became *the* most important agent in implementing and controlling general insurance programs. Health insurance funds became (and are now) responsible for collecting contributions not only for health insurance but for public pension schemes and the unemployment program as well. Unlike the broader range of responsibilities they exercise in the implementation of health insurance *and* the delivery of health services, the responsibilities for the other programs are primarily confined to the collection of payroll contributions and the transfer of these funds to other agencies. Under national legislation, income ceilings for participation, conditions of membership, and the payroll contribution of employers and employees have progressively changed (Altenstetter, 1982a, p. 58).

By the 1960s, almost 80 years after social security was first enacted, even experts had difficulty keeping up with all the statutory changes and court rulings. Extensive research is required to answer a simple question about the legal status of a program. When the previous Bonn coalition assumed office in 1969, it undertook a major effort to consolidate the kaleidoscope of separate rules and stipulations scattered in numerous legal and administrative sources in order to restore a comprehensive survey of German health and social policy.[4]

SELECTED CHARACTERISTICS OF FOUR SOCIAL SECURITY PROGRAMS: A LEGACY OF INSTITUTIONAL AND FINANCIAL MECHANISMS FOR TODAY'S PROGRAM OPERATIONS

The Health Insurance Program

The health insurance program, over 100 years old, insured 26% of the labor force, or 10% of the population in 1885. By 1970, 97% of the labor force, or 43% of the population, were active members of insurance funds (Flora and Alber, 1981, p. 75). Including dependents, a total of about 90% of the German population was covered in 1983 (Der Bundesminister für Arbeit und Sozialordnung, 1983). The GKV (*Gesetzliche Krankenversicherung*) provides virtually total coverage of all risks relating to chronic or temporary sickness and mental and emotional disability, as well as some preventive care and generous income maintenance. In fact, one can argue that the GKV of today is an all-inclusive health-protection and income-maintenance program, and that the term "insurance" is a misnomer. Clients now have similar rights to receive benefits under each source of entitlement, whether welfare, general assistance, or insurance (Altenstetter, 1982a). These rights constitute a departure from the long tradition of individual agency care for separate needs.

A national fixed income ceiling determined eligibility in this compulsory insurance program in 1883, and it continues to do so today. The income ceiling rose from 2,000 RM in 1883 to 48,600 DM in 1984. From 1904 to 1968, ceilings were raised periodically, and each ceiling was valid for several years. Since 1969 ceilings have been raised annually and by larger amounts than those previously mandated. The national policy of raising income ceilings has affected the status of local insurance funds. For example, the total number of mandatory members increased from about 25 million in 1955 to about 33 million in 1975. General local sickness funds (AOKs), which were the most important funds in the 1880s, have not been the beneficiaries of national policy. Their competitors, especially the enterprise, guild, and agricultural funds, as well as the substitute funds for white-collar and blue-collar workers, have absorbed the increases (see Table 1).

Although the formulation of the most important provisions of health insurance policy, such as benefits, eligibility, and the like, has been centralized since 1883, the implementation of the program has always been decentralized. Since 1945, however, consolidation has been rapid, ex-

Table 1. Members by Type of Insurance Carrier, in Thousands

Year	AOK	LKK since 10/1/1972 Landw. KK	BKK	IKK	SeeKK	KnK	Ersantzkassen Blue collar	White collar	Total
1938	13,524	1,817	4,097	676	59	762	2,887		23,222
1950	13,838	617	2,300	398	21	1,128	81	1,764	20,200
1955	16,143	540	2,960	660	46	1,335	145	3,070	24,800
1960	15,433	469	3,600	936	70	1,402	231	4,919	27,000
1965	15,442	418	3,874	1,244	71	1,318	290	6,082	28,740
1970	15,954	434	4,177	1,472	78	1,124	335	7,072	30,646
1975	16,136	942	4,268	1,587	67	1,076	363	9,064	33,503
1980	16,495	861	4,287	1,824	61	980	434	10,395	35,339
1983	16,240	822	4,198	1,895	58	986	493	11,110	35,805

*August 1976

Key:

    AOK = local sickness fund organized on a geographic basis
    LKK = agricultural fund
    BKK = factory fund
    IKK = fund for craftsworkers and tradeworkers
 SeeKK = fund for mariners
    KnK = fund for miners
Ersatzkassen = substitute funds
Sources: Der Bundesminister Für Arbeit und Sozialordnung, *Übersicht über die Soziale Sicherung*, Bonn, no
  publisher, July 1976, p. 188.
  Der Bundesminister für Arbeit und Sozialordnung, *Die gesetzliche Krankenversicherung in der
  Bundesrepublik Deutschland im Jahre 1983*, Bonn, no publisher, p. 14.

tending the trend that started in 1914, when the total number of local
health insurance funds was cut almost in half, from 20,000 in 1911 to
13,500 in 1919 (Altenstetter, 1982a). In 1975 the GVK was administered
by about 1,400 different funds (see Table 2). Since then about 200 funds
were closed or merged.

Since its inception, the GKV (except for a few funds) has been largely
financed by a payroll tax levied equally on employers and employees.
But total contributions today vary from region to region and from fund
to fund. They even vary within the same type of insurance fund. For
example, contributions to the general sickness funds (AOKs) varied in
1983 from a low of 10.2 percent to a high of 15.7 percent (Der
Bundesminister für Arbeit und Sozialordnung, 1983, T11).

As a result of their heterogeneous membership, the funds draw revenues from four different sources. Active members of the program, who
contribute for their own and their dependents' health bills, constitute
the bulk of all revenues. Until 1982 the federal social insurance program
paid the contributions of retired people to the GKV—an increasingly
higher proportion of total membership. Starting in 1983 the elderly also
contribute and their share has been rising ever since. The distribution of
the elderly among the different insurance funds is uneven, and local

Table 2. Institutional Development of Sickness Funds (RVO) in the Federal Republic of Germany

Year	General Sickness Funds	Enterprise Funds	Guild Funds	Agricultural Funds[a]	Total Number
1951	396	1,336	134	102	1,968
1957	398	1,397	134	102	2,040
1960	400	1,348	155	102	2,005
1967	401	1,205	178	102	1,886
1970	400	1,133	178	102	1,813
1975	313	935[b]	164	19[c]	1,431
Federal Republic Gain or Loss	−83	−401	+30	−83	−537

[a]Agricultural funds were called Rural Funds until 1972.
[b]The national data include funds for railway employees (BKK Bundesbahn), for post office employees (BKK Bundespost), and for employees of the Federal Ministry of Transportation (BKK Bundesverkehrsamt). The latter fund has jurisdiction over all employees of the ministry irrespective of their residences in Germany, whereas the former covers regional or local populations or employees of one enterprise only.
[c]The figure applies to a nationwide fund for all those who work in horticulture (Gartenbau).
Source: Bundesverband der Ortskrankenkassen, *Die Ortskrankenkassen 1975*, (1976, p. 9).

sickness funds (AOKs) include an unusually high proportion of the aged, ranging from 30 to 35 percent of the total membership of a fund (AOK). The federal government pays the contributions to the GVK for the unemployed from the unemployment insurance program. These contributions are derived from two sources: contributions to unemployment insurance, and federal transfers. Federal subsidies for maternity allowances and maternity and child care provide the final revenue source. Despite numerous and restrictive changes on details of each program since 1982, the overall pattern of financing remains the same.

The expenditure side is equally complex. Local funds pay for all medical, dental and hospital bills, including medical aids and medication. Except for medication and dental care and since 1983 for hospital care, there is no cost-sharing component in the GVK. Since the entitlement of a patient/client may be rooted in insurance, welfare or assistance, and because the fund is usually the first contact agency under the Rehabilitation Law of 1974, health insurance agencies may have to advance funds for which they will eventually receive reimbursements from other carriers. In order to recover advanced funds, these agencies often have to enter into long and controversial negotiations to determine which agencies are financially responsible.

Health funds have little to say about how to extract or allocate resources. In general, the funds do not control how contributions are collected or the number of citizens obligated to make such contributions. The funds can raise or lower the percentage of the payroll tax in line with local financial needs and within a nationally set maximum; however, they have little leeway in deciding for whom the money shall be spent, how much shall be spent, what provider will be used, and under what conditions. These decisions are all negotiated elsewhere by others.[5]

The Accident Insurance Program

The accident insurance program was enacted in 1884–1885 and covered accidents at work. The imperial legislation of 1900 extended coverage to workers in agriculture, industrial enterprises, construction business, and in the merchant marine (Peters, 1974, p. 64). But unlike the revision of other social security programs, few fundamental changes were made except for the inclusion of occupational diseases in 1927. Disability and survivors' benefits were indexed after the indexation of public pensions in 1957. The 1963 federal legislation required all businesses with more than 20 employees to hire a safety inspector.

Even though the liability of industrial enterprises had been a recognized principle since before 1885 (Peters, 1974, p. 47), not all enterprises were subject to liability. Those enterprises to which liability was extended by the 1885 legislation became responsible for providing disability and survivors' benefits. But the burden of proving negligence of the employer rested with the victims or the survivors. Arbitration courts (*Schiedsgerichte*) were responsible for setting claims. Today benefits are paid irrespective of the cause, the negligence or special circumstances. The determination by a certified physician (*Durchgangsarzt*) under contract to the program that the injury, the impaired working capacity, or the death of the claimant resulted from an accident or an occupational disease establishes the financial responsibility of the program. Since 1974, rehabilitation and medical services have been included in disability benefits, but during the first six weeks, the GKV picks up medical and hospital bills.

In 1885, some industrial enterprises were required to insure their workers and employees who earned less than 2,000 RM a year. In 1978, the accident insurance program provided coverage for a total of 31 million employed individuals and approximately 14.6 million high school and university students. Since 1971, children attending kindergarten have also received coverage (Lampert, 1980, pp. 42, 241). In 1885, 18% of the labor force, or 7% of the population, had become members of the work-injury program, as it was called then, but by 1970, 98% of the working population, or 42% of the entire population, was directly covered (Flora and Alber, 1981, p. 74).

Industrial insurance corporations (*Berufsgenossenschaften*) administered the accident insurance program in the last century and do so today. Like other insurance carriers, they are quasi-public agencies with delegated responsibilities discharged by their own governing bodies. These insurance corporations cover all enterprises in the same industrial sector, craft, or profession and provide them with risk insurance for liabilities resulting from accidents at work or occupational diseases.

Institutional consolidation has been important for the accident insurance program, but the organizational complexity is immense. In 1908 the program was implemented by a total of 66 corporations, 48 agricultural insurance carriers, and 540 provincial and municipal agencies (Peters, 1974, p. 64). Today there are 35 insurance corporations, one insurance corporation of seamen, 19 agricultural corporations, 13 corporations or associations of local governments in each *Land* (state). Six funds in Hamburg, Hannover, Oldenburg, Düsseldorf, Kiel, and Münster provide accident insurance for fire departments. Six communities—Düsseldorf, Dortmund, Essen, Frankfurt, Köln, and München—are recognized as insurance carriers and administer their own accident insurance. The federal government, the ten *Länder* (states), and West Berlin administer accident insurance for employees in their respective public enterprises and agencies. The federal agency of labor in Nuremburg also provides accident insurance. Although most carriers provide insurance for their employees alone, some carriers are responsible for other target groups such as children, students, and trainees. In many instances, field offices are responsible for specific industrial sectors. Although the federal government is considered one unified insurance carrier, four separate federal agencies provide protection for railway, maritime, and postal workers (Der Bundesminister für Arbeit und Sozialordnung, 1977, pp. 230–233).

With a minor exception, only one revenue source, namely, employer payroll contributions, provide funds for the accident insurance programs. Contributions are calculated on the basis of expenditures made during the past calendar year. The methods and criteria for calculating contributions by individual groups of employers vary considerably. The wages of workers *and* the rating of each employer group determine the rates. Specifically, the wages and salaries obtained in a particular industry, craft, business, or public service are important criteria. The rating of an industry or a group of businesses depends on the number and the severity of accidents in that industrial or business branch. Because ratings can be volatile, they are revised and adjusted every five years. Rates in agriculture depend on additional factors such as manpower needs, property values, and other criteria that the statutes of agricultural corporations may specifically prescribe.

The employment status in the labor force determine eligibility, entitlement, and benefits. Employment status is independent of the kind and the length of employment and the amount of income. As Töns (1980, pp. 408–418; 1974, pp. 829–841) explains, the understanding and the legal interpretation of what constitutes employment status are liberal.

The Social Insurance Program

The social insurance program, or the public pension and disability scheme, was set up by law in 1889, and included all blue-collar workers over the age of 16. The scheme provided modest economic protection against temporary or permanent disability as well as retirement income, but dependents and survivors' benefits were initially excluded (Lampert, 1980, p. 129). Amendments have extended benefits to larger and more diversified occupational and professional working people and have integrated hitherto separate schemes by harmonizing benefits for diverse groups (see Table 3). Although the indexation of the program in 1957 undoubtedly constitutes one of the most important changes, the program has been subjected to further amendments. In the 1960s and the 1970s, the contribution rates and the income limits for contribution purposes were raised almost annually (Der Bundesminister für Arbeit und Sozialordnung, 1977, pp. 61–178).

Although the formulation of policy governing the social insurance program has been centralized since 1889, the implementation of the program never has been. This is in part because the program differentiates among social strata of the working population, and in part because the historical roots of highly decentralized mechanisms for administering the program have been respected. For example, in 1908, 31 insurance agencies, all organized outside the regular system of public administration, were responsible for the blue-collar workers in designated local or regional districts. In addition, 10 certified carriers (*Kassen*) insured workers employed by the empire, regional authorities, or municipalities (Peters, 1974, p. 66). Career bureaucrats worked under the supervision of existing administrative agencies in Prussia and other *Länder* (Jacob, 1963, p. 41). Although the central government provided some subsidies to the program, it did not exercise authority or control until 1911, when the central government obtained authority over the white-collar component of the insurance program. But according to Jacob, this authority never matched the political control and authority associated with other central programs.

Control over the blue-collar insurance program remains in the hands of 18 state insurance agencies (LVA) serving people in territorial districts that conform to those established in the nineteenth century, not to the territorial entities created after 1945. One federal agency administers the program for federal railway workers. A seamen's fund caters to marine seamen, a federal miners' fund serves the miners. The federal insurance agency for white-collar workers in Berlin (BfA) is responsible for white-collar population (Der Bundesminister für Arbeit und Sozialordnung, 1977; Lampert, 1980, pp. 247–278). In addition to the miners' insurance program, about 1.6 million civil servants, including dependents, are covered by a separate retirement program financed by outlays from the federal, the state, or the local government (Lampert, 1980, p. 259). Another retirement scheme provides social insurance for all registered craftsmen—about 113,000 individuals. About 700,000 individuals are covered by agricultural pension schemes. Finally, several pension schemes provide benefits for the self-employed: physicians, dentists, tax accountants, architects, veterinarians, pharmacists, and lawyers (Lampert, 1980, p. 260).

Since its inception, the program has been financed by payroll taxes levied equally on employers and employees. The percentage of contributions calculated from gross earnings has steadily increased. In addition to payroll contributions, the program has always received central subsidies first paid by the empire, then by the central government during the Weimar Republic, and finally, since 1949, by the federal government in Bonn. Data compiled since 1950 indicate that although federal subsidies to individual program components began to decline two years before indexation was inaugurated in 1957, the federal purse, as well as retirees who have obtained greatly improved retirement incomes since 1957, has been the major beneficiary of indexation.

The Unemployment Insurance Program

Unlike the pioneering efforts undertaken to develop health, retirement, and accident insurance in the 1880s, which were aimed at securing the stability of the political regime, Germany did not enact an unemployment insurance program until 1927. The program replaced the welfare program for the unemployed that was passed in 1919. Designed to protect the workers against a fluctuating economy, it reflected, among other things, an important political priority of the Weimar coalition parties, especially of the Social Democratic party and the trade unions. In 1930, the first year for which statistics are available, 44% of the labor force and 32% of the population were covered (Flora and Alber, 1981, p. 77; Alber, 1981, pp. 151–183).

With the exception of civil servants, all employed individuals and trainees, irrespective of salary or wage levels, are covered by the pro-

Table 3. Common Aspects of German Insurance Programs—1980

	Health Insurance	Accident Insurance	Social Insurance	Unemployment Insurance
Benefits	cash and in-kind benefits are improved in quantity and quality	cash and in-kind benefits are improved in quantity and quality	cash and in-kind benefits are improved in quantity and quality	cash cash amounts are increased
Risks	A comprehensive definition of sickness and health that includes total coverage for all risks of chronic or temporary ill health and mental and emotional disability. It also includes prevention and income maintenance	A comprehensive coverage for accidents and occupational diseases and income maintenance	retirement income and early retirement income because of disability and health insurance coverage	unemployment and health insurance and social-insurance coverage
Method of Inclusion	steady increases in income limits for compulsory coverage and/or contributions	dependent employment status and special risk groups	steady increases in income limits for compulsory coverage and/or contributions	dependent employment status
Target Populations	expansion	expansion	expansion	expansion
Contributions as % of gross wages—1978*	11.4%	information on % not available	18%	3%

Dominant Mode of Financing	equal employer-employee payroll contributions increase steadily	employer payroll contributions	equal employer-employee payroll contributions increase steadily	equal employer-employee payroll contributions adjusted to fluctuations in the economy and the labor market
Single or Multiple Funding	multiple funding	single funding	multiple funding	multiple funding
Operating Agency	health funds	insurance corporations and other cost carriers	because of segregation of the labor force institutional division: state insurance agencies (LVA) for blue-collar, and federal insurance agency (BfA) for white-collar workers	local labor offices under state control
Governance Model**	Labor-management control	labor-management control	labor-management control	labor-management control in addition to control by the federal government, the states and the municipalities

*Data are from Heidenheimer (1981).

**Despite formal recognition of employers and employees as representatives, in reality their control translates into labor-management control in the majority of insurance carriers of the various programs.

gram. In 1980 it provided two kinds of compensation: (1) unemployment compensation (*Arbeitslosenversicherung*) of 68% of prior net earnings up to a maximum of 52 weeks provided that the unemployed had worked for 104 weeks before being laid off. When entitlement was exhausted, (2) aid to the unemployed (*Arbeitslosenhilfe*) was paid for an unlimited period (Lampert, 1980, pp. 262–263). Moreover, irrespective of the kind of entitlement, unemployed people are entitled to continued benefits under the health and the social insurance programs. As the mission agency, the federal agency of labor pays contributions to both parties.

A three-tiered administrative structure deals with the unemployment insurance program and other labor-market policies. The federal agency of labor (*Bundesanstalt für Arbeit*) in Nuremberg serves as the primary agent, but administration is dispensed through 9 state labor agencies and 146 local labor offices (Der Bundesminister für Arbeit und Sozialordnung, 1977, p. 273).

Unemployment insurance was the most important labor market program. In 1957 it was revised substantially to reflect economic and employment conditions of the time. New programs addressed particular groups of working people, especially in the construction industry. However, the most important change occurred in 1969 when a new law (*Arbeitsförderundgsgesetz*) strengthened a myriad of complementary programs linked to employment policies, occupational opportunity and the protection of social rights. Despite these additions, payments for the unemployed and special groups, such as construction workers, represents the bulk of the agency's expenditure (Lampert, 1980, pp. 296–297).

No single source finances the program. The most important contributions are from employers and employees (in 1980 set at 1.5% of base salary). In 1979 they constituted 79% of total program revenues (Lampert, 1980, pp. 296–297). Another crucial revenue source, especially in times of economic stress, is subsidies that the federal government is obliged to pay to the federal labor agency when reserves are totally depleted.

Since 1980 the unemployment insurance program has undergone two major changes: considerable restrictions of benefits and increases of the contribution rate to over 4 percent of base salary. Depending on the fluctuations of unemployed persons this rate was adjusted upward to 4.6 percent in 1983 and 1984 and downward to 4.1 percent in 1985. *Arbeitslosenhilfe* was also restricted subject to special provisions.

Unlike the labor-management partnership that governs the administration of the other insurance programs, the members of the two governing bodies of the federal agency of labor—the administrative council (*Verwaltungsrat*) and the board (*Vorstand*)—represent the federal government, the state and local governments, businesses, and trade unions. The committee attached to the 9 state labor agencies and 146 local labor offices follow the same principle of representation.

The multi-tiered structure of the German social insurance system has been evident since its origins. In his historical analysis of German administration, Jacob (1963, pp. 38–40) writes:

> Bismarck's plan for Reich administration of the insurance programs met the concerted opposition of the Catholic Center party and many Liberals. These groups shared a lively distrust of German bureaucracy. They demanded that the insurance programs be operated by autonomous agencies instead of centrally directed Reich offices . . . . The Liberal and Catholic demands were coupled with opposition to Reich agencies and Reich contributions from Bavaria and Baden and coolness to the entire scheme by the Conservatives. The consequent lack of support in the Reichstag forced Bismarck to accept compromises proposed by the Catholic and Liberal opposition. As a result, the Reich authorized the Länder to establish autonomous administrative agencies for each of the insurance programs. The Reich contributed only a small share to the disability and old age insurance; the others were supported by contributions from workers and employers. The Länder received authority to supervise the agencies, but laymen rather than career civil servants controlled their daily operations.

In fact,

> the Reich was denied *direct* control of the insurance programs until 1911 when the Reichstag established the White Collar Insurance. As white collar workers constituted a small and widely scattered group, the Reich overcame Land objections to the establishment of a centralized Reich Insurance Authority. The Authority operated under the Chancellor's direct control and was staffed by Reich civil servants. (Jacob, 1963, p. 42)

> Lay administrators become especially entrenched in the Health Funds which administered the health insurance fund and the Industrial Insurance Corporations (Berufsgenossenschaften) which operated the accident insurance. There were seven types of Health Funds, each of which had slightly different administrative arrangements. The most prevalent type, the Local Health Fund (Ortskrankenkasse), was controlled by workers. (Jacob, 1963, p. 40)

However, this control seems to have been on paper in the initial years (Tennstedt, 1977, p. 230). Jacob states, "Employers controlled the Industrial Insurance Corporations" (1963, p. 40).

Despite these differences, two general points need underscoring. First, the institutional mechanisms, methods of financing, and operations chosen remain the same. Second, the political forces that were originally entrusted with authority, responsibility, and accountability for administering the program control it today. Despite changes since the 1880s, Table 4, on the governance and control model of insurance funds, demonstrates continuity in what was hailed as an important insti-

Table 4.   The Governance and Control Model of Insurance Funds

Agency	Employer	Employees	Self-Employed
Retirement	1/2	1/2	—
Exceptions :			
Federal Railway Ins. Agency	1/2[a]	1/2[a]	
Federal Miners' Fund	2/3	1/3	
Health Insurance Funds	1/2	1/2	—
Exceptions:			
Enterprise Funds	1/2[a]	1/2[a]	
Federal Miners' Fund	2/3	1/3	
Substitute Funds	1/1	—	
Accident Insurance Agencies	1/2	1/2	
Exceptions:			
Agricultural Insurance Corp.	1/3	1/3	1/3

[a]Although the employer sends one representative only, he has the same number of votes as all employee representatives.
Source: Lampert, (1980, p. 337).

tutional and political innovation in the nineteenth century. But the mixed model of finance and control has become more nationalized. For example, sickness insurance contracts were negotiated directly between individual physicians and the funds. Now these contracts are negotiated by the respective national or regional spokesmen of peak associations. It can be argued that labor-management bodies rubber-stamp decisions made at the center and in the regions. Except for political forces of the extreme right and left, all political groupings of the Bonn democracy believe in the continued virtues of *Selbstverwaltung* or the labor-management control of implementing agencies.

Table 4 summarizes the representational mix in the agencies that administer the retirement, the health, and the accident insurance programs. With few exceptions, an equal number of trade union and management representatives sit on the assembly and the boards and on their specialized committees. Employee representation now means trade union representation, a point accepted in contemporary political debate (von Ferber, 1977; Tennstedt, 1977).

Before 1974, several national programs, including health and social insurance, granted services and benefits to handicapped individuals; yet neither the benefits nor the definitions of disabled persons were uniform. Depending on the origin of a disability (accident at work, birth, etc.), persons disabled before 1974 may or may not have received similar service benefits. For example, sickness funds usually granted fewer benefits than did social insurance or assistance programs. Service benefits for an injured person varied widely depending on the agency that was responsible for providing assistance. Similar disparities existed under the social insurance program.[6]

The 1974 rehabilitation legislation did away with the cause of a disability as the sole element that established entitlement to cash benefits or services. By doing so it crosscut and made more interdependent several formerly distinct policy areas, such as policies on manpower, employment and unemployment, education, and occupational and professional training. Most important for the receipt of services, the 1974 legislation abolished distinct categories of target groups, but did not eliminate such categories for administrative purposes and financing.

The most crucial aspect of the legislation is the retention of the provision that cash benefits continue to provide differentials for different target groups. The provisions of the 1974 legislation no longer distinguish between blue-collar and white-collar workers with a steady and long employment record. Instead, it differentiates between both categories of workers from nonworking groups—survivors and dependents, especially widows, and single family, female households—and those with irregular employment records. Since 1980 these differences have intensified (Leibfried and Tennstedt, 1985).

Six national agencies have been charged with responsibilities for one or all four distinct kinds of rehabilitation services. The identities of the agencies have been preserved, but they were ordered to coordinate the implementation of the new rehabilitation program. In addition to legislation and administrative regulations, mandated joint interagency agreements among the six national agencies and their respective field offices enforce the rehabilitation program. Although the 1974 legislation did not do away with the previous legislation on implementation, it attempted to move toward uniform programs by doing three things:

1. setting national norms and criteria for the delivery of services;
2. mandating uniform administrative procedures for all participating agencies;
3. mandating the provisions of uniform bundles of services to different groups of handicapped individuals.

The elimination of jurisdictional disputes over agency responsibility and of delays in receiving services is another objective of the new program. In the past interagency disputes over jurisdiction and financial responsibility for particular client groups became insurmountable barriers to the delivery of services to eligible individuals. Instead of placing the burden of proving eligibility on clients, the new legislation placed the burden on participating agencies. Individuals were no longer required to apply separately for different forms of rehabilitative assistance (medical, occupational, educational, or social). Instead, they were required to deal with only one agency. Agencies were to work out ways to transfer funds among themselves; for example, in the event that such transfers became necessary to finance health services. To achieve this goal, the legislation mandated that all mission or local line agencies of the national social, health, accident and unemployment insurance, plus several general assistance programs, inform handicapped persons about their rights to benefits. The agencies must also assist them in obtaining such services. At the local level, these institutions usually had been organizationally and politically fragmented. The new approach was designed to prevent organizational complexity from jeopardizing clients by requiring horizontal cooperation among district programs whose organization had been primarily vertical.

However, mandating and implementing cooperation are two distinct things. The local implementation device was to be the global rehabilitation plan for each client served. However, the federal program did not place responsibility on a single agency. Instead, it based responsibilities on existing jurisdictional and administrative structures. Hence, responsibility continues to be bureaucratically and administratively fragmented: a maze of federal, state, and local agencies administer entitlement and related matters, whereas a maze of public, quasi-public, voluntary, and private institutions provide necessary bundles of client services.

The profiles of local implementation networks are hardly as simple or as orderly as this schematic presentation indicates. Much wider, more diversified, and fragmented organizational infrastructures exist both for the administration and the financing of services and for their delivery as well. Implementation networks for the administration and the financing of these programs may include the following organizational components:

1. local assistance offices (*Versorgungsämter* and *Hauptfürsorgestellen*), which administer the general assistance program covering persons injured or handicapped in the line of government service;
2. industrial insurance corporations (*Berufsgenossenschaften* and *Eigenunfallversicherungsträger*), which administer the program of benefits to persons injured at work or suffering from an occupational disease;
3. state insurance agencies (LVA) for blue-collar workers, the federal insurance agency (BfA) for white-collar workers, the federal agency for miners (*Berufsknappschaft*), and the agricultural "chests" for the elderly (*Landwirtschaftliche Alterskassen*);
4. local labor agencies (*Arbeitsämter*) and state labor agencies

(*Landesarbeitsämter*), which administer federal employment programs;

5. county governments (*Landkreise*), unincorporated cities (*Kreisfreie Städte*), and regional agencies (e.g., voluntary charitable organizations, such as *Landeswohlfahrtsverbände, Landschaftsverbände*), which may be involved in administering a kind of welfare program (*Sozialhilfe*) that provides medical and economic aid to physically, mentally, and emotionally disabled persons who are not entitled to assistance under any other program.

A critical element in the operation of this complex structure is the health insurance funds (AOK, BK, IK, LK, and EK) that are major sources of payment for services for a myriad of public, quasi-public, and private agencies. Efforts to impose a "seamless web" of medical services, especially for those about to be discharged from treatment facilities to enter a rehabilitation phase, are fraught with complications and difficulties (Altenstetter, 1982a, pp. 78–106). The staff of local sickness funds may have to interact with a wide range of different service institutions, such as medical rehabilitation centers, rehabilitation hospitals, regular hospitals, specialized health facilities, child and youth centers, occupational training centers, homes for disabled persons, and nursing care centers.

SUMMARY AND CONCLUDING COMMENTS

The scope of this paper does not allow a close examination of the politics of policymaking within the context of specific programs or at particular time periods. Although politics certainly matters for the passage of each amendment, it seems to matter little in a long historical perspective. Politics has not generated the political momentum that could have initiated major departures from the status quo ante. Possibly there might not have been any intention to do so at all.

Moreover, in light of the cumulative development, it is difficult to attribute the objectives and the directions of these programs to any single set of political actors and politics and, more importantly, to any particular political regime or government. If, for example, the explanation that the type of regime determines the scope and nature of these kinds of programs were to hold universally, it would be reasonable to expect that the four political regimes, different in terms of political values and major actors, would have made more substantial departures from the pattern of development. But, with few exceptions, and despite temporary economic and political crises and changes in government, gradual evolution prevails.

Commenting on trends and problems of public expenditure in Europe and America, Jürgen Kohl suggested "that dynamics of coalition governments override left and right differences" (Kohl, 1981, pp. 324–325). In light of the dominance of coalition parties in the Weimar Republic and the dominance of different coalition governments in the Bonn democracy, which included the two largest parties in the Grand Coalition from 1966 to 1969, Kohl's explanation has considerable appeal in the German case. Indeed, the need for consensus formation and compromise among ideologically different parties has been influential in formulating German social policy since 1918.

In the case of the German programs, no polarized political authority appears to have influenced major decisions. Decision-making on social security was centralized in the Bismarck regime, during the Weimar Republic, and reached its zenith under Hitler. The social security policies of the Bonn democracy make a striking contrast with the decentralized decision-making for health policy, hospitals, and other social policies. But the synchronization of social security programs tends to be counterbalanced by the vertical and the horizontal fragmentation of responsibilities for operating the program and for their finance. In terms of operational responsibilities, there is vertical and horizontal fragmentation between federal and social security bureaucracies, across governmental levels, and between a myriad of field agencies. With such complex implementation networks, it is difficult to pinpoint the accountability of any agency. Control over the field operations of implementing agencies is also divided between the federal and the state governments, control over expenditures is even more difficult to identify. Given the multiple revenue source of most programs and the central mandates to spend funds for heterogeneous target groups, how can government be held accountable for social expenditures?

To the extent that German citizens and residents have been able to assert their economic rights through administrative and judicial action, uniform laws and procedures have protected them. In that sense Weber's legal rational authority is operative. At the same time uniform law and court rulings have also maintained differences among social classes, as is most apparent when entitlement is assessed not in legal terms but in terms of actual benefits and services received by different client groups. In general, entitlement to insurance and assistance, especially for long-term contributors, yield higher benefits than welfare with sporadic or no employment record.

The development of the four health programs used since 1945 suggests ways of assessing implementation in other countries, especially in the United States. Implementation strategies are weak for old programs and old social institutions. Decisions made decades ago still exert influence on present operations. We often assume that an implementing agency, especially at the community level, has a choice of deciding with whom to interact, for what activity, and through what particular approach or method. Such choices hardly exist for these programs. Even with major regime changes, programs retain the distinctions and decisions of earlier periods. Differences were seldom scrapped, but were absorbed into an expanding system.

NOTES

1. Of the many public programs that provide the contours of the German welfare state, we focus only on four core insurance programs. Other programs of the welfare state include housing, manpower policy, family allowances, and so forth.

2. During the 14-year period from 1919 to 1939, the cabinet was reshuffled 14 times, or one cabinet change took place per year.

3. Court rulings have also contributed to increased costs. For example, the GKV was required to pay for the treatment of alcoholism, obesity, renal dialysis, heart transplant, and the like. According to one study on the rehabilitation program quoted in Redler and John (p. 12), two far-reaching rulings of the federal social court in 1969 and 1976 translated into additional costs to the rehabilitation program. These costs amounted to 15 percent of the total budgets of these agencies.

4. By 1977 two books of an anticipated ten-volume series on social legislation (Sozialgesetzbuch) were published (SGB I and SGB IV). In 1983 the tenth volume was completed (SGB X).

5. Hospital rate setting and possibly the setting of rates from specialized health facilities are exceptions because insurance funds participate—directly or indirectly—in the actual negotiations. But regional variations in the methods of negotiating hospital rates are impressive; so are the differences in rates for different groups of hospitals (Altenstetter, 1982b). In some instances rates are set more or less to conform to actual costs. In other cases rates are negotiated on the basis of what one can consider a politically defined formula that has some relationship but not in all cases to costs. The provisions of the German hospital law of 1972 facilitate the transfer of multiple costs because of the different ways of cost accounting, as Thiemeyer (1979) systematically examined and demonstrated.

6. Definitions of the scope of disability and the scope of benefits differed. The social insurance program operated with a definition of disability that included "measures to maintain, improve, and restore the ability to work." Another law (*Arbeitsförderungsgesetz*) spoke of the "promotion of work and occupational skills of disabled individuals." The welfare program (*Sozialhilfe*) spoke of "aid to reentry" (*Eingliederungshilfe*). According to Redler and John, important differences in cash income exist, which can be primarily attributed to employment status, length of employment, and skills. The more "normal" the work record and the better the skills, the higher the income payments. Disability payments for veterans (*Kriegsopferfürsorge*) are high also.

REFERENCES

Aichberger, Friedrich (no date), *Sozialgesetzbuch. Reichsversicherungsordnung*, Textsammlung, München: Verlag C. H. Beck.

Alber, Jens (1981), "Government Responses to the Challenge of Unemployment: The Development of Unemployment Insurance," in Peter Flora and Arnold J.

Heidenheimer, eds., *The Development of the Welfare States in Europe and America*, New Brunswick, NJ: Transaction Books, pp. 151–183.

Altenstetter, Christa (1982a), *Implementation of German Health Insurance Seen from the Perspective of General Sickness Funds* (AOKs), Berlin: Science Center.

Altenstetter, Christa (1982b), *Ziele, Instrumente und Widersprüchlichkeiten der Deutschen Krankenhauspolitik, Vergleichend Dargestellt am Beispiel der Implementation der Bundespflegesatzverordnung*, (Goals, Instruments and Ambiguities of the German Hospital Policy: A Comparative Analysis of the Implementation of the Federal Regulation on Hospital User Charges), Berlin: Science Center.

Altenstetter, Christa (1985), *Krankenhausbedarfsplanung*, München: Oldenbourg Verlag.

Ashford, Douglas E. (1981), "The Growth of Social Security in Britain and France: Welfare States by Intent and by Default," Paper prepared for the Western Societies Program Conference on "Post-Keynesian Politics: The Origin of the Modern Welfare State," Cornell University, September 17–19.

Ashford, Douglas E. (1978), "Structural Analysis of Policy or Institutions Do Matter," in D. E. Ashford, ed., *Comparing Public Policies*, Beverly Hills: Sage Publications, pp. 81–98.

Blankenburg, Erhard and Uta Krautkrämer (1980), "Ein Verwaltungsprogramm als Kaskade von Rechtsvorschriften: Das Arbeitsförderungsgesetz," in Renate Mayntz, ed., *Implementation Politischer Programme*, Königstein/TS, Verlagsgruppe Athenäum, Hain, Scripton, Hanstein, pp. 138–153.

Bundesverband der Ortskrankenkassen (1976), *Die Ortskrankenkassen 1975*, Bonn: Bad Godesberg.

Der Bundesminister für Arbeit und Sozialordnung (1977), *Übersicht über die Soziale Sicherheit*, Bonn: no publisher.

Der Bundesminister für Arbeit und Sozialordnung (no date), *Die gesetzliche Krankenversicherung in der Bundesrepublik Deutschland im Jahre 1983*, Bonn: no publisher.

Flora, Peter and Jens Alber (1981), "Modernization, Democratization, and the Development of Welfare States in Western Europe," in Peter Flora and Arnold J. Heidenheimer, eds., *The Development of the Welfare States in Europe and America*, New Brunswick, NJ: Transaction Books, pp. 37–80.

Flora, Peter and Arnold J. Heidenheimer, eds., (1981), *The Development of the Welfare States in Europe and America*, New Brunswick, NJ: Transaction Books.

Hanf, Kenneth and Fritz W. Scharpf, eds. (1978), *Interorganizational Policy Making: Limits to Coordination and Central Controls*, London: Sage Publications.

Heclo, Hugh (1974), *Modern Social Politics in Britain and Sweden*, New Haven, CT: Yale University Press.

Heclo, Hugh (1981), "Toward a New Welfare State?" in Peter Flora and Arnold J. Heidenheimer, eds., *The Development of the Welfare States in Europe and America*, New Brunswick, NJ: Transaction Books, pp. 383–406.

Heidenheimer, Arnold J. (1981), "The Indexation of Pension Entitlements: The West German Initiative in Comparative Perspective," Paper prepared for the Western Societies Program Conference on "Post-Keynesian Politics: The Origins of the Modern Welfare State," Cornell University, September 17–19.

Hull, Christopher and Benny Hjern (1983), "Policy Analysis in Mixed Economy: An Implementation Approach," *Policy and Politics*, 3:295–312.

Jacob, Herbert (1963), *German Administration Since Bismarck*, New Haven, CT: Yale University Press.

Jung, Karl (1974), "Grundgedanken Zum Rehabilitations-Angleichungsgesetz," *Die Ortskrankenkasse*, vol. 20-21:797–98.

Kaim-Caudle, P. R. (1973), *Comparative Social Policy and Social Security: A Ten-Country Study*, New York: Dunellen.

Kaufman, Herbert (1976), *Are Government Organizations Immortal?* Washington, D.C.: The Brookings Institution.

Kastner, Fritz (1974), "Rehabilitation. Die Neue Aufgabe der Krankenversicherung," *Die Ortskrankenkasse*, vol. 20–21: 785–91.

Kohl, Jürgen (1981), "Trends and Problems in Postwar Public Expenditure Developments in Western Europe and North America," in Peter Flora and Arnold J. Heidenheimer, eds., *The Development of the Welfare States in Europe and America*, New Brunswick, NJ: Transaction Books, pp. 307–344.

Lampert, Heinz (1980), *Sozialpolitik*, Berlin: Springer Verlag.

Leibfried, Stephan (1977), "Die Institutionalisierung der Arbeitslosenversicherung in Deutschland," *Kritische Justiz*, 3: 289–301.

Leibfried, Stephan and Florian Tennstedt, eds. (1985), *Politik der Armut und Die Spaltung des Sozialstaats*, Frankfurt a.M: Suhrkamp.

Maxwell, Robert (1975), *Health Care: The Growing Dilemma*, (2nd ed.), New York: McKinsey.

Mayntz, Renate (1980), "Executive Leadership in Germany: Dispersion of Power or Kanzler-demokratie?" in Richard Rose and Ezra N. Suleiman, eds., *Presidents and Prime Ministers*, Washington: American Enterprise Institute, pp. 139–179.

Mayntz, Renate, ed. (1980), *Implementation politischer Programme*, Königstein/Ts, Verlagsgruppe Athenäum, Hain, Scripton, Hanstein.

Mayntz, Renate and Fritz W. Scharpf (1975), *Policy-Making in the German Bureaucracy*, Amsterdam: Elsevier.

Mommsen, W. J. in collaboration with Wolfgang Mock (1981), *The Emergence of the Welfare State in Britain and Germany 1850–1950*, London: Croom Helm.

Peters, Horst (1974), *Die Geschichte der Sozialen Versicherung*, Bonn-Bad Godesberg: Asgard Verlag.

Pressman, Jeoffrey L. and Aaron Wildavsky (1979), *Implementation*, (2nd ed., expanded), Berkeley: University of California Press.

Redler, Elisabeth and Jürgen John (1981), "Ökonomische Aspekte der Behindertenpolitik: Die Deutsche Erfahrung," unpublished manuscript.

Scharpf, Fritz W. (1977), "Public Organizations and the Waning of the Welfare State: A Research Perspective," *European Journal of Political Research*, 7: 339–362.

Scharpf, Fritz W., Bernd Reissert and Fritz Schnabel (1976), *Politikverflechtung: Theorie und Empirie des kooperativen Föderalismus in der Bundesrepublik Deutschland*, Kronberg: Scriptor Verlag.

Schattschneider, E. E. (1960), *The Semi-Sovereign People*, New York: Holt and Rinehart.

Tennstedt, Florian (1977), *Soziale Selbstverwaltung*, vol. 2, Bonn: Verlag der Ortskrankenkassen.

Thiemeyer, Theo (1979), "Krankenhauswirtschaft in Rahmen gesamtgesellschaftlicher Zielsetzungen," *Krankenhaus-Umschau*, 10: 783–788.

Töns, Hans (1974), "Das Unfallheilverfahren in der Gesetzlichen Krankenversicherung," *Die Ortskrankenkasse*, 20–21: 829–41.

Töns, Hans (1980), *Grundausbildung für den Krankenkassendienst*, Sankt Augustin: Asgard Verlag, 12, überarbeitete Auflage.

Van Langendonck, Jozef (1975), *Prelude to Harmony on a Community Theme: Health Care Insurance Policies in the Six and Britain*, London: Nuffield Provincial Hospital Trust.

Von Ferber, Christian (1977), "Soziale Selbstverwaltung. Fiktion oder Chance?" in Harald Bogs and Christian von Ferber, eds., *Soziale Selbstverwaltung*, vol. 1, Bonn: Verlag der Ortskrankenkassen.

Wilensky, Harold L. (1975), *The Welfare Society and Equality*, Berkeley: University of California Press.

PART II

CRITICAL DECISIONS TOWARD
NATIONALIZATION

INTRODUCTION TO PART II

Douglas E. Ashford and E. W. Kelley

Well before the recent crisis of funding social security, advocates, professionals and bureaucrats had taken most social security programs in hand and they were an accepted component of democratic governance. In retrospect, the curious change was that growth in these stages was not politically more controversial than it was. In general, the nationalization of social security originates with the bureaucracies of modern states, not with politicians. Leibfried's chapter on the intergovernmental administrative struggles of the Weimar Republic reminds us how intense and complex these struggles could be. There were some vitally important changes in the design, operations and assumptions of social security in nearly all the democracies, but these decisions were increasingly taken by national government, not through party or electoral debate.

In this section we provide several clues to the strange decline of political salience of social security within governments, if not to the public. Of course, a major factor was the relative economic stability and prosperity of most Western economies, but this hardly seems a sufficient explanation when taking into account the important policy decisions made during the interwar years in most democracies. One of the most important decisions leading toward nationalization in the United States before the war was Secretary of the Treasury Morgenthau's case to Roosevelt to index the American system. Stein analyzes this decision and its implica-

101

tions in his chapter. Equally important decisions were made about the expansion and organization of unemployment benefits, outlined by Harpham how the controversy arose over state politics. His essay may help solve the depoliticization riddle because it was the influence of organized labor combined with state politics that shaped policy. The financing of unemployment benefits was a joint task of the federal and state governments. Paradoxically, under President Nixon, now recognized as a major figure in the escalation of social spending over the 1970s, the federal government agreed to take on all costs of the Emergency Unemployment Compensation Act of 1971.

No less intricate than the combination of state politics and state interests as they came to bear on unemployment insurance in the United States is the intense struggle in Germany between the wars to establish fixed guidelines for poverty assistance. Long before the powerful welfare interest groups of the 1980s, Germany had a national Welfare Federation linking together a determined body of local assistance officials. As Leibfried describes, these officials were able to work through their states to frustrate national aims. The battle took place over the approved limits to the "breadbasket" formula for mineral subsistence in an earlier welfare era, but it reveals both the immense influence of the localized German bureaucracy and the political delicacy of attempting radical welfare reforms without local support.

Indexing is, of course, an important instrument for nationalization which avoids direct clashes with local interests. As Heidenheimer describes, the indexing of German social security in 1957 was the decision of a strong conservative leader, Adenauer, who was trying to reconcile the complex German system of social security with the politics of the "Grand Coalition" of the late 1960s. By then the intricate bureaucratic structure of German social security was virtually immune to change by the federal government.

A number of changes were occurring simultaneously in the political context of social security policies. As is well known, social spending and finance were becoming a highly technical problem and less readily made into political ammunition except in the obvious sense of immediate rewards for politically active groups, largely pensioners. The actuarial study and delicate negotiations needed to help integrate public and private pensions in Britain, for example, took nearly a decade. Second, the bureaucracies and their clients and experts had forged strong links over the generation or more that it took for the welfare state to reach its contemporary proportions. Many of these people, including trade unions and business, preferred to settle their problems in the comparative peace and quiet of officialdom rather than take the more costly and often more risky route of new legislation. While the welfare state had prospered, there had been few institutional, legal and constitutional changes that facilitated political intervention through the democratic process. The major ideological battles were actually fought and usually won by social security advocates as the major needy groups had established their identities and footholds within government. Political mobilization and political access lost importance.

FUNDING SOCIAL SECURITY ON A CURRENT BASIS:
THE 1939 POLICY CHANGE
IN THE UNITED STATES

Bruno Stein

Social insurance systems in the developed world are encountering increasing strains. Beginning as what, in hindsight, were relatively modest income maintenance programs that dispensed with the stigma of charity and means tests, some flowered into comprehensive programs that, together with a concurrent growth in means-tested income maintenance, marked the transition of free labor market economies into welfare states. Much of this flowering occurred after World War II, when a period of sustained economic growth made income transfers from taxpayers to taxgetters relatively painless. This growth has, at least for the time being, slowed to a crawl. What was once affordable now looks expensive.

To complicate matters even further, the postwar period saw a remarkable demographic development. Fertility rates that had been depressed by the prior Depression and war leapt upward, as if to make up for previous losses. Then, as suddenly as the phenomenon appeared, it re-

versed itself sharply. As a result, public retirement programs, almost all
of which are currently funded, have begun to face a demographic time
bomb. A large cohort, with longer life expectancies than their predeces-
sors, will need to be supported by a relatively small cohort of economically actives.

The United States, although not a welfare state if compared to
Sweden or the Netherlands, has not been immune from these strains. Its
public assistance programs for non-aged underwent an astonishing expansion during the prosperous 1960s. However troublesome the "welfare mess" might have seemed, it did not occasion large drains on the
national fisc because the population at risk was relatively small. The
fragmented nature of public assistance *did* result in considerable fiscal
strains on regions that received large migrations of poor people and, not
long thereafter, began on the road to economic decline because of sectoral shifts in the economy. Be that as it may, public assistance claimants
are disproportionately black (and Hispanic) and, as minorities, are not
popular subjects for income transfers from a predominantly white and
non-Hispanic majority.

The income maintenance program that currently covers, and worries,
most Americans is popularly known as Social Security. Based on social
insurance principles that are common to the industrial world, it consists
of non-means-tested provisions for old age, survivors, total disability,
and health insurance for the aged. Unlike most social insurance programs in other countries, it is financed exclusively (except for
Medicare–Part B) by a payroll tax divided equally between employers
and workers (the self-employed pay 75% of the combined rate). Revenues from the tax (called "contribution") are apportioned among three
funds: Old Age and Survivors Insurance (OASI) Trust Fund, Disability
Insurance (DI) Trust Fund, and Hospital Insurance (HI) Trust Fund.
These are contingency reserves, invested in special issues of U.S. government obligations. Coverage is virtually complete, at 90% of the working population. The principal exclusions are federal employees, and
some state and local government employees—these are provided for
separately, and in most cases, more favorably.[1] Cash benefits are wage
related, but skewed to favor low income workers. Since 1975, cash benefits have been indexed to the Consumer Price Index.

The current crisis in Social Security dates back to the mid-1970s, when
the depletion of the Trust Funds, principally OASI, began to ring alarm
bells. This compelled Congress to make some politically unpleasant decisions. It could raise the rates at which payroll taxes were to be increased,
increase the taxable maximum, lower benefits, or dip into general revenues. It also had to correct a serious technical error built into the system
by the 1972 amendments which, in a period of falling real wages,

overcompensated for inflation at the point of retirement, thus driving benefits up at a faster rate than contemplated.[2] Congress rejected the option of using general revenues, possibly for ideological reasons and because of the federal budget's already chronic deficits. This left little choice but to raise the payroll taxes and the taxable maximum (effective *after* the 1978 Congressional elections) and to cut relative benefits for future retirees, but only to the extent that they would have risen but for the technical error. It also solved the decoupling problem, choosing the costlier of two options, i.e., the one that would have the effect of maintaining rather than reducing future benefits relative to future wages (Stein, 1980, pp. 194–195).

The relative benefit cut went unnoticed. The tax increase, which was labeled as the greatest in American history, did not go unnoticed, especially in the face of a growing tax revolt among the voters. When Congress rested from these difficult labors, it believed that it had saved Social Security for the next 75 years. In point of fact, it had not, since it left an actuarial deficit that a future generation could worry about.

The amendment was passed in late 1977. By 1979 it became apparent that short-term forecasts of unemployment and inflation had been too rosy. The system is acutely sensitive to these factors, because unemployment reduces payroll tax revenues and inflation raises benefit disbursements. A combination of the two is deadly. In consequence, the OASI Trust Fund began a new decline. After considerable political agony, Congress was compelled to act to avoid the impending insolvency of the Old Age and Survivors Insurance Trust Fund.[3]

One by-product of the crisis was an upsurge of interest in Social Security by economists. Until the 1970s, the economics literature on the subject was sparse. There were a few textbooks, such as Rejda (1976), and Turnbull, Williams and Cheit (1974), that were standard references on income maintenance in the 1960s (Burns [1956] was the standard work in the late 1950s), and Pechman, Aaron and Taussig, published in 1968, was generally accepted as the definitive study of Social Security. Suddenly, Social Security became a hot topic. An outpouring of studies resulted. As economists approached the subject anew, many did not like what they saw. One of the aspects that troubled some of them, especially those who were led by Martin Feldstein, was the pay-as-you-go nature of the financing. Although modern economists tend to be ahistorical, they inevitably tripped across a piece of ancient history and duly recorded it in their footnotes: the original 1935 Social Security Act had provided for a (more or less) fully funded system of old age benefits, to begin payments in 1942. Before it actually went into effect, the system was amended in 1939 and, *inter alia*, was shifted to a pay-as-you-go (PAYG[4]) basis. And thereby hangs a tale.

FULL FUNDING VERSUS PAY-AS-YOU-GO

Before delving into the nature of this apparently crucial policy decision, it may be useful to sketch out the difference between full (or advance) funding and PAYG. To minimize the degree of complexity, I shall confine myself to social insurance old age benefits that are public, i.e., administered by a central government. In a fully funded system, earmarked taxes are levied and invested in securities—generally, but not inevitably, obligations of the central government.[5] At the inception of such a system, benefit payments are low, rising to the targeted replacement ratio of benefits to prior earnings only when the system matures. That is, the first cohort that enters retirement gets a return based only on its contributions plus interest, and only when the cohort that has spent its full work life in the labor force retires do full benefits become available. The analogy is with private annuity schemes, except that contributions need not come solely from equi-divided payroll taxes, and benefits need not be fully related to individuals' contributions or earnings histories.

Under PAYG, today's taxes pay today's benefits. Since revenues and disbursements are not necessarily equal at any one point in time, a contingency fund is used to even out the differences. The fund (in the United States, the several funds) commonly holds government obligations. Relatively speaking, it need not be very large, since its function is to ensure the liquidity of the system at times when cyclical or other economic shocks unexpectedly increase net outflows.

In principle, PAYG is a chain letter of virtually infinite duration. The first cohorts that retire receive a gift and, if things work smoothly, only the last generation alive at the end of time loses.[6] More elegantly, PAYG is called a compact between generations in which each working generation supports its elders in the expectation that it will, in turn, be supported by the following generation. Seen in this light, a PAYG-based old age system socializes what was common practice in the past, when children supported their aged parents. The reader will note, however, that a compact to which one generation is not a signatory has some potential for being broken.

The rate of return of payroll tax contributions under a fully funded system is the yield on its portfolio. If the obligations are acquired at market rates of return, there is no subsidy from other taxes unless explicitly introduced. For a PAYG system supported by payroll taxes, there is an implicit rate of return equal to the rate of population growth plus the rate of growth of per capita earnings (Munnell, 1977, pp. 127–128).

This immediately raises an interesting question. If market rates are higher than implicit rates, is not a fully funded system preferable to PAYG? In fact, market rates have exceeded implicit rates (even after taxes) in the United States, so that the question is a cogent one. The answer, however, is not obvious.

PAYG permits the system to begin paying full benefits immediately without levying enormous taxes. It thus bypasses that aspect of the maturation stage that reserves full benefits for full life workers. If the first cohort of retirees is supported by some other public assistance program—and this was contemplated by the original 1935 Act—then PAYG is in effect during the maturation stage in any event, although it ultimately phases itself out. Hence, the benefits of full funding are postponed for quite a long time. Note that the last generation alive, if you worry about things like that, does not get benefits under either system; someone must be alive and working to pay the taxes that yield the interest on the public debt held by the Fund.

This brings us to an important point. In a real sense, the economically active population always supports its dependents. The goods and services consumed by the retired population are, by and large, currently produced with an existing stock of labor and capital. Active and dependent persons appear on the marketplace with money claims on real output. The dependent persons may do so by spending from their accumulated assets or from public income transfers that they receive. In the first instance, they are spending their own money, that is, the equivalent of a fully funded pension. They do not, of course, believe themselves to be supported by others because in a private property society, their claim is established by law and consensus. Beneficiaries of currently funded transfer payments may similarly believe that they have earned (and thus own) their benefits, and they are likely to hold to this belief even though their prior social insurance tax contributions were (a) used to support others, not themselves, and (b) were not great enough to cover the size of their benefits. However, if we pierce the veils of money and of institutional arrangements that pertain to property and/or statutory rights, we can see that the goods taken up by the dependent population are not available—or foregone by—the active population. Something foregone is in the nature of a cost.

If this is the case, then both full funding and PAYG result in intergenerational transfers. In PAYG, the transfer is obvious: today's working population taxes itself to pay today's benefits. With full funding, the transfer is less obvious, being clouded by institutional considerations. Nonetheless, it is there. Today's working population pays taxes for the interest payments on the debt from which part of today's benefits are paid. In a static sense, the difference between the two systems is distributional; its effects depend on how different taxes affect different segments of the population.

In a dynamic sense, the difference pertains to the differing effects that the systems may have on capital accumulation and future output. As Munnell (1977, p. 127) said:

> a funded system is preferable to a pay-as-you-go system if the real rate of return on capital exceeds the implicit rate of return in a currently financed program. In fact, deciding whether or not to have a funded system is really equivalent to deciding whether or not there is an optimal supply of capital in the economy. If the real rate of return on capital exceeds the implicit return for a pay-as-you-go program, the capital supply is suboptimal and society would gain by accumulating reserves in a trust fund.

Needless to say, capital accumulation ultimately comes from saving, that is, from foregoing present consumption and diverting resources to capital. If the stock of capital is, by some definition, believed to be suboptimal, full funding can be used to increase it. But this will work only if the foregone personal consumption reallocates the freed-up resources to capital. Government's bonds are not real wealth to an economy: they are merely claims against its future taxing power. If government borrows for its current expenditures and runs persistent deficits, then all that has happened is that current public consumption has been favored over current private consumption.

In short, if a full funding mechanism is to achieve a goal of capital accumulation, the net revenues from a social security must be diverted directly or indirectly into real capital formation. At the inception of such an arrangement, the older cohorts are losers and the younger cohorts reap the gains of the sacrifices made by their elders.[7] This capital formation is needed so that future output can be great enough to satisfy, in some political sense, the needs of both the active and dependent populations. A poor society is less likely to be generous to its dependents than a wealthy one.

HISTORICAL BACKGROUND

The Social Security Act of 1935 was, in hindsight, a remarkably conservative document. Until that time, public income maintenance programs had followed the general traditions derived from the English Poor Laws (Stein, 1971, pp. 42–73) which, like other poor laws, were designed to cope with social needs generated by a marginal segment of the population. The Depression had widened that margin considerably. To be sure, the New Deal's initial response to the mass impoverishment of the Depression was a dole, pure and simple (the Federal Emergency Relief Act), but the notion that people should earn their support was deeply embedded in the American political ethos. This is reflected by the fairly quick shift from straight relief for the unemployed to work relief programs such as the WPA.

By the same token, a social insurance program that is contributory and whose benefits are related to prior labor earnings also has a conservative ring to it. Those who receive benefits have "earned" them by their own contributions and those made in their behalf by their employers. No means test is required, although it is necessary to establish whether the conditions of eligibility have actually been met by the claimant.

The roots of social insurance were first implanted in the tory soil of Bismarckian Germany, and turned out to be adaptable for transplant into other countries. Cates, in his provocative and revisionist view of American Social Security, dubs the founders of our Social Security system as conservatives, fighting off the "liberal" alternative offered by the Townsend movement (1981, p. 121).[8] Although I would not characterize the Townsend plan as liberal—utopian or crackpot might be better descriptors—it may be argued that demogrants are more likely to be favored by the left than by the right. As will be seen below, the modifiers "liberal" and "conservative" have elusive meanings when applied to Social Security. The 1939 Amendments which liberalized the program by adding coverage for dependents and survivors, and by moving away from "sound" principles of funding toward PAYG, received much of their impetus from "conservative" sources (Derthick, 1979, pp. 132–133).

Unemployment was undoubtedly the principal political issue in the early 1930s, and a program to provide unemployment insurance as a long-term replacement for work relief was high on the New Deal agenda. Individual states were afraid to enact such programs, out of fear that the necessary taxes would put their businesses at a competitive disadvantage. However, relief for the aged was also an issue, as state-financed relief programs groaned under the growing burden. The second issue rapidly snowballed under the pressure of the Townsend Movement. The plan developed by Dr. Francis Townsend initially proposed a pension of $200 per month for persons over sixty, with the proviso that it be spent within the month. It was to be financed by a turnover tax of 2% and it promised not only to take care of the aged (at what would then have been a very high standard of living) but also to create prosperity for everyone else.[9]

The strength of the Townsend Movement, which flourished in an environment that fostered other radical populist ideas,[10] awoke both Congress and the administration to the need for an old age benefit system and, indeed, for the need to establish a more comprehensive income security system. Indeed, the Movement frightened both liberals and conservatives and led some of the latter to a search for an income security system that would be acceptable to them. The issue of how to fund such a system evolved from this search. In any event, Roosevelt's response to these pressures was to appoint a cabinet Committee on Economic Security, with a staff of distinguished experts, to develop a coherent program that could be submitted to Congress.[11]

The basic old age provision that emerged from the Committee's deliberations consisted of two parts:

1.   An old age insurance[12] program covering about 60% of the labor force, to be financed by a payroll tax of 2% of covered wages up to $3,000 per year (divided equally between employers and employees), rising in gradual stages to 5% in 1957. Benefits were to be based on total covered earnings after 1937 (when the tax was to go into effect). The benefits were to begin in 1942. A reserve would be accumulated, and held in U.S. government obligations (or obligations guaranteed by the government) with an interest payment of 3%. This interest rate, it may be noted, was above prevailing market rates;

2.   An old age assistance program (OAA) to be administered by states on conventional poor law principles, but adhering to the minimum standards established by the Act. This was perceived to be transitional. As the old age insurance program matured, the younger cohorts would be moving toward the full benefit goal of about 50% of prior earnings, and OAA would phase down and confine itself to the residual aged poor, largely those who were not covered by old age insurance (e.g., agricultural workers, domestics, and a few other exclusions).

Two things about the old age insurance program should be noted here. One is that the benefit unit, like the taxing unit, was the individual. The second is that the financing provision in the original bill did not reach full funding. By the actuarial calculations made at the time, a deficit would appear in about thirty years, with the implication that contributions from general revenues would be needed thereafter (U.S. Social Security Board, 1937, p. 212).

At the last minute, Treasury Secretary Morgenthau called Roosevelt's attention to the projected deficits (Altmeyer, 1966, p. 29; Witte, 1962, pp. 148–151). Roosevelt wanted a fully funded program. Although it was too late to make the change in the administration bill, it was made clear to Congress that an alternative financing scheme would be forthcoming for consideration by the House Ways and Means Committee. The actuaries went back to work and revised the schedule of taxes to reach a joint rate of 6% by 1949. The effect was intended to make the system self-supporting until 1980. It would also have raised the size of the ultimate reserve from $14 billion to about $50 billion (Witte, 1962, pp. 151–152). This was no mean sum, at a time when the publicly held federal debt was about $29 billion. The new schedule was presented to Congress. Popularly known as the Morgenthau Amendment, it was adopted.[13]

Let us recap for a moment. The original policy proposal for old age insurance developed by the Committee on Economic Security envisioned full funding during much of the maturation period of old age insurance, with PAYG entering in 1965 to top up the system. If it is considered together with OAA, the picture changes somewhat. OAA is financed from federal and state general revenues; hence, it is in the nature of PAYG. If OAA was to phase down through time, its demands on general revenues would diminish as the insurance program's demands on general revenues would commence. Qualitatively, the net result would have been a partially funded old age benefit system with a reserve considerably larger than needed for mere contingency purposes.

The Morgenthau Amendment was closer to full funding in spirit, although it would have required general revenues by 1980. The gain of fifteen years would have involved an increase of $36 billion in the ultimate size of the reserve, thus more than doubling the national debt. Although "sounder" in the usual actuarial sense, it would still have fallen short of the ideal of full funding or self-support. Since the amendment did not touch OAA, its PAYG element was unaffected by the change.

Inevitably, the question arose: why such a large reserve if self-sufficiency was not achievable even at the then astonishingly high payroll tax rate of 6%? If Morgenthau envisioned still higher payroll taxes (if, for that matter, he thought that far ahead), he was politically too astute to suggest them to Congress. It is not surprising, therefore, that no sooner was the Act passed, than policymakers began to have second thoughts.

Their alternatives were limited. Higher payroll taxes were out of the question. Overall lower benefits were impossible. The older cohorts were not going to get much and those reaching age 65 before 1942 would only get their taxes back, plus interest. The nation had developed a taste for Social Security, as evidenced by the adverse reaction to Alf Landon's negative speech on the subject during the 1936 presidential campaign. The continued liveliness of the Townsend Movement attested to the existence of an organizable constituency with considerable clout.

If anything, the challenge faced by the policymakers was how to develop a program that yielded more and did so at no higher cost. Ordinarily, that is a pretty neat trick and commonly achievable only by using deficits to put off the evil day. In this case, however, the reverse appeared to be possible. By reducing the reserve to a contingency level, one could pay better benefits and pay them sooner. Due to the paucity of free lunches, what was really accomplished by the policy change of 1939 was: (1) a diversion of part of the payroll tax from general purposes to benefits; and (2) a reduction of certain future benefits and, for some classes of people, their elimination.

THE TROUBLESOME RESERVE

The Old Age Insurance provisions of the 1935 Act turned out to displease a good many influential persons. Townsendites were obviously not satisfied with a program that, ultimately, would provide only minimum necessary support. Liberal supporters of the program wanted contributions from general revenues, as well as an early start of benefits and the extension of benefits to survivors, dependents, and invalids. "But most serious of all was the attack, made by insurance men and business organizations, on the financing of old age insurance, centering on the slogan 'pay as you go' " (Witte, 1957, p. 257).

This attack may have reflected a conservative fear that the large reserve would induce an unwarranted expansion of the program, presumably by offering a temptation to future Congresses to sweeten the program by dipping into the reserve fund. The attack had the ironic effect of laying the basis for an immediate and expansive reconstruction of the program. Program executives who had never favored a large reserve conceded the criticism regarding financing and came up with a program to spend more money sooner. Thus, "a conservative critique had paved the way for a liberal outcome, one of many illustrations of the ambiguity and adaptability of social insurance policy, in which it is often hard to tell the sides apart or who won" (Derthick, 1979, p. 143).[14]

Senator Arthur Vandenberg started the ball rolling by persuading the Senate Finance Committee of the desirability of having an external Advisory Committee study the possibility of revising the 1935 Act. After much political pulling and hauling, an Advisory Committee was jointly chosen by the Senate Special Committee on Social Security and the Social Security Board in May, 1937.[15] The Committee consisted of representatives of employers (mostly "enlightened" types such as Marion B. Folsom and Gerard Swope, and insurance industry representatives), unions (both AFL and CIO) and the public. The last group included people who were active in developing the 1935 Act, such as J. Douglas Brown, Edwin E. Witte, and interested persons like Paul H. Douglas.

The Committee's recommendations conformed fairly closely to those developed by the Social Security Board,[16] which was not exactly a coincidence. For the purposes of this essay, one important thing is that the Advisory Committee *unanimously* agreed that full reserve funding was not feasible.[17]

Although Roosevelt's message to Congress on January 16, 1939 skirted the issue of full financing (U.S. Congress, 1939, pp. 1–2), there is no doubt that he had made a 180-degree turn on the subject. A program that paid benefits sooner, extended them to dependents and survivors, and was said to cost no more in the long run than the skimpier 1935 Act, was politically irresistible. The postponement of the scheduled payroll tax increases made the program even more popular. Both conservative businessmen and the newly-emerging Keynesians wanted to avoid a tax increase in a recessionary year. Indeed, Marriner Eccles, Chairman of the Federal Reserve's Board of Governors, had laid part of the blame for the 1937–1939 recession of the payroll tax (Cates, 1981, p. 106).

The ever-faithful Morgenthau, author of the famous (or notorious) Morgenthau Amendment, explained his change of mind to the House Ways and Means Committee. The large reserve was no longer necessary because new information showed that actual coverage of the population would be close to 80% rather than the originally estimated 50–60%.[18] Since so great a proportion of the population would benefit, direct contributions from general revenues would be an equitable substitute for interest earnings on the reserve. These would not, he stressed, be needed in the near future. He was careful to point out that, in the future, PAYG would require other taxes (i.e., general revenues) or higher payroll taxes. In the meantime, he asked for a contingency reserve limited to three times the prospective benefit obligations accruing in the ensuing five years, as well as regular actuarial reports to Congress, and special reports whenever the reserve (to be called a Trust Fund) rose above or fell below this figure (U.S. Congress, 1939, pp. 2111–2113).

It can be argued that this apparent about-face did not constitute a change from his (and FDR's) fundamental fiscal conservatism. In 1935, Morgenthau had supported reforms like old age insurance, but wanted to keep a firm hand on the budget (Blum, 1959, p. 300). He still wanted this firm hand on the budget in 1939, but was willing to trade off lower Social Security taxes for greater excise taxes, taxes on government salaries, and on the interest on all government securities, including federal, municipal and state obligations. He made this position clear in his testimony on the Revenue Act of 1939. In reference to his suggestion to postpone the increase in the Social Security tax, he stated, "Any tax reduction must be offset by tax increases. We should take no step which the public may interpret as moving away from the objective of a balanced budget" (Blum, 1965, p. 30).

It is interesting to note that by 1942 Morgenthau wanted to raise Social Security taxes as an anti-inflation measure, in exchange for better postwar benefits. The Senate stood with Vandenberg in opposing this move, and the tax remained frozen at the original level. He tried again in 1944, and his failure to achieve the increase is characterized by Blum as a "great defeat" (Blum, 1967, pp. 50, 53–54, 68–74).

According to Cates (1981, pp. 109–110), Vandenberg wanted to hold the line on Social Security taxes until the excess reserve was gone. He was even willing to support authorization from general revenues, knowing full well that they would not be needed in the foreseeable future. The strategy worked, and in 1950, when the tax was raised for the first time, the authorization for general revenues was withdrawn, and has not been relegislated to this day.

PAYG, SAVINGS AND ECONOMIC GROWTH

Although the payroll tax was advertised by its advocates as a form of compulsory saving[19] which helped people and averted indigence in old age, it was no such thing. From both a legal and an economic point of view, a tax is a tax. Most serious policymakers understood this, notwithstanding its relabeling in 1939 as a contribution to make it conform to the insurance image that the Social Security Board and its successor agency tried to stress.[20]

Under pure PAYG, the tax is more or less earmarked to pay current benefits. Under full or partial funding, the excess of revenues over disbursements is used for current government expenditures. In the latter case, the *quid pro quo* is a claim against future general taxes, but the claim is not held by the individual saver; it is held by a government agency and is, in no sense, anyone's private property. This was made amply clear by the Supreme Court in *Fleming* v. *Nestor* (363 U.S. 603). In that case, the Court upheld a law depriving Communists and their dependents of benefits. The Court stated that "it is apparent that the non-contractual interest of an employee . . . cannot be soundly analogized to that of a holder of an annuity . . . " (363 U.S. 603, at 616). What Congress gives, Congress can take, regardless of the nature of the funding.

Still, the existence of Social Security can affect personal saving behavior. The tax reduces disposable income available for saving, and the anticipated benefits can displace the need for saving. The latter is part of the celebrated and controversial Feldstein thesis, first propounded in 1974, which attempts to show that Social Security reduces saving, thus depressing capital formation and GNP, and thereby redistributing income from wages to capital.[21] Feldstein has proposed to correct this malfunction by shifting from PAYG to full—or substantially full—funding, while curtailing or ending government deficits (Feldstein, 1974b, 1976).

While the issue of savings and capital formation was largely overlooked in the 1939 debates, it did not altogether escape notice. In his testimony before the House Ways and Means Committee, J. Frederic Dewhurst came to grips with the question of whether a reserve fund was really a form of collective saving.[22] Although he strongly supported PAYG (with some contributions from general revenues), Dewhurst anticipated many of the issues underlying the Feldstein thesis. His views can be summarized as follows.

Wage earners were not great savers. To the extent that Social Security led them to expect a pension, they would curtail their saving: the greater the pension the greater the reduction in saving. The portion of the tax levied on employers would have uncertain impacts on saving, depending on the shifting and incidence of the tax. If it fell on employers, it would reduce profits and thereby the savings of the people most able to save. However, if it were passed backward in the form of lower wages, or forward to consumers through higher prices, it *would* have a savings effect, squeezing the savings from income groups who could least afford it (including workers not covered by the Act and not eligible for benefits).

Moreover, even assuming that net savings ensue, much depends on what is done with them. If these are used to retire the national debt, then net saving occurs only if the private sellers of the debt reinvest the purchase money (this is precisely what Feldstein assumes would happen). Should government engage in deficit financing, there would be no net saving (Feldstein would agree), but merely a shift in the burden of public expenditures toward wage earners.

The gist of the argument is that the only way that the present sacrifice entailed by accumulation of a reserve would lighten the burden of the next generation is for it to generate savings that are invested domestically in capital that would enhance future production (U.S. Congress, 1939, pp. 811–816).

Dewhurst expressed doubts as to whether the mechanism of the reserve fund would achieve the goal of capital accumulation, and went on to worry about the effect that an increase in saving by low income workers would have on economic stability and cyclical fluctuations.

This last point was not merely a touch of Keynes. At a time when the U.S. economy had an excess supply of capital and labor, it seemed commonsensical to oppose an exogenously determined decrease in demand. After ten years of Depression, recovery was higher on the social agenda than growth. A demand-led recovery, which put idle capital and labor to work, would (to Keynesians) generate savings for future investment.

Even so, the American Keynesians who followed Alvin Hansen were to be more concerned with stagnation than growth. As war began to engender recovery, this group predicted bad times to follow. To them, saving in a mature economy was a vice, not a virtue. As they became influential in policy circles, they brought with them their predilections in favor of consumption. Keynes himself, in 1946, told them that Social Security would depress saving, and that their fears of stagnation were therefore unwarranted (Munnell, 1977, p. 554). If so, they might have received some reassurance for a preference for PAYG, but it is doubtful that they gave the issue much thought.

WAS IT A PSEUDO ISSUE?

In opting for PAYG, Congress did not really make a conscious decision regarding the optimal size of the nation's capital stock. The level of economic sophistication is not high among politicians, although economists are prone to underestimate it. My reading of the House Ways and Means Committee hearings shows that the question barely surfaced in the form of Dewhurst's testimony, which put the issue negatively. The purpose of his presentation was to provide ammunition against the Townsendites, ammunition that Congress sorely needed.

Moreover, the principals in the Advisory Council and Congressional debates understood that each generation supports its own elderly. I have noted above that full funding can disguise the cost because, when the system matures, part of the benefits are paid out of interest on bonds. Most persons do not particularly associate their income tax burdens with this budgetary item—an item that is considered to be a non-discretionary part of the federal budget.

From a shorter term perspective, however, full funding can be perceived as making the cost more obvious and explicit in the early stages of the program. The initial social insurance benefits are lower. The tax either begins at or quickly rises to the level premium needed to sustain the system through time, provided that benefits remain unchanged and that actuarial assumptions turn out to be correct. The reserve that must be accumulated is a concrete statement of the size of future benefit obligations. As the system matures, these obligations grow as the number of eligible beneficiaries grows relative to the working and taxpaying population.

Altmeyer and Witte, who leaned to the full funding principle[23] said that the purposes of the reserve account were to give the public an accurate statement of future liabilities ("it is merely honest bookkeeping"), and to budget the costs over a long period. The latter would encourage future Congresses to appropriate enough money to cover currently accruing liabilities (U.S. Congress, 1939, pp. 2205, 1757). To put it another way, the reserve would depoliticize the system, removing it from the annual whims of future Congresses. Note that the motivation was political, not economic.

But the reserve account was not the only way to keep the books honest. The alternative that lay at hand was periodic actuarial estimates of both short and long run obligations. These would have to be made in any event, regardless of the methods of financing. Congress knew that future obligations would rise and, given the actuarial estimates, could legislate future tax increases in advance, thus dispensing with the mechanism of the reserve.

The only reserve needed was the contingency reserve, which became the system of Trust funds. If the Funds became larger than needed, tax increases could be postponed or benefits added and extended. Should they be smaller than needed, the scheduled tax increases could be accelerated. Each proposal to improve benefits could have a price tag attached to it, based on actuarial estimates. In this fashion, PAYG would be as sound and as fiscally responsible as full funding. And it could be self-supporting, not really needing general revenues.

The 1939 Congress, and its successors, felt more comfortable with this option. Psychological reinforcement was provided by the sharp net inflow of revenues caused by the war, as taxable payrolls rose above, and retirements fell below, previous estimates. This enabled Congress repeatedly to defer the scheduled tax increases, so that the next step did not become effective until 1950.

SUBSEQUENT DEVELOPMENTS

By 1950, when Congress next gave serious thought to Social Security, the issue of full funding versus PAYG had receded and the Townsend Movement was largely gone. Proposers of "flat plans" (basic universal pensions) and "double deckers" (basic pensions with earnings-related supplements) found their cries unheeded. The structure established in 1939 was in place. It only remained to build on it.

The growth of Social Security after 1950 paralleled the growth of social insurance schemes elsewhere. It may be that social insurance programs have a dynamic of their own, especially during periods of economic growth. The explanation for this dynamic is best left to others,[24] and I shall not dwell on it here. Suffice it to say that the American system's expansion in scope, its provision of a transfer-in-kind (Medicare), and the advent of indexation, all made actuarial projections increasingly chancy. Too many variables needed to be forecast, and the forecasts were wrong.

Back in 1939, Witte had warned that if deficits arose under PAYG, Congress would have four choices: (1) increase payroll taxes, (2) reduce benefits, (3) levy new taxes, or (4) go on incurring deficits. He feared that future Congresses would not be willing to levy the higher taxes which would have been unnecessary had earlier Congresses levied taxes to meet the real cost of benefits and not merely the cost of current outlays (U.S. Congress, 1939, p. 1767). Whether by chance or foresight, he forecast the dilemma that faces American Social Security today.

CONCLUDING COMMENTS

The Social Security Act of 1935 established an old age insurance system, ostensibly to be financed on a full funding basis. A joint payroll tax would be levied, beginning in 1937, at 2% (joint) of covered wages (up to $3000), rising in stages to 6% in 1948. Benefits would begin in 1942, based on covered earnings between 1937 and age 65, payable on condition of retirement. The excess of revenues over disbursements would be invested in government bonds, constituting an interest-bearing reserve that would ultimately reach $47 to $50 billion.

The amendments of 1939 altered the benefit structure by including survivors and dependents, and by basing benefits on average wages, so that full benefits would become available in 1940. The financing, however, was shifted to a current basis. The policy change in financing occurred because of great opposition to the concept of a large reserve, an opposition that came from a wide spectrum of political opinion

On the surface, full funding would have been sounder by conservative canons. That is why, at the last minute, Morgenthau persuaded Roosevelt that the concept be embodied in the 1935 bill. Hence, conservative opposition to it may strike one as surprising.

An underlying conservative fear was that full funding would have the effect of compelling government to engage in deficit spending. The alternative possibility, that other taxes might be reduced as an offset, must have struck conservatives as politically unlikely. If this was their thinking, then they were probably correct. Thus, given a choice between full funding and PAYG, they supported the latter. The debate in 1939 is replete with solemn references to the "soundness" of PAYG, made by various representatives of the business community. Needless to say, liberals agreed.

From an economic point of view, full funding might have been an engine for forced saving and capital accumulation. However, a necessary condition or this would have been a conscious fiscal policy that severely restricted the growth of the national debt past the point needed to fund the system. Hindsight suggests that such fiscal discipline would have been unlikely. The ascending Keynesians would certainly have objected to such a fiscal straightjacket. It would have foreclosed vigorous use of countercyclical fiscal policy. Furthermore, it would have hampered the use of a monetary policy that relies on open market operations, since this device is possible only if publicly held government debt is available for trading by the Federal Reserve.

Politically, full funding might well have slowed the expansion of Social Security. Excluded groups would have been less eager for inclusion in the absence of the windfalls that blanketing-in created for them— enormous windfalls in the case of the older cohorts. Benefit increases would have to be constrained if they required increases in an already high (relatively speaking) "level premium" tax rather than the low (but still upward moving) tax needed during the period of maturation.

On the other hand, full funding might have acted to depoliticize Social Security. While restraining the growth of benefits, it would, at the same time, have made the benefits more akin to contractual rights. The Trust Fund would have been the "owner" of assets whose yield would have financed a significant part of the benefits, and a default on government bonds would, in all likelihood, have been more unthinkable than a reduction in statutory benefits.

Either way, the bottom line remains the same: each generation supports its elders. There are alternative ways of accomplishing this task, and there are alternative ways of inducing or compelling national saving. In retrospect, one concludes that, given the political, economic and historical forces at play from 1935 to the present time, the choice between full funding and PAYG was inevitably resolved in favor of the latter.

These forces are now undergoing a process of change. Social Security has been forced to adapt in order to avoid the more difficult process of radical change. The principal adaptive policy options can be grouped into: (1) those involving more taxes (either higher payroll taxes, contributions from general revenues, or other taxes such as a Value Added Tax), or (2) lower benefits (such as higher ages of eligibility, lower maximum benefits, elimination of the minimum benefit, taxation of benefits, and similar devices).

These policy choices are reflected in the 1983 amendments that provide for greater revenues, principally by accelerating the scheduled payroll tax increases, and reducing benefits in a variety of ways, including a delay in the payment of the cost of living adjustment, an increase in the eligibility age that affects younger workers, and the partial taxation of benefits received by higher income retirees. In addition, the new law has an automatic mechanism for reducing the cost of living adjustments whenever the Trust Funds fall to dangerously low levels.[25]

The radical policy option of phasing out Social Security has not been adopted or even seriously considered, but the 1982 tax legislation introduced the thin end of the wedge by giving favorable tax treatment to individual retirement savings. In short, it has been easier to make incremental changes, albeit negative ones, in an existing and time-honored institution, than to start anew. As a final irony, it is quite conceivable that the system will—temporarily—approach levels of full funding in the 1990s. Perhaps the 1939 debates will be renewed at that point.

ACKNOWLEDGMENTS

The author is indebted to the late Eveline M. Burns, J. Douglas Brown, and the participants of the Conference on Post-Keynesian Politics for their helpful comments.

NOTES

1. For a brief but more complete description, see Stein (1980, pp. xvii–xx). Coverage of state and local employees is optional, for constitutional reasons that are no longer important. Most states and localities opted in, but may no longer opt out. Non-profit institutions were allowed to opt in voluntarily; since 1983, however, all must be covered. New federal employees are also covered, but those hired before 1983 remain under the existing federal retirement system.

2. The "decoupling" problem, as it was called, is incredibly arcane and dealt with the benefit computation formula introduced in 1972. A good explanation is found in Kaplan (1977).

3. This should sustain the OASI Trust Fund through the 1980s, if all goes well. Thereafter, it will (given the existing schedule of tax increases and barring some other catastrophe) rise substantially until the war babies retire after the turn of the century. This is because increases in the labor force will substantially exceed withdrawals by the smaller number of older cohorts.

4. I have borrowed the acronym from Barr (1973). It is not in common use in the United States, but it is handier than constantly repeating "pay-as-you-go."

5. In Canada, obligations of provincial governments are also used. Sweden is atypical in its use of private sector securities.

6. The exact theoretical conditions that are necessary are found in Paul Samuelson's (1958) classic exact consumption loan model.

7. This abstracts from a host of practical problems, not the least being the effective investment of the forced savings into productive capital. Keynesians may doubt that the mere existence of a pool of savings assures its investment.

8. Page references to Cates are to his dissertation (1981). A revised work, entitled *Insuring Inequality*, was published in 1982.

9. It is almost impossible to ascertain the economics of this plan. The most charitable thing that can be said is that it reflected an under-consumption view of the Depression, and that it relied on a sharp increase in the velocity of circulation of money to increase GNP.

10. Such as Huey P. Long's Share-the-Wealth movement and Upton Sinclair's Program to End Poverty in California (EPIC). The Long machine controlled Louisiana and, before his assassination, Long was seen as a threat to FDR's renomination. Sinclair came close to winning the governorship to California.

11. The story has been told too often to bear repetition here. The classic work is Witte (1962), which was a confidential memorandum of the events that led to the passage of the Act. It was written in 1936 and not published until 1962. Also see Altmeyer (1966).

12. The word "insurance" was carefully avoided for constitutional reasons and did not come into play until after the Supreme Court upheld the Act in *Helvering* v. *Davis*, 301 U.S. 619. The word used instead was "benefits."

13.   Brown, a staff member of the Committee on Economic Security, made a statement to the House Ways and Means Committee that departed from Morgenthau's position. Although he personally favored PAYG, he circumspectly limited himself to an argument against the accumulation of large reserves (see Brown, 1977, pp. 40–41). The amendment also included a provision that further skewed benefits in favor of low wage earners (Witte, 1962, p. 152).

14.   Derthick's work (1979) is an excellent analysis of the peculiar politics of Social Security and of the roles of the policy-influential groups that have shaped the development of the system, including the program executives. For a critical view of the early program executives, see Cates (1981).

15.   Arthur Altmeyer, the Chairman of SSB, played a delicate political game in shaping the framework of the Committee's deliberations in the direction that he desired. For his recollection of the events, see Altmeyer (1966, pp. 88–98). A view of Altmeyer as a politically skilled and dedicated program executive is found in Derthick (1979, pp. 19–20).

16.   For the text of both reports and FDR's message to Congress recommending changes, see U.S. Congress (1939, pp. 1–43).

17.   See Witte (1957, p. 258). Witte also notes that the 1935 Act did not really provide for full reserve funding (Witte, 1957, p. 273, fn. 15).

18.   The original estimates had not taken into account movement between covered and uncovered employment.

19.   Labor Secretary Frances Perkins saw it as providing an "almost compulsory habit of slight saving . . . which I think most of us find very difficult unless there is some systematic way by which we can compel ourselves to do so" (Perkins, 1946, p. 284).

20.   For analyses of the importance of this imagery, see Cates (1981, pp. 84–87), Derthick (1979, pp. 224–227) and Stein (1980, pp. 171–172).

21.   The original version is Feldstein (1974a). The discovery of a programming error led to a corrected version (Feldstein, 1980). For various critiques of the thesis, see Barro (1978), Darby (1979), Esposito (1978), Leimer and Lesnoy (1980), and Munnell (1977, pp. 116–124).

22.   Dewhurst was an economist for the Twentieth Century Fund and testified on the report of its Committee on Old Age Security. Most of the committee members had been directly or indirectly involved in the development of the Social Security Act. The purpose of the report and testimony was to oppose the Townsend Plan.

23.   Not really *full* funding. Witte estimated that the $47 billion reserve to be accumulated by 1980 ($47 billion was the figure in the 1939 debates) would not suffice, and doubted that would even be attained (U.S. Congress, 1939, pp. 1758–1761). However, he did not propose the higher taxes that would produce full funding. Altmeyer cared more about getting the system under way than about how it would be financed (Derthick, 1979, pp. 249–250).

24.   For some divergent views on this, see Browning (1975), Derthick (1979, chaps. 15–18) and a prescient analysis by Burns (1944).

25.   A summary of the provisions of the 1983 amendments can be found in Social Security Administration, Office of Legislation and Regulatory Policy, *Legislative Bulletin* No. 98-15, March 28, 1983.

REFERENCES

Altmeyer, Arthur J. (1966), *The Formative Years of Social Security*, Madison, WI: University of Wisconsin Press.
Barr, Nicholas A. (1973), "Myths My Grandpa Taught Me," *The Three Banks Review* 129 (Feb.):27–56.
Barro, Robert (1978), "Social Security and Private Saving—Evidence from the U.S. Time

Series," in *Studies in Social Security and Retirement Policy*, Washington, D.C.: American Enterprise Institute.

Blum, John Morton (1959), *From the Morgenthau Diaries: Years of Crisis, 1928–1938*, Boston: Houghton Mifflin.

Blum, John Morton (1965), *From the Morgenthau Diaries: Years of Urgency, 1938–1941*, Boston: Houghton Mifflin.

Blum, John Morton (1967), *From the Morgenthau Diaries: Years of War, 1941–1945*, Boston: Houghton Mifflin.

Brown, J. Douglas (1977), *Essays on Social Security*, Princeton, NJ: Industrial Relations Section, Princeton University.

Browning, Edgar K. (1975), "Why the Social Insurance Budget Is Too Large in a Democracy," *Economic Inquiry*, 13:373–387.

Burns, Eveline M. (1944), "Social Insurance in Evolution," *American Economic Review*, 24 (March, Part 2):199–211.

Burns, Eveline M. (1956), *Social Security and Public Policy*, New York: McGraw-Hill.

Cates, Jerry R. (1981), *Social Security: Organization and Policy*, Ph.D. Dissertation, University of Michigan.

Cates, Jerry R. (1982), *Insuring Inequality*, Ann Arbor: University of Michigan Press.

Darby, Michael (1979), "The Effects of Social Security on Income and the Capital Stock," Washington, D.C.: American Enterprise Institute (mimeo).

Derthick, Martha (1979), *Policymaking for Social Security*, Washington, D.C.: The Brookings Institution.

Esposito, Louis (1978), "Effect of Social Security on Saving: Review of Studies Using U.S. Time-Series Data," *Social Security Bulletin*, 41 (May):9–17.

Feldstein, Martin S. (1974a), "Social Security, Induced Retirement and Aggregate Capital Accumulation," *Journal of Political Economy*, 82 (Sept.-Oct.):905–925.

Feldstein, Martin S. (1974b), "The Optimal Financing of Social Security," Discussion Paper No. 388, Harvard University, Institute of Economic Research.

Feldstein, Martin S. (1976), "Response to Pechman," in *Funding Pensions: Issues and Implications for Financial Markets*, Boston: Federal Reserve Bank of Boston.

Feldstein, Martin S. (1980), "Social Security, Induced Retirement and Aggregate Capital Accumulation: A Correction and Update," Working Paper No. 579, National Bureau of Economic Research, November.

Kaplan, Robert S. (1977), *Indexing Social Security: An Analysis of the Issue*, Washington, D.C.: American Enterprise Institute.

Leimer, Dean R. and Selig D. Lesnoy (1980), "Social Security and Private Saving: A Reexamination of the Time Series Evidence Using Alternative Social Security Wealth Variables," Working Paper No. 1, Social Security Administration, Office of Research and Statistics, November.

Munnell, Alicia H. (1977), *The Future of Social Security*, Washington, D.C.: The Brookings Institution.

Pechman, Joseph A., Henry J. Aaron and Michael K. Taussig (1968), *Social Security: Perspectives for Reform*, Washington, D.C.: The Brookings Institution.

Perkins, Francis (1946), *The Roosevelt I Knew*, New York: Viking Press.

Rejda, George E. (1976), *Social Insurance and Economic Security*, Englewood Cliffs, NJ: Prentice-Hall.

Samuelson, Paul A. (1958), "An Exact Consumption-Loan Model of Interest With or Without the Social Contrivance of Money," *Journal of Political Economy*, 66 (Dec.):467–482.

Social Security Administration, Office of Legislation and Regulatory Policy (1983), *Legislative Bulletin*, No. 98-15 (March 28).

Stein, Bruno (1971), *On Relief: The Economics of Poverty and Public Welfare*, New York: Basic Books.

Stein, Bruno (1980), *Social Security and Pensions in Transition: Understanding the American Retirement System*, New York: Free Press/Macmillan.

Turnbull, John G., C. Arthur Williams, Jr. and Earl F. Cheit (1974), *Economic and Social Security*, (4th ed.), New York: Ronald Press.

U.S. Congress, House of Representatives, Committee on Ways and Means (1939), *Hearings Relative to the Social Security Act Amendments of 1939*, 3 vols., Washington, D.C.: U.S. Government Printing Office.

U.S. Social Security Board (1937), *Social Security in America*, Washington, D.C.: U.S. Government Printing Office.

Witte, Edwin E. (1957), "Organized Labor and Social Security," in Milton Derber and Ewin Young, eds., *Labor and the New Deal*, Madison: University of Wisconsin Press.

Witte, Edwin E. (1962), *The Development of the Social Security Act*, Madison: University of Wisconsin Press.

THE CONTINUING POLITICAL CHARACTER OF THE SOCIAL SECURITY SYSTEM IN THE UNITED STATES

E. W. Kelley

The 1972 Social Security Act and the 1983 amendments to the Social Security Act are responses to diametrically opposed problems. The 1972 amendments are an attempt to regularize what previously had been a political adjustment of the incomes of older Americans in response to inflation. The 1983 amendments are an attempt to fund a system which is in financial peril; a situation not clearly envisioned at the time the 1972 amendments were passed. Yet, we can argue that both sets of amendments represent the continued dominance of political interests in determining the structure of the social security system. This is true both of the contents of the act and the process by which the amendments were passed. Such politicization of social security is not new; it has existed since the system began.

As Stein implies in his chapter, the 1935 Social Security Act was not designed to alleviate the immediate misery of the elderly. Payments were not to commence until the 1940s. Under the system Stein discusses, it was assumed that social security would replace at least part of other forms of retirement insurance already in place. The original legislation appears to be a declaration of principle: the principle that there should be and will be (even if not in the immediate present) a publicly supported scheme for providing for the welfare of the elderly and incidently those other groups included in the full act. In Teune's chapter, he has described the ideological orientations and intellectual backgrounds of those individuals around Roosevelt who advocated a social security program.

The gradualistic and symbolic aspects of social security are particularly clear when one notes that the congressional testimony shows that the 1935 act was not passed with macroeconomic or countercyclical intentions in mind. Stein also implies that the shift in 1939 to pay-as-you-go (PAYG) system from the normal kind of fully funded insurance scheme was not motivated by attempts at microeconomic management. The shift in the method of funding occurred for a more pragmatic political reason. The issue was not one of managing the economy, but one of who was going to manage the capital available to the economy. Under a fully funded program the public sector could have had a significant impact on investment, and thus on the private economy as the whole. Given the historic American mistrust of government (central governments, not state and local governments), this was not a particularly palatable option. At the same time, as Stein argues, the 1939 shift to pay-as-you-go accumulation of funds also represents a shift in who bears the cost of supporting the elderly. As Stein so clearly states, this assumes that each generation effectively supports its elderly in one way or another. The political question of how to divide the cost within the present generation was resolved by the political response to fears of publicly controlled capital formation dominating the private markets.

The period of rapid expansion of the social security system from post-World War II until the end of the 1960s is punctuated by a series of benefit increases and extensions of coverage that became closely associated with the Democratic Party which controlled the Congress for almost this entire period of time (Rothouse, 1983, pp. 26–27). In fact, the expansion of the system could have been even more rapid except for the fact that social security legislation is considered in the House Committee on Ways and Means. This committee was and is the only generally representative committee in the House. In 1935, Ways and Means jurisdiction allowed the executive to avoid the conservative and southern dominance of other committee chairmanship and leadership positions. In the 1960s, Ways and Means jurisdiction provided a more fiscally conservative appoach to social security than would be true in the Democratic dominated, specialized committees in an era of economic expansion.

Hence, while the expansion of benefits in response to inflation and the expansion of coverage occurred with approaching elections, the magnitudes of the increases were not as great as they might have been had similar legislation been considered in some other committee. The Democrats on Ways and Means were not trading in the usual system of floor reciprocity which does not regard party affiliation strongly; rather, they were engaged in passing legislation which on average was electorally beneficial to Democrats while maintaining responsible fiscal posture. However, in looking at the politics of the development of the social security system we must consider electoral politics and bureaucratic politics as well.

Historically, major changes have been made in the social security system when there has been a confluence of opinion across the business community, elected officials, and, when developed, the bureaucracy that administers social security. In 1939, even liberal Congresspeople agreed with business fears that a fully funded social security system would put a tremendous accumulation of funds in one place and that such an accumulation was inconsistent with their conception of democracy (*Congressional Record*, March 17, 1937).

Expansion of the social security system was in the interest of many organized groups. For the liberal business community, labor, and Congressional politicians, particularly Democrats, expansion provided electoral security or currency for politicians; it allowed for a regularized turnover of labor which was to the benefit of both labor unions and the business community. The elderly could retire with long-term security, and their place in the work force could be taken by those who might otherwise be unemployed or underemployed. This business support is not an unusual phenomenon if one recalls that among the major proponents of the Wagner Act were heads of major U.S. corporations. Business support for the legislation also involved regularizing relations with labor (Rothouse, 1983, p. 121).

Those federal bureaucrats involved in social security had incentives that were similar to those of the business community. Essentially businesses wished to control risk at both ends of their markets, the supply side and the sale or demand side. This can be done through contracts with labor, contracts with distributors, federal loan guarantees, etc. The techniques are numerous. Their use makes the economic world predictable and jobs secure. To expand the level of benefits, to extend and complicate eligibility, and to introduce technology into the social security network, all have the effect of making the administration of social security more rule-governed and predictable.

All social security administrators through the 1960s supported expansion of the system. As Derthick (1979, p. 17) points out, this was particularly true of Arthur Altmeyer, who administered the system almost as long as all other administrators combined. Additionally, since social security had been originally justified as a self-insurance scheme, the arguments available to both social security bureaucrats and Congressional politicians for expanding benefits were often based on the work ethic. The argument is that individuals have worked and contributed to the social security system. The benefit is earned if benefits are not adjusted. Inflation takes away part of what one is entitled to because of one's work. So long as the economy was expanding and contributions to the Old Age and Survivors Insurance Program in particular were increasing, there was little difficulty in adjusting benefits for inflation.

THE INDEXING OF SOCIAL SECURITY

The issue of indexing social security benefits first came to public attention during the presidential election of 1968. Richard Nixon proposed that benefits be indexed and persisted in this position in his messages to Congress in 1969. The indexing issue was not a new one to Social Security Administration officials. In fact, they had been tempted to present to House Ways and Means legislation to that effect even before 1969, and to go public with that position (Rothouse, 1983, p. 30). However, so long as the Democrats controlled both legislative branches, social security administrators could not be sure of the reception of such proposals. At that time the executive branch allowed the Social Security Administration to administer its programs with little oversight. At the same time there was a biannual confluence of interests as Congresspeople sought re-election. This led to the continued upward adjustments of benefits. Indexing could jeopardize the autonomy of the congressional "benefit" system since it would remove the legislative rewards for passing bills that provide voter benefits in the future.

Nixon, however, had no particular desire to allow social security to continue to be electoral fodder for Democratic Congresspeople. Further, the benefits of indexing to the Social Security Administration are clear. The risk to the system due to partisan politics, by the Congress in particular, are greatly reduced. The administration of social security becomes a rule-governed activity with almost all subsequent major changes flowing from problems identified by bureaucrats. Social security would become an administered system, divorced from the political needs of those individuals who must legislate funding for it: ideal for a Republican administration and for social security bureaucrats.

Indexing legislation had to pass a Democratic Congress. To obtain Democratic congressional compliance, an irresistible package of proposals was assembled. The old assumption that wage rates would remain static was changed. A dynamic wage assumption was more consistent with postwar experiences. This assumption allowed for an apparent short-term reduction in social security taxes, while at the same time providing for indexing benefits (Derthick, 1979). The then social security chief actuary, Robert Myers, presented a plan which appeared impossible to oppose. Taxes were lowered, benefits were increased, and the aged never again had to worry about losing their rightful retirement income due to excessive current inflation. Myers' proposals, however, only worked on the basis of demographic projections which had been known to be incorrect since 1966. Additionally, his proposals would unintentionally produce a modest windfall of benefits to the aged under a variety of conditions, most of them occurring if annual earnings increased less than 2.25% or if inflation levels were above 5% (Moorhead and Trowbridge, 1977, pp. 433–434). The conditions for destabilization, then, in terms of recent experiences, are easily attained. These unfortunate facts could not derail the 1972 legislation. The political needs of the administration, social security officials, and legislators were minimally met. The legislation did not pass because of the desire on the part of the participants to produce a sensitive, actuarily sound system that would work for the indefinite future. Behind the rhetoric of planning, entitlements, and fairness to the elderly lay the political interests of these political groups.

An even clearer example of the demands of politics on social security legislation was the 20 percent increase in benefits that Congress voted to take effect before indexing. If one questions how such legislation as well as the indexing proposal could have come from House Ways and Means, one must remember that Wilbur Mills, the Committee's chairman, was a candidate for the presidency in the Democratic primaries in 1972. In fact, the increase combined with the indexing legislation was passed just a month before the major primary season began. Under normal circumstances it is most unlikely that the prudent Mills would have allowed legislation through the committee that represented such a commitment on future resources. The legislation itself was technically imperfect and provided a unjustifiable windfall of retirement benefits. Inflated (not real) wages, as well as benefits, were to be indexed; this virtually doubled benefits for future retirees. This problem was "fixed" by legislation in 1977.

THE 1983 SOCIAL SECURITY AMENDMENTS

The political character of the 1972 changes was recognized by the 1977 amendments. A national commission was to investigate all aspects of the program, but the consequences on inadequate planning came to fruition sooner than most people thought was likely. Between 1977 and 1980 there was a tremendous difference in the estimated and actual increase in the Consumer Price Index, the real wage differential, and the unemployment rate. With a social security system based on somewhat inaccurate and misleading premises, the adverse economic climate of the late 1970s persuaded the trustees of the system to advise Congress in 1980 that the Old Age and Survivors Insurance Programs would be bankrupt in 1981. The national commission report of March 12, 1981, demonstrated a long-term actuarial imbalance under any reasonable cost estimates (*Report of the National Commission on Social Security*, 1981, p. 2).

After Republican gains in the 1980 Congressional elections, the social security crisis was an issue that the Democrats could use to the disadvantage of the Republican party in 1982. Democrats were concerned with only a short term "fix" to prevent immediate bankruptcy. That fix occurred in October 1980 when the 1980 amendments allowed the borrowing of next year's payroll tax receipts from the Disability Insurance Trust Fund to bolster the Old Age and Survivors Insurance Trust Fund. Since this borrowing was to be repaid with interest, and since it occurred between funds included under the original legislation, little political controversy surrounded it (Derthick, 1979).

The Social Security Administration (SSA) could afford to remain neutral between short- and long-term solutions because the issue was not whether the system would be funded in either the short or long run. In retrospect, the principle point of issue was who was to bear the cost. The SSA saw both the short-term and long-term solutions working to their bureaucratic interest. Who actually bore the costs was of less concern to them than that the disagreements be resolved.

After the 1982 Congressional elections, in which the Democrats gained 26 seats in the House of Representatives, the long-term problem of social security funding still had to be faced. Rothouse describes in detail the positions of the various Democratic, Republican and business interests in facilitating a solution to the funding problem. Succinctly put, the Republicans favored restricting benefits in various direct and indirect ways, while the Democrats favored increasing taxes and in some cases using general revenues to fund the system as it currently existed. Many, but not all, Republicans and most of the business community opposed the use of general revenues in the social security system.

In the resulting compromise, the Republicans gave up more than the Democrats. Of the "new" money to be found, 75 percent came from increasing the social security tax structure, while 25 percent came by reducing future benefits although in somewhat surreptitious ways (Rothouse, 1983; Harpham, 1984). In order to come up with a compromise acceptable to both the legislative and executive branches, however, the overall size of the savings did not work out to the correct amount. In order to construct a proposal that was politically acceptable to Congress and the Executive, unrealistic economic assumptions and projections were made, just as in 1972. The Republicans were concerned with making sure the system was at least adequately funded through the 1984 presidential elections. Hence, if one looks carefully at the cash flow in this system and reserves in the trust fund, a financial crunch could arise again as early as 1985 and 1986. Whether this occurs or not, a crisis is likely after the turn of the century. The legislative politics surrounding the 1983 amendments are somewhat different from those surrounding previous amendments. Since the pie to be taxed was not expanding when the amendments were passed, any shifts that benefited one group either by providing benefits or shifting costs represented costs to some other group lobbying against it. The proposal to raise the retirement age, for example was lobbied against by the elderly. Business lobbied against the hidden rate increases. Both Republicans and some business people lobbied against the one time provision for covering some costs out of general revenues, because they believed that it might set a precedent for future funding of the system. Federal employees objected to their required inclusion in the system in the future.

It is clear that in the end Congress and the Executive have again produced a short-term political fix. This fix was more difficult to arrive at because the increased cost of the system could not be balanced off against anticipated revenue increases from economic growth. This is not to suggest that the system was actuarily sound before the recessions of the late 1970s and early 1980s. However, the crisis would not have arisen as quickly if a recession had not exposed the weaknesses of the 1972 and 1977 amendments. No matter how much the rhetoric of entitlement, the justification of social security as self-insurance, or the principles of actuarial soundness are invoked, legislation affecting the amount, scope of benefits, beneficiaries and the allocation of the costs of social security is intimately entrenched in the political process as is any allocation or reallocation of public goods or services. There is no reason to believe that planning, actuarial considerations, or general principles will override the short-term of interest groups and politicians. The entire electoral and legislative system is designed to respond to all these dimensions of change.

This does not mean that democracies, particularly those which elect their legislatures to short terms in office, cannot meet the social security demands of citizens in a welfare state. What we might alter is our expectations as to how such problems will be dealt with in the future. There is nothing inherently bad about using the legislative process to produce continual short-term corrections in the financing of the system. Whether planned by apparently neutral bureaucrats or legislated by Congress, any system of transfers inevitably imposes costs on some individuals in order to support the elderly at some given level of subsistence. If the entire system were planned, this fact would not be altered. To plan the system without legislative involvement would remove the elected representative from decision-making concerning the allocation of current costs for supporting the elderly generation. In some ways such a shift would be the very antithesis of what democratic responsiveness is about.

However, there is a potential problem which democratic regimes may not so effectively handle. There is no reason to believe that the packages of goods and services that people demand across Western industralized democracies are going to be sufficiently labor intensive as to allow for the gainful employment of all those who desire employment. If we generalize from the consideration of social security to the inclusion of unemployment compensation and welfare in Western systems, a time might arrive in the next twenty years when all those who want to work cannot and therefore must be recipients of one or more type of transfer. At the same time, the work ethic is sufficiently strong in at least the United States, northern Europe and Japan, that citizens receiving such transfers are often viewed and often view themselves as second class-citizens (Goodwin, 1972). While there is no overall growth in the economy, considerable resentment, usually expressed at the local level, arises concerning levels of taxation generally. All this could lead to a confrontation among the work ethic, the systems of transfers within a society, and the allocation of work among individuals. If a situation arises in which people who want to work cannot and these people view themselves as less than full citizens, then we are back to the situation Roosevelt faced when he took office. A large number of people who invest in preparing for work are left adrift and viewed as freeloaders by those who both work and contribute to the cost of welfare.

REFERENCES

Altmeyer, Arthur J. (1968), *The Formative Years of Social Security,* Madison: University of Wisconsin Press.
Ball, Robert M. (1973), "Social Security Amendments of 1972: Summary and Legislative History," *Social Security Bulletin,* (March): 3–25.
Congressional Record (March 17, 1927), p. 2324.
Derthick, Martha (1979), *Policymaking for Social Security,* Washington, D.C.: The Brookings Institution.
Goodwin, Leonard (1972), *Do the Poor Want to Work?* Washington, D.C.: The Brookings Institution.
Harpham, Edward (1984), "Fiscal Crisis and the Politics of Social Security Reform," Unpublished article.

Kaplan, Robert S. (1977), *Indexing Social Security: An Analysis of the Issues,* Washington, D.C.: American Enterprises Institute.

Moorhead, Ernest and Charles Trowbridge (1977), "The Unresolved OASDI Decoupling Issue," *Transaction, Society of Actuaries* 29:433–434.

Munnell, Alice H. (1977), *The Future of Social Security,* Washington, D.C.: The Brookings Institution.

Rejda, George E. (1976), *Social Insurance and Economic Security,* Englewood Cliffs, NJ: Prentice-Hall.

Report of the 1971 Advisory Council on Social Security (1971), Arthur S. Fleming, Chairman, Washington, D.C.: U.S. Government Printing Office.

Report of the National Commission on Social Security (1981), Milton Gwirtzman, Chairman, Washington, D.C.: U.S. Government Printing Office, March 12.

Report of the National Commission on Social Security Reform (1983), Allan Greenspan, Chairman, Washington, D.C.: U.S. Government Printing Office, January.

Rothouse, Neil (1983), *Social Security's Financing Crisis: The Subordination of Economic Principles to Political Interests,* Honors Thesis, Department of Government, Cornell University, Ithaca, NY.

Social Security Administration, Office of Legislation and Regulatory Policy (1983), *Legislative Bulletin,* N. 98-115, March 23.

U.S. Congress, House (1978), *1978 Annual Report of the Board of Trustees of the Federal Old Age and Survivors Insurance and Disability Insurance Trust Funds,* H. Doc. 95-336, 95th Congress, 1st session, Washington, D.C.: U.S. Government Printing Office, p. 37.

WELFARE GUIDELINES IN THE 1920s:

REGULATING WEIMAR'S POOR

Stephan Leibfried

We contrast the defamatory description of the state as a welfare establishment to the state as a mutual support organization, a state that protects the weak, cares for the sick and provides for the elderly. We want a state that takes care of the anxieties of existence for those that have nothing and gives the worker the certainty that he can rely on the society he built by work in good times in the days when he is unfit for work and is old . . . (Albert Hofmann, a functionary of the Weimar welfare rights movement, 1932, p. 469)

The conflict over levels of social assistance in German welfare should be seen in relation to the social and political structure of welfare policies in the Federal Republic. Though not always better solved or even resolved, problems of the contemporary welfare state may be better defined when related to historical precedents, even though such precedents are largely forgotten. The historical problem of central-local differences over social assistance is found throughout the history of social policy in all western countries, especially Britain and the United States (Leibfried, 1979, 1978; Branson, 1979). The central-local problem arises necessarily as the welfare systems are related to differing local labor markets and local political cultures which are only slowly and partially overlaid by national/ unitary structures.

Important concerns of the Weimar period still affect the Federal Republic. First, the welfare rate structure that was introduced nationally during the Weimar period still applies throughout Germany under the name "standard of support" (*Regelsatz*) (Hofmann and Leibfried, 1980), though the differences among areas have decreased. Then as now the goal of a uniform social policy toward the poor had not been achieved. Welfare assistance differentials (urban/rural and north/south) still exist (Leibfried, 1982, pp. 264–267) because of different municipal social and political cultures and the long-standing municipal responsibility for the delivery of social assistance. Second, in some ways the present situation is worse than in the Weimar period because uniform provision is no longer the aim of the National Welfare Federation (*Deutscher Verein fuer oeffentliche und private Fuersorge,* or NWF), the most important semi-public "welfare cartel" in the Federal Republic. The NWF determines the "poverty level," which becomes both the standard of *and* the statistical base for social assistance in West Germany.[1] The extra-parliamentary and bureaucratic powers of Weimar no longer press for welfare improvements, nor do they directly help the poor by questioning federal support scales. In particular, there is no longer an equivalent to the social movements of the national insurance pensioners and other pensioners found under Weimar. The interests of pensioners have changed, and under the Third Reich (Leibfried et al., 1984b) their organization was "conquered" to become a quasi-governmental organization to provide social services.

As a result, the efforts of the NWF and by the Federal Labor Ministry under Weimar to establish statistically precise definitions of welfare disparities were only partially implemented. The methods of collecting and analyzing data are still not well developed, and serious differentials among areas still exist under the constitutional guise of equality in the welfare state. Awareness of welfare problems as well as the range of political interests of the NWF has diminished. Socialist or social-democratic interests are far more marginally represented than in the Weimar period because the poverty level issue was suppressed during the 1930s. The postwar bureaucracy had no recollection of the welfare struggle and was more susceptible to narrow professional concerns (Tennstedt, 1981).

The loss of professional and bureaucratic concern for innovation has many side effects. During the Weimar period the search for a "biological method" to calculate subsistence needs on a scientific caloric base was a formula to restructure middle-class society itself. Today the possibility of conceiving such "socio-political Utopias" are virtually excluded. The development of the market basket principle of the "biological method" under Weimar is seen today as an issue of providing marginal security to the poor, but without the potentially disruptive socio-political force of the 1920s. Thinking today about functional equivalents for social assistance then involves sharing wealth in a more direct way. The shift from direct methods of calculating social need to more general social standards is not peculiar to Germany. For example, the historical poverty debate in England (Townsend, 1979; Leibfried, 1983) and early welfare policy in the United States (Leibfried, 1985; Aronson, 1982) are similar to physiological and nutritional analysis of welfare needs begun in Germany around the turn of the century.

In brief, the dispute between the major German welfare organization, the NWF, and the Reich over the 1920s laid the foundations for national German welfare assistance and reveals many continuing political conflicts inherent in seeking acceptable levels of assistance for the poor. Much as today, it was impossible for the Weimar government to overrule the German states and municipalities, but nonetheless vitally important precedents were made in the search for agreement on national guidelines for poverty assistance. As the depression deepened, it became more and more difficult to justify diverse poverty benefits, and, as we see in may contemporary social welfare programs, the conflicting problems of wages, unemployment assistance and contributory assistance steadily grew. Throughout the decade of the 1920s the NWF acted as the main spokesman for the localized interests, and the gradual erosion of its influence was a major step toward nationalizing the German welfare state.

INFLATION IN THE 1920s: EXPERIMENTATION WITH THE "POOR TARIFFS" UNDER ECONOMIC AND SOCIAL PRESSURES

One must make it clear to the masses that the price of bread or meat is not an economic price alone, but a political price as well which is determined by the political balance of power. Even weekly wages are political wages. When they vote, they vote on bread and meat and the wage-level all at the same time . . . we have an organized economy which is governed by the society and by the state in ever increasing degrees of organization. (Rudolf Hilferding at the Kiel party conference of the German Social Democratic Party, 1927, in Wachenheim, 1928, p. 258).

A special feature of German welfare until 1924 was the purely local determination of "poor tariffs" or social assistance, but this tradition gave way to the social and political upheaval and rapid inflation of the 1920s. The old procedure was particularly vulnerable to socio-political tensions. A "sliding scale" was supposed to ensure an "automatic" improvement in benefits to the poor during inflation, though adequate adjustment was often delayed. Before and during the First World War local authorities complied with the established system: assistance scales were usually revised monthly but remained wholly a matter of local discretion. An indexed system of calculating social assistance was found in nearly every large city and district and was a response to the inflation period. Berlin played a pioneering role because it maintained automatic adjustment even after the serious postwar inflation when other municipalities had discontinued periodic local review.

In 1923 the Prussian Ministry of Public Welfare, among others, urged the presidents of the local administrative districts to instruct the communities to keep social assistance closer to the cost of living. The Reich selectively introduced automatic adjustment of welfare rates as well as national pensions and unemployment relief. These changes put the NWF under unavoidable pressures and social assistance began to lag behind other forms of assistance. As the NWF wrote, the differential between forms of assistance has continued to grow:

> Though it was an unwritten law before the Second World War that assistance rates for a single person almost equalled the lowest wage of an unskilled female worker, the rates cannot be maintained today because recent wage rates for the unskilled approximate those of the skilled laborers. Above all, because the wages of female workers approximate those of male workers, the disparity between wage increases for unskilled workers and the assistance for the unemployed, as well as for national insurance pensioners and the poor receiving relief, in the last few weeks has reached a condition which urgently requires adjustment. (*ND* or *Nachrichtendienst*, official journal of the NWF, August 1923, p. 390)

Nevertheless, the NWF accepted indexing by the end of the inflationary period only to withdraw support after 1924 with price and wage stabilization. Berlin kept indexing much to the disfavor of the NWF. In general, by the early 1920s the welfare debate favored a more generous definition of subsistence for welfare benefits, while, as a consequence of a series of court decisions before the war, the whole official welfare discussion favored minimal subsistence (*ND*, October 1925, p. 408). The upward trend began during World War I when better assistance for families of servicemen was provided (see *ND*, September 1932, p. 232).

The municipal welfare policies responded to social and economic pressures in different ways. For example, in some cities there was a major expansion of payments-in-kind. Forced by inflation to increase social assistance, the municipalities used various ways to calculate need and its adjustment: some municipalities relied on civil servants' wages; the majority used the lowest local wage for workers; a minority made use of the "biological method" or the market basket principle. On the basis of the calculated need for food, a local monetary equivalent was fixed. The pioneers of the "biological methods" at the beginning of the Weimar Period were Cologne and Offenbach. Later Elberfeld, Darmstadt and other cities followed.

But the NWF took another direction, favoring a less easily politicized form of distribution. The NWF feared the complications with wage policies.

> Because the wage levels [are] . . . to a large extent result of economic and party power struggles, it is to be feared that wages will be subject to large fluctuations in the future; if so, adjustment of assistance to this norm appears to be inappropriate. It would be unfortunate if welfare work were used as a catch-word in wage disputes, which could easily happen. (*ND*, November 1923, p. 431 f.)

The NWF's feeling was that a "minimum wage" standard for welfare created conflict because the low wage level "is vague and only noticeable when continually exceeded." Because of poor income data, it cannot even be determined. "Setting assistance at the lowest local wage would be especially dangerous if small increases in the assistance rates were used as a prime driving factor for wage policy—a risky undertaking that in the end is always a disadvantage for welfare" (*ND*, June 1925, p. 304). The NWF argued that even the lowest wages exceeded assistance needs from public funds (*ND*, August 1923, p. 390).

Although there was no comprehensive system for determining subsistence levels as there is today, the NWF felt it knew "instinctively" what exceeds minimum need. As it wrote, discrepancy in the determination of the poor relief rates did not arise from local differences, but from the fact that basically no clarity exists in setting "exclusion rates" (the prewar expression for standard support rates) (*ND*, September 1923, p. 413). The NWF favored the reduction of welfare support by limiting benefits to the "level of wages of the most poorly paid worker as the upper limit . . . One thus assumes as self-evident that the minimum wage, to some extent a consequence of the iron wage law, always slightly exceeds the absolute necessities of life in each cultural situation" (*ND*, May 1925, p. 276). Necessities of life and wage limits were the "two poles between which assistance must generally remain" (*ND*, May 1925, p. 276). The NWF argued that keeping within these limits does not permit formulating fixed assistance scales. They can only be determined post hoc. It preferred a variable threshold, "which affects welfare only when it is continually too low (in the case of absolute necessities) or exceeded (in the case of wage limits)" (*ND*, May 1925, p. 277). While one can and must experiment with the biological or Darwinian method to determine the "life-line," the NWF tolerated no experiments with wage limits. "On the contrary, the welfare payment must not violate wage standards under any circumstances because the incentive for work would be destroyed; welfare must adopt a wage limit as low as possible so that the differential from minimum wages would become smaller" (*ND*, May 1925, p. 277).

THE "MARKET BASKET" AS A PROGRESSIVE MODEL TO RATIONALIZE WELFARE POLICY IN THE WEIMAR PERIOD

The "market basket" principle could have become a path toward social reform for the NWF in the Weimar period because it did not directly raise the political question of choosing between redistribution or distribution. The market basket principle also enhanced professional influence over welfare by relying more on nutrition, social hygiene and statistics. A strategy such as this avoids politicization and would have been opportune for the NWF since depoliticization removed welfare from the influence of federal politics (Tennstedt, 1981). For this reason, the NWF emphasized the role of science at that time in this and other cases.

The "biological method" persisted through the Weimar period, but only in certain municipalities. The NWF devoted its 1925 conference to the idea, and reported with detachment on the practical value of such a rational standard.

> Today, as is well known, one tries to arrive at a generally valid absolute subsistence level through purely biological principles where one works from the number of calories which are deemed necessary for the maintenance of vital functions. The real value of this method, however, lies in the fact, that it traces the *price movement*, which differs in time and locality, for provision of this number of calories. (*ND*, June 1925, p. 303)

At the 1925 NWF conference national models for scales using scientific nutritional findings were discussed for the first time. The most favored model not only made use of nutritional, but economic and statistical data as well. Each model presented was supported by an expert from the NWF (*ND*, June 1925, p. 303). The assistance level for each of these models was substantially higher than the average rates used in the Reich, and the NWF did not adopt any of these models. Later the NWF journal reported on the "biological method" in Elberfeld and Cologne. The latter "market basket experiment" was considerably refined to include a continuous check on prices of food and other necessities; it included refinements such as practical cooking experiments and a model shopping list; and it provided in a book nutritional instruction for recipients. Needy housewives were also to be asked to participate occasionally in cooking instruction given in the kitchens of the welfare establishments (*ND*, November/December 1927, p. 301).

In short, the "scientific calculations" of welfare needs would indeed have been possible, but it would have led to assistance levels which were generally too high for the municipalities. Even more, it would have generated criticism of wage policies and possibly would have stimulated radical social reform. The significance of these concerns to social development must not be overlooked. These welfare designs were part of a general aspiration to set "practical" and self-regulating limits to capitalistic developments. The full meaning of welfare reform and the search for scientific welfare standards in the Weimar period can only be assessed by looking in more detail at the social problems encountered from 1919–1933, in particular from 1919–1923.

The pioneer of the market basket principle in the Weimar period was Robert Kuczynski (Robert Kuczynski, 1921, pp. 1–31; Juergen Kuczynski, 1957). For the entire Weimar period, he or his son regularly estimated a differentiated monthly subsistence level on the basis of Nathan Zuntz's (1847–1920) calorie scheme, published in his *Political Finance Correspondence*. The work of Robert Kuczynski (1876–1947) was received with hostility. Responding to arguments against the principle, he replied:

> unfortunately it is true that very many people must live with a very low income. But we do not have enough food and clothing to guarantee subsistence to the total population. That should not be misconstrued as setting the subsistence level even lower ... One must, in the final analysis, make the subsistence costs equal to the usual earnings from employment in the cities where the population is not literally starving or freezing or does not live in luxury... (R. Kuczynski, 1921, p. 16 f.)

According to the estimates by Juergen and Robert Kuczynski, the *average net wage* never went beyond the subsistence level, so that a reform based on the market basket principle would always have had a sizeable effect on distribution even at that time. Only in the Federal Republic of Germany in the 1950s, when more rapid and continuous economic growth and a shrinking poverty population allowed benefits to rise to the subsistence level, the market basket principle gained support from social and political reformers and was eventually established nationwide. But under growth conditions, the potential social effects of the market basket strategy also diminish and principles of sharing social wealth and increased participation are substituted. Such new reform principles should have effects similar to those anticipated by the market basket discussion of the Weimar period: to ensure a more even distribution of social wealth, now based more generally on "normal" living standards, in order to protect society from "poverty" as once understood in a more encompassing sense (Leibfried, 1982; Townsend, 1979).

THE DEVELOPMENT OF GUIDELINES AND THEIR REGULATION AS FORMS OF POLITICAL COMPROMISE

From the outset, the basic position of the NWF was that "schematized assistance rates" threatened to squander public resources. The market basket approach violated basic principles of individualized, subsidiary welfare work. The NWF adhered to this position throughout the Weimar period in order to resist nationalizing social assistance standards and limiting municipal discretion. In 1923, the NWF wrote, "The question is whether, in the proposed federal skeleton law, welfare based on measures of need should be introduced despite disagreement over providing standards for uniform assistance scales." The NWF made three points. First, municipal standards should be rejected because they do not assure better payment and will vary widely. Second, legal minimal scales are essential "in order to guarantee cost-of-living to the needy in socially uninterested communities." Third, legal maximum scales are also needed in order "to have federal support in the face of unjustified demands by the needy" (*ND*, November 1923, p. 431).

The NWF chose this comparatively reserved approach in order to protect the municipalities against nationalization. Politically, the situation was still unclear. The aftermath of the uprisings of 1918 and 1919 was still felt so that it appeared necessary to build an agreed position ("maximum rate") into the basic norm. Thus, the strategy to avoid centralized intervention in social assistance was not well-differentiated or adequately developed. Still, in NWF publications there are frequent references to such "scales" as a binding assistance requirement, a condition the NWF later abandoned.

A firm definition of the NWF position first appears during a dispute at a training seminar in August, 1924, on implementing the National Decree on Welfare Obligations. The decree did not stipulate social assistance guidelines, but provided federal authority to specify principles (*Reichsgrundsaetze*). For this reason, a municipal officer, Ewald Sasse (1888–1970), reported on the "practical application and possibilities for legal regulation under guidelines for assistance." Sasse spoke against exclusive cash assistance because such payment would erode discretionary authority for individual needs. He also opposed a minimum income since it would standardize the lowest levels of need. In contrast, he stressed the need for "standard guidelines" and framed the issue in a legally opaque way: "not minimum or maximum rates, but rather on a middle ground, regulated scales ... could be lived with more easily." Thus, an element of legal evasion and municipal discretion was built into the discussion of the anticipated "binding" federal intervention. In fact, the federal decree did not contain any obligation to introduce scales, although it was included in drafts of such a decree. By 1928, the NWF made its apprehensions clear. "The subsistence scales, which by nature are only vague indicators for determining a basic livelihood, run the risk of becoming regulating rates" (Polligkeit, *ND*, August 1928, p. 268).

CURRENCY STABILIZATION: CHANGING GUIDELINES UNDER NATIONAL PRESSURE

With currency stabilization, three processes began which were important for the later development of welfare guidelines: the criteria for determining the welfare levels became diffuse; political and social pressures were redirected from the Reich to municipalities; there was more regulation (*Verrechtlichung*) and bureaucratization of municipal welfare work. Under strong and direct political pressure local principles for social assistance yielded to national needs. Nevertheless, the economic collapse of trade and industry especially in the Rhine and Ruhr areas, enormously increased unemployment in a very short period. By December, 1923, the welfare burden of the big cities (unemployed, old-age pensioners, other pensioners, war victims, large families, and the poor) had grown enormously and welfare services had reached 40% of the population, and in many cities 80% (*ND*, December 1923, p. 439).

The national strategy was to direct political pressures of welfare onto the municipalities. In welfare work, the "local community becomes the balancing point between mass demands and the service capacity of the state, a balance which may all too often break down in a direct clash with mass preferences. While party representatives attempted to push the most extreme demands through municipal councils, the masses demonstrated in front of the city halls in order to emphasize their demands. The state used the communities as safety valves and deflection points, so to speak, against the assault which the masses, in reality, directed against the state itself" (*Zwangslaeufige Gemeindepolitik*, 1925). The problem was aggravated by federal legislation "disregarding" the income of certain groups in granting welfare. The social effect was to create a privileged group within the population receiving social assistance.

The principal motive of the federal strategy to expand benefits through "disregards" was described as follows: "Given the situation of local welfare authorities, especially in the countryside, and aside from relatively few large cities, welfare organizations simply have not passed on increases in national insurance pensions" (*ND*, August 1925, p. 339). For that reason, disregarding national insurance pensions provided a new basis for a centralized subsistence policy. National guidelines were extended in order to have a firm baseline to measure the "privileges" of the poor. Thus, the social and political pressures on municipalities extended federal control, but also lead to increased assistance payments and increased efforts to integrate the poverty population.

Because of its impact on municipal authority, the "schematized" system became controversial. It implied a right to welfare or a legal claim to subsistence, and justified the integration of welfare administration into the constitutional structure of the state. Shifting the conflict to muncipalities created the need to protect city government. Its passive relationship to welfare administration was dismantled. The welfare bureaucracy and the representatives of welfare organizations became part of the "national" welfare system, but these procedural changes and their legal implementation directed social conflict again toward the municipalities.

Although the complex formula of the NWF protected the highly differentiated pattern of local welfare, the issue was not fully settled. Under pressure from the Social Democrats, the German parliament decided in July 1925 that national pensions should be placed on the same tax basis as private pensions and passed legislation to disregard national pension income for welfare purposes. Although resisted by parts of the Center Party and the German Nationalists, the Social Democratic measure passed. The NWF used every means at its disposal to oppose the decision. It complained about the "demonstration of distrust in local communities and their organizations" (*ND*, July 1925, p. 318) and protested "decisions made possible by a constitutional loop hole" (*ND*, August 1925, p. 337). The NWF also hoped that the bureaucracy would use its powers to raise a constitutional issue and wrote, "Perhaps the constitution should be altered; in such cases and under certain conditions a right of veto should be given to the federal government (cabinet)."

The NWF protest was not totally ineffective. Ignoring constitutional requirements, the federal government refused to endorse the new law and to submit it for promulgation. The Ministry of Labor was in a particular dilemma, for, on the one hand, it did not want to support the NWF, but, on the other hand, the Ministry felt pressure from pension organizations to liberalize pension "taxation." Hence, the Ministry sought a compromise by replacing a uniform "tax" break for national pensions with a sliding scale. In effect, the NWF wanted to change a question or principle into an organizational problem where it knew its own network would prevail. The organizational strategy is similar to the later development of welfare in the United States (Piven and Cloward, 1971). In any event, by this indirect method a national claim to regulate welfare was partially affirmed in the late Weimar Republic.

THE OUTCOME: DIFFERENTIAL ASSISTANCE IN SIMILAR COMMUNITIES AND THE PROPOSED REFORM OF 1925

To the NWF the change from a uniform disregard to a differentiated "tax deduction" was a lesser evil in order to avoid the greater evil of a universal disregard or national compulsory minimum scales. The NWF turned the problem inside out by recasting the issue of inegalitarian payment structures in rural areas and in smaller cities into an organizational question, and in doing so protected municipal interests. As the NWF reported, "In the (welfare) organizations unwilling to make payments, increasing payments is not primarily a question of institutional force but an educational measure. Through instruction, awareness, discussions, courses and further gradual reforms must be attempted" (*ND*, September 1925, p. 379). The Federal Labor Ministry countered "the states must try to accept the scales as fundamental to muncipal surveillance" (*ND*, October 1925, p. 410), but did not take the next logical step of appointing inspectors.

With one exception, all members of a special welfare commission agreed with the NWF. Their professional and practical concerns were displayed by Wilhelm Polligkeit (1876–1960), who argued "parliament must realize that it may not continually interfere in administrative matters. Nothing is achieved by legal force, but rather through understanding and consultation, and further professional schooling of the municipal supervisors." Nevertheless, the federal government, the Federal Ministry of Labor, Prussia and Bavaria boycotted the commission. The Ministry of Labor wanted to introduce national scales and not to be hindered in any way by sharing reform with the NWF. The Federal Labor Minister and the Federal Minister of the Interior made their purpose clear with regard to the NWF: "The guidelines should alleviate the task of verifying through supervising bureaus and the appeals tribunals whether appropriate welfare is granted. They should protect clients against arbitrary determination of welfare payments because unjustified deviation from the guidelines has to be justified if there are complaints" (*ND*, November 1925, p. 429).

The result was another move toward a national welfare policy. In order to obtain statistical information to implement the new policy, the NWF had to request of its members that the Federal Labor Ministry be informed of the guidelines set and about the income tax returns of the local welfare organizations. This was a decisive step toward nationalizing the guidelines and helped launch an advisory and complaint service that further mobilized social pressures for nationalization. The Federal Labor Ministry made clear that it seriously advocated national guidelines, and shortly thereafter national guidelines were adopted by parliament. The issue did not die with this unceremonious takeover by the ministerial bureaucracy, but it created new layers of controlled participation through legislation (Diefenbach, 1926, col. 480).

THE FIGHT FOR "GENERAL WELFARE" AS A DISGUISED DEFENSE OF FLEXIBLE MUNICIPAL SOCIAL POLICIES

Since the first attempts by the NWF to create a "Federal Poor Law" in the Weimar period, its main position had hardly changed. In their view, the national opinion that general welfare only helped the irresponsible was erroneous (*ND*, August 1924, Special Section, p. 10). In theory, the NWF fought against welfare "differentiated by levels" and also against "elevated or privileged welfare." Actually, though, the NWF favored differentiated benefit levels, with benefits never legally defined but delegated to the local authorities (*ND*, October 1925, p. 408). The NWF wanted to adjust to diverse local demands within a framework of regional requirements. As different as these requirements were across the Reich, NWF solidarity rested on the defense of local choice, stabilized and modified according to locally set priorities. On this point there was unity of rural and urban welfare unions, as well as all the regions. The NWF claimed "the demand is for sufficient freedom for local welfare organizations to individualize welfare. This demand not only adjusts to the fact that welfare payments are individually decided, but also differentiated in regard to local conditions and local welfare structures" (*ND*, August 1928, p. 263 f.).

Until the economic crisis completely overtook the welfare structure, the conflict of Reich and local welfare organizations continued under the aegis of the NWF. With assistance of the NWF the welfare organizations tried to implement their concept of flexible social policies for municipalities and opposed fixed national standards. The Federal Ministry of Labor attempted to enforce the general guidelines and published its findings. It also helped more privileged clientele outside the framework of social assistance and supported other welfare interest groups.

Through legal appeals other organizations could force the implementation of national guidelines. The combination of political unrest and standardization of guidelines inevitably raised subsistence scales, in part because the Ministry of Labor compiled figures revealing sizeable disparities among areas. The first compilation was published in early 1927, and helped crystallize pressure to eliminate municipal differences throughout the country (*Reichstag Press*, IIIrd Reichstag, 1924/26, No. 2810, enclosure I).

A glimpse of the debate shows how difficult the process of nationalizing the guidelines became. A municipal welfare expert reported:

> Although total payments in most cases cannot be calculated numerically . . . it is clear that the welfare payments from a large number of welfare organizations are insufficient. No one can live for one month on an assistance rate of 10 to 15 Reichs-Marks per person, and 15 to 20 Reichs-Marks for a married couple with additional children, not even in the rural areas. . . (Baak, 1929, p. 567).

The strategy of the district welfare organizations was to circumvent uniform assistance scales by differentiating social classes. The NWF vehemently reacted to new attacks on municipal demands for more flexible and more generous assistance. With the Federal Ministry of Labor, the NWF attempted to build a new defense by asking for a commission to study welfare laws with the hope of enlisting support from the National Association of Cities and Counties as well as the Organization of Prussian Provinces. In addition, the NWF tried to limit the effects of judicial interpretations of the welfare decree. Prussia was successful in being exempted from the terms originally set by the Federal Labor Ministry. Predictably, the review committee also came to the conclusion:

> that centrally determined guidelines as well as centrally determined assistance rates are unacceptable for social assistance because they are incompatible with the principles of individualization. By making centrally set minimum rates effectively maximum rates, such control would not be in the interests of the needy and is a development which must be guarded against. (*ND*, October 1929, p. 443)

Imposing a national procedure on the local setting of the basic subsistence standard was successful even though not as effective as binding minimum rates would have been. The ministry reported to the German Parliament on February 4, 1931, that a general review:

> shows that the 'guideline regulations' in 1930 were generally enforced, that in industrial states and provinces, as in the Rhineland and Westphalia, Thueringen and Saxony, the rates were generally accepted, while in the agricultural states, for example Bavaria, Wuerttemberg, Hessia, great disparities existed due to the various liv-

ing standards. In some districts, especially in rural districts, political influence on the
rates is unmistakable. (Kleindinst, *ND,* October/November 1931, p. 316)

THE GLOBAL ECONOMIC CRISIS: MANIPULATION
OF THE GUIDELINES TO UNDO SOCIAL REFORM
AND TO INCREASE NATIONAL CONTROL

The international economic crisis, which started in 1928, was used by the
NWF to seek a global settlement with the Federal Labor Ministry. It interpreted the crisis as "pressure for maximum individualization" and defended itself as the national authority on welfare politics which had with-
stood "schematization" since 1919 (*ND,* October/November 1931, p.
318; September 1932, pp. 281–285). Returning to its old position, the
NWF wrote, "levels of assistance should be justified only on the basis of a
locally determined guideline and in consideration of individual circumstances and with allowances for all income" (*ND,* October/November
1931, p. 318). Wilhelm Polligkeit, the NWF's leading administrative
official, said in 1931: "Since 1919, our Federation has warned again and
again to beware of exaggerations. Experience in private life shows that
only he who stands on his own feet responds decisively and at the right
time" (*ND,* October/November 1931, p. 324).

The times favored the NWF and all welfare state guarantees were lowered. The situation deteriorated on various fronts: the benefits were "individualized"; the shortlived minimum guidelines ended; and "elevated"
or "privileged welfare" fell apart. The first direct national intervention
in the social assistance crisis came in June, 1931. Thereafter, federal or
state grants towards local welfare expenses were only guaranteed if the
"scales did not exceed standards deemed to be required and acceptable."
Compared to earlier periods, the NWF took little exception. It reported,
"the executive committee saw a regrettable intrusion into the self-
government and self-reliance of the welfare organizations, and expressed the fear that a standard policy would be enforced by the
supervising bureaus, which, if directed to fiscal cuts, would infringe
upon welfare principles" (*ND,* July 1931, p. 203). Even in 1919, economic decline affected welfare nationally. Nevertheless, the NWF did
not see any particular problems in the depression, and as in the past,
relied more on the protection of the "weakest links" in the structure of
welfare administration rather than on nurturing reform and innovation
and on protecting the level of support for "the weakest" nationally.

The NWF's understanding of the situation was so isolated from the
needs of the poor that it resisted strengthening the right of appeal and
the participation by beneficiaries in appeals procedures that the Federal
Labor Ministry had built in to limit assistance cuts. For the NWF these

were "typical examples of overorganization" and a "duplication of the successive appeals." It called for intervention by the Federal Commissioner for Economy and Efficiency (*ND*, August 1931, p. 249; Gutzeit, 1931, p. 269). In 1931 there were no benefit increases by any of the welfare organizations. As the NWF elegantly paraphrased it, several districts considered the guidelines only a piece of paper, "allowing for the decline of living costs through an individualized adjustment of the assistance levels" (*ND*, May 1931, p. 130).

How did the severe reduction of welfare payments affect municipal welfare policy? A welfare worker, Martha Wedel (1892–1963) from Hannover, provides an illustration:

> The guidelines are cut again and again. Repeatedly, welfare funds were reduced and rationed. Everyone knew and feared the days when notices about assistance cuts went out. Complaints and reproaches rang in our ears the whole day long: How can I feed a child with 10 Marks? I cannot get a cheaper place to live. I cannot even send my child to school if it does not have shoes! (Wedel, 1932, p. 255)

The director of the Hannover welfare office, Wilhelm Schickenberg (1876–1971), reported:

> we hang on the words of our city treasurers as we ask the timid question of whether we can rely next week on the budgetary allotments for an already decreased assistance. There are no longer special payments, special rest benefits are flatly rejected, and dentures only permitted when some appeals tribunal out of touch with reality intervenes. The costs for a cataract operation are denied unless the applicant is already blind. . . (Schickenberg, 1931, p. 281)

If the NWF had been as shrewd in opposing cuts as it was in attacking the guidelines, its proposal to link welfare to the standard of living index (*ND*, May 1931, pp. 130 ff.) should have troubled its conscience. The index was constructed on a pre-World War I base, and did not correspond in any way to the living habits of the late 1920s. Further, the index had been tailored to general social categories and showed no special consideration for the eating habits of workers or the poor, nor for particular tastes. The NWF was reactionary throughout the crisis. In September, 1932, the NWF reported: "One of the most disastrous errors in the development of social assistance in recent years was to use national scales as a base for the judgment of the adequacy of the assistance rates" (*ND*, September 1932, p. 232). In 1931, the NWF admitted "the low levels set for public welfare by the index affect at least a fifth of the population, which creates the danger that such levels might not be determined so much by the actual subsistence needs of those receiving assistance as by the public coffers of the welfare authorities . . ." (*ND*, July 1932, pp. 179f.). But the welfare state under Weimar could not succeed against such a professional and biased organization representing all public and private local welfare agencies with no political interest in the social meaning of the guidelines, i.e., in the effective protection of the weakest members of society.

SCALING WELFARE: RESULTS FROM THE WEIMAR PERIOD

Declining welfare funds lead to new controls. They focused not only on the guidelines but also on actual payments. What was never achieved in the mid-1920s, a binding and consistent national minimum for all groups, was readily attained when fiscal control demanded to undercut it. While such developments occurred at the state level, the Emergency Decree for the Restoration of Social Payments of October 19, 1932, did not lower the guidelines directly, but the jurisdiction was definitely withdrawn from local influence. Thus, the Reich continued in the direction of earlier changes that it had made in local scales and in distribution standards. Gradually, social assistance became indistinguishable from incomes policy and unemployment relief. "Today the scales have become an important factor in revenue sharing. If the welfare scales were lower than the normal assistance rates of 'Alu' (unemployment assistance), and 'Kru' (emergency assistance), people would receive assistance calculated according to the subsistence scales. These scales would thus also determine the extent to which federal resources (unemployment insurance) or community assistance (emergency welfare) could be claimed for assistance for the unemployed" (*ND*, September 1932, p. 233).

Because the NWF swam with the tide during the financial crisis, it did not try to protect welfare by enlisting support from labor unions and other social groups. On the contrary, the political parties and national policy did additional damage by trying to dismantle flexible social security institutions. All bear a measure of responsibility for the erosion of the welfare structure under Weimar. Similarly shaped developments in the 1980s (cf. Leibfried and Tennstedt, 1985) give reason to doubt that this lesson was learned from history.

ACKNOWLEDGMENTS

This article was written in cooperation with Eckhard Hansen and Michael Heisig and is part of a project funded by the German Research Foundation (Deutsche Forschungsgemeinschaft) entitled "Socio-Political Intervention and Subsistence." For a more comprehensive version of this text with more specific references to the German context, see Leibfried, 1981 and Leibfried et al., 1984a. A more comprehensive study of public assistance under Weimar is being undertaken. Meanwhile all historical and comparative work undertaken by this research group has been collected in Leibfried et al., 1985. The actual development of welfare politics in the Federal Republic of Germany is reviewed in Leibfried and Tennstedt, 1985.

NOTES

1. The NWF is a *national* association with all public local welfare authorities as core members. Other members are the private charities and the states and the federal government. It was founded in 1881 to substitute for an inexistent national ministry of welfare by coordination through association. Due to its filling a functional gap and its unique national standing, it came to acquire a unique importance in the steering of local social policy or in regulating the poor, cf. Tennstedt, 1981. The NWF's "cartel" position in welfare politics has been challenged in the 1980s, cf. Leibfried and Tennstedt, 1985.

REFERENCES

Aronson, Naomi (1982), "Social Definitions of Food Entitlements: Food Needs 1885–1920," *Media Culture and Society*, 4 (1): 51–61.

Baak, Bernhard (1929), "Die Fuersorgetarife im Deutschen Reich," *Zeitschrift fur das Heimatwesen*, 34 (35):564–569.

Branson, Noreen (1979), *Poplarism, 1919–1925. George Landsbury and the Councillor's Revolt*, London: Lawrence & Wishart.

Diefenbach, Friedrich (1926), "Besteht ein Rechtsanspruch des Hilfsbedürftigen auf Unterstützung?" *Zeitschrift fuer das Heimatwesen*, 31, (17), col. 477–480, (18), col. 500–504, (19), col. 538–542, (20), col. 568–571.

Gutzeit, Erwin (1931), "Das Einspruchs - und Beschwerdeverfahren im Fuersorgewesen auf Grund der Notverordnung vom 5. Juni 1931," *Die Landgemeinde*, 40 (15):269–270.

Hofmann, Albert (1932), "Finanznot und oeffentliche Fuersorge," *Arbeiterwohlfahrt*, 7 (15):467–470.

Hofmann, Albert and Stephan Leibfried (1980), "Historische Regelmaessigkeiten bei Regelsaetzen; 100 Jahre Tradition des Deutschen Vereins?" *Neue Praxis*, 10 (3):253–285.

Kuczynski, Juergen (1957), (Robert) *Rene Kuczynski*, Berlin: Aufbau Verlag.

Kuczynski, Robert (1921), *Das Existenzminimum und verwandte Fragen*, Berlin: H. R. Engelmann.

Leibfried, Stephan (1978), "Public Assistance in the United States and the Federal Republic of Germany—Does Social Democracy Make a Difference?" *Comparative Politics*, 11 (1):59–76.

Leibfried, Stephan (1979), "The United States and West German Welfare Systems: A Comparative Analysis," *Cornell International Law Journal*, 12 (Summer): 175–198.

Leibfried, Stephan (1981), "Existenzminimum and Fuersorge-Richtsaetze in der Weimarer Republik," *Jahrbuch der Sozialarbeit* 4 (1982), Reinbek near Hamburg: Rowohlt, pp. 469–523.

Leibfried, Stephan (1982), "Zur Sozialpolitik der Verteilungsformen in der Sozialhilfe. Einige Anmerkungen zur Regelsatzdiskussion," in *Nachrichtendienst des Deutschen Vereins fuer oeffentliche and private Fuersorge*, 61 (9):261–271.

Leibfried, Stephan (1983), "Sozialpolitik und Existenzminimum. Anmerkungen zur Geschichte der englischen Entwicklung," *Zeitschrift für Sozialreform*, 27 (2):72–100.

154   STEPHAN LEIBFRIED

Leibfried, Stephan (1985), "The Development of the 'Moral Economy' of the Welfare State: U. S. Poverty Lines in Comparative Perspective," in *Forschungsschwerpunkt Reproduktionsrisiken, soziale Bewegungen und Sozialpolitik,* ed., Sozialpolitik und Sozialstaat, Bremen: University, pp. 513–553.

Leibfried, Stephan, Eckhard Hansen, and Michael Heisig (1984a), "Politik mit der Armut. Notizen zu Weimarer Perspektiven anläßlich bundesrepublikanischer Wirklichkeiten," *Prokla,* 14 (56):105–126.

Leibfried, Stephan, Eckhard Hansen, and Michael Heisig (1984b), "Geteilte Erde? Bedarfsprinzip und Existenzminimum unter dem NS-Regime: Zu Aufstieg und Fall der Regelsätzë in der Fürsorge," *Neue Praxis,* 14 (1):3–20.

Leibfried, Stephan and Florian Tennstedt, eds. (1985), *Politik der Armut und die Spaltung des Sozialstaats,* Frankfurt a.M.: Suhrkamp.

Leibfried, Stephan, et al. (1985), *Armutspolitik und die Entstehung des Sozialstaats. Entwicklungslinien sozialpolitischer Existenzsicherung im historischen und internationalen Vergleich,* Bremen: University.

Piven, Frances Fox and Richard Cloward (1971), *Regulating the Poor: The Functions of Public Welfare,* New York: Pantheon.

Schickenberg, Wilhelm (1931), "Brutale Sparsamkeit," *Wohlfahrtswoche,* 6 (33):281.

Tennstedt, Florian (1981), "Fürsorgegeschichte und Vereinsgeschichte. 100 Jahre Deutscher Verein in der Geschichte der Deutschen Fürsorge," *Zeitschrift für Sozialreform,* 27 (2):72–100.

Townsend, Peter (1979), *Poverty in the United Kingdom: A Survey of Household Resources and Standards of Living,* Middlesex: Penguin.

Wachenheim, Hedwig (1982), "Reichstags—und Landtagswahlen und die Wohlfahrtspflege," *Arbeiterwohlfahrt,* 3 (9):257–262.

Wedel, Martha (1932), "Ablehnen," *Wohlfahrtswoche,* 7 (31):255–256.

Zwangsläufige Gemeindepolitik (1925), *Kölnische Zeitung,* November 13 (846): 1.

FEDERALISM, KEYNESIANISM, AND THE TRANSFORMATION OF THE UNEMPLOYMENT INSURANCE SYSTEM IN THE UNITED STATES

Edward J. Harpham

I

Unemployment has been a chronic problem plaguing western societies since the rise of commerical economies in the sixteenth century. Until the late nineteenth century the traditional responses to the unemployment brought on by either a cyclical downturn in the economy or technological innovation were public welfare and conscription into the work force. These poor law approaches to the problem of unemployment found their clearest articulation in Great Britain in such acts as the Elizabethan Poor Laws (1602), the Speenhamland System (1795), and the Poor Laws Act of 1834 (see Polanyi, 1944).

Unemployment insurance only emerged as an alternative approach to the problem of unemployment in a capitalist society in the late nineteenth century. The basic idea behind unemployment insurance was that during times of economic prosperity reserves would be accumulated that would be used to compensate workers who had involuntarily lost their jobs during harder times. Unlike the traditional welfare programs, compensation from these reserves was to be a matter of right, not simply need, and would be discontinued after a specified period of time. As the reserves were built up over time, it was hoped that the need for traditional unemployment relief measures would be significantly curtailed.

This study investigates the institutional transformation of the unemployment insurance system in the United States from 1935 to the early 1980s. Its primary concerns are twofold: first, to show how specific political interests transformed a highly decentralized unemployment insurance system reflecting one set of goals into a much more centralized system reflecting a new set of goals; second, to analyze the political and economic significance of the financial crises which have come to confront the unemployment insurance system in the 1970s. It is argued that these crises are the direct result of the Federal Government's attempt in the 1970s to graft a new set of Keynesian-oriented policies at the national level upon the existing decentralized system. Any attempt to solve these fiscal crises will have to come to terms with the tension that has existed in the past and continues to exist today between the system's decentralized institutional structure and the demands that have been placed upon it in our modern Keynesian era.

II

Under Part II of the National Insurance Act of 1911, Britain became the first major European country to institute an unemployment insurance program. This program covered approximately 2.25 million workers in certain industries of chronic high unemployment and was financed by contributions from employers and employees as well as a state subsidy that matched one-third of the amount collected from the other groups. As Daniel Nelson explains:

> This tripartite system of contributions became the distinguishing characteristic of the British plan. Although the emphasis of the act was on compensating the jobless, relatively strict limitations prevented unnecessary benefit payments, and modest incentive provisions allowed the workers and employers with good employment records to claim refunds [a provision that was dropped in 1920]. . . . While it rejected prevention, the 1911 act was sound financially, limited, moderate, and based, insofar as possible, on insurance methods. (Nelson, 1969, p. 10)

From 1919 to 1932, ten other European countries drew upon the British experience and adopted their own version of unemployment insurance to meet the needs of their particular political economies. By the early 1930s unemployment insurance had become one of the most unique and important institutions in the evolving welfare state in Europe.

Despite the growth of considerable support for an unemployment insurance program in the United States, little progress was actually made in bringing such a program into existence through the late 1920s. The reasons for this lay in the unique political and economic environment found in America prior to the 1930s. Organized labor remained staunchly opposed to unemployment insurance. According to Samuel Gompers, unemployment insurance was a dole which, along with other forms of social insurance promoted by the government, threatened to coopt the labor movement. As the American Federation of Labor's convention platform explained in 1919, "Place in the hands of the government the right to determine who is and who is not entitled to governmental insurance" and "the government will determine then what will constitute justifiable reasons for unemployment" (Garraty, 1978, p. 151). The decentralized federal system in the United States—which left responsibility for welfare programs such as unemployment insurance in the hands of the state and local governments—also tended to undermine support for unemployment insurance. Opponents to unemployment insurance argued that the state taxes which would be needed to finance such a program would unfairly handicap employers who sought to compete for interstate markets against employers from states without a similar tax. These arguments were complemented by the widely held belief among state and local political leaders that the European experiments in unemployment insurance had failed dismally. It was pointed out that in Britain, the unemployment insurance system had lost all but the pretense of actuarial soundness by 1920 and had been transformed for all intents and purposes into a new form of public assistance which paid out benefits with little regard to previous contributions. Given the relatively low levels of unemployment in the United states during the 1920s, few state politicians were willing to take the risk of instituting an unemployment insurance system in their state alone.[1]

This environment underwent a fundamental transformation during the Great Depression. By early 1930, 4 million wage earners had lost their jobs, and by late 1932, 9.5 million. While it is difficult to document, changing public demands for some sort of program multiplied as more and more people became involuntarily unemployed. During its 1932 national convention, the AFL finally abandoned its earlier opposition to social insurance legislation and came out in support of unemployment insurance. While intense conflicts raged over the feasibility of unemployment insurance in many state legislatures during the 1920s and early 1930s, it was not until 1932 that Wisconsin passed the first state unemployment insurance act in the United States. Few states followed Wisconsin's lead. The problems of interstate competition and strong interest group opposition, particularly that of business, were simply too great to overcome. By the mid 1930s, it appeared to many knowledgeable observers that only a national program would be able to circumvent these problems.

The first bill concerned with national unemployment insurance was introduced in the House of Representatives in 1916 by Representative Meyer London, a Socialist from New York. It was not until 1933, however, that there emerged any considerable support for an unemployment insurance bill in either the House or the Senate. This support ultimately led to the introduction of the Wagner-Lewis Unemployment Insurance Bill in both the House and the Senate on February 5, 1934. While President Roosevelt initially came out in support of the Wagner-Lewis Bill on March 23, on June 8 he sent a message to Congress announcing that he planned to present to Congress in the next session a comprehensive plan for economic security in which an unemployment insurance program would play a central role. Only with the passage of the omnibus Social Security Act of 1935 did unemployment insurance become a permanent feature of the American political economy.

The Social Security Act basically provided for four things in regard to unemployment insurance. First, it established a 3% federal unemployment tax on the taxable payroll of all subject employers. Although this tax originally applied to the total payroll of all subject employers, beginning in 1940 it was limited to the first $3,000 of each employee's annual wages.[2] Second, the act provided for a 2.7% tax offset for employers who participated in a federally approved state unemployment insurance program. To receive federal approval, state systems had to meet a number of important requirements, including provisions for the payment of unemployment benefits through public employment offices and the depositing of all umemployment tax receipts in a state Unemployment Trust Fund set up in the United States Treasury. In effect, through the tax offset provisions of the act, the federal government was compelling states to set up acceptable programs or the entire 3% tax would go to the federal government. Third, the Social Security Act stated that the remaining .3% payroll tax would go to the national Treasury and be used to meet the costs that states would incur in the administration of their own unemployment insurance programs and in the operation of their public employment offices. Fourth, provisions were made for "experience rating" which permitted states to grant tax credits to employers who maintained good employment records.

In contrast to the unemployment insurance systems found in Britain and in other European countries, the system established by the Social

Security Act was radically decentralized. While the federal government was responsible for approving all state programs and for keeping the book accounts for the trust funds of the separate state programs, the individual states were responsible for making most of the important specific decisions such as determining coverage, eligibility, levels and duration of benefits, and state unemployment tax rates. The reasons for giving the federal government such a minimal role were both constitutional and political. Roosevelt, as well as several key advisors both inside and outside of Congress, believed that a purely national system would have been declared unconstitutional by the courts. Just as importantly, they wanted to make sure that the individual states would be given the greatest latitude in determining the specific program best suited to their local economic conditions. Few political leaders wanted to strip states completely of their traditional responsibility for maintaining welfare programs. Moreover, the last thing any of the supporters of the Social Security Act wanted was a bitter controversy over the details involved with unemployment insurance.

While state legislatures were delegated the authority to decide upon the specifics of unemployment insurance in their state, national policymakers did articulate three general goals for unemployment insurance in the United States as a whole: (1) to protect regular workers from some of the financial hardship which accompanied short-term unemployment; (2) to help stabilize the economy during periods of economic decline by maintaining the purchasing power of laid off workers; and (3) to encourage employers to stabilize employment practices through certain tax incentives.

Not surprisingly, key political leaders and important interest groups tended to focus attention more upon one goal than upon another. Roosevelt was particularly interested in using unemployment insurance in order to help stabilize employment practices over the long run. As he explained in his message to Congress on the Social Security Act on January 15, 1935:

> An unemployment compensation system should be constructed in such way as to afford every practical aid and incentive towards the larger purpose of employment stabilization of private employment. Federal legislation should not foreclose the States from establishing means for inducing industries to afford an even greater stabilization of employment. (*Congressional Record*, 1935, p. 545)

In contrast, the unemployment insurance experts who helped draft the unemployment insurance provisions of the Social Security Act tended to focus attention on the way in which the program would help maintain purchasing power during economic downturns. Organized labor, on the other hand, was interested primarily in the benefits provisions of the program, and sought to expand these provisions as far as was politically and financially possible. Business interests tended to focus on the employment stability provisions of the program, not so much because they believed that tax incentives could stabilize employment practices, but because they recognized the potential usefulness of the experience rating provisions in minimizing their tax burdens (see Nelson, 1969, Chapter 9; Witte, 1963; Altmeyer, 1968).

Significantly, the goals set out for unemployment insurance were not completely compatible with one another. Indeed, as would become strikingly apparent over the next twenty years, the pursuit of one goal often tended to limit or even to undermine the pursuit of one of the other goals. For example, to the degree to which state legislatures tailored unemployment insurance towards the needs of regular, rather than all, workers, unemployment insurance was a very limited countercyclical tool. Similarly, to the degree to which employers were encouraged to stabilize employment practices through state experience rating provisions, the ability of the unemployment insurance system to finance additional regular benefits or to maintain purchasing power during periods of economic decline was seriously undermined. While the state legislatures initially were left to decide how these goals would be balanced, it was recognized that the Federal Government probably would have to take up the problem at a later date. As the President's Committee on Economic Security, the committee which drafted the initial version of the Social Security Act, noted, "The plan of unemployment compensation we suggest is frankly experimental. We anticipate that it may require numerous changes with experience, and, we believe, is set up that these changes can be made through subsequent legislation" (*Congressional Record*, 1935, p. 546). How subsequent legislation would balance the contradictory goals built into the program was a question no one dared to ask.

III

The constitutionality of the unemployment insurance provisions of the Social Security Act was upheld by the Supreme Court on May 24, 1937. By June 30, unemployment insurance had become nationwide with the passage of approved laws in all states. By 1938, approximately one third of the civilian work force was covered under the new state-federal program.

Two developments in the operation of the unemployment insurance system between 1938 and 1959 revealed much about the goals that were being pursued and the interests that were being protected in the existing state-federal system. First, the level and duration of benefits provided by most state programs remained low. While the average weekly benefit received by unemployed workers was only 43% of the weekly wage in 1938, it fell to 39% in 1946 and to 33% in 1954. During the same period, the average available duration for benefits increased only minimally from 19.6 weeks in 1946 to 22.4 weeks in 1954. Unemployment insurance simply did not protect regular workers against the income loss of short-term unemployment. These limited benefits were a direct reflection of the business controlled politics that had evolved out of the decentralized policymaking system which was in charge of the specifics of unemployment insurance in the United States. Most states had been able to accumulate large trust fund reserves during World War II because of low levels of unemployment. Business groups, in turn, had been able to lobby successfully at the state level that it was perfectly reasonable for states to lower state unemployment insurance taxes in order to maintain a favorable tax climate. As a result, from 1938 to 1948 the average state unemployment insurance tax rate dropped from 2.69% to 1.01%. With tax rates low and business influence high, few state politicians were willing or able to expand the benefits or coverage provided by the unemployment insurance system during the postwar period.

Second, some of the state programs began to experience severe financial difficulties. The constant worry over interstate competition for business in state legislatures had left some state unemployment insurance systems facing chronic fiscal crises. These financial problems were exacerbated further by the unexpected demands that were forced upon state unemployment insurance systems by the postwar recessions of 1948–1949 and 1953–1954. While these recessions were national in scope, they had a much more severe impact upon certain regions of the economy than upon others. Certain states, particularly those of the industrialized northeast and midwest, found their state trust funds being rapidly depleted during the recessions, and this despite the fact that most were willing to impose higher state unemployment insurance taxes than the national average.

A number of important attempts were made through the 1940s and early 1950s to respond to these developments by giving the federal government a larger and more central role to play in determining the specifics of unemployment insurance in the United States.[3] No permanent changes were introduced at the national level, however, until 1954 when two major pieces of unemployment insurance legislation passed Congress. The first piece simply extended the mandatory coverage provided by the unemployment insurance system to include a considerably larger portion of the work force.[4] This legislation fundamentally redefined who was considered to be a regular member of the work force. The second piece of legislation established a separate $200 million account, the Federal Unemployment Account or the so-called Reed Fund,

in the Treasury's Unemployment Insurance Trust Fund that would be
financed by excess proceeds from the .3% Federal Unemployment Tax
and would be used to provide interest-free loans to state trust funds that
were unnecessarily low.[5] In effect, this act established a new paper account in the Unemployment Trust Fund to help to alleviate some of the
financial pressures that threatened to undermine parts of the state-
federal unemployment insurance system. Significantly, even with this
new institutional feature, the decentralized character of the system as a
whole remained intact. Individual states, not the Federal Government,
continued to remain responsible for determining the level of benefits,
the duration of benefits, and the financing of their specific programs.
They essentially continued to remain responsible for financing the goals
towards which unemployment insurance was directed.

Behind these rather conservative reforms lay a controversial and revealing debate over the goals and the institutional structure of the
unemployment insurance system. Congressional critics, with the support
of organized labor, pointed out that for all intents and purposes the existing decentralized system did little to promote employment stability or
to provide what they considered to be adequate benefits. Indeed, some
argued that the device that was supposed to promote employment stability, experience rating, actually undermined the ability of state systems to
provide adequate benefits. As Senator Lehman of New York explained:

> There is no justification at all for the merit system. Those employers that benefit by
> a merit system deserve little credit for maintaining stable employment. They are
> usually firms whose product is in great demand and who, therefore, can operate
> continuously; they are not affected by the seasonal fluctuation of employment. But
> the fellow whose product sometimes falls off in demand, or the man whose business
> is seasonal, not only does not receive the recognition of the merit system, but also is
> put to a greater tax burden, which further jeopardizes the continuity of the fund,
> since large sums of money are being paid to those who under the law benefit by the
> merit system. If the merit system did not exist, considerably increased benefits, of
> course, could be paid to the unemployed. (*Congressional Record*, 1954, p. 10345)

Critics argued further that unemployment was not simply a local problem subject to local conditions but a national problem brought on by
nationwide economic forces that should be dealt with on a nationwide
basis. According to Senator Pastore of Rhode Island:

> to say that the employment problem in any particular State is strictly the responsibil-
> ity of that State and of no concern to the Nation . . . begs the question somewhat and
> shows a complete misunderstanding of our American economy . . . if economic mis-
> fortune strikes any one of our States or any particular area, the rest of the Nation
> cannot afford to remain complacent and unconcerned under the delusion that this
> ailment will remain localized. Whether we like it or not, we are all in the same eco-
> nomic boat. The disaster that befalls one area today can and probably will strike
> some other area tomorrow. (*Congressional Record*, 1954, p. 10325)

In their rejection of the existing decentralized unemployment insurance system, opponents to the 1954 reforms articulated a strikingly Keynesian understanding of the role of unemployment insurance in the nation's economy that went far beyond the limited countercyclical goals embodied in the Social Security Act of 1935. They argued that the principle goal of unemployment insurance should be the maintenance of purchasing power in the nation as a whole, not simply to assist unemployed individuals in times of need, but to buttress the entire business structure. Further, they concluded that in order to pursue this countercyclical goal certain mandatory federal standards for unemployment insurance had to be established that would guarantee certain minimum benefit payments, extend potential coverage up to 39 weeks, and expand coverage to include all employed workers. As Senator Morse of Oregon, one of the most outspoken critics of the existing system, explained, any reform of the unemployment insurance system "should follow the intent and purpose of the Full Employment Act of 1946" (*Congressional Record*, 1954, p. 10348). Despite intense debate, proposals embodying such provisions were defeated decisively in roll call votes in both the House and Senate.

Significantly, neither the Eisenhower Administration nor congressional supporters of the 1954 reforms explicitly rejected the idea that the existing system should be geared to help maintain purchasing power during periods of economic decline. Both, in fact, recognized that the existing system should be upgraded in order to provide adequate benefits and coverage that would support aggregate purchasing power throughout the nation as a whole. But beyond the limited institutional reforms embodied in the 1954 legislation, they argued that such upgrading should remain the responsibility of the various states. As the House Report on the bill which extended coverage explained:

> While the problem of unemployment must always be one of national concern, geographic variations both in economic conditions and in employment practices make it essential that actual implementation of an unemployment insurance system be carried out by State action. . . .
>
> Your committee believes that the further coverage is extended in this area, the further the Federal Government is moving into an area where the differences in State and local conditions becomes a significant factor. There is a twilight zone where needed flexibility can only be maintained through State action. It may be appropriate that unemployment protection be extended in this fringe area, but your committee believes that such extension should be left to State determination in light of local variation in employment patterns. (U.S. Congress, House, 1954, pp. 2–3)

In essence, supporters of the 1954 reforms wanted unemployment insurance to be a countercyclical tool, but only within the confines of a highly decentralized system. Far from resolving the tensions and contra-

dictory goals built into the original program, the 1954 reforms only
added another institutional mechanism through which they might come
into conflict.[6]

IV

Dissatisfaction with the decentralized unemployment insurance system
remained high during the late 1950s. Supporters of organized labor
continued to argue that the existing system still could not meet effectively the problem of unemployment in the United States because of its
antiquated institutional structure. Their concerns were well founded.
Beginning in 1955, six states became eligible to borrow money from the
Reed Fund in order to keep their trust funds solvent. While only Alaska,
Pennsylvania, and Massachusetts actually drew upon the Reed Fund for
assistance, their financial troubles focused attention upon the fact that
some states faced more severe unemployment problems during economic downturns than other states. Ironically, those very states which
appeared to need an expanded unemployment insurance program the
most, could afford it the least.[7]

The inability of the existing employment insurance system to act as an
effective countercyclical weapon of the federal government was highlighted during the 1957–1958 recession when the number of individuals
who had exhausted their regular state benefits rose from 1.1 million to
2.5 million. In response to this immediate problem of long-term
unemployment, the Eisenhower administration pushed through Congress the Temporary Unemployment Compensation Act of 1958
(TUCA). This program basically made available non-interest bearing
loans from the Federal Treasury to states that wanted to extend the duration of regular state benefits up to an additional 50%. These loans
were to be made available until April 1, 1959, and to be repaid by January 1, 1963. Failure by a state to repay its loan on time was to lead to a
reduction in the employer's tax offset privilege that would continue until
the full loan was repaid to the Federal Treasury.

The TUCA reflected the fundamental assumptions on which the
unemployment insurance system had rested since 1935. Not only did the
federal government's role in the system as a whole continue to remain
minimal, but full financial responsibility for benefits and coverage continued to lie with the individual state governments. All the Federal Government actually did with the TUCA was provide states with the opportunity to expand their current benefits programs and to defray the costs
of such expansion into the near future when financial pressures upon
the system hopefully would have decreased.

Much as during the 1954 debates, there existed strong support in Congress for giving the federal government a much larger role to play in the unemployment insurance system as a whole. In the House, for example, the Ways and Means Committee reported a bill that would have provided non-repayable federal grants to states that wanted to extend current coverage an additional 16 weeks. This bill was overturned on the floor by a vote of 223–165. In the Senate, Senator John Kennedy of Massachusetts pushed for an extension program that would have forgiven states for repaying the federal government for aid if their trust funds were unnecessarily low. Both the original House proposal and the Kennedy bill would have marked a major break with the existing system by removing certain financial responsibilities from the hands of the states. As the minority report of the Ways and Means Committee's original bill explained:

> U.I. cannot give complete and unlimited compensation to all who are unemployed. Any attempt to make it do so confuses unemployment insurance with relief, which it is designed to replace in large part. It can give compensation only for a limited period and for a percentage of the wage loss. (U.S. Congress, House, 1958, p. 23)

In 1958, as in 1954, attempts to restructure the decentralized unemployment insurance system to meet a new set of Keynesian goals were soundly defeated.

All together, 17 states borrowed a total of $445.6 million from the Federal Treasury under the TUCA. The bulk of these funds went to the hard-hit industrial states of the northeast and midwest. Michigan, New Jersey, New York, and Pennsylvania alone borrowed over 65% of the funds made available under the program. Unfortunately, far from solving the problems confronting the existing unemployment insurance system, the TUCA ultimately only exacerbated them. By January 1963, only Washington, D.C. had begun to repay voluntarily any of these funds. As provided in the legislation, temporary tax increases went into effect in those states which had borrowed money under the program. While provisions were added in 1963 to extend the repayment period and to freeze the level at which the federal unemployment tax had been raised, the net effect of the TUCA was to place additional burdens upon those states that were experiencing serious financial problems during the late 1950s and early 1960s.

These financial problems took on renewed importance early in the Kennedy administration during the recession of 1960–1961. From December 1960 to September 1961, national unemployment hovered between 6.6% and 6.9%, up from a yearly average of 5.6% during 1960. In addition, long-term unemployment (individuals unemployed for 16 weeks or more) rose from 987,000 in November 1960 to 2.1 million in

April 1961. In response, the Kennedy administration proposed—and the Congress enacted—a second temporary extension program, the Temporary Extended Unemployment Compensation Act of 1961 (TEUC). Like the Eisenhower program, the TEUC provided for advances to states that would enable them to extend their regular benefits programs by 50%. Unlike the Eisenhower program, the Kennedy program was financed by a temporary increase in the federal unemployment tax from 3.1% to 3.5%. The extra .4% was earmarked for a separate loan account that was established in the federal government's Unemployment Trust Fund and would make the advances to the individual states when necessary. In other words, under the TEUC federal taxes collected from employers all over the country were to be pooled together to pay for all advances made to the states. There would be no necessary relationship between the amounts advanced to a particular state and the amount employers from the state would pay into the TEUC account. In effect, the TEUC program provided for a temporary regional transfer of unemployment insurance tax funds from states with low unemployment to states with high unemployment. Before it expired, over 2,763,000 individuals had received $770,838,000 under the program.

Not surprisingly, the pooling features of the Kennedy program engendered considerable controversy. Opponents in both the House and the Senate argued that the program represented a dangerous step away from the existing system which had left the individual states with the responsibility for financing all regular unemployment insurance benefits. In the Senate, a Finance Committee-sponsored amendment, which would have eliminated the pooling features, was narrowly defeated by a vote of 42–44. Opposition came from 39 Democrats and 5 Republicans, mainly from states in the industrial north and midwest as well as the far west that were experiencing severe unemployment problems. The Temporary Extended Unemployment Compensation Act of 1961 set an important precedent in the development of the unemployment insurance system. Its financing provisions were an important step toward acceptance of long-term unemployment as a national responsibility, at least during recession. In sharp contrast to the Eisenhower program of 1958, the TEUC was for all intents and purposes a federal program grafted upon the existing decentralized unemployment insurance system. It gave the federal government a new, albeit temporary, role to play in mobilizing the unemployment insurance system into an effective countercyclical weapon. While the TEUC did not permanently alter the relationship that existed between the Federal Government and the individual state governments in the current system, it nevertheless marked a fundamental break with the institutional principles which had been established by the Social Security Act of 1935 and reaffirmed by the Reed Act of 1954 and the TUCA of 1958 (see Malisoff, 1963).

It is important to note that the TEUC was only part of a larger set of proposals supported by organized labor and the Kennedy administration to restructure permanently the unemployment insurance system into a powerful countercyclical weapon of the federal government. Among these proposals were minimum federal standards that would have required states to raise benefit levels of up to 30% of a worker's regular salary, a permanent extension program that would have provided regular benefits up to 39 weeks when necessary, and a broadening of the coverage of unemployment insurance to include almost all employed workers. As President Kennedy explained in his February 2, 1961 message to Congress, such a major overhaul of the system was imperative if unemployment insurance was to perform its proper role in the American political economy.

> Our permanent Federal-State unemployment insurance system, which has become an institution essential to the effective functioning of our labor markets as well as a strong defense against economic contraction, is in need of permanent reform . . . it would be a tragic mistake to embark upon a Federal supplementation program without also strengthening the underlying system. A mere stopgap approach ignores the role our permanent unemployment insurance system was intended to play, and establishes instead a precedent for falling back on temporary remedies whenever the system is really needed. (Kennedy, 1962, p. 46)

Despite repeated attempts by the Kennedy and Johnson administrations to restructure the existing decentralized unemployment insurance system, no major overhaul of the system took place between 1961 and 1968. The reasons for this were twofold. First, serious conflicts emerged between organized labor and business groups over exactly how far the reforms should go. Labor groups such as the AFL-CIO lobbied heavily for increased nationalization of the system through the imposition of federal standards regarding benefit levels and duration of benefits. Business groups such as the Chamber of Commerce and the National Association of Manufacturers pressured Congress to reject any reform proposals that amounted to an effective nationalization of the existing decentralized system. This conflict reached its peak during 1966 when separate versions of a reform bill passed both houses of Congress. While the Senate version contained the controversial federal standards, the House version did not. The bill finally died in Conference Committee because neither house was willing to back down on the issue of federal standards. Second, business conditions throughout the mid and late 1960s were prosperous for the most part and kept unemployment rates low throughout most of the nation. This economic prosperity helped to relieve much of the financial pressure which had threatened state systems throughout the 1950s and early 1960s. Indeed, 1969 represented a symbolic watershed in the history of unemployment insurance in the United States for it was the first year since 1955 that all outstanding loans by the Reed fund to state trust funds had been repaid. On the surface, the state federal unemployment insurance system appeared to be a sound social insurance program that had met the economic and political needs of the nation for forty years. In fact, such was far from the case. Within three years it became strikingly clear that 1969 actually only marked the calm before the storm.

V

The supposedly fiscally conservative, states' rights oriented administration of Richard Nixon was responsible for getting through Congress the first permanent institutional changes in the unemployment insurance system since 1954, in the form of the Employment Security Amendments of 1970. Like the earlier Democratic administrations, the Nixon administration believed that unemployment insurance should play a major role in protecting workers from the financial hardships of unemployment and in maintaining aggregate purchasing power during economic downturns. Similarly, it recognized that:

> unemployment insurance fails to serve its intended purpose completely either in aiding unemployed individuals or in bolstering the economy because of several major deficiencies in the program. Large groups of workers are excluded from UI coverage. The weekly cash benefits are inadequate in amount and too limited in duration. And there are serious problems connected with the statutory requirements for eligibility and disqualification, and their administration and with the financing of the program. (U.S. Dept. of Treasury, p. 141)

Unlike the Kennedy and Johnson administrations, however, the Nixon administration rejected the idea that a wholesale nationalization of the existing system through the imposition of federal standards was either desirable or necessary. "Unemployment insurance," explained Nixon in a message to Congress on July 8, 1969, "is one of the foremost examples of creative federal-state partnership . . . . This makes the system far more flexible and attuned to local needs and special circumstances of local economies" (Nixon, 1970, p. 496). While calling upon the individual states to provide adequate benefits to achieve the welfare and countercyclicial goals of the unemployment insurance program within two years, the Nixon administration continued to argue that the existing system could be reformed into a more effective countercyclical tool without completely altering the decentralized institutional structure upon which it traditionally had been based.

The Employment Security Amendments of 1970 transformed the existing unemployment insurance system in three ways. First, they raised the federal unemployment insurance tax from 3.1% to 3.2% (thereby raising the effective federal tax after the offset from .4% to .5%) and the taxable wage base from $3,000 to $4,200. Second, they extended coverage to an additional 4.8 million workers to bring the percentage of the workforce covered under all state and federal unemployment insurance programs up to approximately 84%.[8] Third, they established a permanent program that would extend the duration of regular unemployment insurance benefits up to a maximum of 39 weeks during serious regional and national economic recessions. The program was to be triggered into operation whenever the national insured unemployment rate reached 4.5% for three consecutive months or in specific states according to a slightly more complicated formula. Unlike either the Eisenhower or the Kennedy programs, this new permanent program was to be jointly financed by the federal and state governments. The 50% federal portion of the extended benefits program was to be financed through a new account in the Treasury's Unemployment Trust Fund, the Extended Unemployment Compensation Account (EUCA), which itself would be funded by a portion of the .5% federal unemployment insurance tax. The remaining state portion of the extended benefits program was to be financed by normal state unemployment insurance taxes.

However successfully the Employment Security Amendments met the political demands of the Nixon administration to preserve the decentralized institutional structure of the unemployment insurance system, it became apparent by late 1971 that they had not converted the system into an effective countercyclical tool of the Federal Government capable of dealing with the economic problems of the 1970s. As the nation slipped into the first major recession since 1961, certain state systems found themselves unable to meet either the countercyclical or the welfare demands made upon them even with the new extended benefits program. Unemployment in America's post-Vietnam era of stagflation proved to be of longer duration than that of the 1950s and 1960s, and to be concentrated much more in certain regions of the economy than in others (see Northeast-Midwest Institute, 1978). Rather than resolving the conflicting goals built into the unemployment insurance system since 1935, the 1970 reforms only intensified the tensions between them.

The response of Congress to the economic debacle of the 1970s mirrored that taken by the Kennedy administration in 1961. A series of temporary benefits programs were passed that extended benefits coverage beyond the 39 weeks provided by the 1970 reforms and gave the federal government a major new role to play in the financing of long-term unemployment benefits. The first such program, established by the Emergency Unemployment Compensation Act of 1971, provided 13 additional weeks of emergency benefits coverage between February 1972 and July 1972 for workers in states with particularly high rates of unemployment who had exhausted their regular and extended benefits. In order to trigger the program, a state's unemployment rate had to reach or exceed 6.5% for a 13-week period. Unlike the permanent extended benefits program established by the 1970 Amendments, the Emergency Unemployment Compensation Act was 100% federally financed. While these funds initially came directly from the Federal Treasury, under provisions of another act which extended the program to March 1973, financing was transferred to the federal portion of the unemployment insurance tax through the EUCA. There was also a temporary increase of .08% in the Federal Unemployment Tax going to the EUCA to finance the program. With the return of heavy long-term unemployment during the 1974–75 recession, Congress enacted two additional temporary extension programs that were modeled on the 1971 program and that extended emergency benefits in states with excessively high rates of unemployment to 52 weeks initially and later to 65 weeks. As was the case with the 1971 program, these programs were financed through the EUCA by the federal unemployment insurance tax.

The significance of these temporary extension programs to the institutional development of the unemployment insurance system in the United States was twofold. First, they enabled the federal government to pump large sums of money into various targeted states' economies in a relatively short period of time in order to maintain aggregate purchasing power during periods of severe economic decline (see Table 1). Between 1975 and 1977, these extension programs enabled the Federal Government to pay out an additional $6.2 billion in supplemental benefits to states with particularly high levels of unemployment that was above and beyond the $6.56 billion paid out under the permanent extension program. Second, they helped to push the federal portion of the unemployment insurance system, the EUCA, into serious financial crisis. Under the provisions of the 1970 Amendments, states were not required to adopt the permanent extension program until 1972. Nevertheless, because of high levels of unemployment during 1971, many states did so early. As a result, the extended benefits program was triggered in almost half of the states during the 1971–1972 recession. When the program went into effect nationwide in January 1972, the national trigger already had been superceded and, for a short time, extended benefits were available to all state programs. Given early implementation and early triggering of the extension program, the EUCA had not collected enough

Table 1.   Unemployment Compensation
Benefits Paid by Program
(in billions of dollars)

Calendar Year	Regular Benefits	Extended Benefits	Federal Supplemental Benefits	Total
1971	4.95	.66	a	5.61
1972	4.48	.48	.56	5.52
1973	4.01	.14	.01	4.17
1974	5.98	.54	a	6.52
1975	11.75	2.49	2.13	16.37
1976	8.97	2.29	2.81	14.07
1977	8.34	1.78	1.25	11.37
1978	8.62	.71	.02	9.35
1979	9.26	.25	a	9.51
1980	14.49	1.70	a	16.19
1981	14.11	1.30	a	15.41

[a]Programs not authorized
Source: Hearing Before the Committee on Finance, United States Senate, 97th cong., 2nd sess., July 29, 1982.

funds through the federal unemployment insurance tax to finance fully the federal share of the program. It was forced to borrow money directly from the General Treasury in order to meet its obligations (see Table 2). While these loans were to be repaid by future revenues from the federal unemployment insurance tax, repayment was not quick in coming. Indeed, the temporary extension programs passed in 1971, 1974, and 1975 quite literally overwhelmed in EUCA. In 1974, the EUCA was in debt to the Federal Treasury for $300 million. This debt ballooned to $1.5 billion in 1975 and to $6.5 billion in 1976. Despite a temporary increase in the federal unemployment insurance tax in 1977 of .2%, specifically aimed at repaying these loans, the EUCA continued to face serious financial difficulties throughout the decade. In 1978, the cumulative debt of the EUCA to the Federal Treasury stood at $8.7 billion. $5.8 billion of this debt was attributable directly to the supplemental benefits programs which finally expired in 1978 (Padilla, 1981, p. 35).

The financial crisis confronting the EUCA actually was only one part of the financial crisis that faced the unemployment insurance system in the 1970s. With the emergence of high rates of unemployment the financial problems which threatened to undermine some state programs during the 1950s and 1960s returned with a vengeance. Beginning with Connecticut in 1972, several states began to borrow heavily from the Reed Fund again. Between 1975 and 1977, the peak years of this borrowing activity, 25 states borrowed over $4.6 billion in interest-free loans

Table 2.   Debt Owed by the Unemployment Trust
Fund to the General Fund (in billions of dollars)

Fiscal Year	Regular State Programs	Extended and Supplemental Benefits	Total
1972	0	.2	.2
1973	0	0[a]	0[a]
1974	0	.3	.3
1975	0	1.5	1.5
1976	2.9	6.5	9.4
1977	4.1	8.7	12.8
1978	5.0	8.7	13.7
1979	5.0	7.9	12.9
1980	5.1	7.6	12.6
1981	6.1	7.0	13.1

[a]Less than $50 million

Source: Hearing before the Committee on Finance, United States Senate,
97th cong., 2nd sess., July 29, 1982.

Table 3.   States with Outstanding
Federal Loan Balances to the
Federal Unemployment Account
(the Reed Fund) as of March 1981

State	Amount Outstanding[a]
Arkansas	62.5
Connecticut	368.8
Delaware	49.3
District of Columbia	59.3
Illinois	1280.8
Kentucky	30.0
Maine	36.2
Michigan	886.0
Minnesota	99.8
New Jersey	659.1
Ohio	520.9
Pennsylvania	1530.8
Puerto Rico	84.4
Rhode Island	120.9
Vermont	40.6
Virgin Islands	7.1
West Virginia	99.8

[a]In billions of dollars

Source: Arthur Padilla, "'The Unemployment Insurance System: Its Financial Structure,"
Monthly Labor Review (December, 1981),
p.33.

from the Reed Fund (see Table 3). For the most part, borrowing was concentrated in the industrial states of the northeast and the midwest that were particularly hard hit by the decade's two recessions. Pennsylvania, Illinois, New Jersey, and Michigan alone were responsible for two-thirds of the debt owed to the Reed Fund. Significantly, these financial problems generally were not the result of excessive benefits provisions or underfunded unemployment insurance programs in those particular states. On the contrary, as was discovered in a study conducted by the W. E. Upjohn Institute for Employment Research for the Michigan Department of Labor in 1977, those states with debts to the Reed Fund also were taxing employers at considerably higher levels. The study concluded that "The argument that low tax rates and liberal provisions are the cause of the current unemployment insurance crisis simply does not stand up against the facts. The clear cause of the financing crisis is the extraordinary high level of unemployment in the 1974–75 recession" (Blaustein and Kozlowski, 1978).

Given the intensity of the demands made upon the Reed Fund for loans and its limited financial reserve, the Reed Fund was forced to borrow money directly from the Federal Treasury, much like the EUCA, simply to remain solvent. In 1976, it borrowed $2.6 billion; in 1977, $1.25 billion; and in 1978, $.86 billion. By the end of 1979, the Reed Fund owed the Federal Treasury $4.98 billion (see U.S. Dept. of Treasury, *Annual Report* for appropriate years).

The financial problems which confronted the unemployment insurance system throughout the 1970s revealed with striking clarity the failure of the 1970 amendments to resolve the tensions which had been built into the program since 1935. As the supplemental programs had demonstrated, even the reformed unemployment insurance system did not adequately meet the needs of workers or the concerns of policymakers during periods of severe long-term unemployment. Moreover, the 1970 amendments ultimately intensified the regional disparities which had threatened the system from the late 1940s to the early 1960s. States effectively were compelled to help finance an additional 13 weeks of extended benefits during periods of high unemployment. In order to meet these new burdens, many states turned to the Reed Fund for assistance. This was at best a temporary solution. Under the provisions of legislation passed in 1960, states were required to repay the full amount borrowed from the Reed Fund within 2 years. Failure to do so would lead to an automatic .3% reduction in the employer's tax credit that would increase each year by .3% until the loan were repaid. In other words, states that borrowed money from the Reed Fund and faced high rates of unemployment for any significant length of time in the 1970s soon found themselves facing a most unpleasant situation:

either they could raise state unemployment insurance taxes immediately and thereby repay their loan from the Reed Fund, or they could wait until the two-year period had expired and then have their employer tax offset gradually decreased. In either case, the taxes being paid by state employers would increase at precisely that time Keynesianism said it should not: in the middle of a recession. In the end, the 1970 reform only enhanced the contradictions that had existed historically between the highly decentralized institutional structure of the unemployment insurance system and a Keynesian countercyclical policy orientation.

The financial crises confronting various state trust funds, the Reed Fund, and the EUCA reopened the debate over the role of the Federal Government in the post-1970 unemployment insurance system. Much as during earlier debates over the system, Keynesian arguments played a major role in shaping various groups' perceptions of the problems confronting the system. The AFL-CIO, for example, drew heavily upon Keynesian ideas as it renewed its call for a larger role for the Federal Government in the system as a whole. While reaffirming its traditional support for minimum benefit and financing standards, the AFL-CIO also argued that the permanent state-federal extension program had to be replaced by a 100% federally funded program of 26 weeks. From its perspective, the current program simply did not meet either the welfare or the countercyclical demands that were being placed upon it by the heavy long-term and regionally concentrated unemployment of the 1970s. Business groups, such as the Chamber of Commerce, on the other hand, maintained their traditional opposition to an increasingly nationalized system. They argued that the temporary extension programs represented a dangerous development in the history of the unemployment insurance system. Not only did the programs undermine the financial integrity of the system as a whole, but they maintained that by extending the provision of benefits to more than a year in duration they threatened to transform the system into a new welfare program. In contrast to organized labor, they called upon the Federal Government to stop instituting such ad hoc programs and to return the EUCA to solvency by financing the indebtedness brought on by these programs through General Revenues.[9]

Far more controversial than the debate over the EUCA was that over the problem of state indebtedness. Beginning in 1976, a series of proposals were introduced into Congress by representatives of debt-ridden northeastern and midwestern states that would have had the Federal Government assume a larger role in financing unemployment insurance in states facing serious unemployment problems. Among those were proposals that would have provided for such things as reinsurance for states against excessively high levels of unemployment, cost equalization that would have spread the costs of concentrated high unemployment across the nation, as a whole, and simple debt forgiveness (see Northeast-Midwest Institute, 1978, pp. 3–49). Representatives from debt-free states, such as Congressman J. J. Pickle from Texas, tended to oppose such proposals simply on a cost-benefit analysis to their particular state. Representatives from the northeast and the midwest, on the other hand, argued that the unemployment insurance system had to be restructured to meet the problems of catastrophic high unemployment. As Robert Mulcahy III, the chief of staff to Governor Byrne of New Jersey, explained in testimony before a House subcommitte, "the solution to the problem is beyond the scope of the program as it exists today. We are dealing with a problem that is national in scope and a crisis that clearly requires Federal direction and initiative" (Mulcahy, 1978, p. 185).

Calls by financially strapped states for an immediate resolution to the financial crises facing the unemployment insurance system ultimately were set aside by Congress in favor of a much more cautious strategy. In 1975 and 1977, bills were enacted to delay until 1981 the mandatory federal unemployment insurance tax increases that would have gone into effect in states that had not repaid their loans from the Reed Fund within two years. In 1976, legislation was passed to combat the growing deficits by raising the taxable wage base from $4200 to $6000 and temporarily increasing the federal unemployment insurance tax rate from .5% to .7%. The legislation also required that tax rates return to .5% by the end of the year in which an advance of general revenues to EUCA had been repaid. None of this legislation proposed any fundamental restructuring in the existing unemployment insurance system. It only pushed the day of reckoning facing the system into the not too distant future.

In the place of reform, the 1976 legislation established a national commission to study the problems facing the unemployment insurance system and to present to Congress possible solutions to them. The commission's final report, delivered in the fall of 1980, called for a considerable nationalization of the existing system including the imposition of federal minimum standards for benefits and financing and for certain proposals to alleviate the financial pressures confronting state trust funds with federal monies (National Commission, 1980). For the most part, the commission's recommendations were ignored by Congress. Few congresspersons wanted to grapple with a problem as difficult and conflict-laden as the financial condition of the unemployment insurance system. Fewer still were receptive to the commission's proposals to nationalize the system further in order to solve its current problem.

Calls by the Carter Administration to pass a new supplemental benefits program in 1980 were ignored by Congress even with an election at stake. The Reagan Administration, for its part, began its term in office by taking a hard-line approach by trying to restore some solvency to the unemployment insurance system as a whole. In 1981, states with outstanding debts to the Reed Fund of over three years old found their employer tax offset decreased by .3%.[10] This was to be allowed to increase each year to a maximum of 3.4% until the loan was paid off. In addition, in the 1981 reconciliation bill, the Administration made it more difficult for states to qualify for extended benefits by raising the insured jobless rate needed to trigger the extended benefits program from 4% to 5%.

The impact of the Reagan initiatives on the unemployment insurance system was startling. Unemployment remained unexpectedly high throughout 1981. Far from simply penalizing states from taking out new loans, the interest penalties placed an additional burden on already strapped state systems. Michigan, for example, faced a 17% unemployment rate in early 1983. Despite having raised the unemployment wage base, tightened eligibility, and frozen benefits, Michigan found itself having to request an additional $530 million loan to add to the $2,335 billion already borrowed from the federal government. Michigan was not alone in its plight. It was estimated by the Labor Department that by the end of 1984, the total state debt to the Reed Fund would rise to $23 billion. Significantly, a large portion of this debt would be concentrated in "smokestack industry" states, such as Ohio, Illinois, Pennsylvania, as well as Michigan, that probably would not be able to pay off their debt for some time to come ("Jobless," 1983).

As the 1982 election approached, pressures mounted on both Congress and the Administration to respond to the record levels of unemployment. In August a new extended unemployment benefits program passed Congress as part of a tax bill to reduce the federal deficit. The bill provided an additional 6 to 10 weeks of unemployment benefits on top of the 39 weeks already in effect. The impact of the new program was muted by the fact that the earlier changes in the permanent extended benefits program had made it more difficult for states to qualify for the additional 13-week program. At the very time the new program was taking effect in some states with high unemployment, the permanent program was triggering off.

By the end of 1983, it appeared that the nation's economy was at last moving out of recession for the first time in over two years. Nevertheless, unemployment rates remained stubbornly high and many states found themselves remaining dependent upon the federal government for keeping their unemployment insurance systems in operation. Ironically, Texas, a state with a seemingly recession-proof economy in the 1970s, found itself drawing upon the federal coffers at the very time the economic recovery was being announced by the Administration. As the nation moved closer to the 1984 election, the prospects of alleviating the financial crises confronting the unemployment insurance system in the near future did not appear bright.

VI

The debate over the institutional structure of the unemployment insurance system mirrors, in many respects, the debate which has taken place over the American federal system since the New Deal. The financial crises which currently threaten the system reflect a larger set of political and economic problems which have emerged out of the attempt to restructure the traditional federal system to meet the needs of a modern political economy. The Social Security Act was undoubtedly a major watershed in the institutional development of the modern American state. It consciously sought to balance the requirements of America's traditional federal system of government with the needs and demands of an advanced capitalist society. The Social Security Act did not permanently resolve the question of the role that the national government would play in the modern American state. There have been a series of attempts since 1935 to centralize further the relatively decentralized unemployment insurance system established under the Social Security Act. These attempts have been linked directly to the idea that the existing unemployment insurance system should be transformed into an effective countercyclical tool of the national government. Keynesian arguments have been appealed to time and time again by groups and regions as a way to legitimate their claims that the Federal Government would have to assume a greater role in the unemployment insurance system if the system was going to meet the demands of an advanced industrial society.

The 1970 reforms were the culmination of a series of attempts to transform the unemployment insurance system into a strong countercyclical weapon of the Federal Government which preserved its traditional decentralized structure. The financial crises which have plagued the system throughout the 1970s and early 1980s are the clearest indication of how badly this attempt failed. Whether the existing decentralized system of unemployment insurance can or should be restructured to meet the enormous demands of national countercyclical policy in the 1980s remains one of the most complex and troubling questions facing social insurance policymakers today. However this question is resolved, one point remains clear: the current financial crises confronting the unemployment insurance system will continue to play a major role in shaping the debate over the future structure of the American welfare state in the latter decades of the twentieth century.

NOTES

1. See Nelson for an extended discussion of pre-1935 attempts to establish an unemployment insurance program in individual states.

2. Subject employers under the 1935 act included firms with eight or more employees. This was lowered to firms with four or more employees in 1954 and to firms with one or more employees in 1970. The $3,000 wage base was raised to $4,200 in 1972 and to $6,000 in 1978. Significantly, states can have a higher taxable wage base for state unemployment taxes if they so desire.

3. In 1945, a temporary account, the George Fund, was established in the federal unemployment trust fund from which states might borrow when their own trust fund dropped to a certain level. Authorization for this account was renewed in 1947 to extend until 1949. No states actually borrowed money from the account.

4. Under the Federal Unemployment Tax Act of 1954, coverage was extended to include firms employing 4 or more workers for 20 weeks beginning January 1, 1956. In addition, it permitted states to apply the experience rating reduction to new employers after 1 year's experience rather than three.

5. In effect the Employment Security Administrative Financing Act of 1954 made the temporary loan account established in the late 1940s a permanent feature of the unemployment insurance system.

6. Business groups, however, remained adamant in their opposition to any expansion or "improvement" of the program at either the state or the federal level.

7. The peak period of borrowing for these three states was between 1958 and 1963. All loans were repaid by 1968.

8. Coverage was expanded again in 1976 to include approximately 98% of the workforce.

9. Numerous House and Senate hearings took up this problem from 1976–1980. See in particular *Repayment of Loans Made to State Unemployment Compensation Programs.* Hearing before the Subcommittee on Unemployment and Related Problems of the Committee on Finance, U.S. Senate, 96th Congress, 2nd Session, on H. R. 4007, April 28, 1980.

10. By March 1981, Connecticut, Delaware, the District of Columbia, Illinois, Maine, New Jersey, Pennsylvania, Puerto Rico, Rhode Island, Vermont, and the Virgin Islands were all making repayments through reduced employer credits towards Federal taxes. See "Jobless Benefits: A Vicious Cycle," *Business Week* (February 21, 1983), p. 123.

REFERENCES

Altmeyer, Arthur J. (1968), *The Formative Years of Social Security,* Madison: University of Wisconsin Press.

Blaustein, S. J. and P. J. Kozlowski (1978), "Interstate Differences in Unemployment Insurance Benefit Costs: A Cross Section Study," Kalamazoo, MI: W. E. Upjohn Institute for Employment Research, March.

Congressional Record, January 17, 1935.

Congressional Record, July 15, 1954.

Garraty, John A. (1978), *Unemployment in History,* New York: Harper and Row.

"Jobless Benefits: A Vicious Cycle," *Business Week* (February 21, 1983).

Kennedy, John Fitzgerald (1962), "Special Message to the Congress: Program for Economic Recovery and Growth, February 2, 1961," *Public Papers of the Presidents of the*

United States: John F. Kennedy, 1961, Washington, D.C.: U.S. Government Printing Office, p. 46.

Malisoff, Harry (1963), *The Financing of Extended Unemployment Insurance Benefits in the United States,* Kalamazoo, MI: W. E. Upjohn Institute for Employment Research.

Mulcuhy, Robert, III (1978), "Testimony before the Subcommittee of Public Assistance and Unemployment Compensation of the Committee on Ways and Means," U.S. Congress, House, Committee on Ways and Means, *Hearing Before the Subcommittee of Public Assistance and Unemployment Compensation,* 95th Congr., 2nd sess., August 10 and 11.

National Commission on Unemployment Compensation (1980), *Final Report,* Washington, D.C.: U.S. Government Printing Office.

Nelson, Daniel (1969), *Unemployment Insurance: the American Experience, 1915–1935,* Madison: University of Wisconsin Press.

Nixon, Richard M. (1970), "Special Message to the Congress on the Unemployment Insurance System, July 8, 1969," *Public Papers of the Presidents of the United States: Richard M. Nixon, 1969,* Washington, D.C.: U.S. Government Printing Office, p. 496.

Northeast-Midwest Institute (1978), *The Crisis in Unemployment Insurance: A Regional Analysis,* Washington, D.C.: August.

Padilla, Arthur (1981), "The Unemployment Insurance System: Its Financial Structure," *The Monthly Labor Review* (December).

Polanyi, Karl (1944), *The Great Transformation,* Boston: Beacon Press.

U.S. Congress, House, Committee on Ways and Means (1954), *House Report 83-2001,* 83rd Congr., 2nd sess.

U.S. Congress, House, Committee on Ways and Means (1958), *Minority Report to House Report 85-1656,* 85th Congr., 2nd sess.

U.S. Congress, Senate, Committee on Finance (1980), *Repayment of Loans Made to State Unemployment Compensation Programs,* Hearing Before the Subcommittee on Unemployment and Related Problems, 96th Congr., 2nd sess., on H. R. 4007, April 28.

U.S. Congress, Senate, Committee on Finance (1982), *Hearing Before the Committee on Finance,* 97th Congr., 2nd sess., July 29.

U.S. Department of Labor (1970), *Manpower Report of the President, March 1970.*

U.S. Department of the Treasury, *Annual Reports of the Secretary of the Treasury on the State of Finances* (appropriate years).

Witte, Edwin (1963), *The Development of the Social Security Act,* Madison: University of Wisconsin Press.

THE INDEXATION OF PENSION ENTITLEMENTS:

THE WEST GERMAN INITIATIVE IN COMPARATIVE PERSPECTIVE

Arnold J. Heidenheimer

Consideration of German social insurance, and social security systems in several other Western democracies, often evokes ambiguities similar to those described by Robert Musil in his novel, *The Man Without Qualities*. In the novel we are told about the elaborate preparations to celebrate the 70th anniversary of Emperor Franz Joseph of Austria, when we know that the celebration will be aborted by the outbreak of World War I and the subsequent disintegration of the Austrian empire. If such a scenario is not being paralleled in the current social security anniversary celebration it is because while modern government may exhibit many signs of encrusted traditions, they have proved more capable of adapting and innovating than the Hapsburg system did in its final decades. The West German social security system, the direct heir of the Bismarckian legislation, has made numerous innovations during the post-1945 period. Perhaps the most important of these was the introduction of "dynamic pensions" in the late 1950s, through which the principle of indexation was first implemented on a large scale in a major social insurance program.

In the German pensions system, most of the costs are met by equal contributions from workers and employers, with a state subsidy providing an additional source which has varied between 15 and 19% in recent decades. In the 1950s, prior to the indexation move, worker/employer contributions were slightly above 15% of gross wages, and protected slightly more than two-thirds of the work force. Average pensions then paid about 28% of net after-tax average wages. But in recent years this proportion has risen to about the 45% level, while the money value has increased more than tenfold, from 60 DM in 1949 to 641 DM in 1978. (For a fuller description of the structure of the present West Germany Social Security System and the interdependence of its programs, see Altenstetter's chapter.)

THE POST-1945 SOCIAL SECURITY STRUGGLES

The West German decision to index social security pensions came in 1957, toward the end of Chancellor Adenauer's second term of office. The detailed historical analysis of Hans Günther Hockerts (1981) makes it possible to relate the emergence of this decision from the complicated struggles of the preceding decade over the question of whether the many separate insurance networks and offices could be integrated into one over-arching *Einheitsversicherung*. It also makes possible a more informed judgment on whether this innovation can be considered as more the result of unparalleled age of the German social insurance organizations or more the result of a structural transformation of the post-1945 West German embryo state, emerging from the new constellation of the CDU/CSU and the founding of the Federal Republic.

After 1945, the initial plans of social insurance "integrationists" called for consolidating the sickness, pension and accident insurance funds and offices, and for liquidating the many separate funds which looked after the social security needs of distinct socioeconomic groups, such as white-collar employees. these plans were initially favored by social policy officials within all military governments. They were particularly supported by the trade unions, who sought to regain the strong influence they had exercised on the pre-Hitler sickness and other insurance organizations. The reform plans called for merging the various enterprise and occupational insurance funds into the larger Local Sickness funds, and would have strengthened union influence over more of the insurance system. The integration plans were broadly backed by those on the left and center who saw in the occupational-stratified insurance structures one more impediment to the democratization of German social and economic life.

What happened to the *Einheitsversicherung* goal was eventually rather similar to what happened to the *Einheitsschule* goal in education, and other structural reforms aimed at the departicularization and/or socialization of German institutions. But, whereas education was to again become primarily a *Land* jurisdiction, since the Second Reich, social insurance had always been exclusively subject to national legislation. So the maneuvering was not only over interim degrees and regulations which might affect subsequent legislation, but also over control of the relevant bureaucracies. The infrastructure of the British occupation zone, which favored the rise to West German leadership of party politicians Kurt Schumacher and Konrad Adenauer, seemed to favor an institutional solution promoting national integration. A German-staffed Central Labor office for the British zone, established in summer of 1946 in Lemgo under several veterans of the Reich Labor Ministry, pursued a course closely linked to the union position, and for a while was highly influential.

It was only later that the "traditionalist" opponents of integration captured a strong bureaucratic position, after the CSU took over the Bavarian Labor Ministry in September, 1947. Bureaucrats who had headed the social insurance division of the Reich ministry in the Weimar period made this their base for a campaign to strengthen opposition to integration plans. They exhibited an "almost missionary zeal" in defending the insurance tradition as "a gift of the German people to the world," and found it "shameful" that German reformers had sought Allied intervention in a policy sector in which Germany had exhibited leadership for over sixty years. This attitude was embraced by CDU politicians like Adenauer, who attacked William Beveridge when the latter toured Germany to support the reform position. It also rallied white-collar, medical and other vested interests, and even won resonance among some SPD and union veterans who defended the older institutions.

The five shaping years from 1947 to 1952 were filled with partisan struggles in successive parliamentary settings over the capture of the most influential bureaucratic positions in the inter-zonal and then Federal offices. Personnel from the more highly-developed Lemgo office stiil formed the core of the bi-zonal Labor Directorate established in Frankfurt in 1948–1949, which was headed by a former Christian trade unionist, Anton Storch, who sought compromises between the two entrenched positions. Pressure from the CDU *Sozialausschüsse*, the CDU'S labor wing, also induced Adenauer to name Storch as Federal Labor minister in his 1949 cabinet. But as a concession to the CSU, FDP and DP portions of his coalitions he named the senior traditionalist as State Secretary. One of the "open secrets" of his administration was that he was to serve as watchdog on his own minister. The State Secretary's most dedicated comrade-at-arms was named to head the social insurance section, and it was only a matter of time until the nonconformist former colleague who had headed the Lemgo office was forced to "emigrate" to a position with the International Labor Organization in Geneva.

If one were to characterize the intensity of the German discussion about the organizational questions on social insurance in graphic form, the high point of the curve would lie in the 1946–1948 period. The decisive legislation was passed in the early 1950s, but by then the unions and the SPD realized that they had no hope of getting their principles accepted. Thus the multiplicity of funds was largely maintained, union influence was checked by the adoption of the parity representation in several key funds, and the separate insurances for white-collar workers were maintained. The changed emphasis in the SPD was epitomized by the fact that the individual who had headed the integrated insurance *Anstalt* in Berlin in 1946 had a decade later become the "social policy pope" of the SPD Parliamentary party by pursuing a policy of conciliation toward the white-collar and middle-class groups.

In pointing its efforts away from structural reform and toward substantive benefit questions, the SPD was effectively angling for support among the pensioner and other transfer recipients whose living standards had been held down while Erhard manipulated fiscal and taxation policies so as to favor the investments and labor policies which helped produce the German "miracle." Later, in the 1970s, academic and other critics were to chide the Social Democrats for abandoning the larger reform goals too readily. But by anticipating the spirit of the Bad Godesberg program, the centrist SPD *Sozialpolitiker* depoliticized social policy largely by muting attacks on status based privileges, such as the *Berufsunfaehigheit* principle in disability pensions (Tennstedt, 1976).

THE EMERGENCE OF THE "DYNAMIC PENSION" PLAN

The developments sketched above are more than prelude, but are essential for understanding how the Adenauer government of 1953–1957, based on a slight CDU/CSU majority, and marginally dependent on unstable smaller coalition parties, was able to produce legislation for the "dynamische Rente" in time for the 1957 elections. After permitting profits to rise steeply, Adenauer had to do something dramatic for those who had not benefitted from the economic revival, as the CDU's labor wing strongly demanded. On most issues, German ministers cannot maintain in Bundestag standing committees the kind of control that British ministers are usually able to maintain in the House of Commons.

In that context the possibility of an effective coalition between the CDU left wing and the SPD opposition party, perhaps covertly supported by the Labor Minister, was one that Adenauer could not ignore.

Another unusual characteristic of the mid-1950s was the high price Adenauer had to pay for handing control of the federal machinery back to the old social policy hands. Connoisseurs of German bureaucratic modes would not have expected these old-timers to show their gratitude by being especially responsive to the Chancellory. But they might have thought that Adenauer's state secretary, Hans Globke, would be in a position to make the ministerial bureaucracy fall into line when the Chancellor really wanted it so. This hardly proved to be the case. Referring to the head of the Labor Ministry's social insurance division, Hockerts describes him as having achieved his ultimate goal through the reconstitution of the traditional institutional structures. He all but refused to call a consultive committee into session, cast "sarcastic irony" on most reform talk, and gave the cold shoulder to attempts to follow up on promises which his ministers had given the legislature about the presentation of a comprehensive "Sozialreform" which the Chancellor had announced in the 1953 government program.

The Labor Ministry's failure to produce a plan to rationalize the social insurance sector gave the Finance Ministry under Fritz Schaeffer an opening to seek to take the initiative at the start of the second Adenauer government. The Finance Ministry hoped to limit expenditure increases through relating social security entitlements more to proved need, creating an integrated file of all recipients, and restructuring the social budget. It prompted the creation of an inter-ministerial government commission, and for the next several years it, together with the Economic Ministry and sometimes Adenauer himself, tried to get the Labor Ministry to accede to this idea. For a few months everybody in Bonn outside the Labor Ministry suddenly discovered the virtues of the British Royal Commission, as the push to promote such a structure under "neutral" chairmanship enrolled even some left-wing CDU ministers, like Jakob Kaiser. But by using every stratagem at its disposal the Labor Ministry managed to frustrate this plan, and to keep jurisdiction by creating yet another committee headed by one of its own officials. The Chancellor's repeated admonitions to come up with the promised *Sozialplan* draft had no noticeable affects. Backed by Storch's Christian trade union friends in the Bundestag, and by the pensioner and other lobbyists, the "iron triangle" held firm. The stream of caustic aspersions on the Ministry's efficacy only added to the increasing pollution of the Rhine.

The concept of the "dynamische Rente" gradually emerged out of the ashes of bureaucratic chagrin. Its first contours can be identified in the plan for a pension reform which the Labor Ministry circulated in 1954 in an attempt to divert attention from its larger failure and to capture attention. But in the meantime Adenauer was reaching outside bureaucratic channels, literally by using family connections to elicit proposals from academic social scientists. He was motivated by the fact that while the CDU had been inactive and relied on bureaucratic conflict, the SPD was busy preparing a well-constructed pension reform proposal. During a joint vacation in Switzerland, Adenauer's son, Paul, interested the Chancellor in the pension proposals of a Bonn University economist, Wilfried Schreiber. These went beyond conventional insurance concepts to envision the program as an "inter-generational solidarity contract," which would tie pension levels to both the living standards of wage-earners and to currency fluctuations. But unlike the Labor Ministry's draft, it made the contributions the independent and not the dependent variable in the pension level formula (Hockerts, 1981, p. 314).

Although the cabinet's social policy committee had by no means accepted the Schreiber proposals as the basis for legislative proposals, between Christmas and New Year 1955 Adenauer approved the "dynamic pensions" principles contained in a draft worked out within the Chancellory. His staff passed word of his position on to both the Labor Ministry and the CDU Party committee. Adenauer then personally turned back criticisms in the CDU executive that the proposals favored public pensioners over those enrolled with private insurance companies, by exclaiming that "after all we are not here to crack the private insurance companies' hard nuts" (Hockerts, 1981, p. 323). He supported indexing both because it would engender a long-term political remedy and because it would protect the determination of benefit levels from electoral competition.

The ensuing pensions war lasted to the time of parliamentary approval in January, 1957. Almost all significant Bonn institutions took sides in what the press labelled a pension war of enormous scope. In that conflict, the opponents seemed close to victory on several occasions. We can only allude to some of its overarching characteristics and to a few symptomatic engagements.

What is particularly striking for an observer looking back from the 1980s is how it was possible to defeat an opposition which represented almost all economic and fiscal institutions and interests within and outside the government. On several occasions, Erhard, Schaeffer and their allies "rehearsed a mutiny" against the basic wage-related formula accepted by Adenauer and the Labor Ministry (Hockerts, 1981, p. 348). They were joined by the explicit criticism from the *Bundesbank*. And subsequently all the entrepreneurial interest groups issued dire warnings about inflationary and other consequences. The most persistent opposition theme inside the cabinet was that wage-related pensions would convert the pensioners from adherents of stable money into natural allies of the trade unions in inflationary directions. Even the emergence of a second currency, based on the "Dyn-mark," was anticipated.

The main parliamentary struggle occurred within the CDU/CSU, with the Finance Ministry openly trying to encourage opposition. Adenauer had to repeatedly warn Fritz Schaeffer that the cabinet proposal constituted guidelines (*Richtlinien*), which the Chancellor expected cabinet ministers to respect. He admitted to numerous audiences that the cabinet presented a "disastrous picture" to the public. Since the SPD had endorsed a plan very similar to the government bill, passage of an opposition bill by the SPD and part of the CDU was a likely prospect, and would have undermined the electoral image of Adenauer and the CDU in the coming election campaign. The Chancellory had to almost force the two warring ministries to maintain some contact with each other, and Hockert chides the Finance Ministry for the "stupendous stubbornness" of its position in the autumn of 1956.

The position of Erhard and his Economics Ministry was important because Erhard was the political hero of the day, and because of the emerging question of whether he would become Adenauer's successor as Chancellor. By and large the limited evidence tends to make Adenauer's skepticism about Erhard's larger political capabilities comprehensible. One finds Erhard usually following in the Finance Minister's train, and the Economics Ministry does not emerge as an independent force in assessing macro-economic consequences. Within the cabinet Erhard missed opportunities to press home neo-liberal reservations, and repeatedly caved in when Adenauer undercut his compromise proposals or asked him to withdraw his public statements (Hockerts, 1981, pp. 329, 402, 407).

Alarming questions of financing capability were raised, of course, in the discussions. The government's projections envisioned that the social security tax rate would have to be raised to 14% in the first decade, and to 16.25% in the second and third decades. By contrast, the leading private insurance actuaries projected, in relation to the government draft, that contributions would have to increase to 24.2% in the early 1980s. Actually, the rate was increased to 18% in 1978, and 18.5% in 1982, which was still in line with a revised third-decade estimate by the Ministry in 1957. In contrast to the later American experience (Derthick, 1979), actuarial estimates were not left to the experts to fight over, but were exposed to very wide public discussion. Indeed, journalists identified a battle between the insurance mathematicians as a key component of a very visible large pension war.

The adoption of the pension reform law on January 22, 1957, culminated a process in which the social policy committee had devoted 190 hours to its deliberation and the Bundestag had held the longest debate up to that time. Its passage was overwhelming because both the CDU/CSU and the SPD deputies voted unanimously in favor, with only the rump FDP and some German Party deputies voting no.

The dynamic principle was implemented by relating contribution-based entitlement semi-automatically to the wage level prevailing when the pension begins. Indexation was limited by some built-in lag, and became based on average wages during the preceding three years. The government was obligated to present annual proposals for adjustments based on recommendations made by a *Sozialbeirat* on the basis of the relevant economic data. This method overrode business demands that adjustments be made only every three or five years. In 1957 the final intra-CDU compromise led to the insertion of an escape clause under situations of especially strong fiscal pressure. But the changes of the pension base (*Bestandsrenten*) had to be passed by legislative adjustment acts, of which there were 22 by the end of 1982.

A COMPARATIVE ASSESSMENT

The German indexation case is somewhat similar to the innovations involving income maintenance legislation in Britain and Sweden examined by Hugh Heclo (1974). How does the German case fit the overall conclusions he extracts in the concluding chapter of his book, in which he synthesizes findings on the roles of bureaucracies, parties, elections, interest groups, and so forth in the process of the successful policy initiation?

The Ministerial Bureaucracy

The bureaucratic innovators who developed the programmatic ideas are credited with the greatest share of constructive influence in the British and Swedish situations (Heclo, 1974, pp. 301–304). The much less successful role of their German equivalents constitutes a striking contrast. It is precisely because the rival bureaucratic units prevented promising blueprints from reaching the agenda that Adenauer took the unusual step of reaching entirely beyond the governmental sphere for his initial model. Locked in bitter competition, the bureaucracies devoted so much energy to undermining each others' plans that they lost the initiative. Only in the final phases of the process, when the Labor Minister was able to dominate the turf, did the bureaucrats put their expertise to effective use.

The entrenched traditions associated with the basic programs, the special attributes of the post-Occupation period, and the novel technical challenges of a new policy model all contributed to reducing bureaucratic capability. Indexation posed intellectual policy problems of a new magnitude. Because coordination instruments were so fragile during the early 1950s bureaucratic innovation was frustrated. Their potential influence was handicapped by "restorationist" orientations of the dominant bureaucratic elements. The result was a failure to find the appropriate internal mechanisms necessary to bend German federal bureaucracy toward innovation.

The Role of Parties and Elections

It is less evident how the German case ranks in relation to the moderate role attributed to parties and elections in the British and Swedish development (Heclo, 1974, pp. 288–297). On the one hand, the 1957 pension reform seems a classic case of a Catholic-led party making an impressive attempt to match and out-bid the Social Democrats, thus illustrating a general thesis recently developed by Wilensky (in Flora and Heidenheimer, 1981). On the other hand, the specialist committees of the CDU party organization were hardly significant in the early stages of program development, while the parliamentary group was useful in hammering out the intra-party compromises later in the process. Perhaps even more than in the British and Swedish cases, the party awaited initiatives from the bureaucracy. The CDU concentrated on selling the final product to the public, in which it was successful insofar as the CDU/CSU 1957 election victory reached a peak which was never achieved before or since.

In comparing the record of the CDU-led governments of 1954–1969 with those of the SPD/FDP ones from 1970 to 1978, Alber found that the former were "distinctly more inclined to pursue a policy of election gifts." Under the CDU, social expenditure growth was 2.6% *higher* in election than non-election years, compared to a 1.5% difference for the SPD/FDP (Alber, 1980, p. 25). Much of this difference was accounted for by the 1957 whopper, which had the effect of permitting Adenauer to continue to dominate the political scene. This phenomenon can be better understood in relation to how much more the CDU/CSU of 1957 was structurally still essentially a "Chancellor Party" (Heidenheimer, 1961). The electoral gift had to be impressive because CDU domestic policy had been rather indeterminate and its campaign organization weaker than the SPD.

The Role of the Government Head

For specialists in German politics it may be surprising to learn of Adenauer's extensive and multifaceted role in the pension issue. The

prevalent impression is that he allowed foreign policy concerns to dominate his priorities. Thus Hockerts (1981) explodes the claim, put forward by Wilhelm Hennis, that Adenauer had displayed lack of interest
by never presiding over any sessions of the cabinet's social policy
committee, and claims that the pensions coup enabled Adenauer to
transform the CDU into the party of social integration which it wished to
become.

It would be interesting to pursue this thesis, especially in view of the
fact that the pension reform was itself only a partial substitute for the
comprehensive social security reform which the government had been
unable to produce. An evaluation would have to take into consideration
Adenauer's very different strategy a year later in the case of the health
insurance reform which was put forward by the Labor Ministry under
Theodor Blank.

Contrast with the 1958 Health Insurance Bill

Another test of the Adenauer government's ability to innovate in social policy developed in 1958, the year after the pension act passage and
following the CDU/CSU election victory. It involved numerous proposed changes in the operation of the health insurance system which
had evolved from Bismarck's first social insurance acts in 1883. A health
insurance bill called for changes in both the reimbursement to physicians and in the way in which funds were raised, specifically by
proposing a cost-sharing system under which patients would be expected to make some direct payments to doctors before the insurance
mechanisms began to operate.

The cost-sharing proposal was less innovative than the pension
indexation one in the sense that it was already being practiced in other
countries. But in the German context it had never been used within the
public health insurance system. This helped to mobilize highly organized interests on both the client side, where the trade unions headed opposition to the cost-sharing plan, and on the provider side, where several
physician associations objected both to the additional burden which fee
collection would place upon doctors, and to some changes in the way the
physicians would receive insurance payments for their services (Stone,
1981).

The sharp contrast in the fate of the two bills is significant in terms of
their somewhat countervailing thrusts. It seems that Adenauer initially
endorsed cost-sharing as a partial corrective to the generous indexation
gesture. Referring to it in his government declaration of May 1957, he
emphasized that "The Federal government is resolved to promote the
idea of self-help and private initiative by all means, and to prevent a

slipping into the total welfare state which would sooner or later destroy well-being and prosperity" (Safran, 1967, p. 50).

The health insurance bill was partly shaped by the very same Labor Ministry bureaucrats who had supervised the pensions bill, but they and their new minister dealt poorly with the different sets of organized interests. Blank had weaker parliamentary support among the CDU unionists than Storch had had, and could not protect his draft in the committees. Rather than come to his support, Adenauer granted access to medical association leaders and made them promises which in effect undercut some major aims of the Ministry and the CDU parliamentary leaders. The overall impression was that the Chancellor was cutting the government's losses, choosing not to invest more political capital on an issue which was of lesser electoral importance. Financial pressures generated by the failure to impose effective cost controls were, after all, quite some way down the road.

Why did the indexation succeed and the health insurance cost sharing fail? One reason was that while the former primarily involved distributing additional benefits, the latter was perceived as primarily involving the distribution of additional costs and burdens. Moreover, failure to give financial relief to the health insurance funds would provide uncertain political dividends, whereas the indexation of pensions provided immediate political support at the next election. If the CDU's social legislation of the late 1950s helped it to become more of a party of social integration, this was partly done at the cost of incurring obligations which only would become fully evident during periods of economic downturn. Finally, the health insurance bill involved not only financial transfers, but changed the terms on which professionals would provide services. Policy changes involving perceived professional privileges, especially when they involve a powerful profession like medicine, tend to arouse a determined defense of vested provider interests because professional stakes are less diffuse than those of beneficiaries in other types of income transfer controversies.

THE FISCAL PROBLEMS SINCE THE MID-1970s

German pension entitlements are calculated at the rate of 1.5% of the annual wage base, so that if a worker had forty years of contributions to his credit he will get 60% of his base. As the average wage levels increased by more than half in the seven years after 1957, the level of pensions moved up, too. Responding also to other variables, the proportion of average gross wages constituted by average pension benefits increased from about 28% in 1955 to 40% in 1969, and to 46% in 1978. But the equalization betwen employed and pensioners was not paralleled by any reduction of income differentials *among* pensioners, since the basic concept of status and income maintenance tended to project the wage differentials into similar pension differentials.

Apart from the three-year lag element, little consideration was given to the implications of the new pensions policy for anticyclical fiscal policy. It is indicative that the name Keynes is missing from Hockerts' index. Indeed the leading Labor Ministry official subsequently stressed that "neither the letter nor the spirit of the legislation suggested that pensions should become yet another instrument of government economic policy." This reflected the view of the Social Advisory Council that "pensioners have a right to benefit increases, if productivity and wage increases them, regardless of possibly inflationary effects" (Rimlinger, 1971, p. 183).

How does the German system compare with practices elsewhere? Among the other West European pension index systems, those of France and Austria are most similar to the German one, in that they are semi-automatic and pensions adjust annually to changes in wage levels. The French pension levels are similar to the German ones. Those in Austria are the most generous but the contribution levels were also the highest, 20.5% compared to 18.5% in the Federal Republic in 1983 (Maydell, 1983, p. 384).

Several of the other European systems differ in that they consist of distinct basic pensions and supplementary pension systems. Sweden and the Netherlands adjust their basic pensions automatically, with indexes linked to wages in the former and prices in the latter country. In Switzerland the basic pensions are adjusted automatically in relation to either the price or wage levels (Scheil, 1979, pp. 48 ff.). In the late 1970s, Britain adjusted to wage or price levels, whichever was higher. But this formula was modified under the Thatcher government, and several Scandinavian countries also cut back on the amplitude of indexing rules in the early 1980s (Heidenheimer, Heclo, and Adams, 1983, pp. 233–234).

For one and a half decades the entitlements generated by the German pension legislation built up pressures which exploded in the mid-1970s when economic growth ceased to generate additional funding the easy way. In the preceding seven years pensions had increased by more than 100 percent, compared to wage increases of about 80 percent. The question of whether pension increases could be financed without raising contributions was a key issue in the 1976 election campaign, during which Chancellor Schmidt promised this would be feasible. But shortly after the elections it became clear that impending shortages in both pension and sickness funds could only be met by altering the formulas. When the cabinet postponed the pension increases, Schmidt was accused of welching on his campaign promises. The result was a violent shake-up in the Labor Ministry, which led to the firing not only of the Minister but of a handful of the top officials who had been running social security affairs ever since the mid-1950s.

The budget crunch of the late 1970s forced a return to the discretionary element which had been dropped in the 1960s. Under a 1978 law the annual pension increases for 1978–81 were held to four percent, instead of the seven percent which normal indexation would have called for (Zöllner, 1982, p. 78). The relation of average pensions to average post-tax net wages, which had risen from 56 to 66 percent between 1972 and 1977, dropped for the next several years. In 1980 they constituted 63.5% of net wages, and 44.5% of gross wages. The new CDU government in 1982 delayed by six months the benefit increases due for 1983 and advanced by four months the contributions increase to 18.5 percent. But it avoided a repetition of the departure from the automatic coupling to wages which had been resorted to in the preceding years. It thus sought to conserve the political credit which had accrued to it as the result of Adenauer's 1957 initiative.

CONCLUSION

As various European countries celebrate the centenary of the introduction of social security legislation, West Germany too has had reason to regard indexation as a mixed blessing in a period of demographic and fiscal squeeze. Is there a connection between the fact that Germany was the innovator both in the 1880s and later in regard to the indexation in the 1950s? Only a very indirect one, it seems. The accretion of numerous programs and special provisions caused the German pensions system to become especially complex. In the setting of the 1950s, indexation came to be seen as a political alternative to a radical rationalization of the entire system. The situation of Germany as a defeated country was also relevant insofar as the social security system was held out by German politicians as one of the few "German-made" institutions in which the country could take pride in the wake of the Nazi regime.

Elements of the party political structure, rather than the bureaucratic one, help to explain why West Germany led the field. In contrast to earlier periods, the Bonn party system has been marked by more direct electoral competition between Social Democratic and Christian Democratic parties. As later happened in the Netherlands, this constellation helped bring about relaively large growth in social expenditures. The unusually rapid growth of the West German economy favored those in,

194 ARNOLD J. HEIDENHEIMER

as against those outside of, the labor market, and also helped to acceler-
ate the decision on indexation. The craving for security dominated West
German politics during the 1950s. Government policies had seemed to
provide political and military security by allying the Federal Republic
with the West. In also strengthening the efficacy of social security guarantees the Adenauer government helped to satisfy deeply-felt political
and economic needs.

REFERENCES

Alber, Jens (1980), "A Crisis of the Welfare State: The Case of West Germany," ECPR
Joint Sessions, Florence, March [German version published in Zeitschrift fuer Soziologie,
Vol. 9, No. 4 (October 1980):313–342]. References are to the English version.
Derthick, Martha (1979), Policymaking for Social Security, Washington, D.C.: The Brookings
Institution.
Flora, Peter and Arnold J. Heidenheimer, eds. (1981), The Development of Welfare States in
Europe and America, New Brunswick, NJ: Transaction Books.
Heclo, Hugh (1974), Modern Social Politics in Britain and Sweden: From Relief to Income Main-
tenance, New Haven, CT: Yale University Press.
Heidenheimer, Arnold J. (1961), "Der Starke Regierungschef und das Parteien-system:
Der "Kanzler-Effekt" in der Bundesrepublik," Politische Vierteljahresschrift, 1:626–45.
Heidenheimer, Arnold J., Hugh Heclo and Carolyn Adams (1983), Comparative Public Pol-
icy: The Politics of Social Choice in Europe and America, 2nd ed., New York: St. Martin's
Press.
Hockerts, Hans Günther (1981), Sozialpolitische Entscheidungen im Nachkriegsdeutschland,
Stuttgart: Klett-Cotta.
Maydell, Bernd von (1983), "Alter und Tod," in Peter F. Köhler and Hans F. Zacher, eds.,
Beiträge zur Geschichte und aktueller Situation der Sozialversicherung, Berlin: Duncker und
Humblot, pp. 369–404.
Rimlinger, Gaston (1971), Welfare Policy and Industralization in Europe, America and Russia,
New York: Wiley.
Safian, William (1967), Veto-Group Politics: The Case of Health Insurance Reform in West
Germany, San Francisco: Chandler.
Scheil, Xenia B. (1979), Dynamisierung gesetzlicher Altersrenten, Munich: Tudor.
Stone, Deborah (1981), The Limits of Professional Power: National Health Care in the Federal
Republic of Germany, Chicago: University of Chicago Press.
Tennstedt, Florian (1976), Berufsunfähigkeit im Sozialrecht, Frankfurt: Europäische
Verlagsanstalt.
Zöllner, Detlev (1982), "Germany," in Peter A. Köhler and Hans F. Zacher, eds., The Evolu-
tion of Social Insurance 1881–1981, New York: St. Martin's Press, pp. 1–92.

PART III

COMPARATIVE ANALYSIS OF NATIONAL SYSTEMS

INTRODUCTION TO PART III

Douglas E. Ashford and E. W. Kelley

The politics of social security are a composite of unique and general features of widely differing democratic systems. Within each are found widely differing views on the nature of poverty, need, and the role of the public sector generally. Existing social security systems also vary widely in how they distribute political rewards and incentives. There is little that is surprising in the findings of many macro-level accounts of the growth of the welfare state. Above all, restricting growth was politically unfeasible and unattractive. Democracies have done more for the disadvantaged, but for a variety of political reasons. If social security policies are of more interest for the light they shed on the behavior of modern states than for their functional uncontrollability, then it is important to begin to assess how we can accumulate such comparative knowledge. Three alternative designs are offered in this section.

The comparative design most amenable to quantitative research methods is a single-country design based on a single program. While these restrictions place limits on the political findings that emerge, Ken Judge provides a careful analysis of how the growth of British pensions might be explained. As he discovers, most of the increase is due to demographic and social change, and political support for pension increases in recent years was bipartisan. This is one of the fundamental causes of nationalization of social security programs. No one in elected office can say no. Perhaps more accurately political decisionmakers are increasingly placed in the situation of adjusting social security programs to broad social and economic change. The political change may be more surprising than the social and economic determinants of controversy. In effect, the mediation of social and economic interests through social security programs places these policies in an entirely new context from the more doctrinaire disputes and heavily bureaucratic infighting of the interwar years.

A second important comparative effort that is raised in part by Judge's chapter is the changing pattern of resource allocation that the importance of social security spending generates. As we have seen in Parts I and II, these adjustments were not accurately foreseen nor were the early decisions escalating social security spending the subject of much political debate. In his chapter, Guy Peters analyzes the growth of social spending in relation to taxation in seven countries. As in all comparative designs working with aggregate data at the national level, we lose much of the internal richness of programmatic and local struggles over social security programs. What we gain is an important insight into the trend among all modern democracies to spread the tax burden more equally and to shift toward resource allocation systems that more directly take into account overall income effects. This too is important evidence of the nationalization of social security systems.

Ashford uses another comparative strategy, based on the apparent contradition between the rapid growth of social spending in France, the more conservative country, and Britain, the country thought to be more heavily committed to social spending. The explanation rests with the historical and institutional features of the two countries. The intricacy of the French social security system, as outlined earlier by Lagrange, meant that government had great difficulty grappling with the bureaucratic and statutory preserves within the system. The structure of the British system combined with the power of parliamentary institutions to become a more effective check on growth of spending. Reinforcing these conditions was the pressure on a dominant party system whose anticipatory response to the challenge from the left, finally victorious in 1981, was to preempt the appeal of the Left. In the more competitive British party system, high level consensus could more easily remove social spending from the political agenda.

The common thread of these chapters is perhaps the most crucial political question concerning the future of social security. For different reasons social security programs were depoliticized over their period of rapid growth. This means that among the democratic governments we are only now learning how to handle these giant programs within our normal political process. Though the transition over the coming decade may be very uncomfortable, it is important to remember that integrating the social security debate with our basic institutions and political processes is vitally important to democratic government.

THE GROWTH OF SOCIAL SECURITY IN BRITAIN:

SPENDING ON PENSIONS

Ken Judge

The third quarter of the twentieth century might eventually be seen in retrospect as the golden age of advanced capitalist economies. During this period economic output grew at record levels and welfare states were established and developed to give succor to those citizens who supported, or were left in the wake of, industrial progress. Britain, which was the home of John Maynard Keynes, the architect of the international economic transformation, was no exception to the general experience. Throughout this period of unparalleled prosperity, however, the economic contradictions of the political implementation of Keynesian policies gradually manifested themselves, and inflation in particular became a problem which governments could only ignore at their electoral peril. As a result the economic ideology of the postwar years which had facilitated the expansion of the modern welfare state was increasingly challenged, especially when other indicators of economic performance deteriorated markedly during the 1970s, and radical attempts are now being made to alter the fabric of economic and social life in homage to the new creed of monetarism.

On the face of it, the chief victims of the economic climate characterized by the Thatcher government's stark statement that "public expenditure lies at the heart of Britain's economic difficulties" are the social and
other public services. However, the purpose of this chapter is not so
much to speculate about the future but to try and learn the lessons of
recent history by analyzing the conditions that facilitated the expansion
of the welfare state during the third quarter of the twentieth century.
The focus is on a single program, in contrast with much of the earlier
literature, in the expectation that it will be possible to identify causal factors more clearly. The primary objective of the chapter, therefore, is to
assess the relative importance of different factors in accounting for the
growth of expenditure on national insurance retirement pensions. This
benefit is particularly worth examining because it is the largest component of social security, which itself is the largest item of state spending in
most advanced industrial societies.

The specific purposes of the chapter are to (1) place the growth of
pensions in the context of the expansion of social welfare expenditures
in general and the various explanations associated with it; (2) provide a
brief review of the distinguishing features of the establishment and development of national insurance retirement pensions between the implementation of the revised Beveridge proposals in 1948 and the present day; (3) identify, discuss and assess the relative importance of the
most important causal factors which explain the growth of pensions expenditure; (4) present some preliminary comments about the politics of
changes in the real rate of pension over time; and (5) speculate about
some future trends in spending on state pensions.

THE EXPANSION OF THE WELFARE STATE

One of the most characteristic features of advanced industrial societies
in the post-Second World War period, at least until the late 1970s, was
the rapid growth of public expenditure in general and social welfare in
particular. Table 1 summarizes some of the most salient features of the
British experience between 1951 and 1978.

The most significant feature of Table 1 is that social expenditure increased approximately threefold in real terms between 1951 and 1978.
This expansion of the welfare state was facilitated by three crucial developments. First, the period witnessed historically high rates of economic
growth. Second, the burden of taxation grew both absolutely and relatively and enabled public expenditure's share of GNP to increase from
36 to 44 percent. For example, the proportion of a single man's gross
earnings taken by direct taxes and national insurance contributions in-

Table 1.   Expenditure and Resources, 1951–1978
(£ million at 1975 cost prices)*

Program	1951	Proportion of GNP (Percent)	1978	Proportion of GNP (Percent)	Annual Average Growth Rate (Percent)
Social Expenditure	8,345	16.1	28,418	27.8	4.5
Military Defense	4,735	9.1	5,315	5.2	0.4
Total Public Expenditure	18,743	36.1	44,795	43.8	3.2
GNP at Factor Cost	51,915	100.0	102,302	100.0	2.5

*Deflated by total home costs index (GDP at factor cost)
Source: Central Statistical Office, *National Income and Expenditure 1980* (London: HMSO, 1980), Table 9.4; and earlier years where necessary.

creased from 16 to 31 percent during this period. Finally, within the public sector the persistent relative decline of defense expenditures provided fiscal space for the development of the welfare state.

The growth of state expenditures was, of course, a widespread phenomenon and the British experience was far from being atypical. Consequently the growth of public spending has spawned a vast literature which ranges from descriptive histories to sophisticated theoretical models of varying ideological persuasions. The astonishing variety of causal models and factors which have been advanced make it impossible to refer to them all in a short space, but we can mention some of the most important, and in doing so it is helpful to make a distinction between macro-models and micro-factors.

One of the most famous, and earliest, of the macro-models is Wagner's Law which postulated that an increase in public expenditure was a natural consequence of economic growth and urban development (Wagner and Weber, 1977). Another is Peacock and Wiseman's influential study of the British experience during the twentieth century which highlighted the importance of *displacement* and *inspection* effects during national emergencies (1967). More recently, O'Connor's account of the *Fiscal Crisis of the State* (1973) has stimulated a lively Marxist contribution (Gough, 1979), and Buchanan and Wagner, from the public choice school, have argued that fundamental changes in the "fiscal constitution' of representative democracies associated with the adoption of Keynesian economic policies have had an inflationary effect upon the size of the public sector (1977). More generally, Breton's *Economic Theory of Representative Government* (1974) demonstrates the expenditure consequences of competitive political markets.

At the micro level there are a vast number of factors which are thought to be of causal importance. Included among these are the increases in dependency associated with recent demographic trends

(Ermisch, 1977); the effect of the relative price effect, particularly upon labor-intensive social services (HM Treasury, 1972); the voracious public sector appetite of utility maximizing bureaucrats (Institute of Economic Affairs, 1978); the high income elasticity of demand for some collectively provided social services (Borcherding and Deacon, 1972); the absence of prices to restrict the potentially infinite demands of consumers (Bird, 1976); the fiscal illusion which disguises the true cost of public programs from taxpayers (Morgan, 1977); and the stimulating effect of political advertising on the demand for public sector outputs (Judge and Hampson, 1980).

Despite the plethora of models and factors which can be identified, none of the explanations advanced so far is entirely satisfactory, and this is particularly true if one is interested in assessing the relative contributions of the different elements. One reason for this situation is that many of the analyses which attempt to identify the relative importance of various factors are based on highly aggregated data. For example, Borcherding (1977) has tried to assess the sources of growth of total public expenditure in the United States between 1902 and 1970. His results suggest that relative price changes account for 10 percent, increased affluence for 25 percent and demographic trends for 20 percent of the observed increase (1977, p. 56). However, serious doubts can be expressed about the validity of many of the assumptions which Borcherding has to use in order to produce his conclusions and which reduce their reliability. Moreover, even when attempts have been made to conduct similar analyses at a lower level of generality, they have not been particularly successful (Gough, 1979; Judge, 1981, 1982; Clark and Menefee, 1981).

The Importance of Pensions and Social Security

The starting point for this chapter is the belief that if we are interested in accounting for the growth of state expenditures there is a powerful case for focusing attention upon a particular program or component of expenditure. Table 2 indicates the relative importance of social security in the expansion of the British welfare state between 1951 and 1978.

In fact, it is such a large program that it makes sense to break it down into some of its constituent parts, as shown in Table 3. The dominance of pensions is immediately obvious, and it is therefore an excellent choice for further analysis. A measure of its importance is that pensions alone account for more than 20 percent of the increase in total social spending between 1951 and 1978.

Table 2.　The Growth of Social Expenditure, 1951–1978
(£ million at 1975 cost prices)*

Program	1951	1978	Annual Average Growth Rate (Percent)	Contribution to Total Growth (Percent)
Social Security	2,839	11,150	5.0	41.4
Education	1,880	6,351	4.4	22.3
Housing	1,478	3,725	3.4	11.2
Health and Personal Social Services	2,068	6,416	4.1	21.7
Employment	80	776	8.5	3.4
Total Social Expenditure	8,345	28,418	4.5	100.0

ªDeflated by total home costs index (GDP at factor cost)
Source:　(Central Statistical Office, *National Income and Expenditure 1980* (London: HMSO, 1980), Table 9.4; and earlier years where necessary.

Table 3.　The Growth of Social Security Expenditure,
1951–1978
(£ million at current prices)

Component	1951	1978	Proportion of Total Increase (Percent)
Pensions	270	7,353	49.5
Family Allowances/Child Benefit	66	1,574	10.5
Supplementary Benefit	96	2,096	14.0
Other	208	3,923	26.0
Total	640	14,946	100.0

Source:　Central Statistical Office, *National Income and Expenditure 1980* (London: HMSO, 1980), Table 9.4; and earlier years where necessary

BEVERIDGE AND SOCIAL SECURITY

The British system of national insurance retirement pensions was established in 1948 as a result of the *National Insurance Act 1946* which was based on recommendations made by Beveridge (1942). This system was altered substantially with the implementation of major social security legislation in 1978, but the basic Beveridge pensions continue to be important and the term *pensions* in this chapter refers specifically to them.

There were and are three main eligibility conditions for the receipt of pensions. The claimant must have retired from regular employment, reached the minimum pensionable age of 65 for men and 60 for women, and satisfied the contribution conditions. However, the actual pension paid can be higher or lower than the basic rate. Pensions are reduced if the contribution conditions are not fully satisfied or if the claimant's earned income exceeds a specified amount within five years of the minimum pensionable age. On the other hand, pension increments are available to those who defer retirement for up to five years beyond the minimum pensionable age.

Beveridge's pension proposals were part of a wider social security plan, but they demanded special attention from him because "the problem of the nature and extent of the provision to be made for old age is the most important, and in some ways the most difficult, of all the problems of social security" (1942, para. 233). Two reasons were given for this judgment. First, it was recognized that the numbers of elderly people would grow rapidly both in absolute terms and in proportion to the working population. Second, the design of universal provision was handicapped by the lack of uniformity in the social and economic circumstances of the elderly. Beveridge's pension proposals rested on three central principles: flat rate benefits in return for flat rate contributions; pensions were for retirement primarily rather than old age; and there should be a twenty-year transition period before anyone received a full contributory pension.

One of these principles is particularly worth highlighting in the present context. Beveridge was adamant that "pensions adequate for subsistence without other means should be given only to people who, after reaching a minimum age for retirement, have in fact retired from work" (1942, para. 244). In support of this principle Beveridge suggested the introduction of an earnings rule, but, far from discouraging elderly people from working, he was anxious to promote the postponement of retirement for as long as possible, "and in any case to avoid doing anything which may bring about earlier retirement than at present" (1942, para. 245). The practical manifestation of this concern was the payment of pension increments for deferred retirement.

The pension policies actually enacted in 1946 closely followed the Beveridge Plan, although some of the actual details, such as the initial pension rate, "were the result of internal government analysis, bargaining, and consultation with the TUC" (Heclo, 1974, p. 256). The major exception to this was the relaxation of the transition period in the face of pressure from the Labour government's own backbenchers. Once the modified scheme was implemented in 1948 it remained largely intact for the next thirty years, although some of Beveridge's essential requirements were progressively undermined. The most important changes between 1948 and 1978 were: (1) the introduction of an ill-fated graduated pensions scheme in 1961; (2) the abandonment of the principle of the flat rate insurance contributions by the Heath and Wilson governments in the first half of the 1970s; and (3) the adoption of price and wage indexation for pension upratings in response to political pressure and accelerating inflation for a brief period in the mid-1970s.

THE GROWTH OF SPENDING ON PENSIONS

Between 1951 and 1978 public spending on pensions at constant prices increased by 443 percent. The most convenient way of accounting for this growth is to express it as the product of three factors: the number of pension recipients; the basic rate of pension; and the ratio of average payments to actual rates.

The Number of Pensioners

Between 1951 and 1978 the number of pensioners increased by 108 percent. This was the result of three factors:

1. The number of people at or above the minimum retirement age;
2. The proportion of the above eligible for pensions;
3. The proportion of those in both the above categories actually deciding to retire.

Two of these factors are relatively easy to explain, but the third is more controversial. The impact of demographic trends is simple to establish. Between 1951 and 1978 the number of people over the retirement age increased by 41 percent and this factor accounts for just under half of the increase in the number of pensioners. The proportion of elderly people eligible for pensions hardly changed at all during the period. We are left, therefore, with a little over half of the increase in the number of pensioners to explain by reference to changing patterns of participation in the labor market and take-up of social security benefits. The facts themselves are not in dispute, but there has been a lively debate about their interpretation.

In both Britain and the United States the rapid increase in the proportion of elderly claiming pension benefits has been mirrored by a marked decline in rates of labor market participation. In the United States, the main features have been summarized by Munnell:

participation in the labor force of men sixty-five years of age and over declined from
45.8 percent to 21.7 percent during the twenty-five years from 1950 to 1975. During this same period, the percentage of insured men sixty-five and over receiving
social security benefits rose from 59 percent to 94 percent. (1977, p. 62)

In the United Kingdom the economic activity rates of elderly men declined from 31.3% in 1951 to 15.3% in 1978. During the same period
the proportion of the elderly in receipt of pensions increased from
61.7% to 91% (Central Statistical Office, 1979, Table 5.2).

Why has there been such a rapid withdrawal from the labor force
among elderly men in particular? There are two competing sets of explanations. On one hand, most economists explain the decline in economic activity with reference to the existence of social security benefits,
improvements in the real value of pensions (the replacement rate) and
high marginal tax rates on pensioner earnings. On the other hand, non-
economists, and particularly administrators of social security programs,
emphasize the importance of deteriorating health, poor employment
opportunities and the trend towards compulsory retirement.

In their survey of the economics of the elderly, Clark, Kreps and
Spengler (1978) comment that:

Most examinations of the labor supply decisions of individuals in older cohorts have
found that eligibility for social benefits has lowered market activity rates . . . . [and
that] . . . . the expansion in coverage and level of benefits since 1950 apparently has
resulted in social security benefits playing a major role in determining the proportion of older individuals in the labor force. (p.932)

More recently, in a very careful review of the macro-economic consequences of social security, Danziger, Haveman and Plotnick (1981)
found that all of the empirical studies they analyzed agreed that the
availability of state pensions reduced the labor supply. One of the few
British studies in this area confirms the observations made in the United
States. Zabalza, Pissarides and Piachaud (1978) conclude that:

in Britain the Social Security system has a significant influence on retirement decisions. On the one hand, by providing a pension it has encouraged people to retire
earlier than they would otherwise . . . . On the other hand, the presence of the earnings rule has reduced potential net earnings from work, and so has acted as a
disincentive for continuing work after the statutory retirement age. (p.24)

It is not the purpose of this chapter to provide a comprehensive review
of the literature which addresses the link between social security and retirement. Nevertheless, a number of points which emerge most strongly

are worth repeating in this context. First, although the *existence* of pensions can be taken for granted, it is worth highlighting their relative improvement because high replacement ratios might well have contributed to a decline in economic activity among the elderly.

A comparison of pensions and *net* earnings shows that the replacement rate rose by 40% from 21.6% in 1951 to 30.2% in 1978. The second point worth reiterating is that the effect of the earnings rule on pensioners' earnings is to impose a marginal rate tax on them up to 100%, and although it is difficult to reach a firm conclusion, Marshall, amongst others, believes that the "evidence which is available supports a theoretical analysis consistent with a distinctive effect of the earnings test on the decision to continue in full-time employment past minimum retirement age" (1978, p. 220).

As far as the effect of compulsory retirement is concerned there is some evidence on both sides of the Atlantic that the practice has grown. For example, both Clark and Spengler (1980) and Schulz (1981) have drawn attention to the extent to which this is associated with the expansion of occupational pension schemes. But it needs to be remembered that:

> Even when there is no official policy of compulsory retirement, tradition on both the employers' and the employees' side may be equally effective in dictating retirement at a certain age. It is in this respect that the National Insurance Act may have created a general belief that 65 and 60 are the right retirement ages for men and women respectively. What the Act intended to be minimum retirement ages, the public has come to consider as the normal retirement ages (George, 1968, p. 163).

Finally, there is also some evidence that the contribution of ill health to the retirement, and especially early retirement, decision has been increasing in recent years (Altmann, 1982).

It seems reasonable to conclude, however, that the existence of, improvement in, and constraints associated with the state pension scheme have made a major contribution to the increase in the number of pensioners over and above the consequences of demographic trends. Beveridge's attempt, therefore, to strike a balance in designing his social security system, by providing adequate income maintenance for old age without discouraging people from working for as long as possible, seems to have failed. Not that this would have surprised Beveridge; he recognized that if "pensions are adequate for subsistence they will obviously encourage retirement" (1942, para. 245). The substantial improvements in their real value since then has provided an even greater incentive for the elderly to withdraw from full-time participation in the labor market.

Basic Rates of Pension

In the autumn of 1951 the basic rate of pension for a single person was £1.50 per week. By the autumn of 1978, after seventeen separate upratings, it had risen to £19.50. In 1975 prices, this represents an increase of 159 percent from £5.21 per week in 1951 to £13.50 per week in 1978. In attempting to explain this substantial increase one is handicapped by the absence of a literature similar to that which has been concerned with the labor market participation of the elderly. Nevertheless, one can identify hints and suggestions in a variety of places which might help to explain the phenomenon.

The first, and probably the most obvious, factor is that pensions have improved in real terms as a byproduct of improvements in the standard of living of the rest of the community. For a short period in the 1970s this was guaranteed by a process of indexation, but more typically the real improvements have been spasmodic.

> By and large, decisions on pension increases have been fairly mechanical decisions taken to adjust pensions every two or three years for the intervening price changes; less often, when the Treasury view of economic circumstances permitted, the increases gave some real improvement in benefits. (Heclo, 1974, p. 258)

One consequence of this historical experience is that to understand changes in the real value of pensions in any single year we need to introduce another factor: the responsiveness of governments to changes in prices and wages. Tony Atkinson (1972) reminds us, for example, that "changes in the purchasing power of benefits between reviews is of very real importance to the individual, [and] the extent to which the value is reduced depends on the length of time between reviews and the level of inflation" (p.16).

A completely different kind of factor which has been advanced to account for improvements in the real value of pensions is the existence of what is variously described as an electoral-economic or political-business cycle (Tufte, 1978). The key element of this theory is the proposition that governments can manipulate short-term changes in public perceptions of economic prosperity through fiscal policy in general and changes in transfer payments in particular. Moreover, as pensions are easily the largest of all transfer payments, it might be expected that they should be of crucial importance in political-business cycle theory. If the theory has any explanatory and predictive power, therefore, we should expect to find a relationship between substantial improvements in pension rates and election years. Both Heclo (1974) and Kincaid (1973) argue that this is consistent with the British experience in the postwar period, but perhaps the best example of this phenomenon is one of the pre-Watergate activities of Richard Nixon. A few days before the 1972 presidential election Nixon arranged to gain the credit for a record increase in social security benefit levels by mailing a letter to all 25 million recipients *and voters*. Other political factors which might be thought to influence the level of pension, such as differences in party ideology or the political power of pensioners, are dismissed as irrelevant by Heclo in his historical account of the postwar development of British pensions. Heclo also argues that, despite the growth of pressure groups, such as the National Federation of Old Age Pensions Associations, they "played little substantial part in postwar policy developments" (1974, p. 260).

The final factor that is mentioned most frequently is a financial one. It is argued that "pension increases depended on increases in flat rate contributions" (Heclo, 1974, p. 258). Over and above this simple link, however, Browning has constructed a sophisticated public choice explanation for the growth of spending on pensions by developing a majority voting model to analyze the determination of taxes and transfers in a system of pay-as-you-go social insurance (1975). The major finding is that the equilibrium size of the system will be "too large" if voters are fully aware of the consequences of the policy. Browning's analysis is based upon two assumptions of different degrees of plausibility: that the preferences of a majority of the electorate have the power to influence policy; and, that citizens are capable of making rational choices about their own interests. The model is applicable to a system of social security in which workers provide pensions for the elderly out of current income.

Proceeding from the above assumptions it is relatively easy to demonstrate, *ceteris paribus*, that older workers, at the time when a social insurance system commences or is increased, obtain a higher rate of return on their contributions than do younger workers. It is rational for older workers to support increases in contribution rates, therefore, so as to finance higher benefits from which they will benefit at the expense of later generations. The actual rate of contribution will be determined, in theory, by the median voter, but it is logical to conclude that even in a community with a stable population structure the net effect of a pay-as-you-go social security system is expansionary. This structural characteristic or defect, however, can be easily exacerbated in a society with an aging population. During the postwar period in Britain, of course, the proportion of older workers and the retired in the population increased steadily. Public choice theory, therefore, would explain improvements in pension rates as a consequence of support for higher contributions by a winning coalition of the middle-aged and the elderly. Even if this theory

strikes any chord of plausibility, though, it need not be considered rep-
rehensible. Insofar as sustained economic growth is achievable, the net
result of the phenomenon outlined by Browning, and vigorously defended by him against criticism, is that it effects a transfer to poor generations from richer ones (see Greene, 1977; Bridges, 1978; Browning,
1977, 1978).

Whatever the merits of these different arguments, the easiest way to
represent the increase in the real rate of pension is to make a distinction
between the consequences of *de facto* indexation with net average earnings and improvements in the extent to which pensions replace work income. The first factor accounts for 53 percent and the second for 47 percent of the increase in the real rate of pension.

Average Rates of Pension

The ratio of average pension payments to basic rates (AVRAT) varies
considerably from year to year depending upon a multiplicity of factors.
These include the contribution records of recipients, the mix of different insurance categories, the number of over-80s, and the number and
timing of upratings in any particular year. Not surprisingly, therefore,
AVRAT has fluctuated quite considerably. The two terminal dates of
1951 and 1978, however, have very similar values because they both
witnessed pension upratings in the autumn, and this was an important
reason for conducting the present analysis between those dates. In fact,
the main factor influencing changes in AVRAT appears to be the existence of an uprating and its timing. Consequently, between 1951 and
1978, AVRAT had virtually no impact at all upon the growth of spending on pensions.

Overview

We are now in a position to assess the relative importance of the two
primary causal factors and their separate elements. These are shown in
Table 4. The increased number of pensioners accounted for 43.3% of
the extra social security spending. Changes in demographic trends and
the take-up of benefits were responsible for 20.4% and 22.9% respectively. It was the improved real rate of pension, however, which was the
most important of the two main factors. It explains 56.7% of the total
increase in spending directly, but it also has an indirect effect through its
influence on the decision to retire. "Indexation" accounted for 30% and
improvements in the replacement of work income for 26.7%.

In my opinion, the factor most worth exploring further is the real rate
of pension. It merits closer attention for three main reasons. First, be-

Table 4.   The Growth of Pensions Expenditure,
1951–1978

	Explanatory Factor	1951	1978	Contribution to Total Growth* (Percent)
(1)	Elderly Population, in thousands	6,839	9,650	20.4
(2)	Pension Claimants as a proportion of (1), in percent	61.7	91.0	22.9
(3)	Indexation of Pensions with Net Earnings, £ per worker	5.20	8.62	30.0
(4)	Improvement in the Replacement Rate, in percent	21.5	33.7	26.7
	Total Spending on Pensions, in £ million	937.5	5088.6	100.0

Methodological Note:
Where $\Delta X = \Delta Y \times \Delta Z$ the relative importance of ΔY and ΔZ can be calculated by taking the logarithmic relationship $\Delta \log X = \Delta \log Y + \Delta \log Z$. For example, the proportion of ΔX which can be accounted for by ΔY can be obtained by calculating $\Delta \log Y / \Delta \log X \times 100$.

cause it explains most of the increase in total expenditure via its direct and indirect effects. Second, because by comparison with, say, the labor market participation of the elderly, it has been a neglected topic. Third, because there seems to be some dispute in the literature about the importance of political competition or "pensioneering."

THE POLITICS OF PENSIONEERING

In an earlier paper the results of a multiple regression analysis of changes in the *annual real value* of pensions were outlined (Judge, 1981). The two most important causal variables were shown to be the length of time between upratings and the size of changes in national insurance contributions. However, the most interesting results concerned the variables which were excluded from the equations. There appeared to be no significant statistical relationship between the level of pensions and average earnings, the political party in power or the years in which general elections took place. But the absence of an identifiable relationship with any measure of income does not mean that there is no link between earnings and pensions, merely that it is not a straightforward linear one.

The contradiction can be explained by reference to the record of British governments about the uprating of pensions for most of the period; it "has been one of occasional *ad hoc* increases to give some approximate compensation for price and wage increases" (Heclo, 1974, p.257).

The most surprising results relate to the political variables because it is widely assumed that the adversarial nature of the British political system creates a functional dynamic in which parties have to compete over the issues which are most important to the electorate. For example, MacGregor argues that the "two major political parties have often engaged in a process of competitive bidding—pensioneering" (1981, p.135). Nevertheless, the regression results suggest that political partisanship was not a significant causal variable. There is also no evidence that variables which might stand as proxies for the political power of pensioners were of causal importance. More surprisingly, a statistically significant link between pension upratings and election years could not be found. In the circumstances there is a strong case for examining the historical record a little more closely, and as far as the politics of pensions are concerned there are two questions which are particularly worthy of closer attention.

a.   Is there any evidence that party competition increased the real value of pensions above the trend level?
b.   Do electoral considerations influence pension increases in ways which are not easily discernible?

Party Competition

It is widely acknowledged that relatively few policy issues have had significant political salience in recent British electoral history, but old age pensions is one of them. The public opinion data throughout the period in question consistently provides evidence of the considerable popular support for pensioners and a concern for their welfare (see Butler and Stokes, 1969; Klein, 1974; Lipsey, 1979). Moreover, there is some evidence that the pension proposals put forward by political parties can induce substantial changes in voting behavior amongst some sections of the electorate (Butler and Rose, 1960, p.193). It should not be surprising, therefore, that both of the major political parties paid particular attention to old age pensions in almost all of the manifestos at every general election between 1951 and 1974 (Craig, 1975). But did they attempt to outbid each other?

My analysis of the reference to pensions in postwar election manifestos leads me to the following conclusions. First, there is a tendency for *governments* of both parties to emphasize their past records rather than make specific future promises. Second, *opposition* parties inevitably make critical comments about the record in government of their adversaries but concentrate most attention upon promises and pledges which are often quite detailed. Third, and notwithstanding the two previous observations, there is a tendency for the Conservative Party to draw more heavily upon references to the past performance of governments so as to emphasize their record of good stewardship. In contrast, the Labour Party appears to continually strive to establish more specific targets for future improvements. Finally, and most importantly, I could find no documentary evidence of an auction, with parties bidding against each other with highly specific promises of pension increases, at any election. On the contrary, in one of the election campaigns where this could have been a real possibility it was explicitly ruled out by the Prime Minister. In 1959, the Labour Party invested a great deal in a specific promise to increase pensions by 20 percent, but Harold Macmillan refused to make counter-promises and declared in one of his speeches that:

> I want our party to win this election. Of course I do. But there is a price I am not prepared to pay for victory. I will not enter into any kind of auction with the parties trying to outbid each other in this and every other sphere. For I know that a government which won an election on that basis would either have to duck out of its promises, or if they tried to carry them out would plunge us back into the inflationary mess from which we have rescued ourselves so painfully. (Butler and Rose, 1960, pp. 55–56)

It is my belief that the absence of party competition is explained by the fact that the adversarial nature of British political debate disguises the extent to which popular support for the elderly in general, and old age pensioners in particular, imposes consensual constraints upon the freedom of maneuver available to British parties. In his influential study, Heclo arrived at a similar conclusion.

> Despite prevailing assumptions that pensions have been particularly subject to back-bench political maneuvring, or to "pensioneering" through party competition, or to left-wing pressure in the Labour Party, actual policy development reveals little such adaptability. What has usually been left to the influence of partisan maneuvring has been the timing of pension increases by the government of the day .... But the absolute base from which increases were made has been little affected by partisan competition and, despite general protestations from both parties favouring larger increases in the abstract, party counter-bidding does not appear to have accelerated the rate of increase. (1974, p.257)

More recently, in their study of the influence of pressure groups on social security policy, Whiteley and Winyard (1982) conclude that the differences between parties with respect to income maintenance are of-

ten exaggerated. They report with approval the views expressed by a
senior civil servant in the Department of Health and Social Security:

> The area of consensus is much larger than one thinks; there is little difference be-
> tween the parties on poverty. All politicians agree that fraud is a bad thing. The
> elderly are more politically attractive than children.

Political Business Cycle

Kincaid is one of many British observers who claim that pension increases are timed to maximize electoral advantage:

> It has often been noted that there is a correlation between the timing of general
> elections and the timing of increases in pensions and other benefits. There have
> been seven General Elections since 1948, including the Election of 1970. In each of
> these elections, except in 1950, there was a pension increase during the election year
> or in the year immediately before. Since 1948 there have been nine increases in the
> basic old-age pension and on six of these occasions there was an election expected
> within the following twelve months. (1973, p.201)

Such observations are clearly inconsistent with the statistical results,
but there are grounds for supporting the literature which postulates the
existence of a political-business cycle for two reasons. First, the American experience is conditioned by a regular four-year cycle of presidential elections, whereas in Britain there is typically considerable uncertainty about the timing of general elections. Second, the British
literature is so remarkably imprecise about the nature of the link between upratings and elections that it is difficult to test in any rigorous
way. However, by taking one of the upratings as a case study it is possible
to argue that electoral considerations can operate in more subtle ways
than are often imagined.

The 1958 uprating of 22% in *real terms* was the largest during the
postwar period and, although it was paid more than eighteen months
before the 1959 general election, it is possible that electoral considerations influenced the size and timing of the increase. However, to appre-
ciate this point the uprating needs to be considered in a wider economic
and political context. Harold Macmillan succeeded Eden as Prime Minister at the beginning of 1957 in the aftermath of Suez, and fearing, as he
told the Queen, that his government might not last six weeks
(Macmillan, 1971, p.185). In the months that followed, the survival of
Macmillan's administration remained precarious as the diplomatic and
political crisis was exacerbated by economic problems at home and
abroad. It was during this period that Macmillan made his famous
"never had it so good" speech in which, whilst acknowledging the pros-

perity of the 1950s, he warned of the dangers of price inflation and the need for wage restraint (1971, p.350). Domestic policy during the second half of 1957, therefore, was dominated by the need to establish sound fiscal and monetary policy and limit wage increases. At the same time Macmillan was acutely aware of the political unpopularity of his government and the extent to which it would be further weakened by savage deflationary policies. He wrote that "by-elections continued to go against us" (1971, p.345), and he continually reminded his colleagues that "the main issues were psychological" (1971, p.366) and that demands from the Chancellor of the Exchequer for cuts in welfare state spending were "more I fear, than is feasible politically" (1971, p.362). In these circumstances the fragility of his government meant that Macmillan might have had to call an election at any moment, and as a result there was a premium attached to any policy which would improve his political standing while being consistent with his economic and political objectives. An increase in pensions was an obvious candidate because it provided a counterbalance to wage restraint. Also, there were 500,000 voters waiting in the wings who were due to become late entrants to the national insurance scheme at the beginning of 1958 and who, it might be supposed, would be appreciative of a record increase in the pension rate. Accordingly, Macmillan told the annual conference of the Conservative Party in October 1957 that:

> It is the pensioner, the retired man, the people on fixed or nearly fixed incomes, who have borne the burden . . . . We have a clear duty to those sections of our people who have not shared in this general prosperity and that duty we intend to discharge. (1971, p.359)

A few weeks later, in the Queen's speech at the beginning of the new session of parliament, it was announced that the government was going to rush through legislation to make increased pensions payable early in 1958.

SUMMARY

The purpose of this chapter has been to identify, discuss and assess the most important causal factors which accounted for the rapid growth of public spending on state pensions in Britain between 1951 and 1978. The analysis indicates that the increase in the number of pensioners was responsible for 43.3% of the total growth. This factor was found to have two central components: demographic trends were accountable for 20.4%; the other 22.9% was attributable to the decline in the economic activity of the elderly. The most important factor, however, was the substantial improvement in the real rate of pension, and this accounts for 56.7% of the increase in expenditure. It is more difficult to "explain" why improvements in the real rate of pension have taken place, but it is clear that higher benefits depended upon the extraction of higher national insurance contributions and that both were made possible by improvements in the standard of living of the rest of the community. This is only part of the story, however, because increases in real disposable income only account for 53% of the improvement in pensions. It seems likely, therefore, that the improvement in the replacement rate of pensions for net earnings from 21.5% in 1951 to 33.7% in 1978 needs to be explained by reference to wider political considerations. The view advanced in this chapter is that a modified form of political business cycle theory and wider references to the public choice literature are likely to be more helpful than an elusive search for "pensioneering" as a product of party competition.

REFERENCES

Altmann, R. M. (1982), "Incomes of the Early Retired," *Journal of Social Policy*, 11 (July): 3, 355–363.
Atkinson, A. B. (1972), "Inequality and Social Security," in P. Townsend and N. Bosanquet, eds., *Labour and Inequality*, London: Fabian Society, 12–25.
Beveridge Report (1942), *Social Insurance and Allied Services*, Cmd.6404, London: HMSO.
Bird, R. M. (1976), *Charging for Public Services: A New Look at an Old Idea*, Toronto: Canadian Tax Foundation.
Borcherding, T. E. (1977), "The Sources of Growth of Public Expenditures in the United States, 1902–1970," in T. E. Borcherding, ed., *Budgets and Bureaucrats: The Sources of Government Growth*, Durham, NC: Duke University Press, 45–70.
Borcherding, T. E. and R. T. Deacon (1972), "The Demand for the Services of Non-Federal Governments," *American Economic Review*, 62 (December), 891–901.
Breton, A. (1974), *The Economic Theory of Representative Government*, London: Macmillan.
Bridges, B. (1978), "Why the Social Insurance Budget is Too Large in a Democracy: Comment," *Economic Inquiry*, 16 (January), 133–138.
Browning, E. K. (1975), "Why the Social Insurance Budget is Too Large in a Democracy," *Economic Inquiry*, 13 (September), 373–388.
Browning, E. K. (1977), "Social Insurance: The Constitutional Perspective," *Economic Inquiry*, 15 (July), 455–457.
Browning, E. K. (1978), "Why the Social Insurance Budget is Too Large in a Democracy: A Reply," *Economic Inquiry*, 16 (January), 139–142.
Buchanan, J. M. and R. E. Wagner (1977), *Democracy in Deficit: The Political Legacy of Lord Keynes*, New York: Academic Press.
Butler, D. and R. Rose (1960), *The British General Election of 1959*, London: Macmillan.
Butler, D. and D. Stokes (1969), *Political Change in Britain*. London: Macmillan.
Central Statistical Office (CSO) (1979), *Social Trends 10*, London: HMSO.
Clark, R., J. Kreps and J. Spengler (1978), "Economics of Aging: A Survey," *Journal of Economic Literature*, 16 (September), 919–962.

Clark, R. and J. Menefee (1981), "Federal Expenditure for the Elderly: Past and Future," *Gerontologist*, 21 (April): 2, 132–137.

Clark, R. and J. Spengler (1980), *The Economics of Individual and Population Ageing*, Cambridge: Cambridge University Press.

Craig, F. W. S. (1975), *British General Election Manifestos 1900–1974*, London: Macmillan.

Danziger, S., R. Haveman and R. Plotnick (1981), "How Income Transfer Programs Affect Work, Savings and the Income Distribution: A Critical Review," *Journal of Economic Literature*, 19 (September).

Ermisch, J. (1977), "The Impact of Demographic Change Upon Public Expenditure and Infrastructure Investment," *Studies in Population Change and Social Planning*, Working Paper No.4, Centre for Studies in Social Policy, London.

George, V. (1968), *Social Security: Beveridge and After*, London: Routledge and Kegan Paul.

Gough, I. (1979), *The Political Economy of the Welfare State*, London: Macmillan.

Greene, K. (1977), "Over Expansion in the Social Insurance Budget and the Constitutional Perspective," *Economic Inquiry*, 15 (July), 449–454.

Heclo, H. (1974), *Modern Social Politics in Britain and Sweden*, New Haven, CT: Yale University Press.

Institute of Economic Affairs (IEA) (1978), *The Economics of Politics*, Readings 18, London: IEA.

Judge, K. (1981), "State Pensions and the Growth of Social Welfare Expenditures," *Journal of Social Policy*, 10 (October): 4, 503–530.

Judge, K. (1982), "Federal Expenditure for the Elderly: A Different Interpretation of the Past," *Gerontologist*, 22 (April): 2, 129–131.

Judge, K. and R. Hampson (1980), "Political Advertising and the Growth of Social Welfare Expenditures," *International Journal of Social Economics*, 7:2, 61–92.

Kincaid, J. (1973), *Poverty and Inequality in Britain*, Harmondsworth: Penguin.

Klein, R. (1974), "The Case for Elitism," *Political Quarterly*, 45:3, 406–417.

Lipsey, D. (1979), "The Reforms People Want," *New Society*, 4 October.

MacGregor, S. (1981), *The Politics of Poverty*, London: Longman.

Macmillan, H. (1971), *Riding the Storm, 1956–59*, London: Macmillan.

Marshall, G. P. (1978), "Income Taxation and the UK Flat-Rate Retirement Pension," *Social and Economic Administration*, 12 (winter):3.

Morgan, D. (1977), *Over-Taxation by Inflation*, Hobart Paper 72, London: IEA.

Munnell, A. (1977), *The Future of Social Security*, Washington, D.C.: The Brookings Institution.

O'Connor, J. (1973), *The Fiscal Crisis of the State*, New York: St. Martin's Press.

Peacock, A. and J. Wiseman (1967), *The Growth of Public Expenditure in the United Kingdom*, 2nd ed., London: George Allen and Unwin.

Schulz, J. (1981), "Pension Policy at a Crossroads: What Should Be the Pension Mix?" *Gerontologist*, 21 (February): 1, 46–53.

HM Treasury (1972), *Public Expenditure White Papers: Handbook on Methodology*, London: HMSO.

Tufte, E. (1978), *Political Control of the Economy*, Princeton, NJ: Princeton University Press.

Wagner, R. E. and W. E. Weber (1977), "Wagner's Law, Fiscal Institutions and the Growth of Government," *National Tax Journal*, 30 (March): 1.

Whiteley, P. and S. Winyard (1982), "Influencing Social Policy: The Effectiveness of the Poverty Lobby in Britain," *Journal of Social Policy*, 12 (January): 1, 1–26.

Zabalza, A., C. Pissarides and D. Piachaud (1978), *Social Security, Life-Cycle Savings and Retirement*, Centre for Labour Economics Discussion Paper No. 43, LSE.

THE DEVELOPMENT OF THE WELFARE STATE AND THE TAX STATE

B. Guy Peters

The development of the welfare state in Western Europe and North America frequently has been discussed in terms of the development of benefits and protections for citizens (Flora and Heidenheimer, 1981). However, the development of benefits has, in turn, created a growing need for public revenues to finance those benefits. During periods of affluence demands for increased revenues have been rather unimportant politically; increased benefits could be paid out of the fiscal dividend of growth (Bell, 1974). However, as the economies of most industrialized countries have become less buoyant after the mid-1970s, increasing demands for revenue have become important political issues, and there has been an increasing "backlash" against the costs of government (*National Tax Journal*, 1979).

The two components of the welfare state—taxes and benefits—are inextricably intertwined, and in order to understand the dynamics of one component it is important to understand the dynamics of the other. The ability to exclude certain types of income or to deduct certain types of expenditures is itself a major subsidy, especially for the middle class.

Whether revenue foregone is the same as an expenditure is a political, economic, and, to some extent, philosophical question. However, we must remember that how much a government taxes and what it excludes from taxation defines the range of government beneficiaries as clearly as the decisions to spend the revenue collected from citizens. We will concentrate on the sources of funding for total levels of expenditure. Although some benefits created in the modern state are identified as particular components of welfare expenditures, almost all expenditures create benefits for someone—frequently the middle class (Rose and Peters, 1976, pp. 65–85). One characteristic of the mixed economy welfare state is that everyone benefits and everyone pays for the benefits. It is, therefore, sensible to focus on the growth of total government revenue as it has evolved during the period of the welfare state (Peters and Heisler, 1981).

It is easy to underestimate the extent of the changes which have taken place in the sources and amounts of government revenue (See Table 1). Dating the beginning of the welfare state era is difficult, and this date varies markedly across political systems. However, if we select a convenient date, such as 1900, then the growth of government revenue is quite startling. This is true not only in terms of the proportion of the growing national production (e.g., Gross National Product), but it is even more true if we look at the number of dollars, francs, pounds or whatever that must be collected. While these absolute numbers may appear to be a meaningless indicator of change given inflation and other fluctuations in the "real" value of a unit of currency, it is nonetheless important to note the administrative burden now borne by tax collectors. The sheer volume of revenue to be raised, combined with the complexity of modern economic and financial structures, requires that administrative ease be an important consideration in the design of revenue systems.

EXPLANATIONS FOR REVENUE CHOICES

Before we begin, there are both demand and supply based reasons for revenue growth. Some of these reasons are factors which are economic in character (usually supply-side) and some are political. One explanation for changes in both amounts and patterns of revenue collection has been demand—as more revenues are needed, more revenues will be found. This does not mean that all increases are the product of conscious choices. Several of the most important revenue sources for modern governments tend to increase their yield without any changes in policies, simply because there is more money flowing through the economy. This is true whether the increased volume of money is the result of real economic growth or inflation. These almost automatic increases in revenue have, in fact, led to a set of hypotheses about the growth of public expenditures which are exactly opposite to the demand-driven explanations discussed above. It has been argued that increases in revenue and spending are supply driven, and that as more money becomes available, aggressive political and bureaucratic actors will find reasons to spend the money (Bird, 1970, pp. 107–122). Once the commitments to spend for a particular purpose have been made, it is difficult or impossible to reverse them. Another important feature of increases in revenue resulting from inflation have served as an important safety valve for political leaders with increasing expenditure demands, for they allow them to raise money. Some explanations for revenue patterns depend upon the revenue generation of sources under conditions of economic change. One of the most important features of a revenue choice is the adaptability of revenue sources relative to inflation and economic growth. As we noted above, some of the growth of government revenue has been unintentional and has been a function of the more rapid growth of tax revenues rather than real economic resources. Whether by inflation or economic growth, when incomes increase, a larger proportion of those incomes is taken as taxes, everything else being equal, "because taxes are paid at a higher marginal tax rate" (Aaron, ed., 1976). Attempts to index taxes so that these automatic increases do not occur as a result of inflation are indicative of the attempts of the political system to cope with the increasing taxation associated with the development of the welfare state.

Fundamentally, the level of economic development and the economic structure of the society influences the selection of revenue instruments. As a country industrializes, more "tax handles" are created as incomes and consumption become more readily identifiable (Musgrave, 1969, pp. 126–127). Although we are concerned with a range of "industrialized democracies" in this chapter, all of which are reasonably developed economically, there are still important differences between countries such as Ireland, with a large proportion of its workforce still employed in agriculture, and one such as the United Kingdom with a small agricultural population. Similarly, as more of the population becomes involved in larger organizations with better record keeping, it becomes more difficult for citizens to hide their incomes from taxation.

Another important economic effect of taxation would be on employment. This is especially true in the case of social security and other payroll taxes paid by an employer. Although, as will be discussed later, payroll taxes have many desirable features from a political perspective, they increase the price of employing an additional new worker rather significantly. For example, in Italy, the cost to the employer on top of the direct wage to the employee amounts to 49 percent of the wage price, thus making adding new workers very costly, and arguably slowing the addition of new workers (Salowsky, 1977). Of course, in a tight labor market or in a society attempting to maximize the productive efficiency of its labor force, such a tax policy might be used as a means of encouraging the substitution of capital for labor.

One of the most obvious manifestations of this economic conception of the effects of taxation has been the growth of the ideology of supply-side economics as expressed through the Reagan tax cut. But interestingly, at least in the short run, this ideology is contradictory to another conservative economic doctrine concerning revenue, specifically that everything else being equal, government borrowing is undesirable.

POLITICAL FACTORS EXPLAINING REVENUE PATTERNS

Rather than being entirely economic or technocratic, tax policies are inherently political choices. No practicing politician needs to be reminded of this. We will discuss the politics of making revenue choices from two perspectives. One is the characteristics of different types of revenue instruments which might allow the rational politician to raise revenue while still maximizing his or her possibilities of re-election. The second perspective, related to the large literature on the "determinants" of public policy, will describe some macro-level political characteristics which may be associated with particular choices of revenue policy.

Few, if any, politicians like to be associated with tax increases, and few things bring greater joy to a politician than the ability to cut taxes (especially if services can be maintained). However, given that governments do face pressures to increase expenditures and consequently to increase revenues, politicians are faced with the inescapable choice of not whether to increase revenues, but how to raise them.

The first thing a rational politician would want is to increase revenues without the public being aware that these revenues are indeed being raised. One way of doing this is to engage in deficit financing to cover a significant share of public expenditure. Political leaders have been quite willing to follow this course of action, as shown in Table 1. For the industrialized countries included in this table, there have been deficits in the majority of years following World War II—even though this was a period of very rapid and sustained economic growth. Thus, although some scholars have argued that the Keynesian revolution in economic thinking is responsible for loosening the ideological restraints against unbalanced budgets, it appears that politicians read Keynes rather selectively.

They choose to read the portion arguing for surpluses in good—and, especially, inflationary—times (Rose and Peters, 1976, pp. 135–140).

Of course, all citizens will know that deficit financing is taking place, but the effects of deficit financing are more remote than the effects of taxes. Thus, the clever politician would run deficits as often as possible (see Table 2), limited by a number of factors such as the economic conditions of the country, interest rates, and perhaps the length of time the politician desires to remain in office. The longer the individual politician wishes to remain in office, the less willing he may be to run deficits; present borrowing implies future expenditure for debt service, and this form of expenditure limits the amount of revenue remaining to finance expenditures which are more politically productive. This assumes, however, that the deficit will be financed through borrowing rather than by simply monetizing the debt, e.g., printing money.

A second means of reducing the political impact of revenue collection on the career prospects of our rational politician is to use less visible taxes (Wilensky, 1976). Some taxes, for example, the personal income tax, are quite visible to citizens and consequently engender resistance to taxation. Other taxes, such as the value-added tax, are generally known to the majority of citizens but, as they are not charged separately, they are less obvious and therefore produce less opposition. Others, such as the corporation tax, are almost totally invisible to citizens even though the real incidence of these taxes may be on the consumer rather than on the corporation which nominally pays the tax. Wilensky has pointed to a significant positive correlation between the visibility of taxes and the strength of anti-tax movements in industrialized countries, and some of our own research points to a weak positive relationship between the visibility of taxes and an indicator of tax evasion.

The political consequences of taxation on the politician might also be reduced by dividing the total tax bill among a number of different taxes and a number of different taxing jurisdictions. Thus, in the United States, where an average citizen may pay taxes to five or more (federal, state, county, municipality, school board) taxing authorities, it is difficult to determine what the real tax bill is, even for direct taxation. Moreover, as the apparent fiscal crisis of post-Keynesian economics deepens, there is likely to be a proliferation of taxing authorities and a proliferation of the instruments used to collect revenues. This may be especially pronounced among local authorities attempting to gain access to some more extensible forms of taxation, as the debate over the possibility of a local tax in Britain indicates (Layfield Report, 1976).

If taxes cannot be hidden from citizens, then at least they can be made more palatable. One means of doing this is to identify the particular benefits received by citizens as the result of a particular tax or user charge

Table 1. Changes in Sources of Revenue of Selected Members of Clusters, 1900–1978 (in percent)

Year	Income Tax	Corporation Tax	Social Security	Property Tax	Customs & Excise	Sales & VAT	Fees	Borrowing	Other
Sweden									
1900	10.8	2.4	3.1	26.6	34.4	0.0	14.8	0.0	9.7
1920	13.6	2.8	6.8	19.4	30.8	0.0	12.2	5.8	8.6
1935	38.7	8.9	8.9	10.6	26.6	0.0	6.2	2.0	0.8
1950	46.4	10.9	4.6	3.4	24.5	0.0	6.4	2.6	1.2
1965	44.6	5.6	11.4	1.4	19.1	9.6	3.6	4.1	1.8
1978	39.9	2.6	20.9	0.4	8.3	13.5	4.6	8.2	1.6
France									
1900	6.0	4.6	1.2	2.2	26.7	0.0	51.9	0.0	8.0
1920	5.9	3.9	6.7	0.9	24.2	0.0	44.7	3.1	10.7
1935	5.7	4.1	11.3	4.6	25.4	1.9	38.3	3.6	5.1
1950	5.4	4.2	24.2	3.3	16.9	19.6	18.6	1.6	6.2
1965	9.9	4.6	29.3	3.9	13.8	22.2	8.6	4.6	3.1
1978	12.1	4.4	39.1	3.1	8.4	20.7	8.3	2.2	1.7
Ireland									
1900	—	—	—	—	—	—	—	—	—
1920	—	—	—	—	—	—	—	—	—
1935	3.6	7.4	3.1	12.9	51.9	0.0	11.8	2.1	7.2
1950	15.4	6.9	4.3	17.5	43.3	0.0	9.6	1.8	1.2
1965	15.4	8.4	6.1	14.5	40.1	5.3	5.2	3.9	1.1
1978	24.4	4.1	12.2	5.7	23.8	14.6	4.8	9.6	0.8

Denmark

1900	6.9	0.0	0.4	7.4	61.3	0.0	14.6	7.1	2.3
1920	26.5	16.4	8.6	10.8	17.9	0.0	14.1	-0.6	6.3
1935	34.8	9.8	10.3	9.4	16.9	0.0	13.6	1.4	3.8
1950	40.6	5.2	4.3	8.8	31.9	0.0	4.8	1.9	2.5
1965	38.6	4.1	5.0	7.6	21.4	8.8	4.4	4.5	0.6
1978	46.8	2.8	1.3	5.5	14.2	19.4	4.6	6.1	0.3

Germany[a]

1900	11.2	8.4	1.2	12.6	25.5	0.0	26.8	0.0	16.3
1920	9.8	9.1	6.4	13.1	20.1	0.0	25.2	6.4	9.9
1935	13.6	6.4	14.6	8.9	19.4	2.6	20.9	8.1	5.5
1950	18.1	9.2	23.8	8.3	13.9	18.2	6.6	0.6	1.3
1965	25.2	6.8	25.2	4.5	14.0	14.8	4.9	3.4	1.2
1978	26.6	8.0	30.6	2.6	8.6	11.9	5.1	4.8	1.8

United Kingdom

1900	6.9	1.8	0.0	32.0	38.7	0.0	8.3	2.3	10.1
1920	28.7	19.6	4.2	11.2	29.8	0.0	2.4	0.6	3.5
1935	24.6	12.4	8.0	14.1	28.9	0.0	3.6	3.1	4.3
1950	22.8	15.4	9.6	11.9	26.3	6.0	2.9	2.0	3.0
1965	29.8	5.9	14.7	13.7	23.0	5.1	3.1	4.2	0.5
1978	30.7	7.0	17.6	11.6	14.6	7.7	2.8	7.1	0.9

[a]The definition of Germany changes with the several political changes occurring in that country. From 1950 onward it is the Federal Republic of Germany.

Sources: OECD (1979b); Mitchell (1975). A variety of national statistical and revenue publications were used to derive the figures for the earlier time periods.

Table 2. Deficits and Surpluses in Industrialized Democracies, 1950–1981

	United States	United Kingdom	France	West Germany	Italy	Sweden	Canada
Surpluses	3	3	5	6	0	2	4
Deficits	29	29	27	26	32	30	28

Source: International Monetary Fund (annuals).

(Savas, 1982). Most tax revenue goes into a general fund and then is allocated among the numerous programs of government through the budgetary process. The average citizen, therefore, may perceive little direct relationship between their tax contributions and their benefits. This is especially true, as Downs (1960) has pointed out, when government is heavily involved in providing public goods rather than more divisible and identifiable private goods. The obvious alternative to general taxation is the use of earmarked ("hypothecated") revenue sources. Such earmarking has been common, at least in Anglo-American countries, as a means of financing social security programs, with the payroll tax being "sold" to citizens as a social insurance contribution rather than as simply another tax (Leuchtenberg, 1963). This made both the tax and the pension which it funded more acceptable to many citizens. Such earmarked taxation has been used to fund a variety of programs, such as alcoholism treatment, highways, and education, and user fees can be directly connected to the enjoyment of a variety of public programs. Although economists and politicians complain at times about the rigidity of hypothecated revenue sources, these sources tend to appease citizens who can identify exactly where their tax money is being spent.

Finally, the rational politician would be concerned about the distributional consequences of his or her choice of a revenue system. One of the ostensible purposes of the public sector is to correct inequities in the distribution of goods and services arising from the market, and the selection of revenue instruments is an important means of effecting such corrections. Thus, while fees, charges, and earmarked taxes may appeal to many citizens and may be justified intellectually by the benefit principle of taxation—those who receive the benefit should pay for it—they may be more regressive forms of revenue collection than many citizens would like to see used to finance welfare state programs (Wilson, 1981). This is especially true given that many welfare state programs, such as social insurance, are financed through rather regressive payroll taxes. Therefore, there is a need to justify other forms of taxation, such as the progressive income tax, on the ability-to-pay principle. Those who have more income are assumed to be able to pay more taxes, so that the distribution of income after the operation of the revenue and benefit systems is assumed to be more equitable.

It is interesting to note what little difference the massive volumes of revenue and expenditure of contemporary political systems make in the actual distribution of income in society. As shown in Table 3, change in the proportion of income received by the lowest decile of the population is altered by only an average of 0.2%, while that of the highest decile is reduced by 1.6%. Although many politicians and many citizens might desire a more significant alteration of the income distribution through government, such change is difficult to produce. The explanation for this lack of progressivity on taxation is but one of several features of the revenue system for which we will attempt to offer explanation below.

As well as the vertical distribution of taxation among social classes, a politician must also be concerned about the horizontal impact of taxation among various industries in the economy. Each industry believes itself to be entitled to a special benefit or subsidy. Such subsidies are generally easier to give through the revenue system than through the expenditure system simply because revenue foregone is not as obvious to the average taxpayer as a direct expenditure. Thus, the range of "tax expenditures" which have arisen in almost all Western industrialized countries is a means of providing subsidies to groups without the need to actually appropriate money (Wills and Hardwick, 1978). This aids in explaining the lack of progressivity of revenue systems. The tax laws may appear progressive when only the rates of taxation are examined, but when the many ways that the more affluent individuals and corporations can legally avoid paying taxes are considered, the operational revenue system is much less progressive (Sanford and Walker, 1980).

Table 3. Difference in Pre- and Post-Tax Income Shares,[a] by Decile

Decile	United Kingdom	United States	Sweden	France	Germany	Canada
1	0.4	0.3	0.2	−0.1	0.3	0.3
2	0.5	0.4	0.4	0.1	0.3	0.4
3	0.4	0.3	0.6	0.0	0.1	0.5
4	0.2	0.4	1.1	−0.1	0.1	0.4
5	0.2	0.3	0.6	0.3	0.0	0.3
6	0.1	0.2	0.5	0.2	−0.1	0.3
7	−0.1	0.2	0.3	−0.7	−0.1	0.1
8	−0.2	0.0	0.2	0.4	−0.3	0.0
9	−0.4	−0.1	−0.4	0.5	0.1	−0.3
10	−1.2	−1.8	−3.1	−0.6	−0.8	−2.0

[a]Percentage post-tax income minus percentage pre-tax income.
Source: OECD (1976).

The rational politician operates in an environment which does not value taxation. Therefore, he or she must do everything possible to find means of hiding the real costs of government from citizens, while at the same time raising sufficient revenues to finance the expensive operation of that government. The strategies of disguising and obfuscating described satisfy the desire for re-election but may be quite contradictory both to the prescriptions of economists and to the values of those interested in democratic government. Most economists would argue that citizens cannot make a rational choice about the tax costs of government and their resulting benefits unless they know the real tax "bill" associated with their benefits (Wicksell, 1958). Concerned citizens and politicians would argue either that if citizens knew their real tax bills they would be in revolt within minutes, or if they understood what they received in benefits in return for their taxes—especially in low-tax countries such as the United States—they would be more positively inclined toward government. Regardless of their ideological persuasions, however, there would be agreement that citizens should be informed about what they are really paying for government.

Our discussion of the politics of revenue collection heretofore has assumed that rational politicians maximize their probability of re-election. This is, however, an abstraction from the complex world of policymaking where many politicians weigh tax and expenditure decisions along with a host of other considerations, and interact with a number of other actors in making revenue decisions. Despite the centrality of revenue choices to many citizens, in government those choices may be made in a more technocratic fashion with little direct involvement of politicians. At one end of the continuum, there is the very secretive Budget of the British government which is announced each year by the Chancellor of the Exchequer, sometimes without significant involvement even by most other members of the Cabinet. This may be contrasted to the more open process of tax policymaking in the United States and Scandinavia. For all of the countries, nonetheless, there is more to consider than the re-election of sitting politicians.

A standard hypothesis is that political parties have a significant influence on tax policy. More specifically, we might expect variations in tax policies depending upon whether one party or another was in office. Interestingly, this hypothesis does not appear to be supported empirically for a variety of reasons (Rose, 1980). One is simple political reason related to the interests of the rational politicians we have been discussing. An old tax is a good tax, at least politically. It does not require any overt political action in order to produce revenue. On the other hand, if a party for ideological or other reasons should decide that the existing tax structure is undesirable, it would have to repeal the old taxes—or alter the rate at which they are charged—and compensate for the lost revenues with new taxes or rates of taxation. This is almost exactly what the Thatcher government did in its budget of June, 1979. It reduced income taxes but compensated for the loss of revenue by increasing the value-added tax and excise taxes. The net effect of these changes on the average citizen was minimal—despite rhetoric about tax reductions. However, there was significant political controversy because taxes were being charged at very different rates.

In related fashion, there may not be very much political mileage to be gained by parties in advocating significant changes in the revenue system. Whereas expenditure programs may benefit a voter without *directly* penalizing other voters, the same cannot be said of a tax. Reducing taxation from one source, assuming a constant volume of expenditure, means that there will have to be a corresponding increase elsewhere or borrowing will have to be increased. The clever political party may, therefore, devote more of its attention to the development of benefit programs rather than to the reorganization of the system of revenue collection, as appealing as the goal of "tax reform" may be to rational policy analysis in virtually all developed economies.

The third reason for the apparent lack of a direct relationship between changes in political party in control of government and changes in the revenue system is that many political parties are, or strive to be, aggregative political institutions (Almond and Powell, 1966). As such, they may contain members of different social classes, and, for these purposes, they may contain representative of a variety of interest groups in the society, and a variety of industries. Any decision to assist one group or industry may threaten the internal consensus of the party, and consequently such issues are perhaps best excluded from political discussion. The technocratic nature of a good deal of tax policymaking may be functional for the maintenance of political parties. Likewise, just as parties seek to maintain internal consensus, there is some evidence that the adversarial relationship assumed to exist between political parties may not be apparent on tax issues. Parties may not be related to differences in tax policy because the members—and especially the leaders—of the parties do not believe very differently about issues of revenue collection. Ideologies may not be dead, but on issues such as taxation there may be sufficient national consensus, based upon history, culture, and/or inertia, and parties would not want to make significant innovations (Ardant, 1971).

The need for parties to aggregate the variety of interests points to another, and, perhaps more important, source of influence on tax policies: interest groups. These groups are not contained by the need to represent a variety of interests, nor the desire to hold public office, and, consequently, they are free to seek changes in tax policy which will specifically favor their members (Elvander, 1972). Further, given the specificity and legality of much of tax policy, and the consequent ability to target benefits, pressure groups may be a more logical form of organization for influencing tax policy than political parties.

Any number of interest groups may be involved in the game of tax politics, as almost any group can devise means by which it may be assisted through taxing, or, more precisely, through not taxing. However, tax politics is the special playground of the major economic interests in the society: the major corporate lobbies, the banks, and the labor unions. These interest groups may exert their influence in a variety of ways. Good (1980), for example, argues that the principle influence of interest groups on tax policy does not result from their overt attempts to influence, but rather, from their indirect influences. These indirect influences arise from the anticipation of other actors (politicians) of the positions they may hold and an attempt to accommodate those positions without conflict. Further, in political systems with more corporate political structures, interest groups may have direct influence on tax policies just as they do on a variety of other policy areas. Finally, as Elvander (1972) points out in regard to Sweden, political parties may become the virtual surrogates of interest groups when discussing taxation, especially in multi-party systems. Parties may abandon the aggregative function (which they may never have had in a multi-party system) in preference to serving the interests of particular groups.

Another political determinant of tax policy is bureaucratic politics. There are a number of very powerful organizational actors involved in making tax policy, and these organizations and their perceptions of the proper means of raising revenue may dominate partisan politics in making tax policy. Typically, the Treasury or the Ministry of Finance is one of the most powerful organizations in government, is central to making tax policy, and can almost determine the nature of tax policies. Nonetheless, the Treasury or Ministry of Finance is not alone in its concerns over taxation, and other bureaucratic organizations may also become involved in formulating tax policy. For example, when the British government was considering the move from the Selective Employment Tax and the Purchase Tax to the Value-Added Tax (VAT), the determination of how to make the change involved not only negotiations with the affected businesses, but also negotiations among the several tax-collecting organizations in British government: H.M. Customs and Excise and Inland Revenue (Johnstone, 1975). Such negotiations would be even more heated in instances where the tax is hypothecated to a particular purpose and is collected by the organization which it funds. The control over a tax involves power and additional personnel; hence, the tax collecting organizations in government may be expected to compete over the extension of particular forms of taxation.

In addition to the competition for taxing authority among tax collecting organizations, there may be other forms of "bureaucratic politics" involved in making tax poilcy. One form would be the political confrontations between the tax collecting bodies and the spending ministries. Although they may desire control over the taxes that exist, tax collecting organizations do not tend to favor the general extension of taxation. This brings them into direct conflict with the spending ministries. Moreover, there will be conflicts between the tax collecting bodies which tend to favor simple tax structures and taxes which are equally applied to all, and the clientele-based organizations in government which want to use the tax system as a means of providing benefits for their clients. In each of these instances, the organizational interests of the members of a government may be as important in the determination of tax policies as the demands being placed upon government by political parties or by interest groups. Thus, as we began the discussion of the politics of revenue, we can conclude by noting that taxation must be understood not so much in terms of mass politics but in terms of elite preferences and accommodation.

ADMINISTRATIVE FACTORS AFFECTING REVENUE PATTERNS

A major set of factors affecting the choice of revenue instruments is related to the ease of administration of the revenue instruments and the certainty of collection. These administrative factors are, to some degree, related to our earlier comments concerning the effects of economic development on taxation. When an economy becomes more industrialized, and as government provides more social security, there is much less difficulty in identifying income earned or the exchange of goods and services. Still, there are several other factors which affect the administration of taxation.

One of these is the culture—the willingness of the population to pay taxes. The stereotype of French and Italian citizens is that they evade taxes whenever possible, and that the collection of an income tax in those societies borders on the impossible. This may be one instance in which stereotypes have some empirical validity, for these two countries rely on consumption taxes, fees, and social security taxes to meet the expenditure demands of government (see Duberge, 1961). There is evidence of growing tax evasion in almost all industrialized societies, which implies that there will be a shift in most countries toward the use of consumption taxes and other forms of revenue which are more difficult to evade. Both user fees and any earmarked tax also give the citizen who is paying the tax an incentive to be sure that the tax recipients are delivered to government and that all similarly placed citizens are also being taxed. If he or she is to receive a particular benefit or is to be covered against certain undesired eventualities, the citizen will want to be sure that the tax has indeed been collected. Tax receipts which are paid into a general fund provide few such incentives, and, in fact, everyone has the incentive to be a free rider and avoid paying the tax.

As in so many policy areas, administrative reasons can be used to prevent things from occurring. For example, one part of the argument against more buoyant forms of local revenue in the United Kingdom—specifically a local income tax—is that such a tax would be "impossible" to administer (Hepworth, 1980, pp. 279–320). Much the same has been said about the use of "employment privilege" or payroll taxes in American cities. In both of these instances, there may be less real administrative incapacity as administrative and political unwillingness to adopt the form of taxation proposed.

Administrative considerations may conflict with the other considerations discussed. The easiest taxes to administer are those which are collected on consumption, and especially on goods and services for which the demand is relatively inelastic, such as alcohol, tobacco or food. Likewise, if taxes are to be placed on income, they would be easier to administer if they had few "loopholes" and exceptions. Both of these administrative criteria would conflict with political considerations: the promotion of greater equality of incomes and the favoring of organized interests. However, there may well be instances in which administrative ease will correspond with political considerations. For example, the Pay-As-You-Earn (withholding) approach to collecting income tax has the administrative advantage that the majority of the tax is collected for government by employers and is collected ahead of the time that it is actually due. The political advantage of this form of collection is that the majority of citizens have little or nothing to pay at the time that taxes are actually due. Hence, even with self-assessment as in the United States, the total tax bill may not be as onerous as it would otherwise be. The citizen may see the total taxes paid, but will not have to write out a check for the entire amount at one time.

TAX CHOICES AND SOCIAL SECURITY

The selection of a revenue system is not a simple matter, and in fact much of the above discussion may be excessively rationalistic in its approach to taxation. As with social benefits, a great deal of the choice about taxation is made by inertia and custom. Taxes are not changed very rapidly; in any one year, the yield of the revenue system may be determined more by changes in the tax base (resulting from economic growth and inflation) as from policy changes. Countries tend to persist in one pattern of taxation unless they have some definite reason to alter that pattern. Such reasons may arise from the political, economic, and administrative factors we have outlined, or they may occur by diffusion. The adaptation of the value-added tax in the United Kingdom as a result of membership in the EEC and its subsequent discussion as a means of raising additional revenue in the United States is indicative of the latter types of charges in tax systems.

With these explanations for differences in revenue systems in mind, we will begin to examine some of the differences which exist in patterns of taxation in industrialized countries. As a first step in that direction, the information in Table 4 gives average revenues derived from a number of sources among OECD countries (excluding Greece, Portugal, Spain and Turkey), the percentage of revenues derived from that source, and the range among the 19 OECD countries. What is perhaps the most striking in this table is the variation in revenue patterns among countries which are commonly regarded as being reasonably homogeneous. For five of the nine major types of taxes shown in this table, at least

Table 4. Cross-National Variations in Revenue Components, 1977
(percentages of total revenue)

Revenue Components	OECD Mean	United States	OECD Range
A. *Taxes*			
Personal income	30.2	29.9	56.9 – 13.2
Employers' social security	13.8	13.0	34.9 – 0.
Sales & VAT	12.4	5.9	21.2 – 0.
Custom & Excise	11.4	7.6	28.2 – 7.5
Corporation	6.7	10.4	18.7 – 2.8
Employees' social security	6.4	8.5	15.8 – 0.
Property	2.6	10.1	11.2 – 0.
Wealth & Inheritance	1.8	1.5	2.4 – 0.
Other taxes	3.7	2.7	10.8 – 1.9
Total tax	89.0	89.6	92.8 – 85.4
B. *User Charges* (including fees and net trading income)	5.5	5.7	10.6 – 2.6
C. *Borrowing*	5.4	4.8	21.6 – 4.6
	100%	100%	

Source: OECD (1979a,b). Calculations for 19 countries with competitive political systems throughout the postwar era.

one country does not use the source at all, while some other country uses it to derive up to one-third of its total revenue. Next to personal income, social security taxes on employers are both the most important and most variable tax. Clearly, these countries are not homogeneous in the ways which they choose to collect revenues.

But despite the apparent variation, there is also some interesting regularity in the tax as well. Although some countries do not use particular tax instruments, they are actually few in number. For example, five countries, including two of the most advanced welfare states (Norway and Sweden) do not collect employees' social security taxes, and two (Australia and New Zealand) do not collect employers' social security contributions. Only Japan does not have a general consumption (sales and VAT) tax. Thus, although it is interesting that not every country chooses to use every instrument, it is also important to note that most countries tax in as many ways possible (12 of the 19 countries have at least one form of tax in each of the broad categories in Table 4).

Another important regularity is that no simple source of revenue accounts for as much as one third of revenues, with the exception of income taxes in ten countries, and employers' social security contributions in one country. In only five other cases does a single tax account for as much as one quarter of total taxation. In other words, not only do the governments of these countries use the variety of available tax instruments, but they also tend to spread the burden among the available taxes. There is, of course, greater reliance on the income tax than on any other form of taxation (for 14 of the 19 countries the personal income tax was the largest single source of revenue), but almost all the taxes are expected to produce a significant share of total revenues.

CLUSTER ANALYSIS

In an attempt to develop some understanding of patterns of revenue collection, a cluster analysis was done of revenue data from the 19 OECD countries which had competitive democratic governments over the period of 1955 to 1977. The percentage of revenues derived from each of a number of sources (see Table 3 for a list of sources) will be used as the variables to define the clusters, with the countries being grouped according to their revenue collection patterns.

Unlike many of the methods applied in the social sciences, cluster analysis does not provide a readily interpretable summary statistic. Rather, cluster analysis depends more on the judgment of the researcher to assess the quality of the results. The method generally applied is to decompose a set of data first into two, then three, and then onward to as many clusters as are deemed necessary. The problem is to decide when there are enough clusters to distinguish all significant groupings of cases without allowing too many clusters, something that would defeat the purpose of reducing a number of cases to a smaller number of patterns. Table 5 presents the results of a cluster analysis on the data from the OECD countries for 1977, with the results of the four, five and six cluster solutions being presented.

The two most clearly defined clusters are Norway and Sweden, and France and Italy. These are the first two clusters to be extracted and they remain stable throughout the analysis. Likewise, a somewhat unexpected cluster composed of the two Antipodes and the other two Scandinavian countries is presented at all three levels of decomposition. The similarity of Australia, New Zealand, and the Scandinavian countries is clearly related to their high rates of income taxation and their lack of employees' social security contributions. The six cluster solution appears

Table 5.   Clusters Derived From 1977 Revenue Data

Four Cluster Solution			
1	*2*	*3*	*4*
Norway	France	Belgium	Denmark
Sweden	Italy	Canada	Finland
		Germany	Australia
		Ireland	New Zealand
		Japan	
		Luxembourg	
		Netherlands	
		Austria	
		Switzerland	
		United States	
		United Kingdom	

Five Cluster Solution				
1	*2*	*3*	*4*	*5*
Norway	France	Belgium	Denmark	Japan
Sweden	Italy	Germany	Finland	Luxembourg
		Ireland	Australia	Canada
		Austria	New Zealand	United States
		Netherlands		Switzerland

Six Cluster Solution					
1	*2*	*3*	*4*	*5*	*6*
Norway	France	Ireland	Denmark	Canada	Austria
Sweden	Italy		Finland	Japan	Belgium
			New Zealand	Luxembourg	Germany
			Australia	Switzerland	Netherlands
				United States	
				United Kingdom	

to be the most useful choice for this analysis. The six cluster solution, in particular, appears to be meaningful in terms of cultural and political patterns among the countries.

The countries in the first cluster, Norway and Sweden, have been linked historically, and despite their differences in wealth, patterns of development, and, to some extent, politics, they have developed relatively similar social and economic programs (Peters and Klingman, 1977). Whether for cultural, historical, or political reasons, they also collect revenue in rather similar ways. A large portion of their revenue comes from income taxation and from general consumption taxes (VAT), and both have relatively low rates of social security taxation. In 1977, both countries borrowed a higher than average percentage of their total revenue. This pattern of revenue collection may be explained by the redistributive aims on the part of decision-makers, both past and present; these aims account for the high income tax element and the low social security component, and for the high rates of VAT and borrowing.

The second cluster has fairly obvious explanations. We mentioned previously the difficulties experienced by French and Italian governments in raising revenues for more visible taxes (e.g., the income tax) and their consequent reliance on VAT and social security taxes, especially the employers' contribution to social security. Historically and at the present, these two countries employ user charges and other economic activities of the State to finance a significant portion of their total costs of running government (Mondari, 1965). Both countries have a pattern of revenue collection which is as invisible as possible, although they are confronted now by increasing expenditure demands (especially in Italy). Their populations began the taxpayers' revolt long before it became fashionable, which made adaptation to increased demands quite difficult.

Ireland constitutes a "cluster" by itself. As we have noted, compared to the other countries in this sample, Ireland is relatively underdeveloped economically. This is true of both the structure of its economy and its per capita income. As a consequence, the government has tended to concentrate its revenue collection on indirect mechanisms. This has meant the very extensive use of customs and excise taxes and general consumption taxation, as well as very high levels of borrowing. Also, perhaps as an inheritance from the United Kingdom or merely the relatively ease of identifying the target, property taxation is very important for the Irish government. As a relatively small percentage of the labor force is employed by firms of any size, income taxation and social security are difficult to collect and constitute a relatively small percentage of revenue. Clearly, any effort to expand Irish social security will raise awkward tax choices.

The fourth cluster which emerges is more difficult to explain. It consists of two Scandinavian countries and two members of the British Commonwealth. It is quite logical that each of these groups of two should be linked, but is not so logical that all four should be linked to each other. Although culturally and historically different, their patterns of taxation are quite similar. There are very high rates of income taxation and low rates of social security taxation. The latter point distinguishes the two Commonwealth countries from other "Anglo-American" democracies, and the relatively high rates of property taxation distinguish these two Scandinavian countries from Sweden and Norway. However, the description of the similarities of the tax systems does not explain why they are similar. At least Australia is somewhat similar to the two Scandinavian countries in that it has a relatively powerful union movement, as well as a rather well-developed sense of equality (Coughlin, 1979). In addition, all of the four countries have a rather high degree of reliance on primary and extractive economic activity. Still, there is a great deal to explain about the formation of this particular cluster.

The fifth cluster extracted might be termed the "hard core" of capitalism, although Luxembourg and perhaps even Canada might be somewhat inaccurately characterized by such a description. Although there are marked differences within this cluster in the degree of development of welfare state programs, there is quite a bit of similarity in how those programs are financed. These countries all raise approximately a mean (of the 19 OECD nations) proportion of their revenue from income taxes, have a significant share of their revenue derived from social security taxation, have a lower than average revenue from general consumption taxation and from fees and charges. The distinguishing feature of the revenue patterns of these countries is the collection of very high levels of corporate tax revenues and very high rates of property taxation. It is especially interesting, given the image of great corporate power in the majority of these countries, that there should be such high levels of corporate taxation. One argument is that this apparent weakness of corporate interests is illusory. The incidence of corporation taxes has been debated by economists for years, but if there is a general conclusion to be reached from the debate, it is that at least some portion of corporate taxation is passed on to consumers, and to the employees of the firm (Due and Friedlander, 1977, pp. 305–315). Under the "right" set of economic conditions, the real payers of the corporate tax are not the corporations but the consumers who buy their products and workers who receive lower wages. An alternative explanation might be that given the development of corporate structures in these countries, and the location of many multinational corporations in Switzerland and Luxembourg for tax and other purposes, the corporation tax is a convenient mechanism for extracting revenues. For the United States, the United Kingdom and Canada, the reliance on property taxation is a historical and cultural phenomenon.

The final cluster of countries may be described as corporate in the political, if not the economic sense of the term. Perhaps the best description of the pattern of revenue collection in these countries is that they have a rather balanced pattern of revenue collection. They tend to use almost every revenue source available to them, and tend to be not too far above or below the OECD means for the use of revenue source. The principle exception to that generalization is their higher than average use of consumption taxes (both VAT and customs and excises), and their somewhat lower than average use of the personal income tax and the corporate income tax. Although it should not be carried too far, this pattern of taxation can be seen as related to the need for balance associated with corporate politics, and the necessity of government giving every sector of society a share of the action in government. The converse of this is that redistributive decisions are less likely to be made in corporate politics, and the balanced pattern—dependent upon the consumption decisions of individuals—will be reflected in the revenue system.

These six clusters provide an interpretable and reasonable description of the patterns of revenue collection in these 19 countries in 1977. Furthermore, a preliminary discriminant analysis indicates that the differences among the clusters are statistically significant. However, these patterns contain information only about a single year rather late in the development of the welfare state. If we are interested in the transformation from pre-welfare state forms of revenue collection to the present day and the implications which those changes may have for modern governance, we must extend the analysis backward in time. We can then see the base from which those countries began their development toward their contemporary systems, and explore the dynamics of developments.

We will begin the examination of historical patterns of development with revenue systems as they existed in 1900. This date has been chosen arbitrarily, and we would be among the first to acknowledge the differential patterns of development of welfare states' programs and the political structures of these countries. The choice of a common year removes the necessity of attempting to identify functionally equivalent years across a range of countries and the resultant possibility of introducing even greater error into the analysis. Given the restraints of space we will select on representative country from each of the clusters discerned in the 1977 data. Of course, it is almost certain that the same clusters would not have formed in 1900, and that the selection of a "representative country" is controversial. Even given these caveats, the analysis should provide an insight into the development of revenue patterns during the development of the welfare state.

Although there are certainly differences among the countries, the national patterns of revenue collection in 1900 shown in Table 1 were remarkably similar, especially when contrasted to the data from 1977. The pattern of revenue collection in 1900 might be described as being traditional or underdeveloped, especially in the economic sense of that term. This is, of course, to be expected given the relatively underdeveloped state of their economies at that time. The major sources of revenues were consumption taxes (customs and excise taxes rather than general consumption taxes), the income from various government and user fees, and, to a lesser extent, the property tax. There was some income from an income tax, but this was still a meager contribution to government revenue and differed from contemporary income tax by being primarily a flat-rate rather than a progressive levy. Social security taxes were only beginning to be collected, and even that revenue was not considered to be government revenue at that time. Instead, it was considered to be the income of private, albeit state-regulated and state-subsidized, social insurance programs described earlier in this book. This distinction persists in several European countries today, although paying social security taxes is as mandatory as paying any other type of tax for the majority of workers. Consequently, even the rudimentary forms of development of social security taxation are included in these data for 1900. In addition, the "other" category in the 1900 data is rather large when compared to later years, in part because of the continuing use of old revenue instruments such as capitation taxes which are not a part of the set of categories we have used to describe modern revenue systems.

From relatively similar revenue patterns in 1900, the countries chosen for analysis tended to diverge in later time periods. In our 1920 and 1935 observations, more distinctive national patterns were emerging. France persisted in relying upon consumption taxes, but was also beginning to use the higher rates of social security contributions (see the previous chapter by Ashford). The United Kingdom, Norway and Denmark were all beginning to rely on the income tax as a means of raising large volumes of revenue, even though the income tax was only paid by a small portion of the population. Ireland gained its independence from the United Kingdom by 1935, and was already raising a very large portion of its revenue from customs and excises, a characteristic which would persist into the 1977 data. Finally, Germany, although a very different Germany from that of 1977, was beginning to rely upon a wide variety of revenue sources, a characteristic also noted in the 1977 data. However, Germany also continued to rely more upon the economic activities of the state than did the other countries, although the difference from France was not considerable.

The growing differentiation of national patterns of revenue collection can be seen as a product of growing demands for revenue which reflect cultural differences in the acceptability of certain forms of taxation, and differences in patterns of economic development. The overall level of revenue collection was still not great when compared to available resources—even during the Depression. Arguably, countries had the opportunity to collect revenues in the manner they found the least troublesome, both politically and economically. The development of welfare state funding in that period had not yet placed any pressures on government which would require them to expand their revenue base beyond that which they found most convenient.

The divergence of national revenue systems persisted in the 1950 and 1965 observations, with the countries demonstrating the most differentiated patterns of revenue collection in 1965. The postwar period was one of increasing affluence, and again there was no particular need for nations to make difficult choices about how to increase their revenues. For the most part, revenues increased automatically, as the economies grew and as more income and expenditure became subject to taxation, although some of the newer forms of taxation (the income tax) did not outstrip increases in the volume of revenues coming from the older forms of taxation. As with so much of the development of the welfare state, affluence reduced the need to make difficult choices in revenue collection as well as in the allocation of those revenues among compting purposes of expenditures.

The 1977 data show an increasing convergence of revenue collection patterns in these countries, possibly caused in part by the nationalization of social security programs. Although some countries persisted in eschewing certain revenue sources, the degree of diversity in revenue collection diminished. Some of this convergence arose through the increasing vigor of countries in administering taxes which were already on the book, such as the income tax in Italy, while some arose from the adoption of new taxes, for instance, the VAT in the United Kingdom and Ireland. As with the latter example, some of the convergence may have arisen through the influence of multinational organizations, and some of it may have arisen through economic development in some of the less affluent nations and the associated increase in the number of tax "handles." However, a major impetus for the convergence of patterns of revenue collection is the need to reaise revenue in large volumes as a result of the expanding social programs of the welfare state. As noted previously, one means of disguising higher level of taxation is to spread the tax burden among as many different types of taxation as possible and as many levels of government as possible. This strategy is being followed by governments currently faced with revenue problems. As demands for revenue increase, politicians will attempt to use every means available to finance their popular expenditure programs. Convergence does not mean that all countries will tend toward a single level of collection for each revenue source, but it does mean that few will be able to afford the luxury of foregoing any possible revenue source. The 19 OECD countries are not homogenous with respect to their forms of revenue collection, but they are more homogeneous in 1977 than they have been at any time since 1900.

CONCLUSION: TAXATION AND WELFARE

The welfare state appears to be entering a new period of re-entrenchment, if not retreat. This change has been triggered at least in part by political and economic pressures against taxation. Governmental decision-makers have demonstrated their adaptability in dealing with these pressures through adopting new revenue measures and by increasing the variety of tax instruments. One important tendency in the development of revenue collection will likely be the increasing utilization of user charges and fees. There is renewed discussion of the value-added tax in the United States, and there is discussion in almost all countries introducing charges for public services that can be priced and charged for directly. A common reaction of governments that need more revenue is to increase taxes on the necessities of life (sic) such as alcohol, tobacco, and petrol.

The welfare state may never have been designed as an institution of large-scale redistribution across classes, but these changes in taxation would appear to represent a movement away from even modest attempts at redistribution. They constitute an extension of the benefit principle of taxation to cover a larger portion of government revenue. From the perspective of their proponents, these changes in revenue collection represent both a justifiable shift in the burden of financing public services onto those who consume those services and a natural means of regulating the expansion of public services. However, for many citizens, "post-Keynesian" developments in revenue collection, as well as post-Keynesian developments in expenditure patterns, will represent an important subtraction from their well-being.

The other question which arises with respect to post-Keynesian revenue collection is whether, in fact, there will be the continuing need to raise the large and increasing amounts of revenue. The evidence from the Thatcher government in the United Kingdom is an indication of the difficulties in actually cutting the size of government, while the initial successes of the Reagan administration fade once social security is threatened. The recent economy under a bourgeois government in Sweden produces more inconsistent evidence. If there is a reduction in

the growth of the public sector, then we might hypothesize some movement away from the convergence intimated in our data. If indeed certain patterns of revenue collection are more acceptable to certain cultural, political and economic systems than others and there was reduced
demand for total revenues (relative to resources), we might expect governments to cut back those taxes which would be more objectionable to
their citizens.

REFERENCES

Aaron, Henry, ed. (1976), *Inflation and the Income Tax*, Washington, D.C.: The Brookings
    Institution.
Aaron, Henry J., and Joseph A. Pechman, eds. (1981), *How Taxes Affect Economic Behavior*,
    Washington, D.C.: The Brookings Institution.
Almond, Gabriel A. and G. Bingham Powell (1966), *Comparative Politics: A Developmental
    Approach*, Boston: Little Brown.
Ardant, Gabriel (1971), *Histoire de l'impot*, Paris: Fayard.
Bell, Daniel (1974), "The Public Household," *Public Interest*, 37(Fall): 29–68.
Bird, Richard M. (1970), *The Growth of Government Spending in Canada*, Toronto: Canadian
    Tax Foundation.
Coughlin, Richard M. (1979), "Social Policy and Ideology: Public Opinion in Eight Rich
    Nations," in R. Tomasson, ed., *Comparative Social Research*, Greenwich, CT: JAI Press,
    pp. 3–40.
Downs, Anthony (1960), "Why the Public Budget is Too Small in a Democracy," *World Poli-
    tics*, 12(July): 541–563.
Duberge, Jean (1961), *La Psychologie sociale de l'impot*, Paris: Presses Universitaires d'France.
Due, John F. and Ann R. Friedlander (1977), *Government Finance: Economics of the Public
    Sector*, Homewood, IL: Irwin.
Elavander, Nils (1972), "The Politics of Taxation in Sweden 1945–1970: A Study of the
    Functions of Parties and Organizations," *Scandanavian Political Studies*, pp. 63–82.
Flora, Peter, and Arnold Heidenheimer, eds. (1981), *The Development of the Welfare State in
    Europe and America*, New Brunswick, NJ: Transaction Books.
Good, David A. (1980), *The Politics of Anticipation: Making Canadian Federal Tax Policy*, Ot-
    tawa: Carleton University Press.
Hepworth, N. P. (1980), *The Finance of Local Government*, London: Allen & Unwin.
International Monetary Fund (annuals, 1950–1981), *International Financial Statistics*,
    Washington, D.C.: International Monetary Fund.
Johnstone, Dorothy (1975), *A Tax Shall Be Charged*, London: HMSO (Civil Service Studies,
    No. 1).
Layfield Committee (1976), *Report of the Committee of Inquiry into Local Government Finance*,
    London: HMSO, cmnd. 6453.
Leuchtenberg, W. E. (1963), *Franklin D. Roosevelt and the New Deal, 1932–1940*, New York:
    Harper.
Mitchell, B. R. (1975), *European Historical Statistics, 1750–1970*, London: Macmillan.
Mondari, Aristide (1965), *Basi statistiche e leggi assimatiche della dinamica dellievasione fiscale*,
    Milan: Universita Bocconi.
Musgrave, Richard A. (1969), *Fiscal Systems*, New Haven, CT: Yale University Press.
National Tax Journal (1979), "Tax and Tax Expenditure Limitations," 32 (Supplement,
    June).

Organization for Economic Cooperation and Development (1976), *Public Expenditure on Income Maintenance Programmes,* Paris: OECD, Studies in Resource Allocation, pp. 108–109.

Organization for Economic Cooperation and Development (1979a), *National Accounts of OECD Member Countries, 1960–1977,* Vol. II, Paris: OECD.

Organization for Economic Cooperation and Development (1979b), *Revenue Statistics of OECD Member Countries, 1965–1978,* Paris: OECD.

Peters, Guy and Martin Heisler (1981), "Government: What is Growing and How Do We Know?" *Studies in Public Policy,* no. 89, University of Strathclyde.

Peters, Guy and C. David Klingman (1977), "Patterns of Expenditure Development in Sweden, Norway and Denmark," *British Journal of Political Science,* 7:378–412.

Rose, Richard (1980), *Do Parties Make a Difference?* Chatham, NJ: Chatham House.

Rose, Richard and Guy Peters (1976), *Can Governments Go Bankrupt?* New York: Basic Books.

Salowsky, Heinz (1977), *Personalzusatzkosten in Westlichen Industrielandern,* Cologne: Deutscher Intitutverlag.

Sanford, Pond C. and R. Walker (1980), *Taxation and Social Policy,* London: Heinemann.

Savas, E. S. (1982), *Privatizing the Public Sector,* Chatham, NJ: Chatham House.

Wicksell, Knut (1958), "A New Principle of Just Taxation," in R. Musgrave and A. Peacock, eds., *Classics in the Theory of Public Finance,* London: Macmillan, pp. 72–118.

Wilensky, Harold L. (1976), *The New "Corporatism": Centralization and the Welfare State,* Beverly Hills, CA: Sage Publications.

Wills, J. R. M. and P. J. W. Hardwick (1978), *Tax Expenditures in the United Kingdom,* London: Deinmann.

Wilson, Thomas (1981), "The Finance of the Welfare State," in A. Peacock and F. Forte, eds., *The Political Economy of Taxation,* Oxford: B. H. Blackwells, pp. 94–117.

THE BRITISH AND FRENCH
SOCIAL SECURITY SYSTEMS:
WELFARE STATES BY INTENT
AND BY DEFAULT

Douglas E. Ashford

Since the oil crisis, welfare has obviously become a more central issue in the politics of the West European democracies, but less noticed has been the changing rankings of major European policies in the European welfare league. Contrary to the image that we often accept, France is no longer a pecunious public spender. As early as 1962, French public welfare spending was 17% of the GDP (excluding housing), exceeded only by Austria, Belgium, Sweden and Denmark among the European and North American democracies. At that time Britain spent 12.6% of its GDP on welfare, a full percentage point less than the OECD average (OECD, 1978, p. 25). By 1975 the relative positions of France and Britain were 20.9 and 16.7% respectively when the average was 18.8%. In retrospect, it appears that the French people were fully aware of the change though leaders were surprised and shocked, while in Britain welfare recipients were deeply upset but leaders were working hard to minimize welfare costs.

Not the least of political paradoxes involved in this transformation is that France recently opted for a Socialist president committed to increasing social security, while Britain chose an austere Conservative prime minister dedicated to reducing public spending and marginally reducing social benefits. Thus, France was celebrating the arrival of the welfare state when Britain was deploring its demise. The contrast becomes even sharper when we compare rates of growth of social security revenues. After the shock of the oil crisis, which was a more severe financial blow to France than to Britain, French social security revenues increased at the rate of 37% over 1975–1980 (down 6% from 1970–1975) while British social security revenues increased at 14.6% (down 26.5% from 1970–1975) (Lagrange and Launay, 1980, p. 1147, constant prices). Over the past five years French social spending had the fastest rate of growth of any European democracy. There is every reason to believe that the trend set in motion by Pompidou and Giscard will be continued by Mitterand.

Such a dramatic departure from national stereotypes makes the behavior of France and Britain of particular interest as a comparative study of social policy. There are two conventional approaches to explaining such differences, neither of which appear fully satisfactory. First, we might proceed with an extension of the macro-level comparison using aggregate data which has, of course, been widely applied to some of the policy problems of the modern welfare state (Rose and Peters, 1978). Useful as such analysis is in identifying instructive cases, the logical problems of such explanations are now widely recognized. The macro-data easily conceals important intrasystemic variations, much of which may elude aggregate measurement. While these essentially statistical explanations help us avoid some obvious pitfalls of comparative policy analysis, they may also generate new and no less damaging distortions by eliminating institutional and political features that in fact operate in different ways within each system. One of the most skillful demonstrations of this problem that I have found is an analysis by Gray (1973) showing that the determinants of AFDC spending at national and local levels are in many respects independent.

Second, and perhaps more common in dealing with expanding social security systems, one might consider the rate of growth of benefits as a function of some singular social or political feature. For example, ideological differences, class politics or party competition no doubt tap critical features of Western democracies (Pryor, 1968; Wilensky, 1975). Such studies are certainly a precaution against careless simplification, but again they must make important assumptions of the validity of any given feature as the independent explanatory factor in moving from one society to another. Again, the British and French cases are instructive because one might expect that a conservative coalition in power for over twenty years would have figured out how to limit social security spending, while more competitive, adversarial British politics might have bid up social benefits more rapidly. Validation of simple theories can only be achieved by invoking abstract and often tautological theories of social or political systems. In other words, validation rests on an ideal-type which can be neither confirmed or rejected. Oddly enough, this more doctrinaire or arbitrary approach may be right, but can never tell us why it is right, a problem that plagues explanations of policy differences by both the extreme left and the extreme right (see Ashford, 1981).

A third approach, which I propose to use in examining this intriguing disparity in British and French welfare performance, is to search for the characteristics of the policy process that differentiate the two systems. The politics of policy is of course a function of both external political constraints operating in any particular policy area such as class politics, party alignment, etc., but it is also a function of the structural regularities of the policy area itself. Separating these two influences on policymaking seems to me an essential and logical preliminary to validating our comparisons of policy performance. Having discovered important macro-differences, the politics of policy offers a way of finding out, first, whether the micro-level behavior subsumed in a general measure is or is not significant across systems, and, second, if it is, whether or not it may explain performance better than general features that are often extracted, perhaps uncritically, from more abstract models of society and politics. In a few words, the *politics* of policy is fundamentally different from the study of policy for "policy purposes," i.e., evaluation, impact, etc., and from the general study of politics.

Without doing full justice to the structural theory of politics that Eckstein has outlined (1973), the point of the analysis to follow is that the politics of social security may have little to do with the commonly accepted goals of a social security system or the measures of social security that are often used in macro-level explanations of differences among social security systems. I am not arguing that social security is less concerned with material equality than, for example, local reform, but I am suggesting that we have no reason to assume that the politics of equality will necessarily be better understood analyzing social security rather than local reform. From this perspective, I have argued that the politics of local reform in Britain and France questions many of the stereotypes of British and French political behavior, many of them derived from very abstract models or based on general features of each system whose significance within the policy process has not been fully explored (Ashford, 1982).

A structural approach to comparing the development of social security would place more emphasis on structural features of the policy process in the two societies, and look for the critical disjunction or pressures that caused France to make large increments in social spending in recent years. I would argue that the politics of policymaking must be distinguished from simply observing policy change itself. Over time, policy analysis involves a number of units of an analysis, quite possibly different units at different points in time, and rejects the assumption that the critical or independent causal factors leading to a change are uniform over time. In this respect, it is curious that both more ambitious quantitative analysis and Marxist theories of social change lead us in the same direction (Peacock and Wiseman, 1967; Andrée and Delorme, 1980). In rather different ways, both are structural theories, one relying on statistical associations and the other on assumptions concerning the nature of class conflict.

As I have argued elsewhere (Ashford, 1978), my feeling is that neither deals adequately with the many levels of interaction found in any complex policy change which involve such varied and discontinuous elements as the particular persuasions and prejudices of ruling elites, the evolving structure of party competition, and changing social and economic trends as they may be related to the policy problem in the history of each society. This is not to say that a rigorous statistical or mathematical model is unlikely to uncover intriguing and previously unobserved relationships; nor that a persistent (dogmatic?) concern for a single causal relationship in society may not show interesting contradictions and discontinuities in a society's development. My underlying argument in analyzing the experience of Britain and France is that for any given social or political problem, the continuities can never be more than a partial explanation and that the causal implications of variables cannot be readily separated from their context because causality often reverses direction. Without, I hope, being too enigmatic, the ways in which causal connections are reversed and the evolving importance of various social and political factors constitute the politics of policymaking.

As we shall see in my approach to explaining the recent development of British and French social security, the politics of policymaking does not presume to tell us everything we wish to know about policies. For one thing, non-decisions take on a slightly different meaning from their general usage in political analysis. For example, there were long periods of time when France did little about social security, but these periods may be essential to our understanding of why France was able and willing to make large increments at later times. Non-decisions are not necessarily rejection or neglect of the policy goal, as more linear or functional theories might suggest, but are frequently periods when important policy issues are being debated, refined and gradually reshaped so that change can take place within the institutional constraints of a society. Furthermore, the politics of policymaking recognizes that political and social systems do not have the functional uniformity often attributed to them by those most interested in policy evaluation, organizational behavior or the "final" outcomes (itself an arbitrary decision of the analyst). For these and other reasons, my inclination is to search first for those historical features that helped define the nature of social security (or any other major policy issue) and how such definitions are shaped by political and institutional constraints. In conducting such an exercise on central-local relations in Britain and France (Ashford, 1982), I found that many of the standing clichés or assumptions about centralization for the two countries are misleading, and I would expect the same in doing so in the case of social security or any other major policy issue.

Contrary to our conventional stereotypes of the two countries, the rapid expansion of French social security was neither planned nor controlled to the extent that we might think, and, not unlike the experience with local reorganization, British concern with social security advanced with the concentration of power in the hands of ministers and the cabinet. Though there were certainly times when social security issues created deep division within parties and even within Parliament in Britain, the ease with which Britain was transformed into the model of a welfare state, and the difficulties which plagued the development of social security in France, become the central features of a political analysis of social security in the two countries. Using structural analysis in a more differentiated way than is commonly done in abstract theories, there are perhaps three main structural problems shaping the transformation of the two countries. They are: (1) the link between political and social values as it evolved in the two societies; (2) relationship of social services and benefits to existing political institutions; and (3) the definition of responsibility and authority in relation to the state and its machinery for providing social security.

THE THEMES OF POVERTY AND SOLIDARITY

In defining the basic values justifying social assistance, the two countries took radically different approaches from the earliest stages of the industrial revolution. Many of these differences can still be observed not only in debates over increasing social security, but in the actual definition of rights and obligations in receiving assistance. Of course, the distinctive traditions of helping others were pre-industrial, in that France began to define social assistance goals in relatively precise terms from the Revolution (see Godechot, 1968, pp. 440–442, 601–708), and Britain in even

more precise terms from the Poor Laws of 1601. While it is hardly surprising that in both countries providing additional help for the poor and
disadvantaged was phrased in liberal terms, the political interpretation
of liberal principles in order to relate the state and its activity to social
needs was quite different.

For present purposes, it is perhaps sufficient to point out that the dislocations of industrial development came to Britain first, partly as a result of the land enclosure and partly as a result of rapid industrial
growth in the north of England. The details of these developments have
been carefully recorded elsewhere (Bruce, 1968; Frazer, 1973; Roberts,
1961) and in many ways are in fact the corpus of British social history in
the late eighteenth and early nineteenth century. The brutal social fact
was that Britain first experienced grinding, hopeless poverty. The debate over the reform of the Poor Laws preoccupied British politics for
nearly a generation, and the Poor Law Amendment Act of 1834 was a
monument to the radical Whigs and Benthamite thinking (see Lubenow,
1971, pp. 30–68; MacDonagh, 1977). Operating under Malthusian principles, nearly all leaders believed that increased wages and benefits
would lead to uncontrollable erosion of profits, but the growing numbers of the poor made change imperative. Despite the intense political
debates of the period, the decision to assist the poor was a characteristic-
ally unpolitical decision. Ultimately attracting wide support in the tumul-
tuous Whig regime, the 1834 Act was reviewed with little controversy by
Peel a decade later. Few could see alternatives short of sheer starvation
which was, of course, permissible for Ireland but not for England.

None of the reformers had any intention of violating laissez-faire
principles, but their humane instincts supported protection for women
and children. There were leaders on both sides of the aisle such as
Nassau Senior and Lord Ashley (later Earl of Shaftebury) who wanted to
protect those who could not protect themselves. As for poverty assistance, it was meant to be degrading and meager. From the Poor Law
Amendment Act springs the distinction between the "deserving" and
"undeserving" poor which permeates British social security to the present day in the form of universally available national insurance benefits
and means-tested supplementary benefits. Though technically termi-
nated with the National Insurance Act of 1911, the Poor Law Boards
continued to function until the Local Government Act of 1929. The
1834 Act was the first major attempt at social engineering although the
Chairman of the Royal Commission, Senior, rejected most of the recommendations of Sir Edwin Chadwick, Bentham's disciple, in writing the
law (see Finer, 1957).

As Briggs (1961) has pointed out, the underlying tension between expert and politician was soon exposed in deciding how to help the poor.

Indeed, one of the fascinating characteristics of the development of British welfare later in the century is how this tradition is continued. The Fabians were, of course, no less enthusiastic social engineers than the Benthamites, but the shock that put in motion the next major round of social legislation came from two humanitarian socialists, Booth and Rowntree, whose studies of poverty in London (1889) and York (1901) created a national sensation. Britain again discovered the costs of poverty in recruiting men for the Boer War when one of three recruits were found to be in appalling health. Tempting as it may be to denounce middle-class politics in France, the response was not to launch new programs for the poor but to bolster the support for the "deserving" poor, and to indulge in adversarial political warfare. The Pensions Act of 1908 was an extravagant bid for votes during the temporary decline of the Conservative Party, and the National Insurance Act of 1911, probably the correct starting point of the welfare state as it is presently understood, was clearly aimed to blunt the appeal of a growing Labour Party.

The theme of poverty that runs through the early development of the British welfare state has profound consequences for the politics of policymaking in this area. First, it enhanced the adversarial tendencies of British politics. Not unlike the theme of "town versus country" in local affairs, which Britain has somehow managed to keep alive for a century while becoming one of the most densely populated and most highly urbanized societies of Europe, the tension between the poor and the unemployed gave politicians an easy, low risk target in calculating their political appeal. With no intention of minimizing the importance of poverty relief, the political effect was to give British policymakers a convenient simplification that neatly fit the requirements of adversarial politics. Whatever may be the contemporary excesses of more recent social policy advisors such as R. M. Titmuss, Brian Abel-Smith, and Peter Townsend, their manipulation of the theme had strong appeal to British leaders and helped to disassociate, if not insulate, special assistance from British politics. The rapid growth of the Supplementary Benefits Commission, and its organizational isolation from other components of the British social security system, takes root in the adversarial advantage of playing one type of benefit against another.

A second political effect is that British social security, and in particular assistance for the poor, takes on an elitist cast whether seen from the left or the right, which is, of course, consistent with the strong elitist strain throughout British policymaking. Much as in the case of central-local relations, values were defined to meet the needs of the political system. In striking contrast to France, the paradoxical result is that the enormous concentration of political power in Westminster seldom needed to be deeply involved in social security policy. Had the underlying values been posed more ambiguously, as they were in France, the struggle to find contemporary solutions would have demanded political talent and extracted political resources. In a curious way, the dominant themes of an expanding social security system in Britain facilitated depoliticization of the issue itself.

An unintended effect which can be briefly noted is that the labor movement, which might be expected to become both an advocate and a participant in the development of social policy, was removed if not disinterested in social security. An obvious reason, of course, was that the Trades Union Congress was heavily occupied in the interwar years with unemployment policies (see Middlemas, 1979), while it could rely on the Labour Party to pursue broader social goals on its behalf. This was a convenient division of political labors, but it meant that individual mobilization and awareness of expanding benefits, new needs, and redistributive problems were minimal. Put somewhat differently, the working class which is perhaps best situated to guide the growth of assistance had little reason to take a direct interest in how social security grew. For different reasons, this suited the leaders of both the Labour and Conservative Parties, but it also meant that the social consciousness of British workers and their organizations is extremely low compared to much weaker continental labor movements. The unfortunate consequences of low popular concern were not to appear until the welfare state achieved much larger proportions and until difficult issues such as horizontal and vertical redistribution began to plague the design of social security systems.

The theme of national solidarity runs throughout the much less aggressive history of French social policy, starting from the Revolutionary debates over paupers (*mendicité*) and the poor (*indigence*) and continuing to the present with the newly acquired title of Mitterand's social security ministry, Ministère de Solidarité Nationale, under a distinguished analyst of French social security and social policy, Nicole Questiaux (see Fournier and Questiaux, 1979). Led by Robespierre, at the height of revolutionary fervor France debated providing more assistance, though the major preoccupation was vagabonds. Article 23 of the Rights of Man stated "Society must support unfortunate citizens, by helping them find work and by assuring subsistence to those unable (*hors d'état*) to work" (Godechot, 1968, p. 440). Much the same stipulation is found in the preamble to the constitution of the Fifth Republic. Given the costs of war as well as the distinctly upper-middle-class control of the Revolution, there was not much assistance forthcoming. The *Grande Livre de la Bienfaisance Nationale* only permitted departments to support about 1300 persons each, carefully divided (as social security still is) in categories of invalid farmers, infirm or aged artisans, and neglected mothers (Godechot, 1968, p. 442).

Having defeated the Scots in the seventeenth century and slowly eradicating the Irish in the eighteenth century, the British had little use for such vague formulations of national obligations. But the theme of solidarity runs throughout eighteenth and nineteenth century French history. The way in which the solidarity theme attracted political thinkers and leaders of all colors (Hayward, 1959) is analagous to the poverty theme in the British debate over expanding social assistance. Prominent in the writing of Blanc, it became an issue inspiring the benevolent reforms of the Radical Socialists; it was strongly reaffirmed if nonetheless quickly extinguished during the Second Republic; and it reappears in the social reform debates of the Third Republic in the 1890s (Minnich, 1948). Oddly enough, it appealed to the secular, positivist thinking of the turn of the century radicals, including Waldeck-Rousseau and Clemenceau, as well as to the early French Marxists and anarcho-syndicalists. Everyone could use such a vague reference, though it is interesting to note that Littré's dictionary of 1887 provided no meaning other than "mutual responsibility of two or more persons" (Bourgeois, 1897, p. 6)

To understand the slow development of the idea over the nineteenth century, one must briefly examine the peculiar way in which the French interpreted liberal ideas in relation to social organization. Until late in the nineteenth century any social manifestation of social or national solidarity to assist not only social reform, but to organize business or labor, was crippled by strict laws on association. The *loi le Chapelier* of 1791 inhibited all forms of association that might overshadow the power of the state, and the Napoleonic Civil Code placed severe restraints on the use of contracts. At least at the level of conceptualization, there is a direct line of descent from early resistance to any form of collective activity outside the state to Michel Crozier's "stalled society." Thus, there developed a fierce but impotent form of liberalism which affected all forms of collective endeavor. In relation to social assistance, it was perhaps best voiced by Thiers in 1850 when he asserted that more assistance to a class of persons would become a "rifle" held at the head of French society. In his words, if social assistance was to remain a strength (*virtu*), it should "remain voluntary, spontaneous, free, and if made otherwise would cease to be a strength and become a constraint, a disastrous constraint" (Belorgey, 1976, p. 96).

If the French notion of solidarity was not as fully manifested in nineteenth and even twentieth century France as more progressive advocates of social assistance might wish, it is perhaps some consolation to know that there was less need for help in Britain. As Mendras points out (1970, p. 5), Britain intentionally destroyed her agrarian society, but France "stopped in her tracks" for a century and a half. The vast majority of Frenchmen lived in small communities where the sick, disabled and infirm could find a meager living or call on charity in manageable proportions. Although the peasants rallied under Gambetta to save the Third Republic in 1870 (just as the workers rallied to save it again in 1936), they had few specific demands to place on a state that so carefully protected grain prices, provided good roads, and nurtured middle-class values. The July Monarchy created the Caisse d'Epargne which was, in turn, encouraged by the Second Empire and blossomed under the Third Republic. In 1881 it had 541 offices scattered throughout France, and by 1904 had nearly twelve million accounts valued at four billion francs (Levasseur, 1907, pp. 770–785). Under a law of 1850 from the Second Republic and bolstered by legislation in 1852 under the Second Empire, mutual insurance societies grew from 2600 with 289,000 members in 1853 to 13,677 with 2 million members by 1902 (Levasseur, 1907, pp. 790–793). While these changes failed to assist the disadvantaged, they gave root to the individual self-interest in social assistance that, as we shall see, still pervades French social security.

Thus, the theme of national solidarity in the development of French social security had unforeseen political effects just as the theme of poverty did in British politics. If nothing more, it made the French acutely aware of the costs of social security and motivated French politicians to be involved in the demands later in the century. Reconciling French self-reliance and individualism with social assistance was a more demanding task than reducing the politics of social reform to adversarial self-interest for a small political elite. In the 1901 census, for example, in an active population of 19.7 million, 7 million persons were classified as *patrons* and 11.4 as wage-earners. Industrial concentration came slowly with only 133 firms with over 500 employees in 1845, and 444 in 1896 (Levasseur, 1907, p. 271, 279). As I have argued, need is in itself a poor indicator of the politics of policymaking, but the French economy and society generally were neither organized nor structured so that political demands for increased assistance would assume high priority. Defining the meaning of national solidarity for increased social assistance was not as pressing as in Britain nor did most Frenchmen want to see individual self-reliance (*prévoyance*) replaced by public programs. As we shall see, perpetuating such ambiguities made it much easier than in Britain to expand the system a century later.

STATE, SOCIETY AND SOCIAL SECURITY

The second major structural problem in the evolution of social security was how to integrate the new values of social relief, and eventually social equity, with the authority of the state, and, in turn, its powers over society. Once again we find Britain and France taking very different approaches. The different motives and expectations of political leaders in the two countries are, of course, a function of the political stability and political agenda prevailing at the turn of the century. After roughly a decade of skillful, if patriarchal, rule under Lord Salisbury, the authority and success of British government was never greater. If the two-party system did not (and probably still does not) display all the vigor and initiative that enthusiasts of British parliamentary policies attribute to it, nonetheless most of Britain was assured that they were living in the best of all political worlds. While it had few direct repercussions on French social security, the situation was almost the reverse in France. The authority of the French state never seemed more in doubt than during the long and bitter fight over Dreyfus. The remnants of French aristocracy were making their last stand and thereby absorbing much of the talent and attention that in a more stable Britain could be focused on the poor. Even if social need and political demands had converged at the turn of the century in France to provide the first push toward a social security system, it seems unlikely that these demands could have reached the political agenda.

While important early legislation emerged from political crises in both countries, they were crises of very different dimensions and meaning. France had organized a Directory of Public Assistance in 1886 under the umbrella of the Ministry of the Interior, and Henri Monod, its first director, was himself closely associated with the "solidarity" movement of the Radicals and Radical Socialists (Weiss, 1980, p. 19). But this agency was mainly concerned with the very limited support for the poor available through the departments and communes. In a pattern that is familiar to students of French politics, and which still pervades the French social security system, competing agencies were organized. A law of 1898 relieved mutual insurance societies of some of the restriction on association and created a High Council of Mutual Security Societies. The mutual societies reached new heights with 24,000 represented in the annual conference of 1905, where the President of France addressed an open-air banquet for 50,000 on the Champs de Mars (Levasseur, 1907, p. 795).

The Dreyfus Affair was a political crisis threatening the very legitimacy of the French state, and in the aftermath of full and final separation of church and state, France was free to consider social problems. Although Caisse des Retraites had been organized under the Second Republic, it had never been allowed to develop. But the loss of Church revenues and charitable organizations meant that some form of relief would be needed. While no doubt derisory by contemporary standards, the law of 1905 for Aid to the Aged and Infirm provided monthly support of eight francs, barely enough to buy a few staples. A 1910 law enlarged pensions to 100 francs for contributors (Weiss, 1980, p. 42), but even this was only an eighth of the British pension so extravagantly promised in the 1908 Pensions Act. A series of court decisions quickly undermined the 1910 French pension law and relieved employers of responsibility to contribute (Hatzfeld, 1971, p. 63).

The crisis of authority associated with Britain was less acute than the Dreyfus Affair, but was nonetheless a severe test of British institutions. Again, the National Insurance Act of 1911 was not the central issue, though the parliamentary crisis precipitated by the House Lords' refusal to pass a liberal budget is obviously more clearly focused on the social spending than is the essentially political crisis of France. The 1911 Act was meant to be limited in scope and was confined to workers in heavy industry who were thought more subject to economic cycles (Harris, 1979b, p. 128). But the political significance of the Act is more in its sequel than in the crisis of 1909–1911. Unlike France, the labor movement acquired great strength during World War I, and the terms of the 1911 Act had more influence on later unemployment legislation, such as the Unemployment Acts of 1920 and 1934, than on setting new standards for social security or redefining the social obligations of the state.

Except for the brief period of the Cartel des Gauches, until the 1936 government France was consistently under conservative rule. In Britain, the rise of the Labour Party, the strength of the unions, and cabinet government itself kept the development of a new social security system in ministerial hands (see Skidelsky, 1967). In 1918 a Ministry of Labour was added to the prewar Ministry of Pensions and, as happens in many policy problems in Britain, government effectively institutionalized the divisions among the various components of a complete social security system. Protectionist policies made unemployment a less severe problem in France until the depression struck with full force in the 1930s. In 1925 there were 245,000 unemployed in France while Britain had 2.1 million unemployed in 1921 (Hatzfeld, 1971, p. 48). Moreover, the weight of French economic opinion was firmly opposed to unemployment insurance which did not appear in a nationally organized form until the Fifth Republic created ASSEDIC in 1958. Indeed, de Gaulle's chief economic advisor in the early years of the Fifth Republic, Jacques Rueff, wrote several articles against unemployment insurance (1925; Hatzfeld, 1971, pp. 47–54) though it should be noted that by 1958 he accepted social security as an integral part of planning the economic future (Rueff, 1972, pp. 271–272).

Thus, the substantive pressures of social security were different, but so also was the more fundamental issue of how needs would be accommodated by the state. Both political trends in Britain, most significantly the rise of Labour, and cabinet government meant that the reconciliation of the state to social needs had to be compressed within the existing structure of authority. Given the adversarial quality of British policymaking, this meant that a running battle and at times poor coordination of social problems took place between ministries, not unlike the similar struggle between Chamberlain as Minister of Health and Ministry of Education in reforming local government over the 1920s (Ashford, 1981b). Although the British record is more progressive than France in extending benefits in the early interwar period, both political pressures and social needs were greater. The important political fact was that the power of government could more readily be linked to the new social responsibilities than in France.

Quite apart from the conservativism of French government, the divided party structure, the instability of parliament and the weakness of labor meant that France looked for organizational solutions rather than ministerial solutions in expanding the role of the state.

Whether one accepts the Crozier hypothesis or not, it is clear that, well before the major commitment to social security in 1945 and 1946, the agencies responsible for social assistance in France were divided and dispersed. On the one hand, the mutual insurance societies were encouraged as the best means of advancing *prévoyance* and personal saving was facilitated by the Caisse d'Epargne. In the turbulent political history of the nineteenth century, there is a curious continuity in the creation of semi-autonomous agencies, however impotent, outside the state such as the Caisse de Retraite in 1848, and the precedent of relying on mixed bodies such as the High Council of Mutual Security Societies and the High Commission on Public Assistance to oversee the development of early social relief programs. As suggested by the Crozier syndrome, as these agencies proved inadequate or ineffective, there was little alternative but for the state to take on new responsibilities. These same tensions over allocating authority can be found in the early amendments to postwar social security laws, and again in the various attempts to reorganize social security in the Fifth Republic. As I would argue in the case of local reform, the social security system encompassed political conflicts and differences, while in the British system from its early stages change was imposed from the top down as successive cabinets and ministers found social security a suitable political issue. In a few words, the French system reflected the uncertain authority structure of France, while the British system was simply attached to a stable authority structure.

The political significance of the French struggle to build a modern social security system is that these policies, as those in many other areas of policy change, reproduce the political and authority relationships of France as a whole. In a sense, France cannot make major policy change without reliving all its political turmoil and resurrecting all of its historic political divisions. From this perspective, the politics of policy confirm the views expressed on party and institutional politics in France, a permanent crisis of authority and a continual struggle to reconstruct authority. Putting aside the obvious propensities for polemical and ideological politics, which may in fact be an essential part of the French policy process, one arrives at the intricate bargaining and careful mobilization of support that seems to be continually repeated in French political life. The complexities of the postwar triumvirate of social security agencies, the Caisse Nationale des Allocations Familiales (CNAF), the Caisse Nationale de l'Assurance Vieillesse (CNAV), and the Caisse Nationale de l'Assurance-Maladie (CNAM) repeat the same theme. Unable to find a suitable legal context for the new organizations, they were in fact organized under the terms of the 1898 law encouraging mutual insurance societies (Voirin, 1961, p. 1). Precisely the same intricacy and confusion characterizes the multitude of *régimes* or collection agencies that assemble contributions and manage state assistance.

In Britain social issues could directly hinge on the authority of government, while in France, as Questiaux writes (1978), "social problems never become problems only because they arise as such." Like so many important policy changes in France, the social security system emerged under a government order (*ordonnance*) in 1945 before France had either a legislature or elections. Reflecting the uncertainty about the role of the state that runs throughout French history, the initial intention was to have a system managed by its contributors and only minimally under the *tutelle* of the state (Laroque, 1971). Space forbids recounting the entire story of how the privileged of the past imposed their special claims on the new system once the enthusiasm of Liberation and the stability of *tripartisme* eroded (see Doublet, 1971; Barjot, 1971; Eustache, 1978). Laroque suggests (1971, p. 5) that the middle class could not accept mixing with the working class, but is was also that workers often could not stand cooperating with workers and that professions could not join with other professions. Whether we choose to regret or exploit the *dirigiste* tendencies of de Gaulle, it is hard to imagine how such an intricate and diversified structure could continue as the system expanded throughout the Fourth Republic, and in 1960 a series of decrees aimed to simplify the elaborate consultation procedures and the extended deliberations that had made the system virtually unmanageable. The 1960 decrees increased the powers of the Director of Social Security, giving him "sole authority over personnel and in defining the organization of services" (Voirin, 1961, p. 333). Lest we be too hasty in condemning *étatiste* tendencies in France, a British minister would never expect anything less.

THE ORGANIZATIONAL CHOICE: TOWNS OR OCCUPATIONS

The third structural feature of the two countries relates to the organizational evolution of the two social security systems, essentially how government would link the beneficiaries and their organizations to political decisionmaking at the center. My concern is somewhat broader than that of the conventional organizational behavior approach which would tend to stress internal or environmental organizational interaction. The politics of organization is, I think, somewhat different in that we are mostly concerned with how organizations structure political activity and political institutions which, of course, varies greatly from country to country. In relation to social security, the disadvantaged were, for fairly obvious reasons, always cared for at the local level in the early development of social assistance. In this respect Britain and France are similar, although the impassioned debates over Poor Law reform and active resistance to the 1834 Act has made the relationship a more dramatic one in Britain. In fact, there were important cities of northern England which never applied the new rules, a violation of parliamentary directions that would be barely tolerated in modern Britain.

The simple political explanation for British reliance on localities as the administrative agents of social assistance might well be no more than the predominance of Conservative Party rule over the past 150 years combined with their tolerance of social reform which can be traced back at least to Disraeli. But the full explanation seems to be a bit more complicated. Conservative rule also meant that the towns with their responsibility for the poor were both deprived of resources (Ashford, 1980) while being politically shielded, especially with the rise of the Labour Party. It served Conservative political interests to buttress local government while also keeping it small scale, as can be seen in the Local Government Acts of 1888, 1894, 1929, 1934, 1958 and 1972 (Ashford, 1982). The "Three wise men of Somerset House," the Poor Law Commissioners, were to make rules and standards which the towns were presumably, as so often in British center-local relations, to enforce passively and effectively. Of course, neither of these things happened.

Oddly enough, the instrument for extracting compliance was not unlike the French *grand corps*. Chadwick and many other early nineteenth century reformers passionately believed in the power of inspection. The Poor Law inspectors, along with education, sanitation, road and many other departmentally linked inspection corps were to be the arm of rational and effective national government. But in a period when the British Parliament was much less subordinated to ministerial designs than today, MPs did not passively accept social, and many other, reforms.

The best example is probably the 1848 Public Health Act, itself an early form of protecting society. The Act emerged from Chadwick's monumental study, the *Report on the Sanitary Conditions of the Labouring Population of Great Britain* (R. A. Lewis, 1952; R. Lambert, 1963), which may anticipate the fate of much research on national problems for it both caused a furor and was then ignored by legislators. Unlike the 1834 Act, passed by 299 to 20, the 1848 Act was considered an immense inroad into local and private powers. Not until the 1854 Health Act was a partially agreeable solution found, and not until the 1866 Sanitation Act did the intense controversy subside (see Lubenow, 1971, pp. 69–106). Much of the progress was due to the moderate implementation and quiet persuasion used by Sir John Simon (himself a descendant of Hugenot refugees from France), Medical Officer of the General Board of Health for two decades (see the excellent biography by Lambert, 1962).

The organizational implications for the future of British social legislation can barely be underestimated. There followed an intense debate over the division of powers between national and local government, most vehemently pursued by Toulmin Smith (Greenleaf, 1975). A romantic devotee of German mythology, he hoped to restore a sense of community, and condemned centralization "as the foul Dragon that is ever gnawing at the root of Yggdrasil, the great World Tree of Freedom—Local Self-Government is the true Urda's spring, whose pure waters can alone keep freshened, forever, the strength and growth of Yggdrasil" (quoted in Lubenow, 1971, p. 94). While local autonomy hardly needs such friends, the organizational consequence was that a weak Local Government Act Office, followed by placing a hodgepodge of responsibilities in the Local Government Board of 1871 (see MacLeod, 1968), left the localities defenseless as national ministries acquired functional powers over health, education, and sanitation. Localities had, in effect, demonstrated their unwillingness and inability to implement social reform long before Labour enacted the reforms of 1946 and 1947.

In retrospect, the enactment of the Beveridge Plan seems a reasonable and necessary event in the evolution of the British welfare state, which is no doubt true. But the interesting political question is not the more obvious issue of how parties respond after a century-long development of social awareness, but why it was so easily accepted and why alternative schemes were never considered. More to the immediate point, how did Britain escape the organizational complexity of French social security? In effect, competing political and group interests, except the doctors in the case of nationalization of health, were virtually eliminated from the national scene. As late as 1909, the Chairman of the Poor Law Division of the Local Government Board was arguing that poor relief had to involve "the loss of personal reputation, the loss of personal freedom, and the loss of political freedom by suffering disenfranchisement" (quoted in Fraser, 1973, p. 147). The other main interested party, the unions, were fully occupied with repressive court decisions and adverse labor legislation, not to mention the prolonged British depression of the 1920s. Contrary to the image of an overly technocratic France, it was the British administrative elite, of whom Beveridge was a brilliant product, that was able to follow the path of rationality and arbitrary national ruling on social security.

The French studied the Beveridge Plan carefully. In many ways Laroque's initial hopes for the French system reflect the technocratic urge so often attributed to the *grands corps,* and so often frustrated by the political and administrative complexity of France. Nothing could make more sense in a social security system than to have a single collection agency, a standard set of benefits, and a well-run central office. But as in the case of local reorganization, political complications could not be avoided, and an intricate, cumbersome administrative structure eroded technocratic ideals. At an organizational level one must ask why French social security has been preoccupied with a set of problems, *harmonisation* (standardization of benefits), *généralisation* (universal coverage), and *solidarité* (aid for non-contributors) for thirty years, while Britain enjoyed with little question what seems to be a centralized and standardized system.

One explanation, of course, is that, as in Britain, departments and communes were unable to bear the costs of welfare. There is clearly a tradition of the poor being helped locally that runs back to the *ancien régime.* One branch of the social security system, *aide sociale* or help in special cases of neglect and disadvantage, still rests with the *collectivités locales.* But here I think direct comparison is very misleading because France never expected, as did Britain, that localities would be on the forefront of social reform. As the entire history of local reorganization in France shows (Ashford, 1982), France has never been able to manipulate communes as easily as Britain could restructure local government, and the allocation of resources, if often working to the advantage of mayors, was primarily in the hands of the Ministry of Finance. But in another sense, French social security is remarkably localized, not through the formal structure of government, but through the grip of occupational and social groups on the system. These interventions, in turn, mean, as I have argued throughout, that the French system is considerably more politicized than the British system.

For understandable reasons, social security progressed more slowly in France than in Britain, but this makes the early appearance of special interests and occupational groups even more persuasive as an explanation of later developments. One of the earliest pension plans, for example, was devised for miners in 1894 (Levasseur, 1907, p. 465). Workers were heavy investors in the Caisse d'Epargne. In 1904, Levasseur (1907, p. 786) found 600,000 depositors in the Seine, nearly 400,000 in the Rhone and 300,000 in the Nord regions. From the early development of the mutual insurance, major occupational groups as well as workers with benevolent *patrons* were linked to the private system of protection. There were 51,000 railroad workers receiving both sickness and retirement benefits at the turn of the century, and numerous small occupational groups such as the Lyon silk workers (Levasseur, 1907, p. 795). From an entirely different quarter, large families began to organize over the 1890s, often under the impulse of the *Rerum Novarum* encyclical that encouraged Catholics to enter into collective associations. A Captain Maire, himself the father of ten children, organized the Popular League of Large Families in 1908 which soon spawned 1500 chapters throughout France (Bonnet, 1978).

Developments within the French labor movement also increased the emphasis on occupational distinctions in the early stages of social security. Not only was the movement much weaker than in Britain, and therefore not able to demand universal benefits, but the ideological splits within the movement meant that state assistance to the poor and workers was viewed with great suspicion. In contrast, British trade unions acquired middle-class values, even to the extent that the Friendly Societies, the closest thing in Britain to mutual insurance societies in France, strongly resisted the 1911 National Insurance Act, and helped impose many restrictions on its use. But the political contradictions of French unions are no less numerous than those in Britain, and by the turn of the century miners, railroad workers and civil servants had their own pension plans. There was little differentiation for agriculture until the 1920s, when a separate organization was created in 1924 to protect farmers.

The inadvertent effect of ideological strife among the workers was that occupations with more leverage obtained their own privileges, while the movement itself shaped a number of basically political demands to be imposed on any future system. No such idea existed in Britain. The more militant Marxism of French workers demanded that social security be paid through a *prélevement* or levy on production. They were opposed to state welfare and insisted on a voice in management of the system (Hatzfeld, 1971, p. 252). As initially conceived, the 1945 system met most of these demands. Under the 1945 scheme, the system was to be managed by the beneficiaries. Unions and other professional groups held three-fourths of the seats on the Administrative Council. It is interesting to recall that the CGT favored appointment from nominations of the various groups until the Communist Party found itself in opposition, when it changed to elections. The political demands of workers help explain their vehement denunciation of the 1967 reorganization when employers and employees were to be equally represented and when selection reverted to nomination (Guillaume, 1971; Galant, 1966). More important, perhaps, is that given the internal schisms of the unions, the occupational differentiations and privileges that took root late in the nineteenth century were quickly superimposed on the new system.

While self-interest no doubt explains the many compromises to follow, the French conception of social assistance, rooted in the French concept of the state, is by no means unimportant in providing organizational incentives and opportunity. Neither the opportunities nor the incentives existed under the more centralized British system. The organizational history is, in fact, the reverse. A Ministry of Labor appeared in France first, in 1874 and largely for inspection purposes, while a Ministry of Health did not appear until 1920. But the French have always seen the "social partners" in principle if not in fact as equally related to government. For them it is perfectly natural that a variety of functions are merged under a general ministry. When the Ministry of Labor and Social Protection (*Prévoyance*) was formed by Clemenceau in 1906, for example, it included regulation of working conditions, industrial relations, statistics, and oversight of the early sickness, accident and pension plans (Levasseur, 1907, p. 514).

Organizationally, the recent merger of all social problems in a single ministry by Mitterand is no different than the similar attempt made by de Gaulle in 1967. Whether one wishes to call this *éfficacité* or *solidarité* makes little difference in terms of the complex occupational context that permeates the French social security system.

As often happens with reforms in France, one wonders more how change ever took place as contrasted with the surprising ease with which British cabinets redirect the structure of government and society, Laroque (1971, p. 14) notes that ranged in opposition were the employers, the family associations, the mutual insurance societies, the private insurance companies, and three departments (Bas-Rhin, Haut-Rhin and Moselle) whose early rally to the theme of solidarity when they were Radical Party strongholds left them with highly developed, departmental social services. Although family allocations now represent only about 15% of social security payments in France, the elaborate and influential groups representing family interests managed to have the *caisse* for families made "provisionally separate" in 1946, and in 1949 it was definitely separated. But the important compromises were with the professional and agricultural groups. In 1948 concessions were made to provide individual benefits (most confusing in the case of pensions and the multitude

of *régimes complémentaires*), which were established with special treatment
for small businessmen, merchants, artisans, professions and farmers (see
Doublet, 1971).

Beattie (1974, p. 254) lists nine major complementary pension funds.
The major compromise was to accomodate *cadres* in 1947 when the Association Générale des Institutions de Retraites des Cadres (AGIRC) was
organized under a collective agreement with CNPF (thereby escaping
the *tutelle*). Not until a renegotiated agreement in 1961, one of the early
Gaullist efforts to generalize the social security system, was membership
compulsory. As so often happens in French politics, a separate organization, the Association des Régimes de Retraites Complémentaires
(ARRCO) was also organized in 1960 for lower-level *cadres,* part of the
price of trying to extend pension coverage. Non-contributors were entitled to a minimal pension (AVTS) which had no reliable state support
until 1956 when Mollet created a Fonds Nationale de Solidarité (FNS) to
provide additional allowances to the elderly on inadequate pensions.
Needless to say, benefits vary widely with miners and railroad workers
eligible at 50 years of age, the employees of nationalized companies for
electricity and gas at 60 years, and the basic pensions at 65 years. Numerous prestigious agencies such as Renault Autoworks, the Bank of
France and the Imprimerie Nationale have special plans.

The British system has not escaped similar organizational problems,
but they are not a function of political intervention in the system, but
produced by the idiosyncracies of the system itself. Unlike the complications of generalizing and standardizing benefits in France, the British
system remains basically under ministerial direction. Where
organizational complexity arises, as in the case of the Supplementary Benefits Commission (see Donnison, 1976; Pichaud, 1979), for example, it
is not filtered through the intricate demands of a multitude of occupational groups, each of which has not only a vested interest in benefits,
but also an active role in their supervision. Only the National Health
Service approximates the complexity of the entire French social security
system (see Klein, 1974, 1976). Space prohibits exploring the pitfalls of
French sickness and health care, but it may suffice to note that it remains
demand-determined so that unrestrained pluralist self-interest has
made medical costs, and hence the government burden, increase virtually without control, while British spending on health has actually declined in recent years.

EXTRACTING POLITICS FROM SOCIAL SECURITY

My argument has been that the macro-models of politics are not particularly useful if we wish to develop more discriminating analyses of how
politics influences the growth of welfare. No doubt class politics has been

influential in the two countries, but the more clearly class-based politics of Britain has not managed to expand benefits as rapidly as France, and under the economic pressures of recent years has been able to make substantial cuts with relatively little political dissent. Though more clearly a competitive, two-party system, British parties have not bid up the price of welfare, while the long period of conservative, Gaullist rule in France saw social security benefits increase rapidly, and during the past five years of economic dislocation, benefits actually surged ahead of many European countries. The ideological answer, is, of course, that Labour has simply not been militant enough, but this seems to me to avoid the problem of how we separate the political from the social. We would all like more benefits, but even in the most utopian of regimes there will be problems of how political control will be exercised over welfare and how benefits will be weighed against public expenditures.

An approach through the politics of policymaking is no substitute for more abstract models, but it does help us test their assumptions and enables us to go much further toward linking the expanding activity of government, common to all welfare states, to politics. As noted in the introduction, a structural analysis of the relation of social security to politics in the two countries does not provide us with independent variables commonly associated with statistical and other more rigorous empirical models. The three main features of the social security policy, its value-orientation, its relation to political authority, and its organizational links to government, are clearly not independently determined. Against these disadvantages of any kind of structural analysis one must weigh the inability of conventional empirical models to deal simultaneously with several units of behavior or levels of interaction. Obviously, we could easily find the continuous variables needed for a standard approach, but, as I have argued elsewhere (Ashford, 1978), such a simplification of the policy process, and many other forms of political interaction, runs the risk of being tautological and/or empirically misleading.

In any event, our more rigorous empirical models for separating the unique from the common for comparative purposes, and for comparing policies in particular, have most often been drived from models of party competition, political participation, etc., which, though laudable in themselves, do not represent new departures in integrating policy studies with the general corpus of political knowledge and theory either for single countries compared longitudinally or for several countries compared cross-sectionally. Essentially, a structural analysis accepts that for any one country at any one time the unique and the common are inextricably mixed at all levels of interaction. As I have tried to illustrate with the structural comparison of social security in Britain and France, the three main levels of interaction in each country, political goals, political authority, and political organization, have deep historical roots whose influence repeatedly comes to bear in shaping social security policy. Which of these factors is more important, or more ambitiously, which is "causal," may be less important than how consistency is achieved within the limits of democratic political life in each country. As I stated at the outset, such an approach does not claim to explain everything about the social security system nor everything about any given policy.

Much as I argue in the case of local reorganization, the French political system has peculiar characteristics in trying to devise a modern social security system *because* it must deal simultaneously with three structural problems: *généralisation, harmonisation* and *solidarité*. The same three problems can, of course, be found within the British social security system. The problems of reconciling contributory and non-contributory benefits is very close to the French problem of *harmonisation* and one of the major accomplishments over the past two decades of British social security has been to devise a reasonably satisfactory integration of pension plans (Ashford, 1981). The important difference from France was that Britain could make these changes with virtually no bargaining with occupational groups and while easily excluding privileged civil service and public employee groups from the policy process. The *généralisation* of the British system was accomplished in one swoop by the 1946 National Insurance Act and its management has, for the most part, been relegated to the mysteries of Whitehall where it is entirely under administrative control (something the French have never been able to achieve). *Solidarité* was, of course, the wellspring of Victorian social reform, but the British have always been uncomfortable with flamboyant terms so poor relief was undramatically integrated into the national political agenda at an early date, even though it continued to be a serious bone of contention between national and local government for many years.

The political result was the British could generally deal with social issues on a one-to-one basis which, in turn, enabled them to bring the full force of the concentrated power of Westminster to bear on social security. The French, in contrast, were continually caught in a triangular battle involving the values of society itself, the authority of the state, and organizational complexity of the social security system itself. No sooner would progress be made toward solving one weakness of the system than another political defense would be broached on another front. For this reason, it appears to me that many of the partisan criticisms of "centralizaton" as a result of the 1960 decrees and the 1967 reorganization are misplaced. It is no special defense of Gaullist technocratic excesses, many of which failed to achieve their intended results, to note that most modern social security systems had acquired even more arbitrary and centralized control by 1960. While the return to nominated membership for the Administrative Councils of the various caisse inflamed partisan feelings, we tend to overlook that few social security systems make even this partial concession toward direct involvement of beneficiaries. In fact, the 1967 reorganization (see Ferny, 1972) achieved neither its immediate aim of apportioning social security costs according to risk (a technocratic and actuarial ideal that no system, to my knowledge, has found feasible) nor its long term of balancing social security accounts. Gaullist *dirigisme* was not all that different from what British ministers do everyday.

While we cannot recapitulate the numerous concessions that were made during the "New Society" period, they reflect the difficulties of establishing any firm political control over the system even while making substantial additions and concessions to new groups and new needs. In 1970 a major law protecting the handicapped was passed; in 1971 maternity benefits adding a billion francs to the social security bill were added; in 1972 equal benefits were promised for the self-employed; in 1973 the government undertook raising all pensions to half the SMIC by 1975. Many of these changes were anticipated in the 6th Plan whose Commision des Prestations Sociales noted (France, 1971, p. 12) "the problem is less to reach an equilibrium between receipts and expenditures than to determine what parts of the national income can be used to cover needs." But effort after effort to create a coherent system failed. The effort of Poniatowski to generalize the system in 1973 by creating a *régime unique* is typical. If the grip of the diverse groups and privileged occupations could not be reduced, then, he proposed, the only option is the laborious process of negotiating similar contributions and similar benefits for each element.

Giscard came to office having promised to incorporate into the system many small groups (*les exclus*) whose low occupational status had left them unprotected. There follows a curious procession of new beneficiaries, including *concierges*, prostitutes and priests; a generalization of sickness benefits in 1974; and increased pension benefits for the aged poor in 1975. The high rate of growth of French social security spending in the late 1970s is largely due to these incremental changes plus the soaring costs of medical care, over which the French government has almost no control while paying about two-thirds of the cost of care. However cosmetic Giscard's reforms may have been, he was well served by two ministers, Mme. Veil at Health and Social Security and Boulin at Labor, who managed to persuade employers and *cadres* to pay more into the system by raising the *plafond* (the taxable proportion of personal income) and who helped integrate unemployment benefits (while paying 90% benefits for the first three months of unemployment). Given costly compromises of this kind, it is no wonder that French social spending soared ahead of that of Britain and many other European countries. The salient political fact in this saga is that at no point was political leverage sufficient to achieve many of the structural changes needed in the system or to restrict the increasing rate of expenditure even though France was more severely penalized by the oil crisis and international competition than Britain and Germany.

The structural features of the British social security system had almost precisely the reverse effect. Starting from the Jenkins austerity budget of 1968, the more centralized and uniform British system could be brought under control, and benefits relative to prices and inflation declined. A less differentiated and less dispersed system provided little of the political access in bargaining and reform that is found in France. On the one hand, this led to rather superficial tinkering with the system, perhaps best illustrated by the 1973 Health Act, which the present Conservative government has oddly enough chosen to reverse. On the other hand, government has been free in ways unheard of in France to press for major integration of the system as in the case of pensions, and of course was never faced with as intricate problems of regulating health care once the entire system was nationalized in 1947. Whether either government has done the "right" or "wrong" thing in extending social assistance is not my point, nor is it, as I noted earlier, the objective of the political analysis of any public policy. On the contrary, the aim is to see how the political interaction within major policy areas is affected by, and in turn affects, the political system. From this perspective, in Britain, the politics of social security, as are the politics of nearly all major issues, are confined to cabinet and government and, with less effect, adversarial politics in Westminster.

The structural analysis helps reveal why this is possible. The complications of central-local relations were removed very early in British political development; the early, if not entirely satisfactory, response to poverty depoliticized a major source of political dissent and protest; and the essentially bipartisan approach of the Conservatives and Liberals, later the Conservatives and Labour, confined control to Westminster. There are characteristics of both the elitist administrative system and the development of French social security that had opposite effects. The theme of *solidarité* helped mobilize and identify the political salience of social assistance, but was by its very nature sufficiently ambiguous so that underlying political differences were perpetuated rather than smoothed over; the laborious development of the system around particular occupational groups, some favored intentionally by the state and others asserting their political clout, made imposing uniformity, and therefore more central control, difficult; and the occupational distinctions that consequently riddle the determination of benefits, contributions and even the organization itself easily proliferate. In general, one may say that none of these complications have plagued political exchange in the case of the British social security system. But for the same reasons, there were neither political interests nor political resources outside Westminster and Whitehall to protect social security in a period of economic decline.

My conclusion, then, is that British parliamentary politics has managed to exclude political complicatons from the workings of the system. In a word, British social security is effectively depoliticized which, in turn, makes it possible to reduce spending in ways that are denied France. For economic, social and political reasons, progress toward the welfare state has been slower in France, because the system is more highly politicized. But the system is in many ways structurally similar to French politics itself, and may well be more politically sensitive. Change is hotly debated, and often rejected. Special interests abound, each with its own organization, administrative and political access, and often its own publications and research support. The paradox is that the incrementalist and dispersed political behavior of the French was worked to give a larger share of the national economic pie to welfare than has the avowedly welfare-oriented British system. The growth of social spending in France is the result of a variety of political forces working through the policy process, while the decrease in British social spending occurs in a context where political demands and interests are more easily excluded from policymaking. For this reason, the elaborate and expanding social security system in France seems an unintended consequence of politics, while the less generous system in Britain can be confined to the intentions of the political elite.

REFERENCES

André, Christine and Robert Delorme (1980) *L'Evolution des dépenses publiques en longue période et le rôle de l'Etat en France (1872–1971)*, Paris: CEPREMAP.
Ashford, Douglas E. (1978), "The Structural Analysis of Policy or Institutions Do Matter," in D. Ashford, ed., *Comparing Public Policies*, Beverly Hills, CA: Sage Publications.
Ashford, Douglas E. (1980), "A Victorian Drama: The Fiscal Subordination of British Local Government," in D. Ashford, ed., *Financing Urban Government in the Welfare State*, New York: Methuen, pp. 71–96.
Ashford, Douglas E. (1981), *Policy and Politics in Britain: The Limits of Consensus*, Philadelphia: Temple University Press.
Ashford, Douglas E. (1982), *British Dogmatism and French Pragmatism: Center-Local Relations in the Welfare State*, Boston: Allen and Unwin.
Barjot, Alain (1971), "L'évolution de la Sécurite Socialé (juin 1960–juin 1966)," *Revue Française des Affaires Sociales*, 25:61–79.
Beattie, P. (1974), "France," in T. Wilson, ed., *Pensions, Inflation and Growth*, London: Heinemann, pp. 253–304.
Belorgey, Jean-Michel (1976), *La Politique sociale*, Paris: Seghers.
Bonnet, Charles (1978), "Cents ans d'histoire," *Informations Sociales* nos. 6–7, pp. 13–31.

Booth, Charles (1889–1903), *Life and Labour of the People in London*, 17 vols., London: Macmillan.

Bourgeois, Léon (1897), *Solidarité*, Paris: Colin.

Briggs, Asa (1961), "The Welfare State in Historical Perspective," *Archives Européene de Sociologie*, 2:221–258.

Brown, R. G. S. (1975), *The Management of Welfare: A Study of British Social Service Administration*, London: Fontana.

Bruce, Maurice (1968), *The Coming of the Welfare State*, London: Batsford, 4th ed.

Donnison, David (1976), "Supplementary Benefits: Dilemmas and Priorities," *Journal of Social Policy*, 5:337–358.

Doublet, Jacques (1971), "La Sécurife sociale et son évolution (octobre 1951–juin 1960)," *Revue Française des Affaires Sociales*, 25:27–60.

Eckstein, Harry (1973), "Authority Patterns: A Structural Basis for Political Inquiry," *American Political Science Review*, 67 (Dec):1142–1161.

Eustache, Jeanne (1978), "Une exigence collective: la protection sociale," *Informations Sociales*, 5:9–22.

Ferny, Antoine (1972), "La sécurité sociale depuis les ordonnances de 1967," *Revue d'Economie Politique*, 82:983–997.

Finer, S. E. (1957), *The Life and Times of Sir Edwin Chadwick*, London: Methuen.

Fournier, Jacques, and Nicole Questiaux (1979), *Le pouvoir du social*, Paris: Presses Universitaires de France.

France, Planning Commission (1971), *Rapport de la Commission Prestations Sociales*, Paris: Documentation Française.

Fraser, Derek (1973), *The Evolution of the British Welfare State*, London: Macmillan.

Galant, Henry C. (1955), *Histoire Politique de la sécurité sociale française 1945-1952*, Paris: Colin (Cahiers de la Fondation Nationale des Sciences Politiques, no. 76).

Godechot, Jacques (1968), *Les Institutions de la France sous la Révolution et l'Empire*, Paris: Presses Universitaires de France.

Gray, Lawrence (1973), "Policy Analysis Illustrated by the Decisions in the Aid to Families with Dependent Children Program," *Journal of Politics*, 35(Nov.):886–923.

Greenleaf, W. H. (1975), "Toulmin Smith and the British Political Tradition," *Public Administration* (UK), 53:25–44.

Guillaume, Michel (1971), "L'évolution de la sécurité sociale période 1966–1970," *Revue Française des Affaires Sociales*, 25:81–97.

Harris, José (1979a) "From Cradle to Grave: The Rise of the Welfare State," *New Society*, 18 January.

Harris, José (1979b), "What Happened after Beveridge?" *New Society*, 25 January.

Hatzfeld, Henri (1971), *De Paupérisme à la sécurité sociale: Essai sur les origines de la sécurité sociale en France 1850-1940*, Paris: Colin.

Hayward, J. E. S. (1959), "Solidarity: The Social History of an Idea in Nineteenth Century France," *International Review of Social History*, 4:261–284.

Klein, Rudolf (1974), "Policy Making in the National Health Service," *Political Studies*, 22:1–13.

Klein, Rudolf (1976), "Political Models and the National Health Service," in R. Acheson and L. Aird, eds., *Seminars in Community Medicine*, London: Oxford University Press.

Lagrange, François and Jean-Pierre Launay (1980), "Les comptes sociaux de la nation," in P. Laroque, ed., *Les Institutions Sociales*, Paris: Documentation Française, pp. 1121–1163.

Lambert, Royston (1962), "Central and Local Relations in Mid-Victorian England: The Local Government Act Office, 1858-71," *Victorian Studies*, 6:121–150.

Lambert, Royston (1963), *Sir John Simon and English Social Administration, 1816-1904*, London: MacGibbon and Kee.

Laroque, Pierre (1971), "La Sécurité sociale de 1944 à 1951," *Revue Française des Affaires Sociales*, 25:11–26

Levasseur, E. (1907), *Questions ouvrières et industrielles en France sous la troisième république*, Paris: Rousseau.

Lewis, R. A. (1952), *Edwin Chadwick and the Public Health Movement, 1832–1854*, London: Longmans Green.

Lubenow, William C. (1971), *The Politics of Government Growth: Early Victorian Attitudes towards State Intervention, 1833–1848*, London: Archon.

MacDonagh, Oliver (1977), *Early Victorian Government, 1830–1870*, London: Weidenfeld and Nicolson.

MacLeod, Roy M. (1968), *Treasury Control and Social Administration*, London: Bell (Occasional Papers on Social Administration, no. 23).

Mendras, Henri (1970), *The Vanishing Peasant: Innovation and Change in French Agriculture*, Boston: MIT Press.

Middlemas, Keith (1979), *Politics in Industrial Society*, London: André Deutsch.

Minnich, Lawrence A., Jr. (1948), *Socal Problems and Political Alignments in France, 1893–1898: Leon Bourgeois and Solidarity*, Ithaca, NY: Cornell University, doctoral thesis.

Organisation for Economic Cooperation and Development (1978), *Public Expenditure Trends*, Paris: OEDC.

Peacock, Alan, and Jack Wiseman (1967), *The Growth of Public Expenditure in the United Kingdom*, London: Allen & Unwin, rev. ed.

Pichaud, David (1979), "Who are the Poor and What is the Best Way to Help Them?" *New Society*, 15 March.

Pryor, Frederic (1968), *Public Expenditures in Communist and Capitalist Countries*, Homewood, IL: Irwin Press.

Questiaux, Nicole (1978), "Réflexion pour une action sociale évolutive," *Bulletin de la Caisse National des Allocations Familiales*, no. 2–3, pp. 29–40.

Roberts, David (1961), *The Victorian Origins of the British Welfare State*, New Haven, CT: Yale University Press.

Rose, Richard and Guy Peters (1978), *Can Government Go Bankrupt?* New York: Basic Books.

Rowntree, Seebohm (1901), *Poverty: A Study of Town Life*, London: Macmillan.

Rueff, Jacques (1925), "Les conditions du salut financier," *Revue Politique et Parlementaire*, 32:5–11.

Rueff, Jacques (1972), *Combats pour l'ordre financier*, Paris: Plon.

Skidelsky, Robert (1967), *Politicians and the Slump: The Labour Government of 1929–1931*, London: Macmillan.

Voirin, Michel (1961), *Les Origines des caisses de sécurité sociale et leurs pouvoirs*, Paris: Librairie Générale du Droit et de Jurisprudence.

Weiss, John (1980), "The Third Republic's War on Poverty: Poor Relief in France, 1871–1914," manuscript.

Wilensky, Harold L. (1975), *The Welfare State and Equality*, Berkeley, CA: University of California Press.

CONCLUSION: THE POLITICAL TRANSFORMATION OF SOCIAL SECURITY SYSTEMS

E. W. Kelley

Although many public sector economists were relatively uninterested in social security and social welfare issues per se, the public sector spending on the domestic scale necessary for groups in society to be insured against life risks could not be avoided as a political issue. This is not to say that social security programs are all post-Keynes. As Altenstetter, Ashford, Lagrange, and Stein point out in their chapters, social security systems for large segments of the population of the countries date from the interwar period. Massive spending on social security, however, post-dates Keynes. Since 1950 the macro- as well as the microeconomic consequences of governmental transfers on massive scale were thought through.

Ironically, most of the initial concerns about the macroeconomic effects of social security transfers did not revolve around its obvious economic effects: the maintenance of a base level of consumption and, hence, demand for goods and services in an economy. Rather, in the United States, the macroeconomic concern that shaped the pay-as-you-go feature of the system revolved around capital accumulation in

273

the public sector. There developed a serious concern that a fully-funded system would eventually move major private sector investment decisions into the hands of the government or trustees of the social security fund. As Stein points out, this scared bankers and other private sector capital accumulators and managers. Another macroeconomic concern involving social security is the capacity of an economy to engage in indexed transfers out of the current revenue. Insofar as the indexing does not reflect the change in prices faced by the actual recipients of social security, a redistribution of national income across age groups occurs. Insofar as the indexing does not reflect the rate of growth of income to the public sector or the social security revenues themselves, there is a net increase or decrease in the share of gross domestic product that flows through the public sector for purposes of these transfers. When the insurance funds are collected on a current basis and are autonomous of other public sector revenues, this can lead to an apparent surplus or deficit in those monies available for social security transfers. All of these possibilities and their actualization in both the United States and Britain in recent years has led to what is called the current crisis in social security. Of course, as Ashford, Heidenheimer, Judge and Kelley point out, none of the above macroeconomic considerations which are relevant to the current crisis in social security were at issue when the decision was made in different countries to index benefit levels.

A striking feature of social security and similar benefits in Britain, France, Germany and the United States is the similarity of the systems as they would currently be described. Social security and health insurance for the elderly, health insurance for the poor, and unemployment insurance are found in all four countries. To conclude, however, that very similar needs will be dealt with in a similar fashion by most Western political systems would be mistaken in at least two ways. The first error is to assume that the systems as a whole were put into place at one time. This is clearly not the case. As Lund points out, the British have been putting in their system of social security and allied benefits for several centuries. Tuene and Harpham point out that there is an intellectual legacy and state-level experimentation dating from the early part of this century in the United States; yet federal-level activity is really a consequence of the Great Depression (Piven and Cloward, 1971). Development of the elements of the German social security and health networks date from an intermediate point, as both Altenstetter and Leibfried point out. As Ashford and Lagrange demonstrate, the French were really quite late in nationalizing their system of old age and income security. The elements of all these systems, then, have been put in place piece by piece. To view them as a macroeconomic entity with intended economy-wide effects would be mistaken. There is no evidence that any of the participants in developing these systems in any of our four countries had any clear conception of what these effects would be.

A second difficulty with focusing on the similarity of ends is that it would tend to provide an overly functionalist perspective on what is inherently intentional and political activity. In a political democracy it is not sufficient to say that groups of people have objective needs. Those needs must be translated into potential voting or other forms of political behavior must be perceived as such by politicians, bureaucrats and others participating in competitive politics, and must be responded to within the institutional forms of each country. As Judge and Kelley point out, there is simply no reason to believe that changes in the extent or shape of a social security system, while responding to apparent and declared need, do not also benefit either political or administrative groups in each country in some way (see also Derthick, 1979). The apparent similarity of ends masks many small differences; these differences, as much as the similarities, reflect the different political histories and decisions made by politicians and bureaucrats over the last century in our four countries. The variations and differences can even be seen on the taxing side. Social security and allied benefits must be paid for and, as Peters points out, the way in which Western democracies tax themselves to pay for these benefits varies greatly. He identifies up to five different basic patterns of taxation across the major industrial democracies. Each of the patterns could have a macroeconomic effect in terms of income redistribution or cushioning the effects of either booms or recessions. Yet it is clear that on the income side as on the benefit side, the systems were not put into place as a whole but developed incrementally and for reasons that would be considered more political or microeconomic in their effects.

DEVELOPMENT OF THE SYSTEMS

Particularly after the franchise is widespread, apparent political self-interest is not sufficient to prompt elected politicians or bureaucrats to enact or expand a particular program in competitive electoral systems. Neither is the objective pursuit of the public or quasi-public interest a sufficient reason. Usually the two purposes must be merged: there must be a demonstrated public benefit and there must be some political or other benefit to those politicians or bureaucrats proposing change. In Britain, the key element of justification of social security is that it ought to be provided to the middle classes and those deserving poor who were available for work when work was available. Although at the time of the 1834 Poor Law Amendment Act most of these individuals could not vote, by the time the twentieth century social security and unemployment reforms occurred, they were becoming well-organized parts of the electorate. Hence, in offering benefits to this group of individuals, British political parties could both appeal to an organized constituency and minimize distortions in the marketplace for labor. British social security and welfare systems distinguished among recipients in terms of their role in private sector economic activity. Even as late as the Great Depression, while there were some small planning efforts in British government before the Second World War, none of these occur in the general area of manpower policy. The general orientation of British political parties toward labor was that both employment and its remuneration should be determined by supply and demand. This attitude is certainly held up through the time at which Keynes disciples have successfully infiltrated the treasury during and after the Second World War. The development of the British system, then, is marked by a cumulation of what could be called targeted entitlements to distinguishable elements of labor in the private sector. Up through the end of World War II, the evolution of social security and allied benefits in Britain was one that targeted particular deserving groups and frequently targeted the form of consumption in which those groups could engage.

The early developments of the French social security and health insurance schemes reflect a self-conscious effort not to politicize these issues at the national level or to make an explicit electoral appeal at the national or regional level. The French economy and particularly agriculture has been locally organized around markets for a long time (Kindleberger, 1964). Between the nineteenth and twentieth centuries a major shift in welfare responsibility occurred, moving welfare considerations from the church to the community. The community, however, is locally defined. The villages and towns take care of their unemployed and elderly. In order to do this, the French maintain a very high labor component to agricultural production all the way up until the late 1950s. This inefficiency of production, while necessary to the maintenance of their locally based, somewhat informal system of welfare, also placed them at a competitive disadvantage any time that world trade and agricultural products tended to drop. Hence, in the Great Depression, French agriculture was hurt most of all, and rate of growth (or loss of growth) in France in the period 1930–1939 was just about the worst in Europe. To maintain the villages and towns in somewhat of a cash economy, the French had to place very high tariff barriers on agricultural products, a practice they had followed intermittently over the preceding 200 years. However, so long as welfare can be locally based, there is no need for a center or right party to attempt to nationalize welfare for the deserving poor or any other group.

At the same time, bits and pieces of a social security and welfare system developed in France. This occurred largely around joint businesses and union negotiations and activities (Ashford, Lagrange) and, in the case of retirement in particular, paralleled the organization of labor unions. Hence, the private sector and labor were involved early on in the piece by piece development of the social security system. Eventually, of course, this would lead the French to a situation very similar to that of the Americans: many private sector plans would proliferate; the government's eventual involvement in social security would be viewed as a back-up or minimal sort of social security guarantee, although many individuals in both countries have only that guarantee. In both countries, the greatest public sector subsidies and/or guarantees of retirement plans would involve those for some public sector employees.

The construction of a highly decentralized retirement system in Germany in 1889 reflects both the preemptory nature of Bismarck's political thinking, as well as an understanding that it is difficult for interest groups to make demands of or unrest to be directed toward a decentralized, amorphous service delivery system. Altenstetter points out that the effects of this anticipatory or preemptory activity were seen in the latter part of Bismarck's rule, when social security programs were used to undercut the Social Democrats and labor unions. As in France, the development of the health and retirement insurance systems reflected both occupational and geographical diversity in Germany, a reflection that continues until the present. A major difference, however, is that the state was a more active participant in the organization of health and social security systems at a much earlier stage in Germany. Under state auspices, these regional and occupational distinctions were reinforced. Moreover, the Germans organized their social insurance incrementally. Breaks in regime form are not paralleled by sudden shifts in social insurance. Instead, new levels of bureaucracy and new private sector employees are brought into the state system. The principal role of the state is one of coordination and providing fiscal guarantees to the many funds.

In the United States the rather explicitly federal character to our government and social service delivery systems has colored the development of social insurance of all kinds. It has made national coverage in any of the major insurance areas very late to develop, and then only in response to a shared national crisis. As Harpham and Teune point out, with respect to unemployment and social security benefits, respectively, there is a long legacy of state-level involvement in such activity. As might be expected, and as in the other countries we are considering, the regional variations in such benefits are reflected even in today's structure. While social security represents an individual entitlement and does not vary by state, both Harpham and Kelley point out that many health and almost all unemployment insurance schemes that are funded by or through the public sector have rather extensive state to state variations (also see Kelley, 1982).

In all of these countries, the evidence presented here suggests that most changes and expansions in the social security system and in other insurance schemes developed by or through the public sector were made for clearly political reasons. At the state level in the United States, governments would be responding to the temporary alliances of voters as well as variations in need, particularly for unemployment insurance. At the national level, social insurance is a clear political response to a national situation which could cause potential threat to regime form (Piven and Cloward, 1971). The evolution of the systems at the national level was more gradual in Britain and in France and, as is demonstrated here, each step was in response to some either organized and politicaly expressed need, or was anticipatory of same. In France, the activities of the public sector until the Second World War were largely confined to a minimal level back-up to social security and health care insurance systems, and maintaining the distinctively local or occupationally-based character of the French social insurance schemas.

In fact, a fair description of the development of the social securities systems in the four countries that we considered is that clear or anticipated political demands were met piece by piece by the public sector as the need arose. In meeting these needs or demands, politicians and bureaucrats typically preserved prior distinctions and organizational bases in already existing systems. This is exactly what you would expect in political life. Each new demand requires a new "fix." The fix is often superimposed onto the already existing system, preserving regional private-public and occupational distinctions. Only in times of crisis, usually wars or depressions, is there an opportunity for politicians and bureaucrats to attempt any sort of reorganization or radical alteration of a social security or other insurance system. Even then, as Altenstetter, Lagrange, Leibfried, Lund, Stein and Teune point out, the changes and even the proposed changes are very conserving in character. Politicians are not risk-takers.

THE POLITICAL IMPERATIVES OF ORGANIZATION

Despite national emergencies and wars, the social security and insurance systems of Britain, France, Germany and the United States have preserved a number of distinctions that permeate political and economic life in all these countries. Indeed, the preservation of such distinctions is probably necessary to the successful development of a social insurance system. These distinctions are particularly geographical, occupational and economic. On the economic side, the distinctions that seem to be preserved involve white-collar–blue-collar workers, the deserving and the undeserving poor, and public- versus private-sector activity. Much welfare and insurance is in the private sector itself. In those countries which have a strong private sector and in which the role of the state has historically been conceived of as one which facilitates commerce (principally modern Germany and the United States) distinctions among the different sectors persist in insurance schemas. In Germany, this is done with state support and involvement. In the United States, it is reflected in the fact that major portions of old age income and medical insurance can be found in the private sector itself. Public sector insurance provides a safety net in the United States. France represents an in-between case. Insurance schemas were largely developed in the private sector or within combinations of the private sector and associated labor unions, often with state support.

When the state attempted to nationalize and ratonalize old age and medical insurance, it had to reflect the nationalized differentials that had developed sector by sector. In other words, once groups collectively view their entitlement in social insurance as resulting from their particular role in the occupational or industrial structure, the state cannot easily undo that conception. State action must reflect private-sector and labor distinctions in order to obtain necessary support. This means that private-sector distinctions must persist whether or not an insurance scheme winds up being principally in the public or private sector. Lagrange points out the great difficulties that France had in nationalizing its social insurance schemas after 1958 and how they eventually had to reflect persistent industrial sector differentials. British insurance and health schemes persist in making the distinction between deserving and undeserving poor. There is a peculiarly schizoid element to social insurance in Britain. On one hand, welfare persists in making the distinction between the deserving and undeserving poor, although this has been overtaken by the needs test for supplementary benefits. Income floors for all have been rejected. On the other hand, British national health develops an effective redistribution through the use of a program of a universal entitlement for medical services. Whereas universal entitlement basically gives individuals an effectively equal access to the service, the service is paid for quite differentially in terms of income levels. This is a reflection of the programmatic character of British political parties; the conservative party is not opposed to the prevention of starvation, bad housing, etc., but is concerned with making sure only those who *declare* themselves in need obtain these benefits from the state.

This also induces some degree of fiscal control over the amount to be spent in the public sector for benefits. On the other hand, the British Labour party, like labour parties in Europe generally, consider some of the basic entitlements like health care to be rights.

Geographic distinctions persist in those countries which organized themselves and their social service delivery systems on a subnational level. This is clearly true of the United States. Since social security itself began as a response to a collective catastrophe, the entitlement to social security benefits is a relationship established between the national government and the individual. Other forms of social insurance in the United States, however, existed as part of the process by which various states provided for economic development and general welfare within their respective boundaries. While the public-private sector distincion and occupational distinctions are preserved in American social insurance programs by having a large part of the social insurance occur in a fragmented manner in the private sector, geographic distinctions persist by having national rule-governed contributions to the vastly varying state insurance programs, as Harpham discusses (also see Kelley, 1982). In other words, those social insurance programs that are conceptually developed in an incremental fashion pile one layer of fiscal activity onto another. When national monies began to go into unemployment and health insurance, such monies were added onto existing state monies and used in such a way to reflect at least some of the existing variation in delivery of these services across states. To some degree this occurs in Germany as well. The organization of the various insurance funds is highly occupational and state-based. Yet the differentials in terms of benefits are not so great, principally because they were not large, ongoing state-based insurance systems which could be added onto preexisting systems. The original state-sponsored systems were those within states which reflected occupational and sectoral differences in the private sector.

THE POLITICAL AND STRUCTURAL IMPERATIVES OF CHANGE

One of the difficulties with a potential explanation or perspective on the development of social security systems is that it appears to be difficult to account for indexing social security benefits. Why would politicians or parties throw away the chance to continuously provide "increased" benefits for an important segment of the voting population? However, almost regardless of type of party system, it is difficult not to index social security once it becomes a political agenda item. In (*strong*) party systems, those in which some degree of party discipline obtains in legislatures and in which candidate selection is not entirely local, the poor and aged would tend to vote more predominantly left-oriented parties. In these systems, one finds that more conservative parties are not opposed to indexing. Indeed, as Heidenheimer points out, Adenauer pursued indexing as an anticipatory political strategy vis-à-vis the Social Democrats for much the same reason that Bismarck developed some elements of the social security system. Similarly, Ashford and Judge show that the conservatives in Britain do not attempt to undo the indexing of social security; rather, at most, they attempt to alter its base so that indexed benefits have a dampening effect on swings in demand in the economy and the public sector borrowing requirements. The latter has the effect of keeping a system solvent on a current basis more readily.

In a (*weak*) party system with localized candidate selection and less legislative party discipline, concentration of older individuals receiving social security benefits will provide clear entry of that interest into the system of floor reciprocity in the United States House of Representatives and Senate. In other words, the concerns of concentrated aged populations will be among the agendas of Congress. Once the issue of indexing has been posed as a possible political option, it is both politically and institutionally difficult for legislators in weak party sysems to individually oppose it. In weak party systems, indexing, then, is a consequence of making the issue one on the legislative agenda at all; in strong party systems, indexing is often a preemptory political move. In both systems, it is to the advantage of the administering bureaucracy to put indexing on the political agenda. Survival and expansion are at stake.

Bureaucrats are buttressed in their advocacy of indexing and of many other changes in the social security system through the invocation of two norms. The first is that of bureaucratic expertise. This is consistent with a common delegation of expert and informative roles in Western governments and occurs, as Kelley points out, with health and other social insurances as well. The other norm that obtains is that of fairness. In democratic systems, "hold harmless" arguments work very effectively: why should an entire class of individuals' real disposable income fall due to no choice or activity on their part? This is a particularly stong argument when one realizes that the principal beneficiaries of a social security system have been the deserving poor, not the undeserving poor.

The indexing of social security is not in the long-term interests of elected legislators or parties in power, as Kelley suggests. Indexing precludes their efforts to provide distributive benefits to definable groups of the population in later years. Yet, once indexing has been made an agenda item, to vote against it is to bring about a groundswell of electoral opposition. By the same token, once indexing is passed, politicians cannot pose or vote for legislation that would deindex social security without political cost. The best that can be done is to attempt to change the basis for indexing, as the British have done on several occasions, so that there is a greater capacity to pay on a current basis and greater capacity to dampen wide fluctuations in demand.

The structure of party competition also has an effect on the types of distinctions that social security systems or even other systems of social insurance must make. In countries with weak party systems, Kelley points out that the development of interim, private sector or local public providers of various kinds of social insurance is greater. Any attempt, then, to nationalize the coverage, particularly on the benefit side, invariably has to retain those structural distinctions that have gradually evolved. As Ashford and Lagrange point out, this is true of the nationalization of the French system, in spite of De Galle's apparent desire to abolish most historic distinctions and benefits. In weak party systems, there is also a clearer rhetoric justifying social security as a self-insurance schema. In stronger party systems, there is a greater rhetoric concerning the entitlement of individuals or deserving poor to care in their older age. The latter is not quite the rhetoric of insurance as much as it is the rhetoric of "just deserts."

Recent agenda items in the general area of social insurance include the attempt to control costs as well as control over the distribution of benefits. The German method of deciding on levels of payment for medical care indicates that cost control is more effective in those cases where both the public and private sector payors are included in the group that sets rates. Where negotiations are only between the public sector and representatives of private sector service providers, there is a public sector capacity to pass cost onward that operates effectively against cost control. In weak party systems, when government and many intermediary payors are confronted by well-organized provider groups in negotiations, the bargaining asymmetry mitigates against cost control as well.

Of all the social insurances which are of concern with regard to cost control at present, social security will possibly prove the most difficult to manage over the long run. This is because the transfer is in cash. One cannot say to a group like doctors, who provide a service, "you will provide the next unit of service at a lower per unit cost." There is no set of service providers who can be denied payment by payors of any degree of concentration. Hence, oddly enough, within any particular type of party system and institutional arrangements, indexed social security benefits are that type of social insurance that will be least amenable to the political process with regard to cost control.

Ironically, then, we have come almost full circle. The answer to the question: *Would Keynes have nationalized social security?* is in many ways unknown. As Ashford points out, Keynes was not thinking in terms of provision of income floors or even other forms of social insurance with their social ends in mind. However, insofar as social security systems have been nationalized, they clearly do have a dampening effect on rapid changes in level of aggregate demand. Yet, oddly enough, were we to want to change that dampening effect within any of the countries we are considering, social security would prove to be the least amenable of all social insurances to political manipulation for macroeconomic ends.

REFERENCES

Derthick, Martha (1979), *Policymaking for Social Security*, Washington, D.C.: Brookings Institution.

Kelley, E. W. (1982), "Consequences of Restructuring Governmental Grants in the United States," paper delivered at I.S.A.P. Conference, Milan, October 25–28, and published in the proceedings.

Kindleberger, Charles (1964), *Economic Growth in France and Britain*, Cambridge, MA: Harvard University Press.

Piven, Frances Fox and Richard A. Cloward (1971), *Regulating the Poor: Functions of Public Welfare*, New York: Pantheon Books.

Author Index

Subject Index

Accident insurance, 82
Adenauer, Konrad, 102, 182, 190
Ashley, Lord, 250
Association Générale des
    Institutions de Retraites
    des Cadres (AGIRC), 264
Association des Régimes de
    Retraites Complémentaires
    (ARRCO), 264
Association for Employment and
    Industry and Commerce
    (ASSEDIC), 64

Benefits, 32, 36, 40, 44, 79, 128,
    142, 160, 191, 207, 208,
    246, 267
Bevan, A., 41
Beveridge Plan, 4, 26
Bevin, E., 41
Bismarck, Otto von, xv, xxi, xxv,
    4, 75–76, 281
Boulin, Peirre, 267
Britain, xvi, 25–58, 199–217,
    228, 245–271
    (See also National Health
    Service (NHS); Poor Laws;

Supplementary Benefits
    Commission; Trade
    Unions)
Liberal Party, xviii
Ministry of Pensions, 256
Victorian, xvii
Brown, J. Douglas, 114
Bureaucracy and Social Security,
    xiv, xxii, 84, 183, 185, 189,
    221

Caisse d'Epargne, 257
Caisse Nationale des Allocations
    Familiales (CNAF), 258
Caisse Nationale de l'Assurance-
    Maladie (CNAM), 258
Caisse Nationale de l'Assurance
    Vieillesse (CNAV), 258
Canada, 237
Cartel des Gauches, 256
Carter, James, 175
Chaban-Delmas, Jacques, 61
Chadwick, Sir Edwin, xvii, 250
Chamberlain, Joseph, xviii
Child Poverty Action Group
    (CPAG), 53